The great diversity and scope of these collected articles clearly indicate why Charles Darwin was and continues to be one of the most important figures in western civilization. Darwin's immense impact on scientific theory grew from not only his masterful knowledge of the various branches of science but also from his profound grasp of scientific methodologies.

As these papers make amply clear, he understood the character and role of theory, of postulates, of deductive reasoning, and of experimentation better than many contemporary scientists. His researches involving thousands of laboratory and field experiments with seedlings, flowers, ants, bees, and a host of other organisms are also described. His familiarity with the work of other scientists is beautifully illustrated throughout in the voluminous bibliographical references provided in many of the articles. Finally, his ability to readily assimilate diverse intellectual systems in science, philosophy, metaphysics, and religion is apparent in his utilization of obscure detail as he formulates fresh, creative generalizations.

More than Darwin the scientist, however, these papers reveal Darwin the man. In his eloquent letters with their nice concern for graceful prose mixed with quotations from classical authors, he constantly surprises us with his disarming candor, fundamental trust in human sincerity, and his concern for suffering in both animals and humans. Clearly, Darwin did not regard the world as a deterministic machine devoid of compassion or lacking in love. These pages constantly attest to Darwin's realization that survival through competition is only part of nature's plan and that nature is more than "red in tooth and claw." This is a collection which affords rare insight into the gradual development of the mind of a brilliant scientist and a truly fascinating human being. As such, it will prove to be of inestimable value to scholars of the history and philosophy of science, and to a broad array of geologists, biologists, and humanists.

PAUL H. BARRETT is a graduate of the University of Connecticut and Michigan State University. Currently a professor of natural science at Michigan State University, he is a foremost authority on and author of numerous articles about Charles Darwin. He is co-author, with Howard E. Gruber, of *Darwin on Man: A Psychological Study of Scientific Creativity together with Darwin's Early and Unpublished Notebooks*, which received the Phi Beta Kappa Award in Science.

The Collected Papers of Charles Darwin

Volume Two

The Collected Papers of Charles Darwin

Edited by PAUL H. BARRETT

With a Foreword by Theodosius Dobzhansky

The University of Chicago Press
Chicago and London

The University of Chicago Press, Chicago 60637
The University of Chicago Press, Ltd., London
© 1977 by Paul H. Barrett
All rights reserved. Published 1977
Printed in the United States of America
80 79 78 77 76   987654321

PAUL H. BARRETT is professor of natural
science at Michigan State University
where he has taught since 1947. He is coauthor
with Howard Gruber of *Darwin on Man*.

Library of Congress Cataloging in Publication Data

Darwin, Charles Robert, 1809–1882.
  The collected papers of Charles Darwin.

  Bibliography: p.
  Includes index.
  1. Natural history—Collected works.
QH365.A1   1977   575'.008   76-606
ISBN 0-226-13657-4

Contents

v

Appendix

The Collected Papers of Charles Darwin
Volume Two

Sketch of Charles Darwin by Samuel
Laurence in 1853. From a photograph
of the original by Edward Leigh of
Cambridge. Reproduced by permission
of the Sedgwick Museum, Department
of Geology, University of Cambridge.

✒ On the Tendency of Species to Form Varieties; and on the Perpetuation of Varieties and Species by Natural Means of Selection[1] By Charles Darwin, Esq., F.R.S., F.L.S., & F.G.S., and Alfred Wallace, Esq. Communicated by Sir Charles Lyell, F.R.S., F.L.S., and J. D. Hooker, Esq., M.D., V.P.R.S., F.L.S., &c.

My Dear Sir, —The accompanying papers, which we have the honour of communicating to the Linnean Society, and which all relate to the same subject, viz. the Laws which affect the Production of Varieties, Races, and Species, contain the results of the investigations of two indefatigable naturalists, Mr. Charles Darwin and Mr. Alfred Wallace.

These gentlemen having, independently and unknown to one another, conceived the same very ingenious theory to account for the appearance and perpetuation of varieties and of specific forms on our planet, may both fairly claim the merit of being original thinkers in this important line of inquiry; but neither of them having published his views, though Mr. Darwin has for many years past been repeatedly urged by us to do so, and both authors having now unreservedly placed their papers in our hands, we think it would best promote the interests of science that a selection from them should be laid before the Linnean Society.

Taken in the order of their dates, they consist of: —

1. Extracts from a MS. work on Species,[2] by Mr. Darwin, which was sketched in 1839, and copied in 1844, when the copy was read by Dr. Hooker, and its contents afterwards communicated to Sir Charles Lyell. The first Part is devoted to "The Variation of Organic Beings under Domestication and in their Natural State;" and the second chapter of that Part, from which we propose to read to the Society the extracts referred to, is headed, "On the Variation of Organic Beings in a state of Nature; on the Natural Means of Selection; on the Comparison of Domestic Races and true Species."

2. An abstract of a private letter addressed to Professor Asa Gray, of Boston, U.S., in October 1857, by Mr. Darwin, in which he repeats his views, and which shows that these remained unaltered from 1839 to 1857.

3

3. An Essay by Mr. Wallace, entitled "On the Tendency of Varieties to depart indefinitely from the Original Type." This was written at Ternate in February 1858, for the perusal of his friend and correspondent Mr. Darwin, and sent to him with the expressed wish that it should be forwarded to Sir Charles Lyell, if Mr. Darwin thought it sufficiently novel and interesting. So highly did Mr. Darwin appreciate the value of the views therein set forth, that he proposed, in a letter to Sir Charles Lyell, to obtain Mr. Wallace's consent to allow the Essay to be published as soon as possible. Of this step we highly approved, provided Mr. Darwin did not withhold from the public, as he was strongly inclined to do (in favour of Mr. Wallace), the memoir which he had himself written on the same subject, and which, as before stated, one of us had perused in 1844, and the contents of which we had both of us been privy to for many years. On representing this to Mr. Darwin, he gave us permission to make what use we thought proper of his memoir, &c.; and in adopting our present course, of presenting it to the Linnean Society, we have explained to him that we are not solely considering the relative claims to priority of himself and his friend, but the interests of science generally; for we feel it to be desirable that views founded on a wide deduction from facts, and matured by years of reflection, should constitute at once a goal from which others may start, and that, while the scientific world is waiting for the appearance of Mr. Darwin's complete work, some of the leading results of his labours, as well as those of his able correspondent, should together be laid before the public.

We have the honour to be yours very obediently,

                                        Charles Lyell
                                        Jos. D. Hooker

J. J. Bennett, Esq.,
Secretary of the Linnean Society

I. **Extract from an Unpublished Work on Species, by C. Darwin, Esq.,
Consisting of a Portion of a Chapter Entitled, "On the Variation of
Organic Beings in a State of Nature; on the Natural Means of Selection;
on the Comparison of Domestic Races and True Species"**

De Candolle, in an eloquent passage, has declared that all nature is at war, one organism with another, or with external nature. Seeing the contented face of nature, this may at first well be doubted; but reflection will inevitably prove it to be true. The war, however, is not constant, but recurrent in a slight degree at short periods, and more severely at occasional more distant periods; and hence its effects are easily over-looked. It is the doctrine of Malthus applied in most cases with tenfold force. As in every climate there are seasons, for each of its inhabitants, of greater and less abundance, so all annually breed; and the moral restraint which in some small degree checks the increase of mankind is entirely lost. Even slow-breeding mankind has doubled in twenty-five years; and if he could increase his food with greater ease, he would double in less time. But for animals without artificial means, the amount of food for each species must, *on an average*, be constant, whereas the increase of all organisms tends to be geometrical, and in a vast majority of cases at an enormous ratio. Suppose in a certain spot there are eight pairs of birds, and that *only* four pairs of them annually (including double hatches) rear only four young, and that these go on rearing their young at the same rate, then at the end of seven years (a short life, excluding violent deaths, for any bird) there will be 2048 birds, instead of the original sixteen. As this increase is quite impossible, we must conclude either that birds do not rear nearly half their young, or that the average life of a bird is, from accident, not nearly seven years. Both checks probably concur. The same kind of calculation applied to all plants and animals affords results more or less striking, but in very few instances more striking than in man.

Many practical illustrations of this rapid tendency to increase are on record, among which, during peculiar seasons, are the extraordinary numbers of certain animals; for instance, during the years 1826 to 1828, in La Plata, when from drought some millions of cattle perished, the whole country actually *swarmed* with mice. Now I think it cannot be doubted that during the breeding-season all the mice (with the exception of a few males or females in excess) ordinarily pair, and therefore that this astounding increase during three years must be attributed to a greater number than usual surviving the first year, and then breeding, and so on till the third year, when their numbers were brought down to their usual limits on the return of wet weather. Where man has introduced plants and animals into a new and favourable country, there are many accounts in how surprisingly few years the whole country has become stocked with them. This increase would necessarily stop as soon as the country was fully stocked; and yet we have every reason to believe, from what is known of wild animals, that *all* would pair in the spring. In the majority of cases it is most difficult to imagine where the checks fall—though generally, no doubt, on the seeds, eggs, and young; but when we remember how impossible, even in mankind (so much better known than any other animal), it is to infer from repeated casual observations what the average duration of life is, or to discover the different percentage of deaths to births in different countries, we ought to feel no surprise at our being unable to discover where the check falls in any animal or plant. It should always be remembered, that in most cases the checks are recurrent yearly in a small, regular degree, and in an extreme degree during unusually cold, hot, dry, or wet years, according to the constitution of the being in question. Lighten any check in the least degree, and the geometrical powers of increase in every organism will almost instantly increase the average number of the favoured species. Nature may be compared to a surface on which rest ten thousand sharp wedges touching each other and driven inwards by incessant blows. Fully to realize these views much reflection is requisite. Malthus on man should be studied; and all such cases as those of the mice in La Plata, of the cattle and horses when first turned out in South America, of the birds by our calculation, &c., should be well considered. Reflect on the enormous multiplying power *inherent and annually in action* in all animals; reflect on the countless seeds scattered by a hundred ingenious contrivances, year after year, over the whole face of the land; and yet we have every reason to suppose that the average percentage of each of the inhabitants of a country usually remains constant. Finally, let it be borne in mind that this average number of individuals (the external conditions remaining the same) in each country is kept up by recurrent struggles against other species or against external nature (as on the borders of the Arctic regions, where the cold checks life), and that ordinarily each individual of every species holds its place, either by its own struggle and capacity of acquiring nourishment in some period of its life, from the egg upwards; or by the struggle of its parents (in short-lived organisms, when the main check occurs at longer intervals) with other individuals of the *same* or *different* species.

But let the external conditions of a country alter. If in a small degree, the relative proportions of the inhabitants will in most cases simply be slightly changed; but let the number of inhabitants be small, as on an island, and free access to it from other countries be circumscribed, and let the change of conditions continue progressing (forming new stations), in such a case the original inhabitants must cease to be as perfectly adapted to the changed conditions as they were originally. It has been shown in a former part of this work, that such changes of external conditions would, from their acting on the reproductive system, probably cause the organization of those beings which were most affected to become, as under domestication, plastic. Now, can it be doubted, from the struggle each individual has to obtain subsistence, that any minute variation in structure, habits, or instincts, adapting that individual better to the new conditions, would tell upon its vigour and health? In the struggle it would have a better *chance* of surviving; and those of its offspring which inherited the variation, be it ever so slight, would also have a better *chance*. Yearly more are bred than can survive; the smallest grain in the balance, in the long run, must tell on which death shall fall, and which shall survive. Let this work of selection on the one hand, and death on the other, go on for a thousand generations, who will pretend to affirm that it would produce no effect, when we remember what, in a few years, Bakewell effected in cattle, and Western in sheep, by this identical principle of selection?

To give an imaginary example from changes in progress on an island:—let the organization of a canine animal which preyed chiefly on rabbits, but sometimes on hares, become slightly plastic; let these same changes cause the number of rabbits very slowly to decrease, and the number of hares to increase; the effect of this would be that the fox or dog would be driven to try to catch more hares: his organization, however, being slightly plastic, those individuals with the lightest forms, longest limbs, and best eyesight, let the difference be ever so small, would be slightly favoured, and would tend to live longer, and to survive during that time of the year when food was scarcest; they would also rear more young, which would tend to inherit these slight peculiarities. The less fleet ones would be rigidly destroyed. I can see no more reason to doubt that these causes in a thousand generations would produce a marked effect, and adapt the form of the fox or dog to the catching of hares instead of rabbits, than that greyhounds can be improved by selection and careful breeding. So would it be with plants under similar circumstances. If the number of individuals of a species with plumed seeds could be increased by greater powers of dissemination within its own area (that is, if the check to increase fell chiefly on the seeds), those seeds which were provided with ever so little more down, would in the long run be most disseminated; hence a greater number of seeds thus formed would germinate, and would tend to produce plants inheriting the slightly better-adapted down.[3]

Besides this natural means of selection, by which those individuals are preserved, whether in their egg, or larval, or mature state, which are best adapted to the place they fill in nature, there is a second agency at work in most unisexual animals, tending to produce the same effect, namely, the struggle of the males for the females. These struggles are generally decided by the law of battle, but in the case of birds, apparently, by the charms of their song, by their beauty or their power of courtship, as in the dancing rock-thrush of Guiana. The most vigorous and healthy males, implying perfect adaptation, must generally gain the victory in their contests. This kind of selection, however, is less rigorous than the other; it does not require the death of the less successful, but gives to them fewer descendants. The struggle falls, moreover, at a time of year when food is generally abundant, and perhaps the effect chiefly produced would be the modification of the secondary sexual characters, which are not related to the power of obtaining food, or to defence from enemies, but to fighting with or rivalling other males. The result of this struggle amongst the males may be compared in some respects to that produced by those agriculturists who pay less attention to the careful selection of all their young animals, and more to the occasional use of a choice mate.

II. Abstract of a Letter from C. Darwin, Esq., to Prof. Asa Gray, Boston, U.S., dated Down, September 5th, 1857

1. It is wonderful what the principle of selection by man, that is the picking out of individuals with any desired quality, and breeding from them, and again picking out, can do. Even breeders have been astounded at their own results. They can act on differences inappreciable to an uneducated eye. Selection has been *methodically* followed in *Europe* for only the last half century; but it was occasionally, and even in some degree methodically, followed in most ancient times. There must have been also a kind of unconscious selection from a remote period, namely in the preservation of the individual animals (without any thought of their offspring) most useful to each race of man in his particular circumstances. The "roguing," as nurserymen call the destroying of varieties which depart from their type, is a kind of selection. I am convinced that intentional and occasional selection has been the main agent in the production of our domestic races; but however this may be, its great power of modification has been indisputably shown in later times. Selection acts only by the accumulation of slight or greater variations, caused by external conditions, or by the mere fact that in generation the child is not absolutely similar to its parent. Man, by this power of accumulating variations, adapts living beings to his wants— may be said to make the wool of one sheep good for carpets, of another for cloth, &c.

2. Now suppose there were a being who did not judge by mere external appearances, but who could study the whole internal organization, who was never capricious, and should go on selecting for one object during millions of generations; who will say what he might not effect? In nature we have some *slight* variation occasionally in all parts; and I think it can be shown that changed conditions of existence is the main cause of the child not exactly resembling its parents; and in nature geology shows us what changes have taken place, and are taking place. We have almost unlimited time; no one but a practical geologist can fully appreciate this. Think of the Glacial period, during the whole of which the same species at least of shells have existed; there must have been during this period millions on millions of generations.

3. I think it can be shown that there is such an unerring power at work in *Natural Selection* (the title of my book), which selects exclusively for

the good of each organic being. The elder De Candolle, W. Herbert, and Lyell have written excellently on the struggle for life; but even they have not written strongly enough. Reflect that every being (even the elephant) breeds at such a rate, that in a few years, or at most a few centuries, the surface of the earth would not hold the progeny of one pair. I have found it hard constantly to bear in mind that the increase of every single species is checked during some part of its life, or during some shortly recurrent generation. Only a few of those annually born can live to propagate their kind. What a trifling difference must often determine which shall survive, and which perish!

4. Now take the case of a country undergoing some change. This will tend to cause some of its inhabitants to vary slightly—not but that I believe most beings vary at all times enough for selection to act on them. Some of its inhabitants will be exterminated; and the remainder will be exposed to the mutual action of a different set of inhabitants, which I believe to be far more important to the life of each being than mere climate. Considering the infinitely various methods which living beings follow to obtain food by struggling with other organisms, to escape danger at various times of life, to have their eggs or seeds disseminated, &c. &c., I cannot doubt that during millions of generations individuals of a species will be occasionally born with some slight variation, profitable to some part of their economy. Such individuals will have a better chance of surviving, and of propagating their new and slightly different structure; and the modification may be slowly increased by the accumulative action of natural selection to any profitable extent. The variety thus formed will either coexist with, or, more commonly, will exterminate its parent form. An organic being, like the woodpecker or misseltoe, may thus come to be adapted to a score of contingences—natural selection accumulating those slight variations in all parts of its structure, which are in any way useful to it during any part of its life.

5. Multiform difficulties will occur to every one, with respect to this theory. Many can, I think, be satisfactorily answered. *Natura non facit saltum* answers some of the most obvious. The slowness of the change, and only a very few individuals undergoing change at any one time, answers others. The extreme imperfection of our geological records answers others.

6. Another principle, which may be called the principle of divergence, plays, I believe, an important part in the origin of species. The same spot will support more life if occupied by very diverse forms. We see this in the many generic forms in a square yard of turf, and in the plants or insects on any little uniform islet, belonging almost invariably to as many genera and families as species. We can understand the meaning of this fact amongst the higher animals, whose habits we understand. We

know that it has been experimentally shown that a plot of land will yield a greater weight if sown with several species and genera of grasses, than if sown with only two or three species. Now, every organic being, by propagating so rapidly, may be said to be striving its utmost to increase in numbers. So it will be with the offspring of any species after it has become diversified into varieties, or sub-species, or true species. And it follows, I think, from the foregoing facts, that the varying offspring of each species will try (only few will succeed) to seize on as many and as diverse places in the economy of nature as possible. Each new variety or species, when formed, will generally take the place of, and thus exterminate its less well-fitted parent. This I believe to be the origin of the classification and affinities of organic beings at all times; for organic beings always *seem* to branch and sub-branch like the limbs of a tree from a common trunk, the flourishing and diverging twigs destroying the less vigorous—the dead and lost branches rudely representing extinct genera and families.

This sketch is *most* imperfect; but in so short a space I cannot make it better. Your imagination must fill up very wide blanks.

III. On the Tendency of Varieties to depart indefinitely from the Original Type. By Alfred Russel Wallace

One of the strongest arguments which have been adduced to prove the original and permanent distinctness of species is, that *varieties* produced in a state of domesticity are more or less unstable, and often have a tendency, if left to themselves, to return to the normal form of the parent species; and this instability is considered to be a distinctive peculiarity of all varieties, even of those occurring among wild animals in a state of nature, and to constitute a provision for preserving unchanged the originally created distinct species.

In the absence or scarcity of facts and observations as to *varieties* occurring among wild animals, this argument has had great weight with naturalists, and has led to a very general and somewhat prejudiced belief in the stability of species. Equally general, however, is the belief in what are called "permanent or true varieties,"—races of animals which continually propagate their like, but which differ so slightly (although constantly) from some other race, that the one is considered to be a *variety* of the other. Which is the *variety* and which the original *species*, there is generally no means of determining, except in those rare cases in which the one race has been known to produce an offspring unlike itself and resembling the other. This, however, would seem quite incompatible with the "permanent invariability of species," but the difficulty is overcome by assuming that such varieties have strict limits, and can

never again vary further from the original type, although they may
return to it, which, from the analogy of the domesticated animals, is
considered to be highly probable, if not certainly proved.

It will be observed that this argument rests entirely on the assumption,
that *varieties* occurring in a state of nature are in all respects analogous to
or even identical with those of domestic animals, and are governed by
the same laws as regards their permanence or further variation. But it is
the object of the present paper to show that this assumption is altogether
false, that there is a general principle in nature which will cause many
varieties to survive the parent species, and to give rise to successive
variations departing further and further from the original type, and
which also produces, in domesticated animals, the tendency of varieties
to return to the parent form.

The life of wild animals is a struggle for existence. The full exertion of
all their faculties and all their energies is required to preserve their own
existence and provide for that of their infant offspring. The possibility of
procuring food during the least favourable seasons, and of escaping the
attacks of their most dangerous enemies, are the primary conditions
which determine the existence both of individuals and of entire species.
These conditions will also determine the population of a species; and by a
careful consideration of all the circumstances we may be enabled to
comprehend, and in some degree to explain, what at first sight appears so
inexplicable—the excessive abundance of some species, while others
closely allied to them are very rare.

The general proportion that must obtain between certain groups of
animals is readily seen. Large animals cannot be so abundant as small
ones; the carnivora must be less numerous than the herbivora; eagles and
lions can never be so plentiful as pigeons and antelopes; the wild asses of
the Tartarian deserts cannot equal in numbers the horses of the more
luxuriant prairies and pampas of America. The greater or less fecundity
of an animal is often considered to be one of the chief causes of its
abundance or scarcity; but a consideration of the facts will show us that
it really has little or nothing to do with the matter. Even the least prolific
of animals would increase rapidly if unchecked, whereas it is evident that
the animal population of the globe must be stationary, or perhaps,
through the influence of man, decreasing. Fluctuations there may be; but
permanent increase, except in restricted localities, is almost impossible.
For example, our own observation must convince us that birds do not go
on increasing every year in a geometrical ratio, as they would do, were
there not some powerful check to their natural increase. Very few birds
produce less than two young ones each year, while many have six, eight,
or ten; four will certainly be below the average; and if we suppose that
each pair produce young only four times in their life, that will also be

below the average, supposing them not to die either by violence or want of food. Yet at this rate how tremendous would be the increase in a few years from a single pair! A simple calculation will show that in fifteen years each pair of birds would have increased to nearly ten millions! whereas we have no reason to believe that the number of the birds of any country increases at all in fifteen or in one hundred and fifty years. With such powers of increase the population must have reached its limits, and have become stationary, in a very few years after the origin of each species. It is evident, therefore, that each year an immense number of birds must perish—as many in fact as are born; and as on the lowest calculation the progeny are each year twice as numerous as their parents, it follows that, whatever be the average number of individuals existing in any given country, *twice that number must perish annually*,—a striking result, but one which seems at least highly probable, and is perhaps under rather than over the truth. It would therefore appear that, as far as the continuance of the species and the keeping up the average number of individuals are concerned, large broods are superfluous. On the average all above *one* become food for hawks and kites, wild cats and weasels, or perish of cold and hunger as winter comes on. This is strikingly proved by the case of particular species; for we find that their abundance in individuals bears no relation whatever to their fertility in producing offspring. Perhaps the most remarkable instance of an immense bird population is that of the passenger pigeon of the United States, which lays only one, or at most two eggs, and is said to rear generally but one young one. Why is this bird so extraordinarily abundant, while others producing two or three times as many young are much less plentiful? The explanation is not difficult. The food most congenial to this species, and on which it thrives best, is abundantly distributed over a very extensive region, offering such differences of soil and climate, that in one part or another of the area the supply never fails. The bird is capable of a very rapid and long-continued flight, so that it can pass without fatigue over the whole of the district it inhabits, and as soon as the supply of food begins to fail in one place is able to discover a fresh feeding-ground. This example strikingly shows us that the procuring a constant supply of wholesome food is almost the sole condition requisite for ensuring the rapid increase of a given species, since neither the limited fecundity, nor the unrestrained attacks of birds of prey and of man are here sufficient to check it. In no other birds are these peculiar circumstances so strikingly combined. Either their food is more liable to failure, or they have not sufficient power of wing to search for it over an extensive area, or during some season of the year it becomes very scarce, and less wholesome substitutes have to be found; and thus, though more fertile in offspring, they can never increase beyond the supply of food in the least favourable seasons. Many birds can only exist by migrating, when their food becomes scarce, to regions possessing a milder, or at least a different climate, though, as these migrating birds are seldom excessively abundant, it is evident that the countries they visit are still deficient in a constant and abundant supply of wholesome food. Those whose organization does not permit them to migrate when their food becomes periodically scarce, can never attain a large population. This is probably the reason why woodpeckers are scarce with us, while in the tropics they are among the most abundant of solitary birds. Thus the house sparrow is more abundant than the redbreast, because its food is more constant and plentiful,—seeds of grasses being preserved during the winter, and our farm-yards and stubble-fields furnishing an almost inexhaustible supply. Why, as a general rule, are aquatic, and especially sea birds, very numerous in individuals? Not because they are more prolific than others, generally the contrary; but because their food never fails, the sea-shores and river-banks daily swarming with a fresh supply of small mollusca and crustacea. Exactly the same laws will apply to mammals. Wild cats are prolific and have few enemies; why then are they never as abundant as rabbits? The only intelligible answer is, that their supply of food is more precarious. It appears evident, therefore, that so long as a country remains physically unchanged, the numbers of its animal population cannot materially increase. If one species does so, some others requiring the same kind of food must diminish in proportion. The numbers that die annually must be immense; and as the individual existence of each animal depends upon itself, those that die must be the weakest—the very young, the aged, and the diseased,—while those that prolong their existence can only be the most perfect in health and vigour—those who are best able to obtain food regularly, and avoid their numerous enemies. It is, as we commenced by remarking, "a struggle for existence," in which the weakest and least perfectly organized must always succumb.

Now it is clear that what takes place among the individuals of a species must also occur among the several allied species of a group,—viz. that those which are best adapted to obtain a regular supply of food, and to defend themselves against the attacks of their enemies and the vicissitudes of the seasons, must necessarily obtain and preserve a superiority in population; while those species which from some defect of power or organization are the least capable of counteracting the vicissitudes of food, supply, &c., must diminish in numbers, and, in extreme cases, become altogether extinct. Between these extremes the species will present various degrees of capacity for ensuring the means of preserving life; and it is thus we account for the abundance or rarity of species. Our ignorance will generally prevent us from accurately tracing the effects to their causes; but could we become perfectly acquainted with the organization and habits of the various species of animals, and could we measure the capacity of each for performing the different acts necessary to its safety and existence under all the varying circumstances by which it is surrounded, we might be able even to calculate the proportionate abundance of individuals which is the necessary result.

If now we have succeeded in establishing these two points—1st, *that the animal population of a country is generally stationary, being kept down by a periodical deficiency of food, and other checks; and, 2nd, that the comparative abundance or scarcity of the individuals of the several species is entirely due to their organization and resulting habits, which, rendering it more difficult to procure a regular supply of food and to provide for their personal safety in some cases than in others, can only be balanced by a difference in the population which have to exist in a given area*—we shall be in a condition to proceed to the consideration of *varieties*, to which the preceding remarks have a direct and very important application.

Most or perhaps all the variations from the typical form of a species must have some definite effect, however slight, on the habits or capacities of the individuals. Even a change of colour might, by rendering them more or less distinguishable, affect their safety; a greater or less development of hair might modify their habits. More important changes, such as an increase in the power or dimensions of the limbs or any of the external organs, would more or less affect their mode of procuring food or the range of country which they inhabit. It is also evident that most changes would affect, either favourably or adversely, the powers of prolonging existence. An antelope with shorter or weaker legs must necessarily suffer more from the attacks of the feline carnivora; the passenger pigeon with less powerful wings would sooner or later be affected in its powers of procuring a regular supply of food; and in both cases the result must necessarily be a diminution of the population of the modified species. If, on the other hand, any species should produce a variety having slightly increased powers of preserving existence, that variety must inevitably in time acquire a superiority in numbers. These results must follow as surely as old age, intemperance, or scarcity of food produce an increased mortality. In both cases there may be many individual exceptions; but on the average the rule will invariably be found to hold good. All varieties will therefore fall into two classes—those which under the same conditions would never reach the population of the parent species, and those which would in time obtain and keep a numerical superiority. Now, let some alteration of physical conditions occur in the district—a long period of drought, a destruction of vegetation by locusts, the irruption of some new carnivorous animal seeking "pastures new"—any change in fact tending to render existence more difficult to the species in question, and tasking its utmost powers to avoid complete extermination; it is evident that, of all the individuals composing the species, those forming the least numerous and most feebly organized variety would suffer first, and, were the pressure severe, must soon become extinct. The same causes continuing in action, the parent species would next suffer, would gradually diminish in numbers, and with a recurrence of similar unfavourable conditions might also become extinct. The superior variety would then alone remain, and on a return to favourable circumstances would rapidly increase in numbers and occupy the place of the extinct species and variety.

The *variety* would now have replaced the *species*, of which it would be a more perfectly developed and more highly organized form. It would be in all respects better adapted to secure its safety, and to prolong its individual existence and that of the race. Such a variety *could not* return to the original form; for that form is an inferior one, and could never compete with it for existence. Granted, therefore, a "tendency" to reproduce the original type of the species, still the variety must ever remain preponderant in numbers, and under adverse physical conditions *again alone survive*. But this new, improved, and populous race might itself, in course of time, give rise to new varieties, exhibiting several diverging modifications of form, any of which, tending to increase the facilities for preserving existence, must, by the same general law, in their turn become predominant. Here, then, we have *progression and continued divergence* deduced from the general laws which regulate the existence of animals in a state of nature, and from the undisputed fact that varieties do frequently occur. It is not, however, contended that this result would be invariable; a change of physical conditions in the district might at times materially modify it, rendering the race which had been the most capable of supporting existence under the former conditions now the least so, and even causing the extinction of the newer and, for a time, superior race, while the old or parent species and its first inferior varieties continued to flourish. Variations in unimportant parts might also occur, having no perceptible effect on the life-preserving powers; and the varieties so furnished might run a course parallel with the parent species, either giving rise to further variations or returning to the former type. All we argue for is, that certain varieties have a tendency to maintain their existence longer than the original species, and this tendency must make itself felt; for though the doctrine of chances or averages can never be trusted to on a limited scale, yet, if applied to high numbers, the results come nearer to what theory demands, and, as we approach to an infinity of examples, become strictly accurate. Now the scale on which nature works is so vast—the numbers of individuals and periods of time with which she deals approach so near to infinity, that any cause, however slight, and however liable to be veiled and counter-acted by accidental circumstances, must in the end produce its full legitimate results.

Let us now turn to domesticated animals, and inquire how varieties produced among them are affected by the principles here enunciated. The essential difference in the condition of wild and domestic animals is this,—that among the former, their well-being and very existence depend upon the full exercise and healthy condition of all their senses and physical powers, whereas, among the latter, these are only partially exercised, and in some cases are absolutely unused. A wild animal has to search, and often to labour, for every mouthful of food—to exercise sight, hearing, and smell in seeking it, and in avoiding dangers, in procuring shelter from the inclemency of the seasons, and in providing for the subsistence and safety of its offspring. There is no muscle of its body that is not called into daily and hourly activity; there is no sense or faculty that is not strengthened by continual exercise. The domestic animal, on the other hand, has food provided for it, is sheltered, and often confined, to guard it against the vicissitudes of the seasons, is carefully secured from the attacks of its natural enemies, and seldom even rears its young without human assistance. Half of its senses and faculties are quite useless; and the other half are but occasionally called into feeble exercise, while even its muscular system is only irregularly called into action.

Now when a variety of such an animal occurs, having increased power or capacity in any organ or sense, such increase is totally useless, is never called into action, and may even exist without the animal ever becoming aware of it. In the wild animal, on the contrary, all its faculties and powers being brought into full action for the necessities of existence, any increase becomes immediately available, is strengthened by exercise, and must even slightly modify the food, the habits, and the whole economy of the race. It creates as it were a new animal, one of superior powers, and which will necessarily increase in numbers and outlive those inferior to it.

Again, in the domesticated animal all variations have an equal chance of continuance; and those which would decidedly render a wild animal unable to compete with its fellows and continue its existence are no disadvantage whatever in a state of domesticity. Our quickly fattening pigs, short-legged sheep, pouter pigeons, and poodle dogs could never have come into existence in a state of nature, because the very first step towards such inferior forms would have led to the rapid extinction of the race; still less could they now exist in competition with their wild allies. The great speed but slight endurance of the race horse, the unwieldy strength of the ploughman's team, would both be useless in a state of nature. If turned wild on the pampas, such animals would probably soon become extinct, or under favourable circumstances might each lose those extreme qualities which would never be called into action, and in a few generations would revert to a common type, which must be that in which the various powers and faculties are so proportioned to each other as to be best adapted to procure food and secure safety,—that in which by the full exercise of every part of his organization the animal can alone continue to live. Domestic varieties, when turned wild, *must* return to something near the type of the original wild stock, *or become altogether extinct.*

We see, then, that no inferences as to varieties in a state of nature can be deduced from the observation of those occurring among domestic animals. The two are so much opposed to each other in every circumstance of their existence, that what applies to the one is almost sure not to apply to the other. Domestic animals are abnormal, irregular, artificial; they are subject to varieties which never occur and never can occur in a state of nature: their very existence depends altogether on human care; so far are many of them removed from that just proportion of faculties, that true balance of organization, by means of which alone an animal left to its own resources can preserve its existence and continue its race.

The hypothesis of Lamarck—that progressive changes in species have been produced by the attempts of animals to increase the development of their own organs, and thus modify their structure and habits—has been repeatedly and easily refuted by all writers on the subject of varieties and species, and it seems to have been considered that when this was done the whole question has been finally settled; but the view here developed renders such an hypothesis quite unnecessary, by showing that similar results must be produced by the action of principles constantly at work in nature. The powerful retractile talons of the falcon- and the cat-tribes have not been produced or increased by the volition of those animals; but among the different varieties which occurred in the earlier and less highly organized forms of these groups, *those always survived longest which had the greatest facilities for seizing their prey.* Neither did the giraffe acquire its long neck by desiring to reach the foliage of the more lofty shrubs, and constantly stretching its neck for the purpose, but because any varieties which occurred among its antitypes with a longer neck than usual *at once secured a fresh range of pasture over the same ground as their shorter-necked companions, and on the first scarcity of food were thereby enabled to outlive them.* Even the peculiar colours of many animals, especially insects, so closely resembling the soil or the leaves or the trunks on which they habitually reside, are explained on the same principle; for though in the course of ages varieties of many tints may have occurred, *yet those races having colours best adapted to concealment from their enemies would inevitably survive the longest.* We have also here an acting cause to account for that balance so often observed in nature,—a deficiency in one set of organs always being compensated by an increased development of some others—powerful wings accompanying weak feet, or great velocity making up for the absence of defensive weapons; for it has been shown that all varieties in which an unbalanced deficiency occurred could not long continue their existence. The action of this principle is exactly like that of the centrifugal governor of the steam engine, which checks and corrects any irregularities almost before they become evident; and in like manner no unbalanced deficiency in the animal kingdom can ever reach any conspicuous magnitude, because it would make itself felt at the very first step, by rendering existence difficult and extinction almost sure soon to follow. An origin such as is here advocated will also agree with the peculiar character of the modifications of form and structure which obtain in organized beings—the many lines of divergence from a central type, the increasing efficiency and power of a particular organ through a succession of allied species, and the remarkable persistence of unimportant parts such as colour, texture of plumage and hair, form of horns or crests, through a series of species differing considerably in more essential characters. It also furnishes us with a reason for that "more specialized structure" which Professor Owen states to be a characteristic of recent compared with extinct forms, and which would evidently be the result of the progressive modification of any organ applied to a special purpose in the animal economy.

We believe we have now shown that there is a tendency in nature to the continued progression of certain classes of *varieties* further and further from the original type—a progression to which there appears no reason to assign any definite limits—and that the same principle which produces this result in a state of nature will also explain why domestic varieties have a tendency to revert to the original type. This progression, by minute steps, in various directions, but always checked and balanced by the necessary conditions, subject to which alone existence can be preserved, may, it is believed, be followed out so as to agree with all the phenomena presented by organized beings, their extinction and succession in past ages, and all the extraordinary modifications of form, instinct, and habits which they exhibit.

Ternate, February, 1858

1. [Read 1 July 1858.] Charles Darwin and Alfred Wallace. Communicated by Charles Lyell and J. D. Hooker. *Journal of the Proceedings of the Linnean Society (Zoology)* 3 (1859): 45–62.†

2. This MS. work was never intended for publication, and therefore was not written with care.—C. D. 1858.

3. I can see no more difficulty in this, than in the planter improving his varieties of the cotton plant.—C. D. 1858.

↞ On the Agency of Bees in the Fertilization of Papilionaceous Flowers, and on the Crossing of Kidney Beans[1]

In a brief notice published by me on this subject last year, I stated that bees always alight on the left wing-petal of the Scarlet Kidney Bean, and in doing so depress it; and this acts on the tubular and spiral keel-petal, which causes the pistil to protrude: on the pistil there is a brush of hairs; and by the repeated movement of the keel-petal the hairs brush the pollen beyond the anthers on to the stigmatic surface. This complex contrivance led me to suppose that bees were necessary to the fertilization of the flower: accordingly I enclosed some few flowers in bottles and under gauze; and those which were not in any way moved did not set a single pod, whereas some of those which I moved in imitation of the bees produced fine pods. But I then stated that the experiment was tried on much too small a scale to be trusted. I have this year covered up between 3 and 4 feet in length of a row of Kidney Beans, just before the flowers opened, in a tall bag of very thin net. Nothing in the appearance of the plants would lead me to suppose that this was in any way injurious to their fertilization: and I think this conclusion may be trusted; for some of the flowers which I moved in the same way as the bees do, produced pods quite as fine as could be found in the uncovered rows.

The result was that the covered-up plants had produced by August 13th only thirty-five pods, and in no one case two pods on the same stalk, whereas the adjoining uncovered rows were crowded with clusters of pods. There were many flowers still on the plants when uncovered; and it was curious to see how, in a few days afterwards, as soon as the bees had access to them, a number of pods hanging in clusters of three and four together were produced. On August 17th I again put the net on a later crop. The covered plants now produced ninety-seven pods, borne on seventy-four stalks, showing that the same stalk often produced more than one pod. This time I kept an equal length of uncovered beans ungathered; and on this length there were 292 pods, or exactly thrice as many as on the covered plants. Taking this number as the standard of comparison for the first experiment (which, however, is hardly fair, as my gardener thinks the second crop was more productive than the first), more than eight times as many pods were produced on the uncovered than on the covered rows. The Kidney Bean is largely frequented by the *Thrips*; and as I have with some other plants actually seen a *Thrips* which was dusted with pollen leave several granules on the stigma, it is quite possible that the fertilization of the covered-up flowers might have been thus aided.

In the common Bean there is no such obvious relation between the structure of the flower and the visits of bees; yet, when these insects alight on the wing-petals, they cause the rectangularly bent pistil and the pollen to protrude through the slit in the keel-petal. I was led to try the effect of covering them up, from a statement in the 'Gardeners' Chronicle'[2] made several years ago, viz. that when bees bite holes through the calyx of the flower in order to get more easily at the nectar, the crop is injured. This was attributed by the writer to injury of the ovarium, which I am sure is incorrect. But I thought that it was possible that the fertilization would be less perfect, as soon as bees ceased to alight on the wing-petals. I accordingly covered up seventeen plants, just before the flowers opened, moving a few flowers to ascertain that very fine pods, including the full average number of beans, could be, and were, produced on the plants under the net. These seventeen plants produced thirty-six pods; but no less than eight of them, though well formed, did not include a single bean. The thirty-six pods together contained only forty beans, and, if the empty pods be excluded, each produced on an average less than one and a half beans; on the other hand, seventeen uncovered plants in an adjoining row which were visited by the bees produced forty-five pods, all including beans, 135 in number, or on an average exactly three beans to each pod,—so that the uncovered beans were nearly thrice as fertile as the covered.

In an old number of the 'Gardeners' Chronicle' an extract is given from a New Zealand newspaper, in which much surprise is expressed that the introduced Clover never seeded freely until the hive-bee was introduced. This statement may be erroneous; at least, as I shall immediately show, it does not apply to the Canterbury Settlement. But I was induced by it to cover up under the same open sort of net about a yard square of the common White Clover, growing thickly in turf; and I then gathered an equal number of heads from the covered and from some uncovered plants which were growing all round, and which I had seen daily visited by my bees. I collected the seed into a small parcel; and, as far as I could estimate, the uncovered plants produced just ten times as much seed as the covered. Speaking loosely, the covered heads might have been said to have produced no seed.

Lathyrus grandiflorus is very rarely visited by bees in this country; and from experiments which I have tried during the last two summers, and from experiments recorded in 'Loudon's Magazine,'[3] I am convinced that moving the flowers favours their fertilization, even when the young pod falls off, as very often happens almost immediately. Sir W. Macarthur, who did not know of my experiments, told me that he had found that in New South Wales the introduced *Erythrina* did not set its pods well unless the flowers were moved. From the statement in regard to the Clover in New Zealand, I wrote to Mr. Swale, of Christchurch in New Zealand, and asked him whether Leguminous plants seeded there freely before the hive-bee was introduced; and he, in the most obliging manner, has sent me a list of twenty-four plants of this order which seeded abundantly before bees were introduced. And as he states that there is no indigenous bee (perhaps this statement applies to bees resembling hive or humble bees, for some other genera are known to inhabit New Zealand), the fact that these plants seeded freely at first appears quite fatal to my doctrine. But Mr. Swale adds that he believes that three species of a wasp-like insect performed the part of bees, before the introduction of the latter: unfortunately he does not expressly state that he has seen them sucking the flower. He further adds a remarkable statement, that there are two or three kinds of grasshoppers which frequent flowers; and he says he has repeatedly watched them "release the stamens from the keel-petal,"—so that, extraordinary as the fact is, it would appear that grasshoppers, though having a mouth so differently constructed, in New Zealand have to a certain extent the habits of bees. Mr. Swale further adds that the garden varieties of the Lupine seed less freely than any other leguminous plant in New Zealand; and he says, "I have for amusement during the summer released the stamens with a pin; and a pod of seed has always rewarded me for my trouble, and the adjoining flowers not so served have all proved blind." The case of the Lupine in New Zealand not seeding freely now that bees have been introduced may be accounted for by the fact, if I dare trust my memory, that in England this plant is visited by humble-bees, and not by hive-bees.

These several facts, and the foregoing experiments, seem to me rather curious; for who, seeing that papilionaceous flowers are hermaphrodite, have an abundant supply of pollen, which is mature before the flower opens, and that the flower itself is so neatly closed, would have imagined that insects played so important a part in their fertilization? I can hardly doubt that in England, during a season when bees were very scanty, if in any one district large crops of seed-clover were planted, the crop would partly fail, from the flowers not being sufficiently moved.

The foregoing little experiments, however, were not tried in relation to the agency of insects in fertilizing a plant with its own pollen. Andrew Knight many years ago propounded the doctrine that no plant self-fertilizes itself for a perpetuity of generations. After pretty close investigation of the subject, I am strongly inclined to believe that this is a law of nature throughout the vegetable and animal kingdoms. I am well aware that there are several cases of difficulty.

The Leguminosae with papilionaceous flowers have been advanced by
Pallas and others as a case in which crossing could never naturally take
place. But any plant habitually visited by insects in such a manner that
their hairy bodies, to which pollen so readily adheres, come into contact
with the stigma, could hardly fail occasionally to receive the pollen from
another individual of the same species. In all Leguminosae, bees do brush
over the stigma. And the possibility of crossing would be very strong in
the case of any plant, if the agency of insects were necessary for its
self-fertilization; for it would show that it was habitually visited by
them.

From these considerations I was led to believe that papilionaceous
plants must be occasionally crossed. Nevertheless I must confess that,
from such evidence as I have been able to acquire, crossing between
varieties growing close together does not take place nearly so freely as I
should have expected. As far as I am aware, only three or four cases of
such crosses are on record. It is not by any means, I believe, a common
practice with seed-raisers to keep the crops of their leguminous plants
separate. Hence I was led last year, in my short communication to the
'Gardeners' Chronicle,' to ask whether any of your readers had any
experience on the natural crossing of Beans, Peas, &c. Mr. Coe, of
Knowle, near Fareham, Hants, in the most obliging manner sent me some
specimens, and an account that last summer he had planted four rows of
the Negro Dwarf Kidney Bean between some rows of the white and
brown dwarfs, and likewise near some Scarlet Runners. The dwarfs he
had saved for seed. The plants themselves he believes presented nothing
remarkable in foliage, height, flowers, &c.; and he feels sure that their
pods were all alike: but the beans themselves presented an extraordinary
mixture, as I can testify from the sample sent me, of all shades between
light brown and black, and a few mottled with white; not one-fifth of the
beans, perhaps much less, were pure Negroes. Some few of the beans also
in the rows of the white Haricot were affected, but none of the
brown dwarfs.

Hence, then, we apparently have the extraordinary fact, described by
Wiegmann[4] in the case of several leguminous plants experimented on
most carefully by Gärtner[5] in the case of the Pea, and described a few
years ago by Mr. Berkeley in the 'Gardeners' Chronicle,'[6] of the pollen of
one variety having affected not only the embryo but the tunics of the
seed borne by the pure mother. I have said that apparently we have here
a fact of this nature; for I must state that Mr. Coe sent me a dozen of the
pure Negro Beans which produced in 1857 the extraordinary mixture. I
sowed them this year; and though quite like each other in appearance,
the dozen produced plants differing in colour of flower, &c., and beans
of various tints; so that these beans, though not affected in their outer

tunics, seem to have been the product of a cross in the previous year of 1856.

This year I sowed the extraordinary mixture raised by Mr. Coe in 1857 from the four rows of the Negro Bean, which he believes to have been quite pure; and the produce is the most extraordinarily heterogeneous mixture which can be conceived—each plant differing from the others in tallness, foliage, colour, and size of flower, time of ripening and flowering, size, shape, and colour of pods, and beans of. every conceivable tint from black to pale brown, some dark purple and some slightly mottled, and of various sizes and shapes. My gardener remarked, as did Mr. Coe with respect to some of his plants, that some of the seedlings seemed to have been crossed by the Scarlet Runner: one of my plants trailed on the ground for a length of 4 feet, its flowers were white, and its pods were very long, flat, and broad; the beans were pinkish purple, and twice as large as those of the Negro; there were also in two cases brown and purple beans in the same pod. These facts certainly seem to indicate a cross from the Scarlet Runner; but as the latter is generally esteemed a distinct species, I feel very doubtful on this head; and we should remember that it is well established that mongrels frequently, or even generally, are much more vigorous than either of their parents.

Mr. Coe tried the experiment more philosophically, and separated his heterogeneous Negro beans into twelve lots, according to their tints; and keeping a few of each as a sample, he sowed them, and he has now harvested them separately. He has kindly sent me samples of all. The variation is now much greater than it was in the parent lot of 1857. Beans of new colours have appeared, such as pure white, bright purple, yellow; and many are much mottled. Not one of the twelve lots has transmitted its own tint to all the beans produced by it; nevertheless the dark beans have clearly produced a greater number of dark, and the light-coloured beans a greater number of light colour. The mottling seems to have been strongly inherited, but always increased. To give one case of the greatest variability, a dirty-brown bean, nearly intermediate in tint between the darkest and lightest, produced a sample which I have been enabled to divide into no less than a dozen different tints, viz. pure white, black, purple, yellow, and eight other tints between brown, slate, yellow, purple, or black. It has been stated that a few of the white Haricots in the rows adjoining the Negroes were in 1857 slightly affected. Mr. Coe sowed some which were of a very pale brown, or cream-coloured; and he has sent me a pod produced this autumn, which pod includes two beans of the above tint and one of a pale, dirty, purplish brown.

Now it may be asked, are we justified in attributing this extraordinary amount of variation to crossing, whether or not the crossing was all confined to the year 1857? or may not the case be one of simple variation? I think we must reject the latter alternative. For, in the first place, the Negro Bean is an old variety, and is reputed to be very true; in the second place, I do not believe any case is on record of a vast number of plants of the same variety all sporting at the very same period. On the other hand, the Negroes having been planted between rows of white and brown beans, together with the facts which I have given on the importance of insect agency in the fertilization of the Kidney Bean, showing, as may be daily seen, how incessantly the flowers are visited by bees, strongly favour the theory of crossing. Moreover, the extraordinary increase in variability in the second generation strikingly confirms this conclusion; for extreme variability in the offspring from mongrels has been observed by all who have attended to this subject.

As seed-raisers do not usually take any precautions in separating their crops of leguminous plants, it may be asked, how are we to account for the extraordinary amount of crossing in Mr. Coe's plants in 1857, when almost every plant in the four rows of the Negro seems to have been affected? I may here add that, in an old paper in the Journal of the Bath Agricultural Society,[7] there is an almost exactly parallel account of the crossing of several varieties of the common Bean throughout a whole field. Insect agency is always at work: but the movement of the corolla will generally tend merely to push the flower's own pollen, which is mature as soon as the flower is open, on to the stigmatic surface; and even if pollen is brought by the bees from another flower, the chances are in favour of pollen from the same variety being brought, where a large stock is cultivated.

I can explain Mr. Coe's case, and that in the Bath Journal, only on one hypothesis, viz. that from some cause the Negro Beans did not, at Knowle, in 1857, produce good pollen, or they matured it later than usual. This has been shown by Gärtner sometimes to occur, and would explain, with the aid of insect agency, the whole case. Believing, as I do, that it is a law of nature that every organic being should occasionally be crossed with a distinct individual of the same species, and seeing that the structure of papilionaceous flowers causes the plant's own pollen to be pushed on to its own stigma, I am inclined to speculate a little further. It is, I think, well ascertained that very close interbreeding tends to produce sterility, at least amongst animals. Moreover, in plants, it has been ascertained that the male organs fail in fertility more readily than the female organs, both from hybridity and from other causes, and further, that they resume their fertility slower, when a hybrid is crossed in successive generations with either pure parent, than do the female organs. May we not then suppose, in the case of leguminous plants, after a long course of self-fertilization, that the pollen begins to fail, and then, and not till then, the plants are eagerly ready to receive pollen from some other variety? Can this be connected with the apparently short duration and constant succession of new varieties amongst our Peas, and, as is stated to be the case on the Continent, with Kidney Beans?

These speculations may be valueless; but I venture earnestly to request any of your correspondents who may have noticed any analogous facts connected with sudden and large variation in their seed-crops of any leguminous plants (including Sweet Peas), or any facts bearing on such plants having kept true for many consecutive generations when grown near each other, to have the kindness to take the trouble to communicate them to the 'Gardeners' Chronicle,' or to the following address, C. Darwin, Downe, Bromley, Kent.

1. *Annals and Magazine of Natural History, including Zoology, Botany, and Geology*, 3d ser., 2 (1858): 459–65. [Also, *Gardeners' Chronicle*, 13 November 1858, pp. 828–29.]†

2. See vol. 1, p. 142, "Humble-Bees."†

3. See, for example, William Gardiner, "Views on the Uses of the Nectary and Corolla in Plants," *Magazine of Natural History, and Journal of Zoology, Botany, Mineralogy, Geology, and Meteorology* 9 (1836): 195–98. Note: reference is made to observation by Dr. Darwin of two hundred butterflies visiting flowers.†

4. Arend Friedrich A. Wiegmann, *Ueber die Bastarderzeugung im Pflanzenreiche. Eine von der Königl.* Akademie der Wissenschaften zu Berlin gekrönte Preisschrift. (Braunschweig: Vieweg, 1828).†

5. Carl Friedrich Gärtner, *Versuche und Beobachtungen über die Befruchtungsorgane der vollkommeneren Gewächse und über die natürliche und Künstliche Befruchtung durch den eigenen Pollen* (Stuttgart: Schweizerbart, 1844).†

6. M. J. B[erkeley], "Vegetable Pathology," *Gardeners' Chronicle*, 24 June 1854, p. 404.†

7. Reference could not be traced.†

➤ Public Natural History Collections[1]

The following correspondence has just passed with the Chancellor of the Exchequer:—

Sir, —As one of a body of working Naturalists deeply interested in the fate of the Natural History Collections now in the British Museum, I am requested to transmit for your consideration the enclosed Memorial, which we believe to express the views of a large number of persons engaged in the pursuit of science, although it has not been considered necessary to send it round for general signature. We also understand that it has the full concurrence of Sir William Hooker and others whose official situation prevents their actually joining in it.

Should you desire to receive any personal explanation of our views we shall be happy to form a deputation to wait upon you at whatever time you may be pleased to appoint.

I have the honour, &c.,

(Signed) *John Lindley*

To the Right Honourable the Chancellor of the Exchequer

Sir, —The necessity of the removal of the Natural History Departments from the British Museum having been recently brought prominently before the Public, and it being understood that the question of their reorganisation in another locality is under consideration, the under-signed Zoologists and Botanists, professionally or otherwise engaged in the pursuit of Natural Science, feel it their duty to lay before Her Majesty's Government the views they entertain as to the arrangements by which National Collections in Natural History can be best adapted to the twofold object of the advancement of Science, and its general diffusion among the Public—to show how far the Scientific Museums of the Metropolis and its vicinity, in their present condition, answer these purposes,—and to suggest such modifications or additional arrangements as appear requisite to render them more thoroughly efficient.

The Scientific Collections or Museums, whether Zoological or Botanical, required for the objects above stated, may be arranged under the following heads: —

1. A general and comprehensive *Typical* or *Popular Museum*, in which all prominant forms or types of Animals and Plants, recent or fossil, should be so displayed as to give the Public an idea of the vast extent and variety of natural objects, to diffuse a general knowledge of the results obtained by Science in their investigation and classification, and to serve as a general introduction to the Student of Natural History.

2. A complete *Scientific Museum*, in which Collections of all obtainable Animals and Plants, and their parts, whether recent or fossil, and of a sufficient number of specimens, should be disposed conveniently for study; and to which should be exclusively attached an appropriate *Library*, or Collection of Books and Illustrations relating to Science, wholly independent of any general Library.

3. A comprehensive *Economic Museum*, in which Economic Products, whether Zoological or Botanical, with Illustrations of the processes by which they are obtained and applied to use, should be so disposed as best to assist the progress of Commerce and the Arts.

4. Collections of Living Animals and Plants, or *Zoological* and *Botanical Gardens*.

The *Typical* or *Popular Museum*, for the daily use of the general public, which might be advantageously annexed to the *Scientific Museum*, would require a large building, in a light, airy, and accessible situation. The Collections should be displayed in spacious galleries, in glass cases, so closed as to protect them from the dirt and dust raised by the thousands who would visit them; and sufficient room should be allowed within the cases to admit of affixing to the specimens, without confusion, their names, and such illustrations as are necessary to render them intelligible and instructive to the Student and the general Public.

The *Economic Museums* and *Living Collections* in Botany might be quite independent of the Zoological ones.

The *Scientific Museum*, in Zoology as in Botany, is the most important of all. It is indispensable for the study of Natural Science, although not suited for public exhibition. Without it, the Naturalist cannot even name or arrange the materials for the *Typical, Economic*, or *Living Collections*, so as to convey any useful information to the Public. The specimens, though in need of the same conditions of light, airiness, &c., as, and far more numerous than, those exposed in the *Typical* or *Popular Museum*, would occupy less space; and they would require a different arrangement, in order that the specimens might, without injury, be frequently taken from their receptacles for examination. This *Scientific Museum*, moreover, would be useless unless an appropriate Library were included in the same building.

The union of the *Zoological* and *Botanical Scientific Museums* in one locality is of no importance. The juxtaposition of each with its corresponding *Living Collection* is desirable, but not necessary—although, in the case of Botany, an extensive Herbarium and Library are indispensable appendages to the Garden and Economic Museum.

The existing Natural History Collections accessible to Men of Science and to the Public, in or near the Metropolis, are the following:—

In Botany.—The Kew Herbarium, as a Scientific Collection, is the finest in the world; and its importance is universally acknowledged by Botanists. It has an excellent Scientific Library attached to it; it is admirably situated; and being in proximity with, and under the immediate control of the Head of the Botanic Garden, it supersedes the necessity of a separate Herbarium for the use of that Garden and Museum. But a great part of it is not the property of the State; there is no building permanently appropriated for its accommodation, and it does not include any Collection of Fossil Plants.

The Botanical Collection of the British Museum, consisting chiefly of the Banksian Herbarium, is important, but very imperfect. It is badly situated, on account of the dust and dirt of Great Russell Street; and the want of space in the existing buildings of the British Museum would prevent its extension, even were there an adequate advantage in maintaining, at the cost of the State, two Herbaria or Scientific Botanic Museums so near together as those of London and Kew. The British Museum also contains a valuable Collection of Fossil Plants, but not more readily available for Science than its Zoological Collections.

There exists no Typical or Popular Botanical Museum for public inspection.

The efficiency of the Botanical Gardens and Museum of Economic Botany at Kew, as now organised, and the consequent advantages to Science and the Public, are too generally recognised to need any comment on the part of your Memorialists.

In Zoology. —The British Museum contains a magnificent Collection of Recent and Fossil Animals, the property of the State, and intended both for public exhibition and for scientific use. But there is no room for its proper display, nor for the provision of the necessary accommodation for its study—still less for the separation of a *Popular Typical* series for public inspection, apart from the great mass of specimens whose importance is appreciated only by professed Naturalists. And, in the attempt to combine the two, the Public are only dazzled and confused by the multiplicity of unexplained objects, densely crowded together on the shelves and cases; the man of science is, for three days in the week, deprived of the opportunity of real study; and the specimens themselves suffer severely from the dust and dirt of the locality, increased manifold by the tread of the crowds who pass through the galleries on Public Days, —the necessity of access to the specimens on other days preventing their being arranged in hermetically closed cases.

A Museum of Economic Zoology has been commenced at South Kensington.

There is an unrivalled Zoological Garden or Living Collection, well situated in the Regent's Park, but not the property of the State, nor receiving any other than indirect assistance, in the terms on which its site is granted.

The measures which your Memorialists would respectfully urge upon the consideration of her Majesty's Government, with a view to rendering the Collections really available for the purposes for which they are intended, are the following: —

That the Zoological Collections at present existing in the British Museum be separated into two distinct Collections,—the one to form a

Typical or *Popular Museum*, the other to constitute the basis of a complete *Scientific Museum*.

These *Museums* might be lodged in one and the same building, and be under one direction, provided they were arranged in such a manner as to be separately accessible; so that the one would always be open to the Public, the other to the man of science, or any person seeking for special information. This arrangement would involve no more trouble, and would be as little expensive as any other which could answer its double purposes as the *Typical* or *Popular Museum* might at once be made almost complete, and would require but very slight, if any, additions.

In fact, the plan proposed is only a further development of the system according to which the Entomological, Conchological, and Osteological Collections in the British Museum are already worked.

That an appropriate *Zoological Library* be attached to the *Scientific Museum*, totally independent of the Zoological portion of the Library of the British Museum, which, in the opinion of your Memorialists, is inseparable from the General Library.

That the *Scientific Zoological Museum* and *Library* be placed under one head, directly responsible to one of her Majesty's Ministers, or under an organisation similar to that which is practically found so efficient in regard to Botany.

That the Museum of *Economic Zoology* at South Kensington be further developed.

Your Memorialists recommend that the whole of the Kew Herbarium become the property of, and be maintained by, the State, as is now the case with a portion of it—that the Banksian Herbarium and the Fossil Plants be transferred to it from the British Museum—and that a permanent building be provided for the accommodation at Kew of the Scientific Museum of Botany so formed.

This consolidation of the Herbaria of Kew with those of the British Museum would afford the means of including in the *Botanical Scientific Museum* a Geographical Botanical Collection for the illustration of the Colonial Vegetation of the British Empire, which, considering the extreme importance of vegetable products to the commerce of this country, your Memorialists are convinced would be felt to be a great advantage.

Your Memorialists recommend further, that in place of the Banksian Herbarium and other miscellaneous Botanical Collections now in the British Museum and closed to the Public, a *Typical* or *Popular Museum* of Botany be formed in the same building as that proposed for the *Typical* or *Popular Museum* of Zoology, and, like it, be open daily to the Public.

Such a Collection would require no great space; it would be inexpensive, besides being in the highest degree instructive; and, like the *Typical* or *Popular Zoological Collection*, it would be of the greatest value to the public, and to the Teachers and Students of the Metropolitan Colleges.

That the *Botanical Scientific Museum* and its *Library*, the *Museum of Economic Botany*, and the *Botanic Garden*, remain, as at present, under one head, directly responsible to one of her Majesty's Ministers.

The undersigned Memorialists, consisting wholly of Zoologists and Botanists, have offered no suggestions respecting the very valuable Mineralogical Collection in the British Museum, although aware that, in case it should be resolved that the Natural History Collections generally should be removed to another locality, the disposal of the Minerals also will probably come under consideration.

November 18, 1858

George Bentham, V.P.L.S.

George Busk, F.R.S. and Z.S., Professor of Comparative Anatomy and Physiology to the Royal College of Surgeons of England

William B. Carpenter, M.D., F.R.S., and Z.S., Registrar of the University of London

Chas. Darwin, F.R.S., L.S., and G.S.

W. H. Harvey, M.D., F.R.S. and Z.S., &c., Professor of Botany, University of Dublin

Arthur Henfrey, F.R.S., L.S., &c., Professor of Botany, King's College, London

J. S. Henslow, F.L.S. and G.S., Professor of Botany in the University of Cambridge

Thomas Huxley, F.R.S., Professor of Natural History, Government School of Mines, Jermyn Street

John Lindley, F.R.S. and L.S., Professor of Botany in University College, London

1. *Gardeners' Chronicle and Agricultural Gazette*, no. 48, 27 November 1858, p. 861.†

✦ Cross-bred Plants[1]

I hope that some of your readers will respond to Mr. Westwood's[2] wish,
and give any information which they may possess on the permanence of
cross-bred plants and animals. Will Mr. Westwood be so good as to give
a reference to any account of the variability of the Swedish Turnip? I did
not even know that it was reputed to be a cross-bred production. I am
aware that this is supposed to be the case with some Turnips; but I have
searched in vain for any authentic history of their origin. No one, I
believe, doubts that cross-bred productions tend to revert in various
degrees to either parent for many generations; some say for a dozen,
others for a score or even more generations. But cannot breeders
adduce some cases of crossed breeds of sheep and pigs (such as the
Shropshire or Oxford sheep, or Lord Harborough's pigs) which are now
true? With respect to the Cottagers' Kale, I was so much surprised at the
accounts of its trueness that I procured seed from the raisers; but in my
soil the plants were far from presenting a uniform appearance. In
addition to the tendency to reversion to either parent form, it is almost
universally asserted that cross-bred productions are highly variable, and
often display characters not observed in either parent. I do not wish to
dispute this common belief, but I suspect it would puzzle any one to
adduce satisfactory cases; and certainly Gärtner has advanced a mass of
evidence on the opposite side. I am not at all surprised at Mr. Westwood
demurring to the belief that occasionally crossing the strain is advantageous or necessary with productions in a state of nature. The subject is
only just alluded to in my volume on the "Origin of Species."[3] I do not
pretend that I can prove the truth of the doctrine; but I feel sure that
many important facts and arguments can be adduced in its favour. The ill
effects of close inter-breeding between the nearest relations, especially if
exposed to the same conditions of life, would be, I believe, the same
under Nature as under domestication,—namely, some degree of sterility
and weakness of constitution. Variability arises from quite independent
causes, and is to a certain extent counteracted in its early stages by the
free crossing of the individuals of the same species. Mr. Westwood
misunderstands me if he supposes that it is my opinion that the Ibis, for
instance, keeps true to its kind "by occasional crosses with individuals of
the same species which have not sprung from the same grandfather or
great-grandfather." I only believe that if individuals of the Ibis did vary,
such crosses would tend to keep the species true; and further, if the
young from a single pair increased so slowly that they all continued to
inhabit the same small district, and if brothers and sisters often united
during successive generations, then the Ibis would rapidly deteriorate in
fertility and constitution. Mr. Westwood advances the hive-bee, as

probably a case of constant intercrossing. Andrew Knight,[4] however, who specially attended to this point, has published his belief (whether founded on sufficient evidence I will not pretend to say) that the queen-bee commonly unites with a drone from another community.

1. *Gardeners' Chronicle and Agricultural Gazette*, no. 3, 21 January 1860, p. 49.†
2. No record of Westwood's communication could be found in the previous fifteen volumes of *Gardeners' Chronicle*.†
3. 1859, pp. 96–97.†
4. Thomas Andrew Knight, "On Some Circumstances Relating to the Economy of Bees," *Philosophical Transactions of the Royal Society of London* 118 (1828): 319–24.†

❦ Natural Selection[1]

I have been much interested by Mr. Patrick Matthew's communication in the Number of your Paper, dated April 7th.[2] I freely acknowledge that Mr. Matthew has anticipated by many years the explanation which I have offered of the origin of species, under the name of natural selection. I think that no one will feel surprised that neither I, nor apparently any other naturalist, had heard of Mr. Matthew's views, considering how briefly they are given, and that they appeared in the appendix to a work on Naval Timber and Arboriculture.[3] I can do no more than offer my apologies to Mr. Matthew for my entire ignorance of his publication. If another edition of my work is called for, I will insert a notice to the foregoing effect.

1. *Gardeners' Chronicle and Agricultural Gazette*, no. 16, 21 April 1860, pp. 362–63. Also *Life and Letters of Charles Darwin*, 2:301–2.†
2. Patrick Matthew, "Nature's Law of Selection," *Gardeners' Chronicle*, no. 14, 7 April 1860, pp. 312–13.†
3. Patrick Matthew, *Naval Timber and Arboriculture* (Edinburgh: Black; London, Longman, 1831).†

❦ Fertilisation of British Orchids by Insect Agency[1]

I should be extremely much obliged to any person living where the Bee or Fly Orchis is tolerably common, if he will have the kindness to make a few simple observations on their manner of fertilisation. To render the subject clear to those who know nothing of botany, I must briefly describe what takes place in our common British Orchids. The pollen-grains form two pear-shaped masses; each borne on a foot-stalk, with a sticky gland at the end. The pollen masses are hidden in little pouches open in front. When an insect visits a flower, it almost necessarily, owing to the position of the parts, uncovers and touches the sticky glands. These firmly adhere to the head or body of the insect, and thus the pollen-masses are drawn out of their pouches, are dragged over the humid stigmatic surface, and the plant is fertilised. So beautifully are the relative degrees of adhesiveness of the gland, and of the grains of pollen to each other and to the stigmatic surface mutually adapted, that an insect with an adherent pollen-mass will drag it over the stigmas of several flowers, and leave granules of pollen on each. The contrivance by which the sticky glands are prevented from drying, and so kept always viscid and ready for action, is even still more curious; they lie suspended (at least in the two species which I have examined) in a little hemispherical cup, full of liquid, and formed of such delicate membrance, that the side projecting over the gangway into the nectary is ruptured transversely and depressed by the slightest touch; and then the glands, sticky and fresh out of their bath, immediately and almost inevitably come into contact with and adhere to the body which has just ruptured the cup. It is certain that with most of our common Orchids insects are absolutely necessary for their fertilisation; for without their agency, the pollen-masses are never removed and wither within their pouches. I have proved this in the case of *Orchis morio* and *mascula* by covering up plants under a bell-glass, leaving other adjoining plants uncovered; in the latter I found every morning, as the flowers became fully expanded, some of the pollen masses removed, whereas in the plants under the glass all the pollen-masses remained enclosed in their pouches.

Robert Brown,[2] however, has remarked that the fact of all the capsules in a dense spike of certain Orchids producing seed seems hardly reconcileable with their fertilisation having been accidentally effected by insects. But I could give many facts showing how effectually insects do their work; two cases will here suffice; in a plant of *Orchis maculata* with 44 flowers open, the 12 upper ones, which were not quite mature, had not one pollen-mass removed, whereas every one of the 32 lower flowers had one or both pollen-masses removed; in a plant of *Gymnadenia conopsea* with 54 open flowers, 52 had their pollen-masses removed. I have repeatedly observed in various Orchids grains of pollen, and in one case *three* whole pollen-masses on the stigmatic surface of a flower, which still retained its own two pollen-masses; and as often, or even oftener, I have found flowers with the pollen-masses removed, but with no pollen on their stigmas. These facts clearly show that each flower is often, or even generally, fertilised by the pollen brought by insects from another flower or plant. I may add that after observing our Orchids during many years, I have never seen a bee or any other diurnal insect (excepting once a butterfly) visit them; therefore I have no doubt that moths are the priests who perform the marriage ceremony. The structure, indeed, of some Orchids leads to this same conclusion; for no insect without a very long and extremely fine proboscis could possibly reach the nectar at the bottom of the extremely long and narrow nectary of the Butterfly-Orchis; and entomologists have occasionally captured moths with pollen-masses adhering to them. If any entomologist reads this, and can remember positively having caught a moth thus furnished, I hope he will give its name, and describe exactly to which part of the moth's body the sticky gland adhered.

We may now turn to the genus Ophrys; in the Fly Orchis (*Ophrys muscifera*), the pollen-masses, furnished with sticky glands, do not naturally fall out of their pouches, nor can they be shaken out; so that insect-agency is necessary, as with the species of the other genera, for their fertilisation. But insects here do their work far less effectually than with common Orchids; during several years, previously to 1858, I kept a record of the state of the pollen-masses in well-opened flowers of those plants which I examined, and out of 102 flowers I found either one or both pollen-masses removed in only 13 flowers. But in 1858 I found 17 plants growing near each other and bearing 57 flowers and of these 30 flowers had one or both pollen-masses removed; and as all the remaining 27 flowers were the upper and younger flowers, they probably would subsequently have had most of their pollen-masses removed, and thus have been fertilised. I should much like to hear how the case stands with the Fly Orchis in other districts; for it seems a strange fact that a plant should grow pretty well, as it does in this part of Kent, and yet during several years seldom be fertilised.

We now come to the Bee Orchis (*Ophrys apifera*), which presents a very different case; the pollen masses are furnished with sticky glands, but differently from in all the foregoing Orchids, they naturally fall out of their pouches; and from being of the proper length, though still retained at the gland-end, they fall on the stigmatic surface, and the plant is thus self-fertilised. During several years I have examined many flowers, and never in a single instance found even one of the pollen-masses carried away by insects, or ever saw the flower's own pollen-masses fail to fall on the stigma. Robert Brown consequently believed that the visits of insects would be injurious to the fertilisation of this Orchis; and rather fancifully imagined that the flower resembled a bee in order to deter their visits. We must admit that the natural falling out of the pollen-masses of this Orchis is a special contrivance for its self-fertilisation; and as far as my experience goes, a perfectly successful contrivance, for I have always found this plant self-fertilised; nevertheless a long course of observation has made me greatly doubt whether the flowers of any kind of plant are for a perpetuity of generations fertilised by their own pollen. And what are we to say with respect to the sticky glands of the Bee Orchis, the use and efficiency of which glands in all other British Orchids are so manifest? Are we to conclude that this one species is provided with these organs for no use? I cannot think so; but would rather infer that, during some years or in some other districts, insects do visit the Bee Orchis and occasionally transport pollen from one flower to another, and thus give it the advantage of an occasional cross. We have seen that the Fly Orchis is not in this part of the country by any means sufficiently often visited by insects, though the visits of insects are indispensable to its fertilisation. So with the Bee Orchis, though its self-fertilisation is specially provided for, it may not exist here under the most favourable conditions of life; and in other districts or during particular seasons it may be visited by insects, and in this case, as its pollen masses are furnished with sticky glands, it would almost certainly receive the benefit of an occasional cross impregnation. It is this curious apparent contradiction in the structure of the Bee Orchis—one part, namely the sticky glands, being adapted for fertilisation by insect agency—another part, namely the natural falling out of the pollen-masses, being adapted for self-fertilisation without insect agency—which makes me anxious to hear what happens to the pollen-masses of the Bee Orchis in other districts or parts of England. I should be extremely much obliged to any one who will take the trouble to observe this point and to communicate the result to the *Gardeners' Chronicle* or to me.

1. *Gardeners' Chronicle and Agricultural Gazette*, no. 23, 9 June 1860, p. 528.†
2. Robert Brown, "On the Organs and Mode of Fecundation in Orchideae and Asclepiadeae," *Transactions of the Linnean Society of London* 16 (1832): 685–746.†

➴ Do the Tineina or Other Small Moths Suck Flowers, and If So What Flowers?[1]

I once saw several individuals of a small moth *apparently* eating the pollen of the *Mercurialis*[2]; is this physically possible? I have during several years watched the smaller clovers, such as *Trifolium procumbens*, and the *Vicia hirsuta*[3] which has such extremely minute flowers, and I never saw a bee visit them. I am, however, aware from experience that it is very difficult to assert that bees do not visit any particular kind of plant. As Mr. F. Bond informs me that he has often seen moths visiting papilionaceous flowers, even such small ones as those of the trefoil, it has occurred to me that small moths may suck the flowers of *T. procumbens* and of *V. hirsuta*. From analogy we must believe that the smaller clovers secrete nectar; and it does not seem probable that the nectar would be wasted. I should esteem it a great favour if any Lepidopterists would communicate their experience on this point.

(In reply to Mr. Darwin's enquiry we may observe that very many of the Tineina are provided with tongues, and that these appendages are naturally used in extracting the sweets of flowers. It is no uncommon sight to see an Umbellifer swarming with the pretty little *Glyphipteryx Fischeriella*, each with its proboscis extended sucking at the flowers. The *Depressariae*, as is notorious to every collector of Noctuae, come very freely to sugar, and no doubt naturally visit flowers.

But the fertilization of flowers may be accomplished by insects in another way. Many species oviposit on the blooming flowers; they do not deposit all their eggs on a single plant, but sparingly a few here and a few there; a female protruding her ovipositor down the corolla of a flower, and then flying off to repeat the operation elsewhere may herself be "the priest who performs the marriage ceremony.")[4]

1. *Entomologist's Weekly Intelligencer* 8 (1860): 103.†
2. A member of the family Euphorbiaceae.†
3. *Vicia* is a large genus of herbaceous plants, often climbing, including vetches.†
4. Parenthetical passage by the editor of the *Gardeners' Chronicle*.†

❧ Note on the Achenia of Pumilio argyrolepis[1]

Mr. James Drummond sent me a packet of seeds of this plant from Swan River,[2] with the following memorandum:—"The achenia[3] of several small composite plants, more especially of that above named, are blown about by the wind till a shower of rain falls, when they attach themselves by a gummy matter to the soil by their lower ends, at the same time setting themselves perfectly upright. They ornament many a barren spot in this country throughout the dry season, and they are not easily removed even when the ground is flooded by thunder storms."

The achenia of the Pumilio[4] are singularly-shaped bodies; the calyx (pappus) consists generally of nine scales or sepals, expanded like a flower, with each sepal beautifully ornamented by branching lines; the lower part, including the seed, is bent towards one side (see Fig. 1) at nearly right angles, and somewhat resembles a human foot in shape. The upper side or instep of this foot is smooth, but the toe and the sole, which is about 1-25th of an inch in length, is covered (see Fig. 2) with from 30 to 40 imbricated little bladders. Each bladder is oval and 1-200th of an inch in length, and is formed of thin structureless membrane, enclosing a hard ball of dry mucus or matter which becomes adhesive when moistened. The sole or the achenium is pitted where the bladders are attached but these do not open into its interior. When the achenia are placed in water or on a damp surface, the bladders in a few minutes all burst longitudinally and discharge their contents, rendering a large drop of water very viscid. This viscid drop does not diffuse itself throughout the water, like gum, but remains surrounding the achenium. When dried it becomes stringy, and will again rapidly absorb moisture and swell. Spirits of wine does not cause the bladders to burst, and it renders the mucus slightly opaque.

If a pinch of these achenia be dropped from a little height on damp paper, the greater number fall like shuttlecocks, upright and rest on the sole; the bladders then quickly burst, and as the paper dries the seeds become firmly attached to it. Many achenia, however, drop so as to rest on one edge of the sole, and in this case the drying of the mucus pulls the upper edge of the sole down, and so places the flower-like calyx nearly upright. Any one looking at a piece of paper over which when damp a number of achenia had been scattered by chance would conclude that

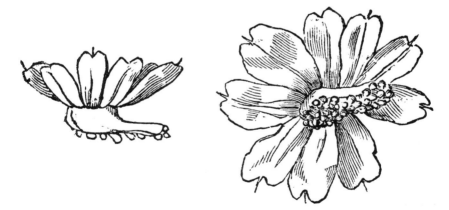

Fig. 1. Side view.　　　　**Fig. 2.** View of under side, seen a little obliquely.

each one had been placed upright and carefully gummed. If an achenium falls upside down, so as to rest on the tips of the calyx, the sole does not touch the damp surface, yet moisture is so rapidly absorbed by the sepals, that in seven minutes I have seen the bladders burst: in this case as the paper dries the exuded mucus dries on the surface of the sole and the seed is not fixed; but if subsequently it be blown the right way up on a damp surface, the mucus will soften and act and attach it firmly. In so dry a climate as Australia the existence of these little bladders of dried mucus, having a strong affinity for water and becoming highly viscid on that side alone of the achenium which alights on the ground, seems a pretty adaptation to ensure the attachment of the seed to the first damp spot on which it may be blown. Whether the tendency of the achenia to place themselves upright be of any service to the plant would be hard to determine; but it seems possible that the salver-shaped calyx, which, as we have seen, so rapidly absorbs moisture and carries it down to the lower surface of the achenia, might aid in utilising dew or showers of fine rain.

1. *Gardeners' Chronicle and Agricultural Gazette*, no. 1, 5 January 1861, pp. 4–5.†
2. Swan River: Western Australia; flows into the Indian Ocean at Perth.†
3. Dry, one-seeded fruit.†
4. *Rutidosis*; plants of Australia, belonging to the family Compositae.†

⬥ Fertilisation of British Orchids by Insect Agency[1]

I am much obliged to Mr. Marshall, of Ely, for his statement that the 15 plants of Fly Orchis (Ophrys muscifera) which does not grow in his neighbourhood, but which flourished in his garden, had not one of their pollen masses removed. The Orchis maculata, on the other hand, which likewise does not grow in the neighbourhood, had all its pollen masses removed. Mr. Marshall is not perhaps aware that different insects haunt different Orchids, and are necessary for their fertilisation. From the wide difference in shape of the flower of Orchis and Ophrys, I should have anticipated that they would be visited and fertilised by different insects. In Listera, for instance, it is chiefly Ichneumonidae,[2] and sometimes flies, which by day perform the marriage ceremony. In the case of most Orchids it is nocturnal moths. Orchis pyramidalis, however, is visited by Zygaena,[3] and I have examined one of these day-sphinxes with three pair of pollen-masses firmly attached to its proboscis. There can hardly be a doubt that the Butterfly Orchis is visited by different moths from most of the smaller Orchids; and I have recognised its peculiar pollen-masses attached to the sides of the face of certain moths. It is probable that the same kind of moths would visit all the species of true Orchis, which closely resemble each other in structure. Thus the Orchis conopsea, planted in a garden some miles from where any native plant grew, had its pollen-masses removed; so this is a parallel case with that of O. maculata given by Mr. Marshall. I have also transplanted the rare Malaxis to a place about two miles from its native bog, and it was immediately visited by some insect, and its pollen-masses were removed. On the other hand, the Epipactis latifolia, growing in my garden and flowering well, had not its pollen-masses removed; though in its own home, several miles distant, the flowers are regularly visited and thus fertilised. We thus see that the seeds of an Orchid might be carried by the wind to some distant place, and there germinate, but that the species would not be perpetuated unless the proper insects inhabited the site. I have now Goodyera repens growing in my garden, and I shall be curious to see next summer whether our southern insects discover or appreciate the nectar of this Highland Orchid.

1. *Gardeners' Chronicle and Agricultural Gazette,* no. 6, 9 February 1861, p. 122.†
2. Wasplike insects whose larvae parasitize other insects.†
3. Burnet moths.†

➤ Phenomena in the Cross-breeding of Plants[1]

Will Mr. Beaton,[2] who has made such a multitude of most interesting observations on the propagation of plants, have the kindness to state whether varieties of the same species of Composite plants frequently cross each other by insect agency or other means? For instance, will any of the Cinerarias, if kept apart from other varieties, breed true? but if standing near other varieties, will they generally, or almost certainly, produce a much greater diversity of coloured seedlings?

I saw an allusion by Mr. Beaton to this subject in The Cottage Gardener of last year with respect to Zinnias; and from this allusion I infer that Zinnia sports much when kept separate.

As I am begging for information on the natural crossing of plants, I will likewise venture to inquire whether the great raisers of Hollyhocks find it necessary to keep each variety far separate from the others for raising seed. The late famous horticulturist, the Hon. and Rev. W. Herbert, when I visited him at Spofforth many years ago, remarked that he was much surprised (considering the structure of the flower and the relative periods of maturity of the pollen and stigma) how true some sorts of Hollyhocks bred, even when growing close to other varieties. I have found this to be the case with some of the varieties, and cannot understand how it is possible. Mr. Beaton might, if he pleased, write an article, very valuable to physiological botanists and of some practical utility, on the natural crossing of varieties. He might indicate in which genera crossing most commonly occurred, and in which it seldom or never occurred. For instance, I have observed Sweet Peas during several years and believe that they never cross; and it is not easy to make an artificial cross, though I succeeded at last, but got no good in a horticultural point of view.

1. *Journal of Horticulture and Cottage Gardener,* n.s., 14 May 1861, 1:112.†
2. D. Beaton, "Phenomena in the Cross-breeding of Plants," *Journal of Horticulture and Cottage Gardener,* n.s., 18 June 1861, p. 211. Darwin's article is part of a larger one by Beaton in which many examples are given in answer to Darwin's questions.†

❦ Fertilisation of Vincas[1]

I do not know whether any exotic Vincas seed, or whether gardeners would wish them to seed, and so raise new varieties. Having never observed the large Periwinkle or Vinca major to produce seed, and having read that this never occurs in Germany, I was led to examine the flower. The pistil, as botanists know, is a curious object, consisting of a style, thickening upwards, with a horizontal wheel on the top; and this is surmounted by a beautiful brush of white filaments. The concave tire of the wheel is the stigmatic surface, as was very evident when pollen was placed on it, by the penetration of the pollen-tubes. The pollen is soon shed out of the anthers, and lies embedded in little alcoves in the white filamentous brush above the stigma. Hence it was clear that the pollen could not get on to the stigma without the aid of insects, which, as far as I have observed in England, never visit this flower. Accordingly, I took a fine bristle to represent the proboscis of a moth, and passed it down between the anthers, near the sides of the corolla; for I found that the pollen sticks to the bristle and is carried down to the viscid stigmatic surface. I took the additional precaution of passing it down first between the anthers of one flower and then of another, so as to give the flowers the advantage of a cross; and I passed it down between several of the anthers in each case. I thus acted on six flowers on two plants growing in pots; the germens of these swelled, and on four out of the six I have now got fine pods, above 1½ inch in length, with the seeds externally visible; whereas the flower stalks of the many other flowers all shanked off. I wish any one who wishes to obtain seed of any other species that does not habitually seed would try this simple little experiment and report the result. I shall sow the seeds of my Vinca for the chance of a sport: for a plant which seeds so rarely might be expected to give way to some freak on so unusual and happy an occasion.

1. *Gardeners' Chronicle and Agricultural Gazette,* no. 24, 15 June 1861, p. 552.†

◆ Fertilization of Orchids[1]

I have been endeavouring during several years to make out the many contrivances by which British Orchids are fertilised through insect agency. I am very anxious to examine a few exotic forms. Several gentlemen have kindly sent me specimens; but I have not seen one of Lindley's grand division of Arethuseae, which includes the Limodorideae, Vanillideae, &c. If any one would have the kindness to send me a few flowers and buds of any member of the group, packed in a small tin canister, by post, addressed as below, he would confer a very great favour on me. Would you have the kindness to inform me, if in your power, whether the late Professor Morren[2] has published anything (and where) on the fertilisation of Orchids by insect agency?—Down, Bromley, Kent.

1. *Gardeners' Chronicle and Agricultural Gazette*, no. 37, 14 September 1861, p. 831.†
2. Charles Francis Antoine Morren. See *Catalogue of Scientific Papers, Royal Society* 4 (1870): 478–84, for list of 157 papers by Morren; several are on orchids and on fertilization by insect agency.†

◆ Vincas[1]

A writer in your columns (p. 699)[2] states that he caused Vinca rosea to seed at the Royal Gardens, Kew, by imitating the action of an insect in inserting its proboscis, as I had succeeded with the common Periwinkle. By implication it may be presumed that V. rosea had not previously seeded at Kew. But another writer, "F. A. P." (p. 736)[3] states that his Vincas seed profusely. Mr. Horwood, gardener to G. H. Turnbull, Esq., of this place, has just been so kind as to bring me a small plant of Vinca rosea with nine flowers fertilised by the insertion of a horse-hair, and it now bears nine fine pods. Mr. Horwood says he has grown many plants for the last eight or nine years, and never before saw a pod. What can be the cause of the difference in the results obtained on the one hand by "F. A. P.", and on the other by the writer from Kew and Mr. Horwood? Will "F. A. P." have the kindness to state, if he sees this notice, whether his plants were in a greenhouse with the windows left open, so that the moths could get access at night?[4]

1. *Gardeners' Chronicle and Agricultural Gazette*, no. 37, 14 September 1861, pp. 831–32.†
2. "C.W.C.," "Fertilisation of Vinca rosea," *Gardeners' Chronicle*, no. 30, 27 July 1861, p. 699.†
3. "F.A.P.," "Vincas," *Gardeners' Chronicle*, no. 32, 10 August 1861, p. 736.†
4. No answer published in *Gardeners' Chronicle* through 12 October 1861.†

◄ Cross-breeding in Plants: Fertilisation of Leschenaultia formosa [1]

Much obliged am I to Mr. Beaton for his very interesting answer to my question. When Mr. Beaton says he does "not know of an instance of the natural crossing of varieties," I presume he intends to confine his remark to the plants of the flower garden; for every one knows how largely the varieties of the Cabbage cross, as is likewise the case (as I know from careful trial) with Radishes and Onions. It was this fact which led me to suppose that varieties of flower-garden plants would naturally cross.

I can quite understand, after reading Mr. Beaton's remarks, that it would be very difficult, perhaps impossible, to detect such natural crossing from the degree to which most of these varieties vary. I should, however, think that those who raise for sale seeds of distinct varieties of the Hollyhock, Stocks, &c., must know whether it is indispensable to keep the parent plants apart.

I will not trouble Mr. Beaton again if he will have the kindness to procure for me answers on one or two points quoted in his paper (June 26, 1860) from the "king of British cross-breeders"—namely, whether I understand rightly that the white *Anemone apennina* seeding in a mass with the blue (*Anemone apennina*?) produced many pale shades? For this seems to be a case of two varieties naturally crossing, though I want to know the fact for another reason—namely, because Anemone does not secrete nectar; and secondly, whether *Mathiola incana* and *glabra*, which the writer speaks of as "crossing freely," were artificially crossed.

Mr. Beaton's statement (July 24, 1860) that if the pollen of five kinds of Geranium (I presume what botanists call varieties, and not what are called species, are here referred to) are placed on the stigma of a flower, one kind alone takes the lead and produces an effect, seems to me a most curious observation. It is, I fear, unreasonable to ask for a few precise cases on this head; for, as I gather from Mr. Beaton, it must be difficult to know whether one or more kinds have produced an effect, owing to the great variability of crossed varieties.

I have been delighted to observe how strongly Mr. Beaton insists that "not a flower in a thousand is fertilised by its own immediate pollen." This is a subject which I have attended to for the last twenty years. From my experiments on a small scale I would not venture to put the case nearly as strongly as Mr. Beaton does; but on the other hand, some of the plants which Mr. Beaton advances as self-fertilisers seem, as far as I can trust my own observations, doubtful. I will give one instance, as it might possibly induce some one to try the experiment. *Leschenaultia formosa* has apparently the most effectual contrivance to prevent the stigma of one flower ever receiving a grain of pollen from another flower; for the pollen is shed in the early bud, and is there shut up round the stigma within a cup or indusium. But some observation led me to suspect that nevertheless insect agency here comes into play; for I found by holding a camel-hair pencil parallel to the pistil, and moving it as if it were a bee going to suck the nectar, the straggling hairs of the brush opened the lip of the indusium, entered it, stirred up the pollen, and brought out some grains. I did this to five flowers and marked them. These five flowers all set pods; whereas only two other pods set on the whole plant, though covered with innumerable flowers. The seeds in these pots were bad, or else I had not skill to make them germinate. I became so strongly convinced that insects would be found concerned in the fertilisation of these flowers, that I wrote to Mr. James Drummond, at Swan River in Australia, and asked him to watch the flowers of plants of this order; and he soon wrote to me that he had seen a bee cleverly opening the indusium and extracting pollen; and a bee with its mandibles thus covered with pollen would very likely effect a cross between one individual and another of the same species. I have been told that this pretty plant, the *Leschenaultia formosa*, never sets seed in this country. I wish some skilful cultivator would rout up the pollen within the indusium in the manner described, and see whether he could not thus get seeds.

1. *Journal of Horticulture and Cottage Gardener*, n.s., 28 May 1861, 1:151.†

✒ Cause of the Variation of Flowers[1]

"D." of Deal, states, and, apparently, he is corroborated by Mr. Lightbody, that when Auriculas[2] throw up side blooms these keep pretty true to their character; but that when they throw up a heart bloom—that is, from the axis of the plant, the flower, no matter what may be the colour of its edging, "is just as likely to come in any other class as in the one it belongs to." This seems to be an extremely curious observation. It shows that some little light could be thrown on the laws of variation, if the many acute observers who read the Journal of Horticulture would contribute their knowledge on such points. I wish "D." would have the kindness to give a few more details, such as out of so many heart blooms so many lost their character, and so many kept true; giving also the proportion in the side blooms which kept true.

As I am appealed to, I will make a few observations on this subject; but I have no doubt others could throw more light on the question. Professor Moquin-Tandon[3] asserts, that with irregular flowers, as Snapdragons, the terminal flower in the axis of the plant is more apt to become regular, or peloric as botanists say, than the other flowers. I once found a Laburnum tree with the terminal flower on each raceme nearly regular, having lost its peablossom structure. With many Pelargoniums[4] (I have one at present in my greenhouse, but I know not its name), the central flower in each truss every year comes regular, loses the two dark patches of colour on the two upper petals, and, what is very curious, loses the nectary, which may be seen in all the other flowers cohering to the flower-stalk. In the common Carrot the central floret in the umbel is dark purple and very different from the others; and I find that this central little flower is extremely variable. Are there not other cases of species which habitually have the central flower different from the others? It must, however, be confessed, that Mr. Masters,[5] a high authority on such subjects, disputes that peloric flowers are apt to be central; but it seems to me extremely improbable that the several recorded cases should be due to chance, and all these facts seem to hang together and to indicate that in the flower nearest the axis there is a tendency to differ from the others, or to be variable, or to revert to a hypothetical regular form— that is, as I should look at it, to revert to the structure of a remote ancestor. The curious case of the Auricula apparently falls into this same group of facts.

I hope that some of your correspondents will state whether in the case of single buds sporting, as has so often occurred with Pelargoniums, it has been observed that such sports occur more frequently on one part of the plant than on another. I suppose it is not so, or it would have been noted. Having alluded to the central flower in certain Pelargoniums which have lost the two dark patches of colour and the nectary, I would venture to ask some skilful observer to try whether this flower could be made by artificial fertilisation and by pulling off *some* of the adjoining flowers to yield seed. The stigma should be fertilised with pollen from, if possible, a peloric flower on another plant; and access of other pollen should, of course, be prevented. Peloric flowers have generally been found quite sterile; but Willdenow[6] got seeds from a peloric Snapdragon, and the peculiarity was inherited: hence it is possible, though not probable, that a new strain of quite symmetrically-flowered Pelargoniums might be thus raised. Experiments are tedious and very often fail; but it would be well worth while for any man endowed with plenty of patience to collect seed from the central floret and from the other florets on the same truss of any ordinary Pelargonium, and sow them separately and see which varied most. Of course, all the flowers should be fertilised by the same pollen and subsequently protected from insects.

The same law which causes the heart bloom on an individual Auricula not to keep so true as a side bloom, might cause the seedlings of the central flower of a Pelargonium or other plant to vary more than the seedlings from the other and exterior flowers. This would be a secret worth discovering and revealing.

1. *Journal of Horticulture and Cottage Gardener,* n.s. 18 June 1861, 1:211.†

2. Yellow-flowered primrose.†

3. Horace Bénédict Alfred Moquin-Tandon, *Éléments de Tératologie végétale, ou, histoire abrégée des anomolies de l'organisation dans les végétaux* (Paris: Loss, 1841).†

4. "Geraniums."†

5. Maxwell T. Masters, "On the Proliferation in Flowers, and Especially on that Form Termed Median Proliferation," *Transactions of the Linnean Society* 23 (1862): 359–70, and, "On the Proliferation in Flowers, and Especially on that Kind Termed Axillary Proliferation," ibid., pp. 481–93. See also additional papers by Masters on plant morphology listed in *Catalogue of Scientific Papers, Royal Society* 4 (1870): 280–81.†

6. Carl Ludwig Willdenow. See "Beschreibung einiger Pflanzengattungen," *Magazin der Gesellschaft Naturforschender Freunde zu Berlin* 5 (1811): 396–402. For additonal titles, see *Catalogue of Scientific Papers, Royal Society* 6 (1872): 372–74.†

On the Two Forms, or Dimorphic Condition, in the Species of *Primula*, and on Their Remarkable Sexual Relations[1]

If a large number of Primroses or Cowslips (*P. vulgaris* and *veris*) be gathered, they will be found to consist, in about equal numbers, of two forms, obviously differing in the length of their pistils and stamens. Florists who cultivate the Polyanthus[2] and Auricula are well aware of this difference, and call those which display the globular stigma at the mouth of the corolla "pin-headed" or "pin-eyed," and those which display the stamens "thumb-eyed." I will designate the two forms as long-styled and short-styled. Those botanists with whom I have spoken on the subject have looked at the case as one of mere variability, which is far from the truth.[3]

In the Cowslip, in the long-styled form, the stigma projects just above the tube of the corolla, and is externally visible; it stands high above the anthers, which are situated halfway down the tube, and cannot be easily seen. In the short-styled form the anthers are attached at the mouth of the tube, and therefore stand high above the stigma; for the pistil is short, not rising above halfway up the tubular corolla. The corolla itself is of a different shape in the two forms, the throat or expanded portion above the attachment of the anthers being much longer in the long-styled than in the short-styled form. Village children notice this difference, as they can best make necklaces by threading and slipping the corollas of the long-styled flowers into each other. But there are much more important differences. The stigma in the long-styled plants is globular, in the short-styled it is depressed on the summit, so that the longitudinal axis of

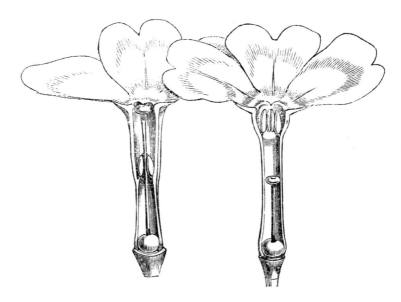

Fig. 1. Long-styled (left) and short-styled (right).

the former is sometimes nearly double that of the latter. The shape, however, is in some degree variable; but one difference is persistent, namely, that the stigma of the long-styled is much rougher: in some specimens carefully compared, the papillae which render the stigmas rough were in the long-styled form from twice to thrice as long as in the short-styled. There is another and more remarkable difference, namely, in the size of the pollen-grains. I measured with the micrometer many specimens, dry and wet, taken from plants growing in different situations, and always found a palpable difference. The measurement is best made with grains distended with water, in which case, the usual size of the grains from short-styled flowers is seen to be 10–11/7000 of an inch in diameter, and those from the long-styled about 7/7000 of an inch, which is in the proportion of three to two; so that the pollen-grains from the short stamens are plainly smaller than those from the long stamens which accompany the short pistil. When examined dry, the smaller grains from the long-styled plants are seen under a low power to be more transparent than the larger grains, and apparently in a greater degree than can be accounted for by their less diameter. There is also a difference in shape, the grains from the short-styled plants being nearly spherical, those from the long-styled being oblong with the angles rounded; this difference in shape disappears when the grains are distended with water. Lastly, as we shall presently see, the short-styled plants produce more seed than the long-styled.

To sum up the differences:—The long-styled plants have a much longer pistil, with a globular and much rougher stigma, standing high above the anthers. The stamens are short; the grains of pollen smaller and oblong in shape. The upper half of the tube of the corolla is more expanded. The number of seeds produced is smaller.

The short-styled plants have a short pistil, half the length of the tube of the corolla, with a smooth depressed stigma standing beneath the anthers. The stamens are long; the grains of pollen are spherical and larger. The tube of the corolla is of the same diameter till close to its upper end. The number of seeds produced is larger.

I have examined a large number of flowers; and though the shape of the stigma and the length of the pistil vary, especially in the short-styled form, I have never seen any transitional grades between the two forms. There is never the slightest doubt under which form to class a plant. I have never seen the two forms on the same plant. I marked many Cowslips and Primroses, and found, the following year, that all retained the same character, as did some in my garden which flowered out of their proper season in the autumn. Mr. W. Wooler, of Darlington, however, informs us that he has seen the early blossoms on Polyanthuses which were not long-styled, but which later in the season produced flowers of this form. Possibly the pistils may not in these cases have become fully developed during the early spring. An excellent proof of the permanence of the two forms is seen in nursery gardens, where choice varieties of the Polyanthus are propagated by division; and I found whole beds of several varieties, each consisting exclusively of the one or the other form. The two forms exist in the wild state in about equal numbers; I collected from several different stations, taking every plant which grew on each spot, 522 umbels; 241 were long-styled, and 281 short-styled. No difference in tint or size could be perceived in the two great masses of flowers.

I examined many cultivated Cowslips (*P. veris*) or Polyanthuses, and Oxlips; and the two forms always presented the same differences, including the same relative difference in the size of the pollen-grains.

Primula Auricula presents the two forms; but amongst the improved fancy kinds the long-styled are rare, as these are less valued by florists, and seldomer distributed. There is a much greater relative inequality in the length of the pistils and stamens than in the Cowslip, the pistil in the long-styled form being nearly four times as long as in the short-styled, in which it is barely longer than the ovarium; the stigma is nearly of the same shape in both forms, but it is rougher in the long-styled, though the difference is not so great as in the two forms of the Cowslip. In the long-styled plants the stamens are very short, rising but little above the ovarium. The pollen-grains of these short stamens from the long-styled plants, when distended with water, were barely 5/6000 of an inch in diameter, whereas those from the long stamens of the short-styled plants were barely 7/6000, showing a relative difference of five to seven. The smaller grains of the long-styled plants were much more transparent, and before distention with water more triangular in outline than those of the other form. In one anomalous specimen with a long pistil, the stamens almost surrounded the stigma, so that they occupied the position proper to the stamens of the short-styled form; but the small size of the pollen-grains showed that these stamens had been abnormally developed in length, and that the anthers ought to have stood at the base of the corolla.

In the two forms of *Primula Sinensis*, the pistil is about twice as long in the one as in the other. The stigma of the long-styled varies much in shape, but is considerably more elongated and rougher than that of the short-styled, the latter being nearly smooth and spherical, but depressed on the summit. The shape of the throat of the corolla in the two forms differs as in the Cowslip, as does the length of the stamens. But it is remarkable that the pollen-grains of both forms, wet and dry, presented no difference in diameter; they vary somewhat in size, as do the pollen-grains of all the species, but in both forms the average diameter was rather above 10/6000 of an inch. There is one remarkable difference in the two forms of this species, namely (as we shall presently more fully see), that the short-styled plants, if insects be excluded and there be no artificial fertilization, are quite sterile, whereas the long-styled produce a moderate quantity of seed. But when both forms are properly fertilized, the short-styled flowers (as with Cowslips) yield more seed than the long-styled. In a lot of seedlings which I raised, there were thirteen long-styled and seven short-styled plants.

Of *Primula ciliata* a long-styled specimen, and of *P. ciliata*, var. *purpurpata*, a short-styled specimen, were sent me from Kew by Prof. Oliver. This case, however, is hardly worth giving, as the variety *purpurata* is said[4] to be a hybrid between this species and *P. auricula;* and the height of the stamens in the one form does not correspond with the height of the stigma in the other, as they would have done had they been the same species. There was, however, the usual difference in the roughness of the stigmas in the two forms, and the pollen-grains, distended in water, measured 6/6000 and 4–5/6000 of an inch in diameter. Single trusses were sent me of *P. denticulata* and *P. Piedmontana* which were long-styled, and of *P. marginata* and *nivalis* which were short-styled; and the general character of the organs leaves hardly any doubt on my mind that these species are dimorphic. In a single flower of *P. Sibirica*, however, which was sent me from Kew, the stigma reached up to the base of the anthers; so that this species is not dimorphic, or not dimorphic as far as the length of the pistil and stamens are concerned, unless indeed this single specimen was anomalous, like that mentioned of *P. auricula.*

We thus see that the existence of two forms is very general, if not universal, in the genus *Primula.* The simple fact of the pollen-grains differing in size and outline, and the stigma, in shape and roughness, in two sets of individuals of the same species, is curious. But what, it may be asked, is the meaning of these several differences? The question seems worthy of careful investigation, for, as far as I know, the use or meaning of dimorphism in plants has never been explained; hence, I will give my observations in detail, though I am far from supposing that all cases of dimorphism are alike. The first idea which naturally occurred was, that the species were tending towards a dioicous condition; that the long-styled plants, with their rougher stigmas, were more feminine in nature, and would produce more seed; that the short-styled plants, with their long stamens and larger pollen-grains, were more masculine in nature. Accordingly, in 1860, I marked some Cowslips of both forms growing in my garden, and others growing in an open field, and others in a shady wood, and gathered and weighed the seed. In each of these little lots the short-styled plants yielded, contrary to my expectation, most seed. Taking the lots together, the following is the result:—

	No. of Plants	No. of Umbels produced	No. of Capsules produced	Weight of seed in grains
Short-styled Cowslips	9	33	199	83
Long-styled Cowslips	13	51	261	91

If we reduce these elements for comparison to similar terms, we have—

	No. of Plants	Weight of seed in grains	No. of Umbels	Weight of seed	No. of Capsules	Weight of seed in grains
Short-styled Cowslips	10	92	100	251	100	41
Long-styled Cowslips	10	70	100	178	100	34

So that, by all the standards of comparison, the short-styled are the most fertile; if we take the number of umbels (which is the fairest standard, for large and small plants are thus equalized), the short-styled plants produce more seed than the long-styled, in the proportion of four to three.

In 1861 I tried the result in a fuller and fairer manner. I transplanted in the previous autumn a number of wild plants into a large bed in my garden, treating them all alike; the result was—

	No. of Plants	No. of Umbels	Weight of seed in grains
Short-styled Cowslips	47	173	745
Long-styled Cowslips	58	208	692

These figures, reduced as before, give the following proportions:—

	Number of Plants	Weight of seed in grains	Number of Umbels	Weight of seed in grains
Short-styled Cowslips	100	1585	100	430
Long-styled Cowslips	100	1093	100	332

The season was much better this year than the last, and the plants grew in good soil, instead of in a shady wood or struggling with other plants in the open field; consequently the actual produce of seed was considerably greater. Nevertheless we have the same relative result; for the short-styled plants produced more seed than the long-styled in the proportion of three to two; but if we take the fairest standard of comparison, namely, the number of umbels, the excess is, as in the former case, as four to three.

I marked also some Primroses, all growing together under the same conditions; and we here see the product:—

	No. of Plants	Total No. of Capsules	Good Capsules	Weight of seed in grains	Or by Calculation:	Good Capsules	Weight of seed
Short-styled Primroses	8	49	40	16		100	40
Long-styled Primroses	9	68	50	10		100	20

The number of Primrose plants tried was hardly sufficient, and the season was bad; but we here again see (excluding the capsules which contained no seed) the same result in a still more marked manner, for the short-styled plants were twice as productive of seed as the long-styled plants.

I had, of course, no means of ascertaining the relative fertility of the two forms of the Chinese Primrose in a natural condition, and the result of artificial fertilization can hardly be trusted; but sixteen capsules from long-styled flowers, properly fertilized, produce 9.3 grains' weight of seed, whereas eight capsules of short-styled flowers produced 6.1 grains; so that if the same number, namely, 16 of the latter, had been fertilized, the weight of seed would have been 12.2, which would have been nearly in the proportion of four to three, as in Cowslips.

Looking to the trials made during two successive years on the large number of Cowslips, and on these facts with regard to common Primroses and Chinese Primroses, we may safely conclude that the short-styled forms in these species are more productive than the long-styled forms; consequently the anticipation that the plants having largely developed pistils with rougher stigmas, and having shorter stamens with smaller pollen-grains, would prove to be more feminine in their nature is exactly the reverse of the truth. If the species of *Primula* are tending to become dioicous, which possibly may be the case, the future hypothetical females would have short pistils, and the males would have short stamens; but this tendency is accompanied, as we shall presently see, by other conditions of the generative system of a much more singular nature. Anyhow, the possibility of a plant thus becoming dioicous by slow degrees is worthy of notice, as the fact would so easily escape observation.

In 1860 I found that a few umbels of both long-styled and short-styled Cowslips, which were covered by a net, did not produce seed, though other umbels on the same plants, artificially fertilized, produced an abundance of seed; and this fact shows that the mere covering in itself was not injurious. Accordingly, in 1861 I covered up under a similar net several plants just before they opened their flowers; these turned out as follows: —

	No. of Plants	No. of Umbels produced	Product of Seed
Short-styled	6	24	1.3 grains, or 50 seeds
Long-styled	18	74	Not one seed

Judging from the exposed plants which grew all round in the same bed, and had been treated in every way exactly the same, except that they were exposed to the visits of insects, the six short-styled plants ought to have produced 92 grains' weight of seed instead of only 1.3; and the eighteen long-styled plants, which produced not one seed, ought to have produced above 200 grains' weight. The production of the 1.3 grain of seed in the smaller lot was probably due to the action of Thrips or some minute insect. This evidence is sufficient, but I may add that ten pots of Polyanthuses and Cowslips of both forms, protected from insects in my greenhouse, did not set one pod, though artificially fertilized flowers in other pots produced an abundance. So we see that the visits of insects are absolutely necessary to the fertilization of Cowslips. As the exposed plants produced an abundance of seed, the tendency to a dioicous condition, previously remarked on, might have been safely carried on, as we see that there is an effective agency already at work which would have carried pollen from one sex to the other.

What insects habitually visit Cowslips, as is absolutely necessary for their regular fertility, I do not know. I have often watched them, but perhaps not long enough; and only four times I have seen Humble-bees visiting them. One of these bees was gathering pollen from short-styled flowers alone, another had bitten holes through the corolla; and neither of these would have been effective in the act of fertilization: two others were sucking long-styled plants. I have watched Primroses more attentively during several years, and have never seen an insect visit them; yet from their close similarity in all essential respects to Cowslips, there can hardly be a doubt that they require the visits of insects. Hence I am led to suppose that both Primroses and Cowslips are visited by moths. All the species which I have examined secrete plenty of nectar.

In *Primula Sinensis*, when protected from insects and not artificially fertilized, the case is somewhat, but not materially, different. Five short-styled plants produced up to a given period 116 flowers, which set only seven capsules, whereas twelve other flowers on the same plants artificially fertilized set ten capsules. Five long-styled plants produced 147 flowers, and set sixty-two capsules; so that this form, relatively to the other, sets a far greater number of capsules: yet the long-styled protected flowers do not set nearly so well as when artificially fertilized; for out of forty-four flowers thus treated, thirty-eight set. These remarks apply only to the early setting of the capsules, many of which did not continue swelling. With respect to the product of seed, seven protected short-styled plants, which bore about 160 flowers, produced only half a grain of seed; they ought to have produced 120 grains: so that the short-styled plants, when protected from insects, are nearly as sterile as Cowslips. Thirteen long-styled plants, which bore about 380 flowers, and which as we have seen set many more capsules, produced 25.9 grains of seed; they ought to have produced about 220 grains in weight: so that although far less fertile than the artificially fertilized flowers, yet the long-styled *P. Sinensis*, when protected from insects, is nearly twenty-four times as fertile as the short-styled when protected from insects. The cause of this difference is, that when the corolla of the long styled plants falls off, the short stamens near the bottom of the tube are necessarily dragged over the stigma and leave pollen on it, as I saw by hastening the fall of nearly withered flowers; whereas in the short-styled flowers, the stamens are seated at the mouth of the corolla, and in falling off do not brush over the lowly seated stigma. In the Cowslip the corolla does not fall off; and both long-styled and short-styled plants are equally sterile when protected from insects. It is a rather curious case, that the falling of the corolla, or its remaining attached when withered, might have a considerable influence on the numbers of a plant, during a year unfavourable to the visits of the proper insects.

In three short-styled plants of *Primula auricula*, protected from insects, the flowers which I fertilized produced seed, but those which were not touched produced none.

In all the species of *Primula* the pollen readily coheres to any object. In all that I have observed, though the stamens and pistils differ in length relatively to each other in the different species, yet, in the two forms of the same species, the stigma of the one form stands at exactly the same height with respect to the corolla as the anthers of the other form. If the proboscis of a dead Humble-bee, or thick bristle, or rough needle be pushed down the corolla, first of one form, and then of the other, as an insect would do in visiting the two mingled forms, it will be found that pollen from the long-stamened form will adhere round the base of the proboscis, and will be left with certainty on the stigma of the long-styled form; pollen from the short stamens of the long-styled form will also adhere a little above the tip of the proboscis, and some will generally be left on the stigma of the other form. Thus pollen will be carried reciprocally from one form to the other. In withdrawing the proboscis from the long-styled form, with pollen adhering near the tip, there will be a good chance of some being left on the flower's own stigma, in which case there will be self-fertilization; but this by no means always occurs. In the short-styled form, on the other hand (and it is important to remember this), in inserting the proboscis between the anthers situated at the mouth of the corolla, pollen, as I repeatedly found, is almost invariably carried down and left on the flower's own stigma. Moreover minute insects, such as Thrips, numbers of which I have observed in Primrose flowers thickly dusted with pollen, could not fail often to cause self-fertilization. We positively know that the visits of large insects are necessary to the fertilization of the species of *Primula*; and we may infer from the facts just given that these visits would carry pollen reciprocally from one form to the other, and would likewise *tend* to cause self-fertilization, more especially in the short-styled (*i.e.* long-stamened) form.

These observations led me to test the potency of the two pollens with respect to the two stigmas in *P. veris*, *Sinensis*, and *auricula*. In each species four crosses can be tried; namely, the stigma of the long-styled by its own-form pollen and by that of the short-styled, and the stigma of the

	Number of flowers fertilized	Total number of pods produced	Number of good pods	Weight of seed in grains	By Calculation: Good pods Weight of seed in grains
Long-styled by own-form pollen (homomorphic union)	20	18	13	5.9	or as 100 to 45
Long-styled by pollen of short-styled (heteromorphic union)	24	18	16	9.3	or as 100 to 58
Short-styled by own-form pollen (homomorphic union)	7	5	4	0.9	or as 100 to 22
Short-styled by pollen of long-styled (heteromorphic union)	8	8	8	6.1	or as 100 to 76
Summary: The two homomorphic unions	27	23	17	6.8	
The two heteromorphic unions	32	26	24	15.4	

Table I   *Primula Sinensis.*

short-styled by its own-form pollen and by that of the other form. It is necessary to use and remember two new terms for these crosses: when the long- and the short-styled stigmas are fertilized by their own-form pollen the union is said to be "homomorphic"; when the long-styled and short-styled stigmas are fertilized by the pollen of the other form, the union is "heteromorphic." I speak of the "own-form pollen," because in the following homomorphic unions, in order to make the experiment perfectly fair, I never placed the pollen of the same flower on its own stigma, but, to avoid the possible ill effects of close interbreeding, I always used the pollen from another plant of the same form. In the following experiments all the plants were treated in exactly the same manner, and were carefully protected from insects as far as that is possible. I performed every manipulation myself, and weighed the seed in a chemical balance. Some of the capsules contained no seed, or only two or three, and these are excluded in the column marked "good pods." First for *P. Sinensis*, as the simplest case.

For the sake of comparison, we may reduce these latter figures as follows: —

	Number of flowers fertilized	Number of good pods	Weight of seed in grains	Number of good pods	Weight of seed in grains
The two homomorphic unions	100	63	25	100	40
The two heteromorphic unions	100	75	48	100	64

In the first part of the upper table, the number of flowers fertilized and the simple result is shown; and at the right hand, for the sake of comparison, the calculated product of the weight of seed from 100 good pods of each of the four unions is given; showing that in each case the heteromorphic union is more fertile than the homomorphic union. Beneath we have a simple summary of the two homomorphic and the two heteromorphic unions. And lastly, for the sake of comparison, a calculation has been made from this summary; first, assuming that 100 flowers of both kinds of unions were fertilized; and then to the right hand, assuming that 100 good pods were produced from both unions. If we compare the result, we see that the flowers of the two heteromorphic unions produced a greater number of good pods, and a greater weight of seed, than the flowers of the two homomorphic unions; and again (and this is the fairest element of comparison, for accidents are thus almost eliminated), that the good pods from the two heteromorphic unions yielded more seed, in about the proportion of three to two, than those from the two homomorphic unions. The difference in weight from 100 capsules of the two forms is 24 grains, and this is equal to at least 1200 seeds.

Beneath we have Table II. of *P. veris*, or the Cowslip. The upper part is exactly the same as in the Table of *P. Sinensis*, and we see in each case that the heteromorphic is more fertile than the homomorphic union. The calculated results from the summary of the two homomorphic and the two heteromorphic unions are more complex than with the last species, and I wished to show that, however we proceed, the general result is the same. We see that the assumed hundred flowers, heteromorphically fertilized by the pollen of the other forms, yielded more capsules, more good capsules, and a greater weight of seed; but I rely little on this, as some whole umbels perished after being fertilized. The fairest element of comparison is to take the good capusles alone; and we here see that the 100 from the two heteromorphic unions yielded seed which in weight was as 54 to 35 from the 100 good capsules of the two homomorphic unions,—that is, nearly as three to two, as in the Chinese Primrose.

	Number of flowers fertilized	Total number of pods produced	Number of good pods	Weight of seed in grains	By Calculation: Good Pods Weight of seed in grains
Long-styled by own-form pollen (homomorphic union)	20	8	5	2.1	or as 100 to 42
Long-styled by pollen of short-styled (heteromorphic union)	22	15	14	8.8	or as 100 to 62
Short-styled by own-form pollen (homomorphic union)	15	8	6	1.8	or as 100 to 30
Short-styled by pollen of long-styled (heteromorphic union)	13	12	11	4.9	or as 100 to 44
Summary: The two homomorphic unions	35	16	11	3.9	
The two heteromorphic unions	35	27	25	13.7	

Table II   *Primula veris.*

For the sake of comparison, we may reduce these figures as follows:—

	Number of flowers fertilized	Total number of pods produced	Number of good pods	Weight of seed in grains	Total number of pods produced	Weight of seed in grains	Number of good pods	Weight of seed in grains
The two homomorphic unions	100	45	31	11	100	24	100	35
The two heteromorphic unions	100	77	71	39	100	50	100	54

With *P. auricula* I was unfortunate; my few seedlings, except one poor plant, all came up short-styled; and of these plants several died or became sick, owing to the hot weather and the difficulty of excluding insects and ventilating the corner of my greenhouse enclosed with net. I finally got only two pods from one union, and three from the other. The result is given in the following table; and, though worth little, we here again see that the heteromorphic are far more fertile than the homomorphic unions.

	Total number of pods produced	Number of good pods	Weight of seed in grains	Good Pods Weight of seed in grains
Short-styled by own-form pollen (homomorphic union)	2	1	0.12	or as 100 to 12
Short-styled by pollen of long-styled (heteromorphic union)	3	3	1.50	or as 100 to 50

Table III   *Primula auricula.*

Whoever will study these three tables, which give the result of 134 flowers carefully fertilized and protected, will, I think, be convinced that in these three species of *Primula* the so-called heteromorphic unions are more fertile than the homomorphic unions. For the sake of clearness, the general result is given in the following diagram, in which the dotted lines with arrows represent how in the four unions pollen has been applied.

We here have a case new, as far as I know, in the animal and vegetable kingdoms. We see the species of *Primula* divided into two sets or bodies, which cannot be called distinct sexes, for both are hermaphrodites; yet they are to a certain extent sexually distinct, for they require for perfect fertility reciprocal union. They might perhaps be called sub-dioicous

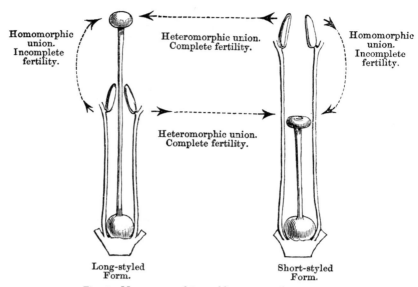

Homomorphic
union.
Incomplete
fertility.

Heteromorphic union.
Complete fertility.

Homomorphic
union.
Incomplete
fertility.

Heteromorphic union.
Complete fertility.

Long-styled
Form.

Short-styled
Form.

Fig. 2. Heteromorphic and homomorphic unions.

hermaphrodites. As quadrupeds are divided into two nearly equal bodies of different sexes, so here we have two bodies, approximately equal in number, differing in their sexual powers and related to each other like males and females. There are many hermaphrodite animals which cannot fertilize themselves, but must unite with another hermaphrodite: so it is with numerous plants; for the pollen is often mature and shed, or is mechanically protruded, before the flower's own stigma is ready; so that these hermaphrodite flowers absolutely require for their sexual union the presence of another hermaphrodite. But in *Primula* there is this wide difference, that one individual Cowslip, for instance, though it can with mechanical aid imperfectly fertilize itself, for full fertility must unite with another individual; but it cannot unite with any individual in the same manner as an hermaphrodite Snail or Earth-worm can unite with any other one Snail or Earth-worm; but one form of the Cowslip, to be perfectly fertile, must unite with one of the other form, just as a male quadruped must and can unite only with a female.

I have spoken of the heteromorphic union in *Primula* as resulting in full fertility; and I am fully justified, for the Cowslips thus fertilized actually gave rather more seed than the truly wild plants—a result which may be attributed to their good treatment and having grown separately. With respect to the lessened fertility of the homomorphic unions, we shall appreciate its degree best by the following facts. Gärtner has estimated the degree of sterility of the union of several distinct species,[5] in a manner which allows of the strictest comparison with the result of the heteromorphic and homomorphic unions of *Primula*. With *P. veris*, for every hundred seeds yielded by the heteromorphic unions, only sixty-four seeds were yielded by an equal number of good capsules from the homomorphic unions. With *P. Sinensis* the proportion was nearly the same—namely, as 100 to 62. Now Gärtner has shown that, on the calculation of *Verbascum lychnitis* yielding with its own pollen 100 seeds, it yields when fertilized by the pollen of *V. Phoeniceum* ninety seeds; by the pollen of *V. nigrum*, sixty-three seeds; by that of *V. blattaria*, sixty-two seeds. So again, *Dianthus barbatus* fertilized by the pollen of *D. superbus* yielded eighty-one seeds, and by the pollen of *D. Japonicus* sixty-six seeds, relatively to the 100 seeds produced by its own pollen. Thus we see—and the fact is highly remarkable—that the homomorphic unions relatively to the heteromorphic unions in *Primula* are more sterile than the crosses between several distinct species relatively to the pure union of those species.

The meaning or use of the existence in *Primula* of the two forms in about equal numbers, with their pollen adapted for reciprocal union, is tolerably plain; namely, to favour the intercrossing of distinct individuals. With plants there are innumerable contrivances for this end; and no one will understand the final cause of the structure of many flowers without attending to this point. I have already shown that the relative heights of the anthers and stigmas in the two forms lead to insects leaving the pollen of the one form on the stigma of the other; but, at the same time, there will be a strong probability of the flower's own pollen being likewise placed on the stigma. It is perfectly well known that if the pollen of several closely allied species be placed on the stigma of a distinct species, and at the same time, or even subsequently, its own pollen be placed on the stigma, this will entirely destroy the simultaneous or previous action of the foreign pollen. So again if the pollen of several varieties, including the plant's own pollen, be placed on the stigma, one or more of the varieties will take the lead and obliterate the effect of the others: but I have not space here to give the facts on which this conclusion is grounded. Hence we may infer as highly probable that, in *Primula*, the heteromorphic pollen which we know to be so much the most effective would obliterate the action of the homomorphic pollen when left on the flower's own stigma by insects; and thus we see how potent the dimorphic condition of the pollen in *Primula* will be in favouring the intercrossing of distinct individuals. The two forms, though both sexes are present in each, are in fact dioicous or unisexual. Whatever advantage there may be in the separation of the sexes, towards which we see so frequent a tendency throughout nature, this advantage has been here so far gained, that the one form is fertilized by the other, and conversely; and this is effected by the pollen of each form having less potency than that of the other on its own stigma.

Bearing on this view of the final cause of the dimorphism of the *Primulas*, there is another curious point. If we look at the right-hand figures of the four first lines in the previous tables of *P. Sinensis* and *veris*, we shall see that one of the homomorphic unions, namely, the short-styled by its own-form pollen, is considerably more sterile than the other; and in *P. auricula*, though here there is no other homomorphic union as a standard of comparison, this union is likewise excessively sterile. That the fertility of this union is really less in a marked degree than in the other three unions, we have an independent proof in the seeds germinating less perfectly and much more slowly than those from the other unions. This fact is the more remarkable, because we have clearly seen that the short-styled form in the Cowslip in a state of nature is the most productive of seed. This form bears its anthers close together at the mouth of the corolla, and I observed long before I had ascertained the relative fertility of the four unions, in passing the proboscis of a dead Humble-bee or bristle down the corolla, that in this form the flower's own pollen was almost certain to be left on its own stigma; and, as I wrote down at the time, the chance of self-fertilization is much stronger in this than in the other form. On this view we can at once understand the good of the pollen of the short-styled form, relatively to its own stigma, being the most sterile; for this sterility would be the most requisite to check self-fertilization, or to favour intercrossing. Hence, also, it would appear that there are four grades of fertility from the four possible unions in *Primula*; of the two homomorphic unions, as we have just seen, one is considerably more sterile than the other. In the wild state we know that the short-styled plants are more fertile than the long-styled; and we may infer as almost certain, that in the wild state, when the flowers are visited by insects, as is absolutely necessary for the production of seed, and when pollen is freely carried from one form to the other, that the unions are heteromorphic; if so, there are two degrees of fertility in the heteromorphic unions, making altogether four grades of fertility.

Two or three other points deserve a passing notice. The question whether the Primrose and Cowslip (*P. vulgaris* and *veris*) are distinct species or varieties has been more disputed and experimented on than in any other plant. But as we now know that the visits of insects are indispensable to the fertilization of these plants, and that in all probability the heteromorphic pollen of a Primrose would be prepotent on the stigma of a Cowslip over the homomorphic pollen of a Cowslip, the numerous experiments which have been made, showing that Oxlips appear amongst the seedlings of Cowslips, cannot be trusted, as the parent plants do not appear to have been carefully protected from insects.[6] I am far from wishing to affirm that pure Cowslips will not produce Oxlips, but further experiments are absolutely necessary. We may also suspect that the fact noticed by florists,[7] that the varieties of the Polyanthus never come true from seed, may be *in part* due to their habitually crossing with other varieties of the Polyanthus.

The simple fact of two individuals of the same undoubted species, when homomorphically united, being as sterile as are many distinct species when crossed, will surprise those who look at sterility as a special endowment to keep created species distinct. Hybridizers have shown[8] that individual plants of the same species vary in their sexual powers, so far that one individual will unite more readily than another individual of the same species with a distinct species. Seeing that we thus have a groundwork of variability in sexual power, and seeing that sterility of a peculiar kind has been acquired by the species of *Primula* to favour intercrossing, those who believe in the slow modification of specific forms will naturally ask themselves whether sterility may not have been slowly acquired for a distinct object, namely, to prevent two forms, whilst being fitted for distinct lines of life, becoming blended by marriage, and thus less well adapted for their new habits of life. But many great difficulties would remain, even if this view could be maintained.

Whether or not the dimorphic condition of the *Primulae* has any bearing on other points in natural history, it is valuable as showing how nature strives, if I may so express myself, to favour the sexual union of distinct individuals of the same species. The resources of nature are illimitable; and we know not why the species of *Primula* should have acquired this novel and curious aid for checking continued self-fertilization through the division of the individuals into two bodies of hermaphrodites with different sexual powers, instead of by the more common method of the separation of the sexes, or by the maturity of the male and female elements at different periods, or by other such contrivances. Nor do we know why nature should thus strive after the intercrossing of distinct individuals. We do not even in the least know the final cause of sexuality; why new beings should be produced by the union of the two sexual elements, instead of by a process of parthenogenesis. When we look to the state in which young mammals and birds are born, we can at least see that the object gained is not, as has sometimes been maintained, mere dissemination. The whole subject is as yet hidden in darkness.

I will now only add that cases of dimorphism, like that of *Primula*, seem to be far from rare in the vegetable kingdom, though they have been little attended to. A large and important class of analogous facts will probably soon be discovered. Professor Asa Gray[9] informs me, that he and Dr. Torrey have described several Rubiaceous genera, in which some plants have exserted stamens, and others exserted pistils. "Mitchella offers an interesting instance of this structure from its relationship, through *Nertera*, to *Coprosma*, one of the few dioecious genera of *Rubiaceae*, and in which the stamens are elongated in the male flowers and the styles in the females." The long-styled hermaphrodite flowers of Mitchella would probably be found more productive of seed than the short-styled; in the same way, but in a reversed manner, as in *Primula*, the short-styled flowers are more productive than the long-styled; from which fact I inferred that, if *Primula* were to become dioecious, the females would have short pistils and the males short stamens, these being the corresponding organs necessary for a heteromorphic union with full fertility. In the dioecious *Coprosma*, on the other hand, the females have long pistils, and the males have long stamens. These facts probably show us the stages by which a dioecious condition has been acquired by many plants.

Prof. A. Gray also informs me that another Rubiaceous genus (*Knoxia*) in India has been described by Dr. Wight, with a similar structure; and this, I am told, is the case with *Cinchona*. Several species of North American *Plantago* are dimorphic, as is *Rhamnus lanceolatus*, as far as its female organs are concerned. In the *Boragineae*, Dr. Torrey has observed a strongly marked instance in *Amsinckia spectabilis:* in some dried flowers sent me by Prof. Gray, I find that the pistil in the one form is more than twice as long as in the other, with a corresponding difference in the length of the stamens; in the short-styled flowers the grains of pollen, as in *Primula*, apparently are larger, in the proportion of nine to seven, than in the long-styled flowers, which have the short stamens; but the difference can hardly be determined with safety in dried flowers. In *Mertensia alpina*, another member of the *Boragineae*, Prof. Gray finds a new and inexplicable case,—namely, some specimens with the stamens and pistil sub-exserted, and other specimens with *both* organs seated low down the tube of the corolla. Dr. Torrey and Prof. Gray have designated all such plants as "dioeciously dimorphous." In the *Labiatae*, Mr. Bentham informs me that several species of *AEgiphyla*, and some of *Mentha*, are dimorphic like *Primula*. The case of *Thymus* is different, as I know from my own observations; but I will not here enlarge on this genus. Again, as I hear from Mr. Bentham, numerous species of *Oxalis* are similarly dimorphic. I can add the genus *Linum*. So that we already know of species (generally several in the same genus) having distinct dimorphic individuals, as far as structure is concerned, however it may prove in function, in no less than eight natural orders.

With respect to *Linum*, I will not here enter on details, as I intend to try further experiments next summer; but I may state, that I observed many years ago two forms in *Linum flavum*, with both the pistils and stamens differing in length. In *Linum grandiflorum* there are likewise two forms which present no difference in their male organs, but the pistil and stigmatic surfaces are much longer in the one form than in the other. The short-styled form, I have good reason to believe, is highly fertile with its own pollen; whether it be more fertile with the pollen of the long-styled form, I cannot at present say. The long-styled form, on the other hand, is quite sterile with its own pollen: several plants grew in my garden, remote from the short-styled plants; their stigmas were coloured blue with their own pollen; but although they produced a vast number of flowers, they did not produce a single seed-capsule. It seemed a hopeless experiment; but I had so much confidence from my trials on *Primula*, that I put a little pollen from the short-styled plants on the stigmas (already blue with their own pollen) of twelve flowers on two of the long-styled plants. From these twelve flowers I got eight remarkably fine seed-capsules; the other flowers not producing a single capsule. The existence of plants in full health, and capable of bearing seed, on which their own pollen produces no more effect than the pollen of a plant of a different order, or than so much inorganic dust, is one of the most surprising facts which I have ever observed.

1. [Read 21 November 1861.] *Journal of the Proceedings of the Linnean Society (Botany)* 6 (1862): 77–96.†

2. Oxlip with many-flowered umbel.†

3. This article, with major deletions, additions, and editorial changes, was reprinted in Charles Darwin, *The Different Forms of Flowers on Plants of the Same Species* (London: Murray, 1877), pp. 14–30.†

4. Sweet's 'Flower Garden,' vol. v. tab. 123.

5. Versuche über die Bastarderzeugung, 1849, s. 216.

6. Mr. Sidebotham (Phytologist, vol. iii. pp. 703–5) states that he protected his plants from crossing; but as he gives in detail all the precautions which he took, and says nothing about artificial fertilization, we may conclude that he did not fertilize his plants. As he raised very numerous seedlings, he would have had to fertilize many flowers, if they had been really well guarded against the visits of insects. Hence I conclude that his results are not worthy of trust.

7. Mr. D. Beaton, in 'Journal of Horticulture,' May 28, 1861, pp. 154, 244.

8. Gärtner, Bastarderzeugung, s. 165.

9. See also Prof. Asa Gray's 'Manual of the Botany of the N. United States, 1856, p. 171. For *Plantago*, see p. 269.

⚓ On the Three Remarkable Sexual Forms of *Catasetum tridentatum*, an Orchid in the Possession of the Linnean Society[1]

The President and Officers of the Linnean Society having kindly permitted me to examine the remarkable specimen, preserved in spirits in their collection, of an Orchid bearing flowers of two supposed genera, and known sometimes to bear the flowers of a third genus, I have thought that the Society might like to hear a short account and explanation of this singular case. The following details will hereafter appear in a small work on the 'Fertilization of Orchids by Insect-agency,' which I am preparing for early publication.[2]

Botanists were astonished when Sir R. Schomburgk[3] stated that he had seen three distinct forms, believed to constitute three distinct genera, namely *Catasetum tridentatum, Monachanthus viridis*, and *Myanthus barbatus*, all growing on the same plant. Lindley[4] remarked that "such cases shake to the foundation all our ideas of the stability of genera and species." Sir R. Schomburgk affirms that he has seen hundreds of plants of *C. tridentatum* in Essequibo[5] without ever finding one specimen with seeds,[6] but that he was surprised at the gigantic seed-vessels of the *Monachanthus*; and he correctly remarks that here we have traces of sexual difference in Orchideous flowers.

The general appearance of the flower of *Catasetum tridentatum*, in its natural position, is given in the diagram, p. 64 (Fig. 1); but the two lower sepals have been cut off. The column is figured separately in an upright position, showing the two curious prolongations of the rostellum, or, as I shall call them, the antennae.

A deep chamber, which from its homological relations must be called the stigmatic chamber, lies between the bases of the antennae; and the anther, with its concealed pollen-masses, is seated above. My object is

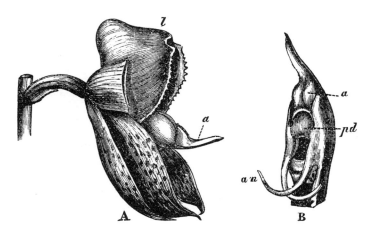

Fig. 1. *Catasetum tridentatum*. A, side view of flower in its natural position with the properly lower sepals cut off. B, front view of column, placed upright. *a*, anther; *pd*, pedicel of pollinium; *an*, antennae; *l*, labellum.

not here to describe in detail the structure of the flower and its curious mechanism. But it must be observed that the ovarium is much shorter, thinner, less deeply furrowed, more solid in the centre, and the bract at its base smaller, than in the two succeeding sexual forms presently to be described. The ovarium is bent so that the bucket-like labellum stands uppermost, instead of forming the lower lip as in most Orchids.

From what I had myself observed previously to reading Sir R. Schomburgk's paper, I was led to examine carefully the female organs of this species, and, I may add, of *C. callosum* and *C. saccatum*. In no case was the stigmatic surface viscid, as it is in all other Orchids (excepting *Cypripedium*), and as is indispensable for securing the pollen-masses on the rupture of the caudicles. I carefully looked to this point in both young and old flowers of *C. tridentatum*. When the surface of the stigmatic chamber and of the stigmatic canal of the above-named three species is scraped off, after having been kept in spirits of wine, it is found to be composed of utriculi (with nuclei of the proper shape), but not nearly so numerous as with ordinary Orchids. The utriculi cohere more together, and are more transparent. I examined for comparison the utriculi of many kinds of Orchids, which had been kept in spirits, and in all found they were much less transparent. Again, in all three species of *Catasetum* the ovule-bearing cords are short, and the ovules present a considerably different appearance, in being thinner, more transparent, and less pulpy than in the numerous other Orchids examined for comparison. They were, however, in not so completely an atrophied condition as in the genus *Acropera*. Although they correspond so closely in general appearance and position with true ovules, perhaps I have no strict right so to designate them, as I was unable in any case to make out the opening of the testa and the included nucleus; nor were the ovules ever inverted. From these several facts—namely, the shortness, thinness, and smoothness of the ovarium, the shortness of the ovule-bearing cords, the state of the ovules themselves, the stigmatic surface not being viscid, the empty condition of the utriculi—and from Sir R. Schomburgk never having seen *C. tridentatum* producing seed in its native home, we may confidently look at this species of *Catasetum*, as well as the other two species, as male plants.

With respect to *Monachanthus viridis* and *Myanthus barbatus*, these two forms are seen, in the specimen sent home by Sir R. Schomburgk, and preserved in spirits in the Society's collection, to be borne on the same spike. They are represented in the diagrams, page 66. The flower of the *Monachanthus*, like that of the *Catasetum*, grows lower side uppermost. The labellum is not nearly so deep, especially on the sides, and its edges are crenated. The other petals and sepals are all reflexed, and are not so much spotted as in the *Catasetum*. The bract at the base of

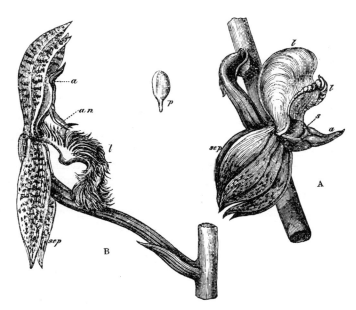

Fig. 2. *Myanthus barbatus* (left) and *Monachanthus viridis* (right). A, side view of *Monachanthus viridis* in its natural position. B, side view of *Myanthus barbatus* in its natural position. *a*, anther; *an*, antennae; *l*, labellum; *p*, pollen-mass, rudimentary; *s*, stigmatic cleft; *sep*, two lower sepals. (The shading in both drawings has been added from M. Reiss's drawing in the 'Linnean Transactions.')

the ovarium is much larger. The whole column, especially the filament at its summit and the spike-like anther, is much shorter; and the front of the rostellum is much less protuberant. The antennae or horn-like prolongations of the rostellum are entirely absent. The pollen-masses are rudimentary: I could find no trace of a viscid disk or of a pedicel; if they exist, they must be quite rudimentary, for there is hardly any space for the imbedment of the disk. The absence of the antennae in this Orchid, which has no pollen-masses to eject, is an interesting fact, as it accords with the view to which I have been led by an examination of three living species of *Catasetum*, namely, that the function of the antennae is to convey the stimulus of a touch to the medial part of the rostellum, causing the membrane round the disk to rupture, and consequently the liberation and ejection of the pollen-masses. Instead of a large stigmatic chamber, there is a narrow transverse cleft close beneath the small anther. I was able to insert one of the pollen-masses of the male *Catasetum* into this cleft, which, from having been kept in spirits, was lined with coagulated beads of viscid matter and with utriculi. The utriculi, differently from those in *Catasetum*, were charged (after having been kept in spirits) with brown matter. The ovarium is much longer, thicker near the base, and more plainly furrowed than in *Catasetum*; the ovule-bearing cords are also much longer, and the ovules more opake and pulpy, as in all common Orchids. I believe that I saw the opening at the partially inverted end of the testa with a large nucleus projecting; but as the specimens had been kept many years in spirits, and were somewhat altered, I dare not speak positively. From these several facts it is almost certain that *Monachanthus* is a female plant; and Sir R. Schomburgk saw it seeding abundantly. Altogether this flower differs in a most remarkable manner from that of the male *Catasetum tridentatum*, and it is no wonder that they were formerly ranked as distinct genera.

The pollen-masses offer so curious and good an illustration of a structure in a rudimentary condition, that they are worth description; but first I must briefly describe the perfect pollen-masses of the male *Catasetum*. These consist of a large sheet of cemented or waxy pollen-grains, folded over so as to form a sac with an open slit along the lower surface; into this slit cellular tissue enters whilst the pollen is in the course of development in the bud. Within the lower and produced end of each pollen-mass a layer of highly elastic tissue, forming the caudicle, is attached, the other end being attached to the strap-shaped pedicel of the pollinium. The exterior grains of pollen are more angular, have thicker walls, and are yellower than the interior grains. In the early bud the two pollen-masses are enveloped in two conjoined membranous sacs, which are soon penetrated by the two produced ends of the pollen-masses, and by their caudicles; and then the ends of the caudicles adhere to the pedicel. Before the flower expands, the membranous sacs including the pollen-masses open, and leave them resting naked on the back of the rostellum.

In *Monachanthus* the two membranous sacs containing the rudimentary pollen-masses never open; they easily separate from each other and from the anther. The tissue of which they are formed is thick and pulpy. Like most rudimentary parts, they vary greatly in size and in form. The included, and therefore useless, pollen-masses are not one-tenth of the bulk of the pollen-masses of the male: they are flask-shaped, with the lower and produced end greatly exaggerated, and almost penetrating through the exterior or membranous sac. The flask is closed, and there is no fissure along the lower surface. The exterior pollen-grains are square and have thicker walls than the interior grains, just as in the proper male pollen; and what is very curious, each cell has its nucleus. Now R. Brown[7] states that, in the early stages of the formation of the pollen-grains in ordinary Orchids, a minute areola or nucleus is often visible; so that the rudimentary pollen-grains of the *Monachanthus* apparently have retained (as is so general with rudiments in the animal kingdom) an embryonic character. Lastly, at the base, within the flask of pollen, there is a little sheet of brown elastic tissue—that is, a vestige of a caudicle—which runs far up the produced end of the flask, but does not (at least in some of the specimens) come to the surface, and could not have been attached to any part of the rostellum. These rudimentary caudicles are, therefore, utterly useless.

We thus see that every single detail of structure of the male pollen-masses, with some parts exaggerated and some parts slightly modified, is represented by these mere rudiments in the female plant. Such cases are familiar to every observer, but can never be examined without renewed interest.

We now come to the third form, *Myanthus barbatus*, often borne on the same plant with the two preceding forms. Its flower, in external appearance, but not in essential structure, is the most different of all. It generally stands in a reversed position, compared with *Catasetum* and *Monachanthus*—that is, with the labellum downwards. The labellum is fringed, in an extraordinary manner, with long papillae; it has a quite insignificant medial cavity, at the hinder margin of which a curious curved and flattened horn projects. The other petals and sepals are spotted and elongated, with the two lower sepals alone reflexed. The antennae are not so long as in the male *C. tridentatum*, and they project symmetrically on each side of the horn-like projection at the base of the labellum, with their tips (which are not roughened with papillae as in the male flower) almost entering the medial cavity. The stigmatic chamber is of nearly intermediate size between that of the male and female forms; it is lined with utriculi, charged with brown matter. The straight and well-furrowed ovarium is nearly twice as long as in *Monachanthus*, but is not so thick where it joins the flower; the ovules are not so numerous as in the female form, but are opake and pulpy after having been kept in spirits, and resemble them in all respects. I believe, but dare not speak positively as in the case of the *Monachanthus*, that I saw the nucleus projecting from the testa. The pollinia are about a quarter of the size of those of the male *Catasetum*, but have a perfectly well developed disk and pedicel. The pollen-masses were lost in the specimens examined by me; but fortunately M. Reiss has given, in the 'Linnean Transactions,'[8] a drawing of them, showing that they are of due proportional size, and have the proper folded or cleft structure; so that there can hardly be a doubt that they are functionally perfect. As we thus see that both the male and female organs are apparently perfect, *Myanthus barbatus* may be considered as the hermaphrodite form of the same species, of which the *Catasetum* is the male, and the *Monachanthus* the female.

It is not a little singular that the hermaphrodite *Myanthus* should resemble in its whole structure much more closely the male forms of two distinct species (namely *C. saccatum* and, more especially, *C. callosum*) than either its own male or female forms.

Finally, the genus *Catasetum* is interesting in an unusual degree in several respects. The separation of the sexes is unknown in other Orchids, excepting probably in the allied genus *Cycnoches* and in one other member of the *Vandeae*, namely, *Acropera*. In *Catasetum* we have three sexual forms, generally borne on separate plants, but sometimes mingled together; and these three forms are wonderfully different from each other—much more different than, for instance, a peacock is from a peahen. But the appearance of these three forms on the same plant now ceases to be an anomaly, and can no longer be viewed as an unparalleled instance of variability.

Still more interesting is this genus in its mechanism for fertilization. We see a flower patiently waiting, with its antennae stretched forth in a well-adapted position, ready to give notice whenever an insect puts its head into the cavity of the labellum. The female *Monachanthus*, not having pollinia to eject, is destitute of antennae. In the male and hermaphrodite forms, namely *Catasetum* and *Myanthus*, the pollinia lie doubled up like a spring, ready to be instantaneously shot forth when the antennae are touched. The disk end is always projected foremost, and is coated with viscid matter, which quickly sets hard and firmly affixes the hinged pedicel to the insect's body. The insect flies from flower to flower, till at last it visits a female or hermaphrodite plant; it then inserts one of the balls of pollen into the stigmatic cavity. When the insect flies away, the elastic caudicle, made weak enough to yield to the viscidity of the stigmatic surface, breaks, and leaves behind the pollen-mass; then the pollen-tubes slowly protrude, penetrate the stigmatic canal, and the act of fertilization is completed. Who would have been bold enough to surmise that the propagation of a species should have depended on so complex, so apparently artificial, and yet so admirable an arrangement?

1. [Read 3 April 1862.] *Journal of the Proceedings of the Linnean Society (Botany)* 6 (1862): 151–57.†

2. *On the Various Contrivances by which British and Foreign Orchids are Fertilised by Insects* . . . (London: Murray, 1862), pp. 236–48 (much revised in book).†

3. 'Transactions of the Linnean Society,' vol. xvii. p. 522. Another account, by Dr. Lindley, has appeared in the 'Botanical Register,' vol. xxiii. fol. 1951, of a distinct species of *Myanthus* and *Monachanthus* appearing on the same scape: he alludes also to other cases. Some of the flowers were in an intermediate condition, which is not surprising, seeing that in dioecious plants we sometimes have a partial resumption of the characters of both sexes. Mr. Rogers, of River Hill, informs me that he imported from Demerara a *Myanthus*, but that when it flowered a second time it was metamorphosed into a *Catasetum*. Dr. Carpenter ('Comparative Physiology,' fourth edition, p. 633) alludes to an analogous case which occurred at Bristol.

4. 'The Vegetable Kingdom,' 1853, p. 178.

5. County, British Guiana.†

6. Brongniart states (Bull. de la Soc. Bot. de France, 1855, tom. ii. p. 20) that M. Neumann, a skilful fertilizer of Orchids, could never succeed in fertilizing *Catasetum.*

7. Transactions of the Linnean Society, vol. xvi. p. 711.

8. This article could not be traced. Darwin probably had an advanced copy, which was later withdrawn.†

✒ Peas[1]

Will any one learned in Peas have the kindness to tell me whether Knight's Tall Blue and White Marrows were raised by Knight himself? If so, I presume that they are the offspring of the crosses described by him in the Philosophical Transactions for 1799.[2] I find that the name "Knight" tacked to a Pea is not a guarantee that the sort was of his production. I will beg permission to ask one other question. Has any one who has saved seed Peas grown close to other kinds observed that the succeeding crop came up untrue or crossed? This certainly occurs rarely if ever; yet from what I have observed on the manner of fructification of the Pea, I should have expected that such crossing would occasionally happen, as in the case of Dwarf Kidney Beans, of which fact I gave a striking example in your Paper of October 25, 1857.[3]

1. *Gardeners' Chronicle and Agricultural Gazette,* no. 45, 8 November 1862, p. 1052.†

2. Thomas Andrew Knight, "Experiments on the Fecundation of Vegetables," *Philosophical Transactions of the Royal Society of London* 89 (1799): 195.†

3. See vol. 1, p. 275, "Bees and Fertilisation of Kidney Beans."†

✒ Cross-breeds of Strawberries[1]

Will any of your correspondents who have attended to the history of the Strawberry, kindly inform me whether any of the kinds now, or formerly, cultivated have been raised from a cross between any of the Woods or Alpines with the Scarlets, Pines, and Chilis? Also, whether any one has succeeded in getting any good from a cross between the Hautbois and any other kind? I am aware that Mr. Williams, of Pitmaston, succeeded in getting some sterile hybrids from the Hautbois and Woods; but whether these were ever at all largely propagated, I cannot find out. I am, also, aware that Mr. Knight and Mr. Williams raised many seedlings by crossing Scarlets, Pines, and Chilis; but what I want to know is, whether any one has crossed these three latter kinds with the Wood or Alpine. I should feel greatly indebted to any one who would take the trouble to inform me on this head.

1. *Journal of Horticulture and Cottage Gardener,* n.s., 25 November 1862, 3:672.†

⚓ Variations Effected
by Cultivation[1]

As you have been so obliging as to insert my query on the crossing of Strawberries, perhaps you will grant me the favour to insert two or three other questions, for the chance of some one having the kindness to answer them. I am writing a book on "Variation under Domestication,"[2] in which I treat chiefly on animals; but I wish to give some few facts on the changes of cultivated plants.

1st. The fruit of the wild Gooseberry is said to weight about 5 dwts.[3] (I am surprised that it is so heavy), and from various records I find that towards the close of the last century the fruit had doubled in weight; in 1817, a weight of 26 dwts. 17 grs. was obtained; in 1825, 31 dwts. 13 grs.; in 1841, "Wonderful" weighed 32 dwts. 16 grs.; in 1845, "London" reached the astonishing weight of 36 dwts. 16 grs., or 880 grains. I find in the "Gooseberry Register" for 1862, that this famous kind attained only the weight of 29 dwts. 8 grs., and was beaten by "Antagonist." Will any one have the kindness to inform me whether it is authentically known that the weight of 36 dwts. 16 grs., has, since the year 1845, been ever excelled?

2nd. Is any record kept of the diameter attained by the largest Pansies? I have read of one above 2 inches in diameter, which is a surprising size compared with the flowers of the wild Viola tricolor, and the allied species or varieties.

3rd. How early does any variety of the Dahlia flower? Mr. Salisbury, writing in 1808,[4] shortly after the first introduction of this plant into England, speaks of their flowering from September, or the end of September, to November. Whereas, Mr. J. Wells, in Loudon's "Gardener's Magazine" for 1828,[5] states that some of his dwarf kinds began flowering in June. I presume the end of June. Do any of the varieties now regularly flower as early as June? Have any varieties been observed to withstand frost better than other varieties?

If any one will give me information on these small points, I shall feel greatly obliged.

1. *Journal of Horticulture and Cottage Gardener,* n.s., 2 December 1862, 3:696.†

2. *The Variation of Animals and Plants under Domestication* (London: Murray, 1868).†

3. Dwt: a pennyweight; 1/20 ounce.†

4. [Read 5 April 1808.] R. A. Salisbury, "Observations on the Different Species of Dahlia," *Transactions of the Horticultural Society of London* 1 (1812): 84–98.†

5. William Smith, "On Dahlias," *Gardener's Magazine and Register of Rural & Domestic Improvement* 3 (1828): 179–81. Smith refers to Wells in the article.†

✒ [Recollections of
Professor Henslow][1]

I went to Cambridge early in the year 1828, and soon became acquainted, through some of my brother entomologists, with Professor Henslow, for all who cared for any branch of natural history were equally encouraged by him. Nothing could be more simple, cordial, and unpretending than the encouragement which he afforded to all young naturalists. I soon became intimate with him, for he had a remarkable power of making the young feel completely at ease with him; though we were all awe-struck with the amount of his knowledge. Before I saw him, I heard one young man sum up his attainments by simply saying that he knew everything. When I reflect how immediately we felt at perfect ease with a man older and in every way so immensely our superior, I think it was as much owing to the transparent sincerity of his character, as to his kindness of heart; and, perhaps, even still more to a highly remarkable absence in him of all self-consciousness. One perceived at once that he never thought of his own varied knowledge or clear intellect, but solely on the subject in hand. Another charm, which must have struck every one, was that his manner to old and distinguished persons and to the youngest student was exactly the same: to all he showed the same winning courtesy. He would receive with interest the most trifling observation in any branch of natural history; and however absurd a blunder one might make, he pointed it out so clearly and kindly, that one left him no way disheartened, but only determined to be more accurate the next time. In short, no man could be better formed to win the entire confidence of the young, and to encourage them in their pursuits.

His Lectures on Botany were universally popular, and as clear as daylight. So popular were they, that several of the older members of the University attended successive courses. Once every week he kept open house in the evening, and all who cared for natural history attended these parties, which, by thus favouring intercommunication, did the same good in Cambridge, in a very pleasant manner, as the Scientific Societies do in London. At these parties many of the most distinguished members of the University occasionally attended; and when only a few were present, I have listened to the great men of those days, conversing on all sorts of subjects, with the most varied and brilliant powers. This was no small advantage to some of the younger men, as it stimulated their mental activity and ambition. Two or three times in each session he took excursions with his botanical class; either a long walk to the habitat of some rare plant, or in a barge down the river to the fens, or in coaches to some more distant place, as to Gamlingay,[2] to see the wild lily of the valley, and to catch on the heath the rare natter-jack.[3] These excursions have left a delightful impression on my mind. He was, on such occasions, in as good spirits as a boy, and laughed as heartily as a boy at the misadventures of those who chased the splendid swallow-tail butterflies across the broken and treacherous fens. He used to pause every now and then and lecture on some plant or other object; and something he could tell us on every insect, shell, or fossil collected, for he had attended to every branch of natural history. After our day's work we used to dine at some inn or house, and most jovial we then were. I believe all who joined these excursions will agree with me that they left an enduring impression of delight on our minds.

As time passed on at Cambridge I became very intimate with Professor Henslow, and his kindness was unbounded; he continually asked me to his house, and allowed me to accompany him in his walks. He talked on all subjects, including his deep sense of religion, and was entirely open. I owe more than I can express to this excellent man. His kindness was steady: when Captain Fitzroy offered to give up part of his own cabin to any naturalist who would join the expedition in H.M.S. *Beagle*, Professor Henslow recommended me, as one who knew very little, but who, he thought, would work. I was strongly attached to natural history, and this attachment I owed, in large part, to him. During the five years' voyage, he regularly corresponded with me and guided my efforts; he received, opened, and took care of all the specimens sent home in many large boxes; but I firmly believe that, during these five years, it never once crossed his mind that he was acting towards me with unusual and generous kindness.

During the years when I associated so much with Professor Henslow, I never once saw his temper even ruffled. He never took an ill-natured view of any one's character, though very far from blind to the foibles of others. It always struck me that his mind could not be even touched by any paltry feeling of vanity, envy, or jealousy. With all this equability of temper and remarkable benevolence, there was no insipidity of character. A man must have been blind not to have perceived that beneath this placid exterior there was a vigorous and determined will. When principle came into play, no power on earth could have turned him one hair's breadth.

After the year 1842, when I left London, I saw Professor Henslow only at long intervals; but to the last, he continued in all respects the same man. I think he cared somewhat less about science, and more for his parishioners. When speaking of his allotments, his parish children, and plans of amusing and instructing them, he would always kindle up with interest and enjoyment. I remember one trifling fact which seemed to me highly characteristic of the man: in one of the bad years for the potato, I asked him how his crop had fared; but after a little talk I perceived that, in fact, he knew nothing about his own potatoes, but seemed to know exactly what sort of crop there was in the garden of almost every poor man in his parish.

In intellect, as far as I could judge, accurate powers of observation, sound sense, and cautious judgment seemed predominant. Nothing seemed to give him so much enjoyment, as drawing conclusions from minute observations. But his admirable memoir on the geology of Anglesea,[4] shows his capacity for extended observations and broad views. Reflecting over his character with gratitude and reverence, his moral attributes rise, as they should do in the highest character, in pre-eminence over his intellect.

1. Leonard Jenyns, *Memoir of the Rev. John Stevens Henslow, etc.* (London: Van Voorst, 1862), pp. 51–55.†

2. About fifteen miles WSW of Cambridge.†

3. Toad which runs rather than hops.†

4. John Stevens Henslow, "Geological Description of Anglesea," *Transactions of the Cambridge Philosophical Society* 1 (1822): 359–452.†

On the Thickness of the Pampean Formation, Near Buenos Ayres[1]

M. Sourdeaux and J. Coghlan, Esq., C. E., have had the kindness to send me, through E. B. Webb, Esq., C. E., some excellent sections of, and specimens from, two artesian wells lately made at Buenos Ayres. I beg permission to present these specimens to the Geological Society, as they would be of considerable service to any one investigating the geology of that country. The Pampean formation is in several respects so interesting, from containing an extraordinary number of the remains of various extinct Mammifers, such as *Megatherium, Mylodon, Mastodon, Toxodon,* &c., and from its great extent, stretching in a north and south line for at least 750 geographical miles, and covering an area fully equal to that of France, that, as it appears to me, a record ought to be preserved of these borings. Southward, at the Rio Colorado, the Pampean formation meets the great Tertiary formation of Patagonia; and northward, at Sta. Fé Bajada, it overlies this same formation with its several extinct shells.

In the central region near Buenos Ayres no natural section shows its thickness; but, by the borings there made in two artesian wells (figs. 1 & 2), the Pampean mud, with Tosca-rock, is seen to extend downwards from the level of the Rio Plata to a depth of 61 feet, and to this must be added 55 feet above the level of the river. These argillaceous beds overlie coarse sand, containing the *Azara labiata* (a shell characteristic of the Pampean formation), and attaining a thickness of about 93 feet.[2] So that

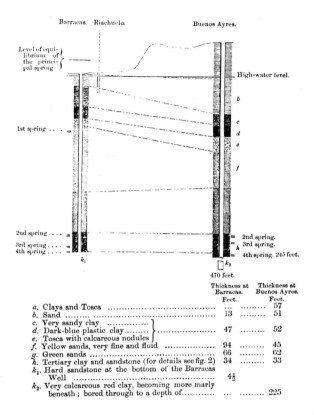

	Thickness at Barracas.	Thickness at Buenos Ayres.
	Feet.	Feet.
a. Clays and Tosca	...	57
b. Sand	13	51
c. Very sandy clay		
d. Dark-blue plastic clay	47	52
e. Tosca with calcareous nodules		
f. Yellow sands, very fine and fluid	94	45
g. Green sands	66	62
h. Tertiary clay and sandstone (for details see fig. 2)	34	33
k_1. Hard sandstone at the bottom of the Barracas Well	4½	
k_2. Very calcareous red clay, becoming more marly beneath ; bored through to a depth of	...	225

Fig. 1. Comparative sections of the artesian wells of Barracas and Buenos Ayres (distance 3¾ miles).

the entire thickness of the great estuarine or Pampean formation near Buenos Ayres is nearly 210 feet.

This formation rests on various marine beds of indurated green clay, sand with corals, sandstone, and limestone, altogether 107 feet in thickness. These beds contain fragments of the great *Ostrea Patagonica*, *O. Alvarezii* (?), *Pecten Paranensis*, and other shells, apparently the same (but they have not been rigorously compared) with those enumerated by M. A. d'Orbigny and by myself as found at Sta. Fé Bajada, as

		Thickness in metres.
a.	Sand	4·33
b.	Very arenaceous clay	8·02
c.	{ Fine clay	1·05
	{ Blue plastic clay	2·90
d.	Tosca with calcareous nodules	2·30
e.	Yellow sand, very fine and fluid, with quartz-pebbles and fluviatile shells	28·60
f.	Green clay, more or less plastic and calcareous, with iron-pyrites, marine shells, and nodules of lithographic stone	20·30
g.	Green sand, with shells and quartz-pebbles	·80
h.	Shelly limestone	·45
i.	Calcareous clay	2·00
k.	Shelly sandstone	·25
l.	Green arenaceous clay	2·00
m.	Shelly sandstone	·30
n.	Speckled sand	·70
o.	Very compact arenaceous clay	2·25
p.	Coarse sandstone	1·40
q.	Green sand, very fine and fluid, with quartz-pebbles and shells	2·35

Fig. 2. Detailed section of the artesian well at Barracas.

well as at various points on the coast of Patagonia. The already enormous continuous extension of the Patagonian Tertiary formation is thus largely increased. Beneath these beds a mass of red calcareous clay, becoming in the lower part more and more marly, containing layers of sand, and of the thickness of 213 feet, was bored through to a depth of 470 feet from the level of the Rio Plata. This lower mass contained no fossils, and its age is of course unknown[3]; but, I may add, that I saw at two points in Western Banda Oriental, beneath the marine tertiary strata, beds of red clay with marly concretions, which, from their mineralogical resemblance to the overlying Pampean formation, seemed to indicate that at an ancient period the Rio Plata had deposited an estuarine formation, subsequently covered by the marine tertiary beds, and these by the more modern estuarine formation, with its remains of numerous gigantic mammalia; and that, finally, the whole had been elevated into the present plains of the Pampas.

1. *Quarterly Journal of the Geological Society of London. Proceedings of the Geological Society* 19 (1863): 68–71.†
2. The following extract from the Report of the borers relates to this bed:—"The bed of yellow, fluid sands between 18.60 m and 47.20 m below the ground contains a subterranean ascending current, the level of which has not varied by a centimètre for three years. The level is 0.60 m (2 feet over the level of the wells at Barracas). This bed ('napa') is powerfully absorbent. At 68.30 m a second subterranean current ('overflowing') was met, which rose one foot over the surface of the ground at Barracas. The discharge was about 50 pipes daily, but the water was salt and undrinkable. At 73.30 m was found a third

subterranean current ('overflowing'), which reached with difficulty the level of the ground. The discharge might be calculated at 100 pipes daily. The water was very salt, and absorbed that of the first overflowing current. The great spring was met with at 77.65 m."

As regards the quality and abundance of the water, Mr. Coghlan remarks that "The quantity of water discharged per hour through a tube of about 4¼ inches in diameter, at a level of 6 feet above high-water mark, was 2658 gallons. Its temperature was 21° Cent., and it had a slightly disagreeable taste, from its being impregnated with salts of lime and magnesia and a small quantity of sulphuretted hydrogen."

3. It was supposed by Dr. Burmeister to be Silurian.

➶ Fertilisation of Orchids[1]

Had Mr. Anderson asked me two days ago for any facts illustrative of his case of unopened flowers of Cattleya crispa and Dendrobium cretaceum producing seed-capsules, I could have given no sort of information; nor can I now explain the fact. By an odd coincidence, yesterday I received a very interesting letter from Dr. Hermann Cruger, the Director of the Botanic Garden at Trinidad, who informs me that certain native species, and native species alone, of Cattleya, Epidendrum, and Schomburghkia, "are hardly ever known to open their flowers, but which nearly always set fruit." In answer to Dr. Cruger, I have asked him to look at the seed or send me some, and inform me whether it appears good.

Will Mr. Anderson have the kindness to send me a few seeds produced by his unopened flowers?

I further asked Dr. Cruger whether these Orchids in their native haunts *never* open their flowers. I can hardly believe that this can be the case, seeing how manifestly adapted the structure of their organs of fructification is to the action of insects. But it is known that several plants, such as Violets, Campanulas, Oxalis, &c., produce two kinds of flowers: one sort adapted for self-fertilisation, and the other sort for fertilisation by insect agency or other means. In some cases the two kinds of flowers differ very little in structure; and it occurs to me as possible that something of this kind may occur with Orchids.

Dr. Cruger further informs me that with certain Orchids, as in those which do not open their flowers, the pollen-masses after a time become pulpy; and though remaining still *in situ*, emit their pollen-tubes, which reach the stigma, and thus cause fertilisation.

An excellent observer, Mr. J. Scott, of the Royal Botanic Gardens of Edinburgh, will, I am sure, permit me to state that he has been making similar observations, and has seen the pollen-tubes emitted from the pollen-masses whilst still in their proper positions.

These facts were all unknown to me when I published my small work on the Fertilisation of Orchids[2]; but I ought, perhaps, to have anticipated their occurrence, for I saw the pollen-tubes emitted from the pollen within the anthers in the Bird's-nest Orchid, and likewise in *monstrous* flowers of the Man Orchis. This latter fact seems related to Mr. Anderson's remark, that flowers of an imperfect character, wanting a petal or sepal, had a great tendency to produce seed-capsules.

These curious observations by Dr. Cruger, Mr. Anderson, and Mr. Scott, convince me that I have in my work underrated the power of tropical Orchids occasionally to produce seed without the aid of insects; but I am not shaken in my belief that their structure is mainly related to insect agency. With most British Orchids this conclusion may be looked on as established.

I will only add that since the publication of my work, a number of persons have set seed-capsules with various tropical Orchids.

1. *Journal of Horticulture and Cottage Gardener*, n.s., 31 March 1863, 4:237.†
2. *On the Various Contrivances by which British and Foreign Orchids are Fertilised by Insects* . . . (London: Murray, 1862).†

⚓ The Doctrine of Heterogeny and Modification of Species[1]

I hope that you will permit me to add a few remarks on Heterogeny, as the old doctrine of spontaneous generation is now called, to those given by Dr. Carpenter, who, however, is probably better fitted to discuss the question than any other man in England. Your reviewer believes that certain lowly organized animals have been generated spontaneously— that is, without pre-existing parents—during each geological period in slimy ooze.[2] A mass of mud with matter decaying and undergoing complex chemical changes is a fine hiding-place for obscurity of ideas. But let us face the problem boldly. He who believes that organic beings have been produced during each geological period from dead matter must believe that the first being thus arose. There must have been a time when inorganic elements alone existed on our planet: let any assumptions be made, such as that the reeking atmosphere was charged with carbonic acid, nitrogenized compounds, phosphorus, &c. Now is there a fact, or a shadow of a fact, supporting the belief that these elements, without the presence of any organic compounds, and acted on only by known forces, could produce a living creature? At present it is to us a result absolutely inconceivable. Your reviewer sneers with justice at my use of the "Pentateuchal terms," "of one primordial form into which life was first breathed": in a purely scientific work I ought perhaps not to have used such terms; but they well serve to confess that our ignorance is as profound on the origin of life as on the origin of force or matter. Your reviewer thinks that the weakness of my theory is demonstrated because existing Foraminifera are identical with those which lived at a very remote epoch. Most naturalists look at this fact as the simple result of descent by ordinary reproduction; in no way different, as Dr. Carpenter remarks, except in the line of descent being longer, from that of the many shells common to the middle Tertiary and existing periods.

The view given by me on the origin or derivation of species, whatever its weaknesses may be, connects (as has been candidly admitted by some of its opponents, such as Pictet, Bronn, &c.) by an intelligible thread of reasoning a multitude of facts: such as the formation of domestic races by man's selection,—the classification and affinities of all organic beings,—the innumerable gradations in structure and instincts,—the similarity of pattern in the hand, wing or paddle of animals of the same great class,—the existence of organs become rudimentary by disuse,—the similarity of an embryonic reptile, bird and mammal, with the retention of traces of an apparatus fitted for aquatic respiration; the retention in the young calf of incisor teeth in the upper jaw, &c.,—the distribution of animals and plants, and their mutual affinities within the same region,—their general geological succession, and the close relationship of the fossils in closely consecutive formations and within the same country; extinct marsupials having preceded living marsupials in Australia, and armadillo-like animals having preceded and generated armadilloes in South America,—and many other phenomena, such as the gradual extinction of old forms and their gradual replacement by new forms better fitted for their new conditions in the struggle for life. When the advocate of Heterogeny can thus connect large classes of facts, and not until then, he will have respectful and patient listeners.

Dr. Carpenter seems to think that the fact of Foraminifera not having advanced in organization from an extremely remote epoch to the present day is a strong objection to the views maintained by me. But this objection is grounded on the belief—the prevalence of which seems due to the well-known doctrine of Lamarck—that there is some necessary law of advancement, against which view I have often protested. Animals may even become degraded, if their simplified structure remains well fitted for their habits of life, as we see in certain parasitic crustaceans. I have attempted to show ('Origin,' 3rd edit. p. 135) that lowly-organized animals are best fitted for humble places in the economy of nature; that an infusorial animalcule or an intestinal worm, for instance, would not be benefited by acquiring a highly complex structure. Therefore, it does not seem to me an objection of any force that certain groups of animals, such as the Foraminifera, have not advanced in organization. Why certain whole classes, or certain numbers of a class, have advanced and others have not, we cannot even conjecture. But as we do not know under what forms or how life originated in this world, it would be rash to assert that even such lowly endowed animals as the Foraminifera, with their beautiful shells as figured by Dr. Carpenter, have not in any degree advanced in organization. So little do we know of the conditions of life all around us, that we cannot say why one native weed or insect swarms in numbers, and another closely allied weed or insect is rare. Is it then possible that we should understand why one group of beings has risen in the scale of life during the long lapse of time, and another group has remained stationary? Sir C. Lyell, who has given so excellent a discussion on species in his great work on the 'Antiquity of Man,'[3] has advanced a somewhat analogous objection, namely, that the mammals, such as seals or bats, which alone have been enabled to reach oceanic islands, have not been developed into various terrestrial forms, fitted to fill the unoccupied places in their new island-homes; but Sir Charles has partly answered his own objection. Certainly I never anticipated that I should have had to encounter objections on the score that organic beings have not undergone a greater amount of change than that stamped in plain letters on almost every line of their structure. I cannot here resist expressing my satisfaction that Sir Charles Lyell, to whom I have for so many years looked up as my master in geology, has said (2nd edit. p. 469):—"Yet we ought by no means to undervalue the importance of the step which will have been made, should it hereafter become the generally received opinion of men of science (as I fully expect it will) that the past changes of the organic world have been brought about by the subordinate agency of such causes as Variation and Natural Selection." The whole subject of the gradual modification of species is only now opening out. There surely is a grand future for Natural History. Even the vital force may hereafter come within the grasp of modern science, its correlations with other forces have already been ably indicated by Dr. Carpenter in the *Philosophical Transactions*[4]; but the nature of life will not be seized on by assuming that Foraminifera are periodically generated from slime or ooze.

1. *Athenaeum. Journal of Literature, Science, and the Fine Arts*, no. 1852, 25 April 1863, pp. 554–55.†

2. See *The Life and Letters of Charles Darwin* ..., Francis Darwin, ed., 3 vols. (London: Murray, 1887, vol. 3, pp. 17–24) for an interesting account of Darwin's public involvement in this controversy.†

3. Charles Lyell, *The Geological Evidences of the Antiquity of Man with Remarks on the Origin of Species by Variation* (London: Murray, 1863).†

4. William B. Carpenter, "On the Mutual Relations of the Vital and Physical Forces," *Philosophical Transactions of the Royal Society of London* 140 (1850): 727–57.†

⚘   Origin of Species[1]

I hope that you will grant me space to own that your Reviewer is quite correct when he states that any theory of descent will connect, "by an intelligible thread of reasoning," the several generalizations before specified. I ought to have made this admission expressly; with the reservation, however, that, as far as I can judge, no theory so well explains or connects these several generalizations (more especially the formation of domestic races in comparison with natural species, the principles of classification, embryonic resemblance, &c.) as the theory, or hypothesis, or guess, if the Reviewer so likes to call it, of Natural Selection. Nor has any other satisfactory explanation been ever offered of the almost perfect adaptation of all organic beings to each other, and to their physical conditions of life. Whether the naturalist believes in the views given by Lamarck, or Geoffroy St.-Hilaire, by the author of the 'Vestiges,' by Mr. Wallace and myself, or in any other such view, signifies extremely little in comparison with the admission that species have descended from other species and have not been created immutable; for he who admits this as a great truth has a wide field opened to him for further inquiry. I believe, however, from what I see of the progress of opinion on the Continent, and in this country, that the theory of Natural Selection will ultimately be adopted, with, no doubt, many subordinate modifications and improvements.

1. *Athenaeum. Journal of Literature, Science, and the Fine Arts,* no. 1854, 9 May 1863, p. 617. Also, Francis Darwin, ed., *Life and Letters of Charles Darwin,* 3 vols. (London: Murray, 1887), 3:22–23.†

⚘   [Yellow Rain][1]

The following interesting letter has been forwarded to us by Mr. Darwin. We have not been able to ascertain precisely to what plant the larger bodies belong, but we believe them to be the pollen grains of some Thistle or Centaurea.[2] They also bear a strong resemblance to the pollen grains of some Malvaceous[3] plant, but they are far larger than those of Malva sylvestris, the only species which could supply pollen in sufficient quantities to tinge the rain with a yellowish tint. Fir pollen is often carried by wind, and deposited by rain on leaves, and we have seen Oak pollen forming yellow spots on leaves after a shower.

A very slight shower, lasting hardly more than a minute, fell here this morning (July 2) about 10 o'clock. My wife gathering some flowers immediately afterwards noticed that the drops of water appeared yellowish, and that the white Roses were all spotted and stained. I did not hear of this circumstance till the evening; I then looked at several Roses and Syringas and found them much stained in spots. Between the petals of the double white Roses there were still drops of the dirty water: and this when put under the microscope showed numerous brown spherical bodies, 1/1000 of an inch in diameter, and covered with short, conical transparent spines. There were other smaller, smooth, colourless sacs about 4/7000 of an inch in diameter. I preserved a minute drop of the water beneath thin glass, cementing the edges, and next morning looked rather more carefully at it. I then observed that the water swarmed with elongated, moving atoms, only just visible with a quarter-inch object glass. Whether these inhabited the rain-drops, when they fell, I cannot of course say; but I suspect so, for the petals, now that they are nearly dry, seem stained with absolutely impalpable matter of the colour of rust of iron. This matter has chiefly collected, in the act of drying, on the edges of each spot. The Rev. M. J. Berkeley could tell us what the larger spherical bodies are which fell this day by myriads from the sky, carried up there, I presume, by some distant whirlwind.

We gathered a leaf spotted with yellow dusty patches a few days since in Mr. Rucker's garden at Wandsworth, but though there were grains of Fir pollen in the spots, and those of some other plant which we could not ascertain, together with a few spores of Fungi, the principal part of the matter consisted of slightly ferruginous apparently siliceous dust.

The ferruginous spots on the white petals of Philadelphus forwarded by Mr. Darwin, consisted of coloured less distinctly siliceous particles, and multitudes of irregular bodies so minute as to present the Brownian molecular motion.

It is quite astonishing what a multitude of bodies are carried about by the wind in the form of dust. Ehrenberg some years since made us acquainted with the dust of the trade winds, but interesting matters may be found at home if we can in any way arrest the bodies which traverse our atmosphere. Flakes of snow bring down various things with them, and it is probable that few showers fall without leaving some sediment, though not so thick as in general to attract notice. An examination of such sediments or deposits with the microscope will soon materially modify our notions of spontaneous generation, and at the same time show a fertile source from which unexpected hybrid forms may arise. Indeed were not Fungi so much the creatures of peculiar atmospheric conditions, there would seem to be no limit to the diffusion of their species.

1. *Gardeners' Chronicle and Agricultural Gazette,* no. 29, 18 July 1863, p. 675. Article by "M. J. B."; quotation by Darwin.†
2. *Centaurea:* Large genus of asteraceous plants, including thistles and bachelor's buttons.†
3. The mallows.†

♠ Appearance of a Plant in a Singular Place[1]

In a hard gravel walk close to my house, my gardener and myself distinctly remember, about five or six years ago, two little rosettes of purplish leaves pushing their way up. We neither of us could imagine what they were; they were soon trampled down and apparently killed. But this spring they have re-appeared in exactly the same spot, and were protected. They have now flowered and prove to be Epipactis latifolia. This Orchid, though by no means a rare plant, I have never seen in this neighbourhood, and have heard only once of its having been found in a wood about a mile and a half distant. The gravel walk was made 20 years ago; and before that time the spot existed as a little-used carriage drive; and about 25 or 26 years ago it was a pasture field. How could this Epipactis, which is so rare a plant here, have come to this spot? The root stock seems to have lain dormant under the gravel for the last five or six years. Could a seed have been blown here from a distance and have germinated during some season when the walk was neglected? The tall stems growing up in the midst of the bare gravel surface present an odd appearance, and the case seems to me a singular one.

1. *Gardeners' Chronicle and Agricultural Gazette*, no. 33, 15 August 1863, p. 773.†

♠ Vermin and Traps[1]

It is a common observation that cases of brutality to horses, asses, and other large quadrupeds, are much less frequently witnessed now than they were some time ago. This is no doubt owing to the general increase of humanity, and to these animals being now under the protection of the law. An English gentleman would not himself give a moment's unnecessary pain to any living creature, and would instinctively exert himself to put an end to any suffering before his eyes; yet it is a fact that every game preserver in this country sanctions a system which consigns thousands of animals to acute agony, probably of eight or ten hours duration, before it is ended by death. I allude to the setting of steel traps for catching vermin. The iron teeth shut together with so strong a spring, that a pencil which I inserted was cracked and deeply indented by the violence of the blow. The grip must be close enough not to allow of the escape of a small animal, such as a stoat or a magpie; and therefore when a cat or a rabbit is caught, the limb is cut to the bone and crushed. A humane game-keeper said to me, "I know what they must feel, as I have had my finger caught." The smaller animals are often so fortunate as to be killed at once. If we attempt to realise the sufferings of a cat, or other animal when caught, we must fancy what it would be to have a limb crushed during a whole long night, between the iron teeth of a trap, and with the agony increased by constant attempts to escape. Few men could endure to watch for five minutes, an animal struggling in a trap with a crushed and torn limb; yet on all the well-preserved estates throughout the kingdom, animals thus linger every night; and where game keepers are not humane, or have grown callous to the suffering constantly passing under their eyes, they have been known by an eyewitness to leave the traps unvisited for 24 or even 36 hours. Such neglect as this is no doubt rare; but traps are often forgotten; and there are few game keepers who will leave their beds on a cold winter's morning, one hour earlier, to put an end to the pain of an animal which is safely in their power. I subjoin the account of the appearance of a rabbit caught in a trap, given by a gentleman, who, last summer witnessed the painful sight many times. "I know of no sight more sorrowful than that of these unoffending animals as they are seen in the torture grip of these traps. They sit drawn up into a little heap, as if collecting all their force of endurance to support the agony; some sit in a half torpid state induced by intense suffering. Most young ones are found dead after some hours of it, but others as you approach, start up, struggle violently to escape, and shriek pitiably, from terror and the pangs occasioned by their struggles." We naturally feel more compassion for a timid and harmless animal, such as a rabbit, than for vermin, but the actual agony must be the same in all cases. It is scarcely possible to exaggerate the suffering thus endured from fear, from acute pain, maddened by thirst, and by vain attempts to escape. Bull baiting and cock fighting have rightly been put down by law; I hope it may never be said that the members of the British Parliament will not make laws to protect animals if such laws should in any way interfere with their own sports. Some who reflect upon this subject for the first time will wonder how such cruelty can have been permitted to continue in these days of civilisation; and no doubt if men of education saw with their own eyes what takes place under their sanction, the system would have been put an end to long ago. We shall be told that setting steel traps is the only way to preserve game, but we cannot believe that Englishmen when their attention is once drawn to the case, will let even this motive weigh against so fearful an amount of cruelty. The writer of these remarks will be grateful for any suggestions, addressed to A. B., Mr. Strong, Printer, Bromley, Kent.

1. *Gardeners' Chronicle and Agricultural Gazette*, no. 35, 29 August 1863, pp. 821–22.†

✒ On the So-called "Auditory-Sac" of Cirripedes[1]

In my work on Cirripedes[2] I have described an orifice, previously unobserved, beneath the first pair of cirri, on each side of the body, including a very singular elastic sack, which I considered to be an acoustic organ. Furthermore I traced the oviduct from the peduncle to a mass of glands at the back of the mouth, and these glands I called ovarian. Dr. Krohn[3] has recently stated that these glands are salivary, and that the oviduct runs down to the orifice, which I had thought to be the auditory meatus. It is not easy to imagine a greater mistake with respect to function than that made by me; but I expressly stated that I could never succeed in tracing the oviducts into actual union with these glands; nor the supposed nerve from the so-called acoustic sack to any ganglion. As Dr. Krohn is no doubt a much better dissector than I am, I fully admitted my error and still suppose that he is right. Nevertheless, several facts can hardly be reconciled with his view of the function of the several parts. To give one instance: if any one will look at the figure of the Anelasma (Lepadidae, Pl. iv.),[4] he will see how extremely difficult it is to understand by what means the ova coming out of the orifices (e) above referred to, could be arranged in the symmetrical lamellae which extend up to the summit of the capitulum: it must be observed that the ova are united together by a delicate membrane enclosing each ovum; moreover the cirri in this animal are in atrophied condition, without regular articulations, so that it is inconceivable how the ova can be transported and arranged by their agency.

I have lately received from an eminent naturalist, Prof. F. de Filippi, a paper (Estratto dall' Arch. per la Zoolog. 31st Dec. 1861), chiefly devoted to the development of the ova of Cirripedes, in which the following passage occurs: —

"The small size of *Dichelaspis Darwinii* has not enabled me to verify the relationship discovered by Krohn between this problematical organ and the termination of the oviduct; but on the other hand the transparency of the tissues has enabled me to perceive a peculiarity of structure which may help to elucidate the question. Fig. 13 represents what I persist in calling a hearing organ. Within a cavity, the walls of which are united to the surrounding tissues, there is a pear-formed sack or ampulla. On the neck of this ampulla, at *a*, are numerous minute lines parallel to each other and to the axis of the ampulla. I doubted at first whether the appearance of these lines arose from folds in the membrane, and therefore I separated some of the sacks, and I could then better convince myself that these lines correspond with true nervous fibres, thin and simple, embedded in the rather thick, resisting, and transparent substance which forms the walls of the ampulla. This circumstance seems to

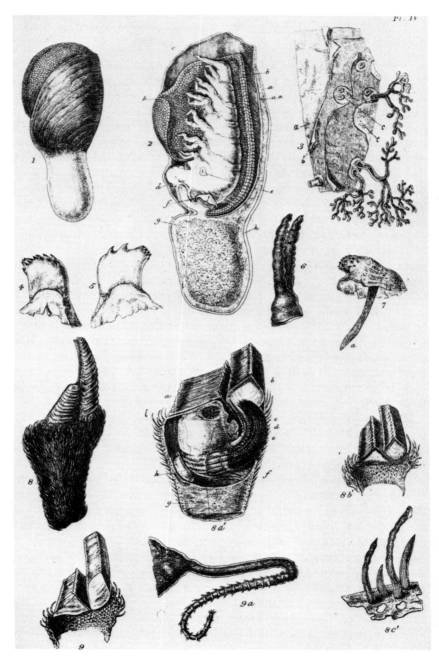

Pl. iv. Anelasma.

me to show clearly the sensitive nature of the organ, and hence to favour Darwin's opinion, who considers them to be organs of hearing."

My object in asking you to publish this note, is to induce some one to attend to this curious organ; to endeavour to discover ova within the so-called auditory sack; for as each cirripede produces so many eggs, assuredly this might be effected without great difficulty. It is, however, possible (as I believe was suggested by Mr. R. Garner[5] at the British Association, but whose paper I have mislaid,) that cirripedes, like certain Entomostraca, may lay two kinds of eggs; one set passing out through the problematical orifices; and another set coming out of the body in sheets, in the manner suggested by me;—namely, the ova collecting under the lining membrane of the sack before the act of exuviation, with a new membrane formed beneath them; so that the layer of eggs becomes external after the act of exuviation. If this view, to which I was led by many appearances, be correct, improbable as it may seem, it ought not to be difficult to find a specimen with the old membrane of the sack loose and ready to be moulted, with the new underlying membrane almost perfect, and with the layer of ova between them. Or a specimen might be found which had lately moulted, with its skin still soft, (and this I believe that I saw) with a layer of eggs still loosely attached to the new lining membrane of the sack.

1. *Natural History Review: Quarterly Journal of Biological Science*, 1863. Pp. 115–16.†

2. Charles Darwin, *A Monograph on the Sub-class Cirripedia, with Figures of All the Species: The Lepadidae; or, Pedunculated Cirripedes* (London: Ray Society, 1851).†

3. August Krohn, "Observations on the Development of the Cirripedia," *Annals and Magazine of Natural History, Including Zoology, Botany, and Geology*, 3d ser., 6 (1860): 423–28.†

4. *Monograph . . . Cirripedia*, 1851.†

5. Robert Garner, "On the Structure of the Lepadidae," *Report of the Thirtieth Meeting of the British Association for the Advancement of Science Held at Oxford June and July 1860*, 1861, p. 130.†

ᴧ [A Review of H. W. Bates' Paper on "Mimetic Butterflies"][1]

The author reveals some curious facts in this memoir, which from its unpretending and somewhat indefinite title we fear may be overlooked in the ever-flowing rush of scientific literature. The main subject discussed is the extraordinary mimetic resemblance which certain butterflies present to other butterflies belonging to distinct groups. To appreciate the degree of dissimulation practised by these insects, it is necessary to study the beautiful plates with which the memoir is adorned. In a district where, for instance, an *Ithomia* abounds in gaudy swarms, another butterfly, namely a *Leptalis*, will often be found mingled in the same flock, so like the *Ithomia* in every shade and stripe of colour and even in the shape of its wings, that Mr. Bates, with his eyes sharpened by collecting during eleven years, was, "though always on my guard," continually deceived. When the mockers and the mocked are caught and compared they are found to be totally different in essential structure, and to belong not only to distinct genera, but often to distinct families. If this mimicry had occurred in only one or two instances, it might have been passed over as a strange coincidence. But travel a hundred miles, more or less, from a district where one *Leptalis* imitates one *Ithomia*, and a distinct mocker and mocked, equally close in their resemblance, will be found. Coloured drawings of seven mocking forms of *Leptalis*, and six mocked forms of *Ithomia*, and one of another genus are given. Altogether no less than ten genera are enumerated, which include species that imitate other butterflies. The mockers and mocked always inhabit the same region; we never find an imitator living remote from the form which it counterfeits. The mockers are almost invariably rare insects; the mocked in almost every case abound in swarms. In the same district in which a species of *Leptalis* closely imitates an *Ithomia*, there are sometimes other Lepidoptera mimicking the same *Ithomia*; so that in the same place, species of three genera may be found all closely resembling a species of a fourth genus. It is highly remarkable that even moths, notwithstanding their dissimilarity in structure and general habits of life, sometimes so closely imitate butterflies (these butterflies being simultaneously mocked by others) that, as Mr. Bates says, when "seen on the wing in their native woods, they deceive the most experienced eye." These several facts and relations carry the strongest conviction to the mind that there must be some intimate bond between the mocking and mocked butterflies. It may, however, be naturally asked, why is the one considered as the mocked form; and why are the others, or two or three other butterflies which inhabit the same district in scanty numbers, considered as the mockers? Mr. Bates satisfactorily answers this question, by showing that the form which is imitated keeps the usual dress of the group to which it belongs, whilst the counterfeiters have changed their dress and do not resemble their nearest allies.

In these facts, of which only a brief abstract has been given, we have the most striking case ever recorded of what naturalists call analogical resemblance. By this term naturalists mean the resemblance in shape, for instance, of a whale to a fish—of certain snake-like Batrachians to true snakes—of the little burrowing and social pachydermatous *Hyrax* to the rabbit, and other such cases. We can understand resemblances, such as these, by the adaptation of different animals to similar habits of life. But it is scarcely possible to extend this view to the variously coloured stripes and spots on butterflies; more especially as these are known often to differ greatly in the two sexes. Why then, we are naturally eager to know, has one butterfly or moth so often assumed the dress of another quite distinct form; why to the perplexity of naturalists has Nature condescended to the tricks of the stage? We remember only one statement, made by Mr. Andrew Murray[2] in his excellent paper on the Disguises of Nature, namely that insects thus imitating each other usually inhabit the some country, which combined with the fact of the imitators being rare and the imitated common, might have given a clue to the problem. Mr. Bates has given to these facts the requisite touch of genius, and has, we cannot doubt, hit on the final cause of all this mimicry. The mocked and common forms must habitually escape, to a large extent, destruction, otherwise they could not exist in such swarms; and Mr. Bates never saw them preyed on by birds and certain large insects which attack other butterflies; he suspects that this immunity is owing to a peculiar and offensive odour that they emit. The mocking forms, on the other hand, which inhabit the same district, are comparatively rare, and belong to rare groups; hence they ·must suffer habitually from some danger, for from the number of eggs laid by all butterflies, without doubt they would, if not persecuted, in three or four generations swarm over the whole country. Now if a member of one of these persecuted and rare groups were to assume a dress so like that of a well-protected species that it continually deceived the practised eyes of an ardent entomologist, it would often deceive predacious birds and insects, and thus escape entire annihilation. This we fully believe is the true explanation of all this mockery.

Mr. Bates truly observes, that the cases of one butterfly mocking another living butterfly do not essentially differ from the innumerable instances of insects imitating the bark of trees, lichens, sticks, and green leaves. Even with mammals, the hare on her form can hardly be distinguished from the surrounding withered herbage. But no case is known of a deer or antelope so like a tiger as to deceive a hunter; yet we hear from Mr. Bates of insects more dissimilar than a ruminant and carnivore, namely, of a cricket most closely resembling a *cicindela*—a veritable tiger amongst insects. Amongst birds, all that habitually squat on the ground in open and unprotected districts, resemble the ground, and never have gaudy plumage. It appears, however, that two cases of birds mocking other birds have been observed by that philosophical naturalist, Mr. Wallace. Amongst insects, on the other hand, in all parts of the world, there are innumerable cases of imitation; Mr. Waterhouse has noted an excellent instance (and we have seen the specimens) of a rare beetle inhabiting the Philippine Archipelago, which most closely imitates a very common kind belonging to a quite distinct group. The much greater frequency of mockery with insects than with other animals, is probably the consequence of their small size; insects cannot defend themselves, excepting indeed the kinds that sting, and we have never heard of an instance of these mocking other insects, though they are mocked: insects cannot escape by flight from the larger animals; hence they are reduced, like most weak creatures, to trickery and dissimulation.

By what means, it may be asked, have so many butterflies of the Amazonian region acquired their deceptive dress? Most naturalists will answer that they were thus clothed from the hour of their creation—an answer which will generally be so far triumphant that it can be met only by long-drawn arguments; but it is made at the expence of putting an effectual bar to all further inquiry. In this particular case, moreover, the creationist will meet with special difficulties; for many of the mimicking forms of *Leptalis* can be shown by a graduated series to be merely varieties of one species; other mimickers are undoubtedly distinct species or even distinct genera. So again, some of the mimicked forms can be shown to be merely varieties; but the greater number must be ranked as distinct species. Hence the creationist will have to admit that some of these forms have become imitators, by means of the laws of variation, whilst others he must look at as separately created under their present guise; he will further have to admit that some have been created in imitation of forms not themselves created as we now see them, but due to the laws of variation! Prof. Agassiz, indeed, would think nothing of this difficulty; for he believes that not only each species and each variety, but that groups of individuals, though identically the same, when inhabiting distinct countries, have been all separately created in due proportional numbers to the wants of each land. Not many naturalists will be content thus to believe that varieties and individuals have been turned out all ready made, almost as a manufacturer turns out toys according to the temporary demand of the market.

There are some naturalists, who, giving up to a greater or less extent the belief of the immutability of species, will say that as the mocked and mocking forms inhabit the same district, they must have been exposed to the same physical conditions, and owe to this circumstance their common dress. What direct effect the physical conditions of life, that is, climate with all its contingencies and the nature of the food, produce on organic beings is one of the most abstruse problems in natural history, and cannot be here discussed. But we may remark that when a moth closely resembles a butterfly, or better still, when a cricket resembles a *Cicindela*, it becomes very difficult to believe that insects so widely dissimilar in their internal structure and habits of life, should have had their external organization alone so largely influenced by their conditions of life as to become almost identical in appearance. Can we believe that one insect comes to resemble the bark of a tree; another a green leaf; another in its larval condition the dead twig of a branch; or that a quail or snipe comes to resemble the bare ground on which it lies concealed, through the direct action of the physical conditions of life? If in these cases, we reject this conclusion, we ought to reject it in the case of the insects which mock other insects.

Assuredly something further is required to satisfy our minds: what this something is, Mr. Bates explains with singular clearness and force. He shows that some of the forms of *Leptalis*, whether these be ranked as species or varieties, which mimick so many other butterflies, vary much. In one district several varieties (which are figured) occur; one alone of these pretty closely resembles the common *Ithomia* of the same district. In a few other cases, this *Leptalis* presents two or three varieties, one of which is much commoner than the others, and this alone mocks an *Ithomia*. In several cases a single *Leptalis*, which sometimes must be ranked, according to the usual rules followed by naturalists, as a variety and sometimes as a distinct species, mocks the common *Ithomia* of the district. From such facts as these, Mr. Bates concludes that in every case the *Leptalis* originally varied; and that when a variety arose which happened to resemble any common butterfly inhabiting the same district (whether or no that butterfly be a variety or a so-called distinct species) then that this one variety of the *Leptalis* had from its resemblance to a flourishing and little persecuted kind a better chance of escaping destruction from predacious birds and insects, and was consequently oftener preserved;—"the less perfect degrees of resemblance being generation after generation eliminated, and only the others left to propagate their kind." This is Natural Selection. Mr. Bates extends this view, supporting it by many facts and forcible arguments, to all the many wonderful cases of mimicry described by him. He adds, "thus, although we are unable to watch the process of formation of a new race as it occurs in time, we can see it, as it were, at one glance, by tracing the changes a species is simultaneously undergoing in different parts of the area of its distribution."

To the naturalist who is interested with respect to the origin of species, the most important parts of this Memoir, together with the descriptive portion at the end, are probably those which treat on the limits of species, on sexual variation, on the variation of important characters, such as the neuration of the wings, &c. We cannot here discuss these points. Mr. Bates shows that there is a perfect gradation in variability, from butterflies, of which hardly two can be found alike, to slight varieties, to well-marked races, to races which can hardly be distinguished from species, to true and good species. Under this point of view, the history of *Mechanitis polymnia* well deserves study: after describing its several varieties, Mr. Bates adds, "these facts seem to teach us that, in this and similar cases, a new species originates in a local variety, formed in a certain area, where the conditions are more favourable to it than to the typical form, and that a large number of such are simultaneously in process of formation from one variable and widely distributed species." It is hardly an exaggeration to say, that whilst reading and reflecting on the various facts given in this Memoir, we feel to be as near witnesses, as we can ever hope to be, of the creation of a new species on this earth.

We will only notice briefly one other point which has an important bearing on the production of new races and species; namely the statement repeatedly made that in certain cases the individuals of the same variety evince a strong predilection to pair together. We do not wish to dispute this statement; it has been affirmed by credible authors, that two herds of differently coloured deer long preserved themselves distinct in the New Forest; and analogous statements have been made with respect to races of sheep in certain Scotch islands; and we know no reason why the same may not hold good with varieties in a state of nature. But we are by our profession as critics bound to be sceptical, and we think that Mr. Bates ought to have given far more copious evidence. He ought also to have given in every case his reasons in full for believing that the closely allied and co-existing forms, with which his varieties do *not* pair, are not distinct species. Naturalists should always bear in mind such cases as those of our own willow wrens, two of which are so closely alike that experienced ornithologists can with difficulty distinguish them, excepting by the materials of which their nests are built; yet these are certainly as distinct species as any in the world.

We think so highly of the powers of observation and reasoning shown in this Memoir, that we rejoice to see by the advertisements that Mr. Bates will soon publish an account of his adventures and his observations in natural history, during his long sojourn in the magnificent valley of the Amazon.[3] We believe that this work will be full of interest to every admirer of Nature.

1. *Natural History Review: Quarterly Journal of Biological Science*, 1863. Pp. 219–24. (A review of "Contributions to an Insect Fauna of the Amazon Valley," by Henry Walter Bates, Esq., *Transactions of the Linnean Society* 23 [1862]: 495–566.)†

2. Andrew Murray, "On the Disguises of Nature: Being an Inquiry into the Laws which Regulate External Form and Colour in Plants and Animals," *Edinburgh New Philosophical Journal* 68 (1860): 66–90.†

3. Henry Walter Bates, *The Naturalist on the River Amazons, a Record of Adventures, Habits of Animals … during Eleven Years of Travel*, 2 vols. (London: Murray, 1863).†

ᐳ   Ancient Gardening[1]

I should be very much obliged if any one who possesses a treatise on gardening or even an Almanac one or two centuries old would have the kindness to look what date is given as the proper period for sowing Scarlet Runners or dwarf French Beans. I am anxious to ascertain, as far as is possible, whether these plants can now be sown at all earlier than was formerly the case. The title, date, and place of publication of any old treatise should be given.

1. *Gardeners' Chronicle and Agricultural Gazette,* no. 41, 8 October 1864, p. 965.†

ᐳ   On the Existence of Two Forms, and on Their Reciprocal Sexual Relation, in Several Species of the Genus *Linum*[1]

The crimson *Linum grandiflorum*[2] presents two forms, occurring in about equal numbers, which differ little in structure, but greatly in function. The foliage, corolla, stamens, and pollen (examined dry, and distended with water) are alike in both forms. The difference is confined to the pistil: in the one form, which I will call "short-styled," the column formed by the united styles, and the short stigmas, together is about half the length of the whole pistil in the other and "long-styled" form. A more important distinction is, that the five stigmas in the short-styled form diverge greatly from each other and pass out between the filaments of the stamens, and thus lie within the tube of the corolla. In the long-styled form the elongated stigmas stand nearly upright, and alternate with the anthers. In this latter form the length of the stigmas varies considerably, their upper extremities projecting even a little above the anthers, or reaching up only to about their middle. Nevertheless there is never the slightest difficulty in distinguishing between the two forms; for, besides the difference in divergence, the stigmas of the short-styled form never reach even to the bases of the anthers. In the short-styled, the papillae on the stigmatic surfaces are shorter, darker-coloured, and more crowded together than in the long-styled form: but these differences seem due merely to the shortening of the stigma; for in the varieties of the long-styled form with shorter stigmas, the papillae are more crowded and darker-coloured than in those with the longer stigmas. Considering the slight and variable differences between the two forms of this *Linum*, it is not surprising that they have been hitherto overlooked.

In 1861 I had eleven plants growing in my garden, eight of which were long-styled, and only three short-styled. Two very fine long-styled plants grew in a bed a hundred yards off, and separated from the others by a screen of evergreens. I marked twelve flowers, and put on their stigmas a little pollen from the short-styled plants. The pollen of the two forms is, as stated, identical in appearance; the stigmas of the long-styled flowers were already thickly covered with their own pollen—so thickly that I could not find one bare stigma; and it was late in the season, namely, September 15th. Altogether, to expect any result from this trial seemed almost childish. From my experiments, however, on *Primula*, which have been laid before this Society ('Journal,' vol. vi. p. 77),[3] I had faith, and did not hesitate to make the trial, but certainly I did not anticipate the full result. The germens of these twelve flowers all swelled, and ultimately six fine capsules (the seed of which germinated this year) and two poor capsules were produced; only four capsules shanked off. These two plants produced, before and after and at the time of the trial, a vast number of flowers, but the germens of not even one swelled. All these flowers, though their stigmas were so densely covered with their own pollen, were absolutely barren.

The nine other plants, six long-styled and three short-styled, grew in the beds of the same flower-garden. Four of the long-styled produced no seed-capsules; one produced two; but the remaining long-styled plant grew so close to a short-styled plant that their branches touched, and this produced twelve capsules, but they were poor. The case was different with the short-styled plants. The plant which grew in juxtaposition with the long-styled plant produced ninety-four imperfectly fertilized capsules containing a multitude of bad seeds, with a moderate number of good seeds. The two other short-styled plants grew in a single clump, and were very small, being partly smothered by other plants; they did not stand very close to any long-styled plants, yet they yielded together nineteen capsules. These facts seem to show that the short-styled plants are far more fertile with their own pollen than the long-styled. We shall immediately see that this is the case in a slight degree. But I suspect that in this instance the difference in fertility between the two forms was in part due to a distinct cause. I repeatedly watched the flowers, and only once saw a humble-bee momentarily alight on one, and then fly away, as if it were not to its taste. If bees had visited the several plants, there cannot be a doubt that the four long-styled plants which did not produce a single capsule would have borne an abundance. But several times I saw small diptera sucking the flowers; and these insects, though not visiting the flowers with anything like the regularity of bees, would carry a little pollen from one form to the other, especially when growing close together; and the stigmas of the short-styled plants, diverging within the tube of the corolla, would be more likely than the upright stigmas of the long-styled to receive a small quantity of pollen when brought by small insects. From the much greater number of long-styled than of short-styled flowers in the garden, evidently the short-styled would be more likely to receive some pollen from the long-styled, than the long-styled from the short-styled.

In 1862 I raised thirty-four plants of this *Linum* in a hotbed; and these consisted of seventeen long-styled and seventeen short-styled forms. Seed sown later in the flower-garden yielded seventeen long-styled and twelve short-styled forms. These facts justify the statement that the two forms are produced in about equal numbers. The first thirty-four plants were kept under a net which excluded insects. I fertilized hetero-morphically fourteen long-styled flowers with pollen from the short-styled, and got eleven fine seed-capsules; these contained on an average 8.6 seeds per capsule, but only 5.6 were apparently good. It may be well to state that ten seeds is the maximum possible production for a capsule, and that our climate cannot be very favourable to this North-African plant. On three occasions I fertilized homomorphically the stigmas of altogether nearly a hundred flowers (but did not separately mark them) with their own pollen, but taken from separate plants, so as to prevent any possible ill effects from close interbreeding; and many other flowers were produced, which, as before stated, would get plenty of their own individual pollen; yet from all these flowers, borne by the seventeen long-styled plants, only three capsules were produced; one of these included no seed, and the other two together gave only five good seeds. Nor do I feel at all sure that this miserable product of the two half-fertile capsules from the seventeen plants, each of which must have produced at least fifty or sixty flowers, is really the result of their fertilization by their own pollen; for I made a great mistake in keeping the two forms under the same net, with their branches often interlocking, and it is surprising that a greater number of flowers were not accidentally fertilized.

Of the short-styled flowers I fertilized heteromorphically twelve with the pollen of the long-styled (and to make sure of the result I previously castrated the majority), and obtained seven fine seed-capsules. These included an average of 7.6 seeds, but of apparently good seed only 4.3 per capsule. At three separate times I fertilized homomorphically nearly a hundred flowers with their own-form pollen, taken from separate plants; and numerous other flowers were produced, many of which must have received their own pollen. From all these flowers borne on the seventeen plants, only fifteen capsules were produced, of which only eleven contained any good seed, on an average 4.2 per capsule. As remarked in the case of the long-styled plants, some even of these capsules were perhaps the product of a little pollen accidentally fallen from the flowers of the other form. Nevertheless the short-styled plants seem to be slightly more fertile with their own pollen, in the proportion of fifteen capsules to three, than the long-styled: the real proportional excess in fertility is probably a little greater, as the short-styled flowers, when not disturbed, do not so surely receive their own pollen as do the long-styled. The greater self-fertility of the short-styled flowers was, as we have seen, also shown by the plants left to themselves, and but sparingly visited by insects, in the flower-garden in 1861, and likewise by those raised in 1862.

The absolute sterility (judging from the experiments of 1861, and which is hardly contradicted by those of 1862) of the long-styled plants with their own-form pollen led me to examine into its apparent cause; and the result is so curious that it will be worth while to give most of the experiments in detail. These experiments were tried on fresh plants, grown in pots and brought successively into the house.

First. —I placed pollen from a short-styled flower on the five stigmas of a long-styled plant, and after thirty hours found them deeply penetrated by a multitude of pollen-tubes, far too numerous to be counted; the stigmas had become discoloured and twisted. I repeated this experiment on another flower, and in 18 hours found the stigmas penetrated by a multitude of long pollen-tubes. All this is what might have been expected, as this is a fertile or heteromorphic union. I likewise tried the converse experiment, and placed pollen from a long-styled flower on the stigmas of a short-styled flower, and in 24 hours found the stigmas discoloured, twisted, and penetrated by numerous pollen-tubes; and this, again, is what might have been expected, as this is a fertile or hetero-morphic union.

Secondly. —I placed pollen of a long-styled flower on all five stigmas of a long-styled flower on a separate plant: after 19 hours I rigorously dissected the stigmas, and found only a single pollen-grain which had emitted a very short tube. To make sure that the pollen was good, I took in this case, and in most other cases, pollen either from actually the same anther or from the same flower, and proved it to be good by placing it on the stigma of a short-styled plant, and seeing numerous pollen-tubes emitted.

Thirdly. —Repeated last experiment, and placed own-form pollen on all five stigmas of a long-styled flower; and, after 19½ hours, not one single grain had emitted its tube.

Fourthly. —Repeated the experiment, with the same result after 24 hours.

Fifthly.—Repeated last experiment, and, after leaving pollen on for 19 hours, put an additional quantity of own-form pollen on all five stigmas. After an interval of exactly three whole days, I rigorously examined the stigmas, which, instead of being discoloured and twisted, were straight and fresh-coloured; and only one grain had emitted quite a short tube, which could be drawn out of the stigmatic tissue without being ruptured.

The following experiments are more striking:—

Sixthly.—I placed own-form pollen on three of the stigmas of a long-styled flower, and pollen from a short-styled flower on the other two stigmas. After 22 hours these two stigmas were discoloured, and slightly twisted, and penetrated by the tubes of numerous pollen-grains: the other three stigmas, covered with their own-form pollen, were fresh, and all the pollen-grains were loose; but I did not dissect the whole stigma rigorously.

Seventhly.—Experiment repeated in the same manner, with the same result.

Eighthly.—Experiment repeated, but the stigmas were carefully examined after an interval of only 5½ hours. The two stigmas with pollen from a short-styled flower were penetrated by innumerable tubes; but these were as yet short, and the stigmas themselves were not at all discoloured. The three stigmas covered with their own-form pollen were not penetrated by a single pollen-tube.

Ninthly.—Put pollen of short-styled on one stigma, and own-form pollen on the other four stigmas; after 24 hours, found the one stigma somewhat discoloured, and twisted, and penetrated by many long tubes: the other four stigmas were quite straight and fresh; but on dissecting their whole lengths I found that three pollen-grains had protruded quite short tubes into the tissue.

Tenthly.—Repeated the experiment, with the same result after 24 hours, excepting that only two own-form grains had penetrated the stigmatic tissue with their tubes, to a very short depth: the one stigma, which was deeply penetrated by a multitude of tubes from the short-styled pollen, presented a conspicuous difference in comparison with the other four straight and bright pink stigmas, in being much curled, half-shrivelled, and discoloured.

I could add a few other experiments; but those now given amply suffice to show that the pollen-grains of a short-styled flower placed on the stigmas of a long-styled flower emit a multitude of tubes after an interval of from five to six hours, and penetrate the tissue ultimately to a great depth, and that after twenty-four hours the stigmas thus penetrated change colour, become twisted, and appear half-withered. On the other hand, the pollen-grains of the long-styled flowers placed on their own stigmas, after an interval of a day, or even three days, do not emit their tubes, or at most only three or four grains out of a multitude emit their tubes; and these apparently never penetrate the stigmatic tissue deeply, and the stigmas themselves do not become discoloured and twisted.

This seems to me a remarkable physiological fact. The pollen-grains of the two forms are undistinguishable under the microscope; the stigmas differ only in length, degree of divergence, and in the size, shade of colour, and approximation of their papillae, these latter differences being variable and apparently simply due to the elongation of the stigma. Yet we plainly see that the two pollens and the two stigmas are widely dissimilar in action—the stigmas of each form being almost powerless on their own pollen, but causing, through some mysterious influence, by simple contact (for I could detect no viscid secretion), the pollen-grains of the opposite form to protrude their tubes. It may be said that the two pollens and the two stigmas by some means mutually recognize each other. Taking fertility as the criterion of distinctness, it is no exaggeration to say that the pollen of the long-styled *Linum grandiflorum* (and conversely of the other form) has been differentiated, with respect to the stigmas of all the flowers of the same form, to a degree corresponding with that of distinct species of the same genus, or even of species of distinct genera.

Linum perenne.—The dimorphism is here more conspicuous, and has been noticed by several authors. In the long-styled form the pistil is nearly twice as long as in short-styled; in the latter the stigmas are smaller and, diverging more, pass out between the filaments of the stamens. I could detect no difference in the size of the stigmatic papillae; in the long-styled form alone the stigmatic surfaces turn round so as to face the circumference of the flower: but to this point we shall presently return. Differently from what occurs in *L. grandiflorum*, the long-styled flowers have stamens hardly more than half the length of those of the short-styled. The size of the pollen-grains is rather variable; after some doubt, I have come to the conclusion that there is no uniform difference between the pollen of the two forms. The long stamens in the short-styled form project to some height above the corolla, and, apparently from exposure to the light, the filaments are coloured blue. These longer stamens correspond in height with the lower part of the stigmas of the long-styled flowers; and the shorter stamens of the latter form correspond in the same manner in height with the shorter stigmas of the short-styled flowers.

I raised from seed twenty-six plants, which proved to be twelve long-styled and fourteen short-styled. They flowered well, but were not large plants. As I did not expect them to flower so soon, I did not transplant them, and they unfortunately grew with their branches closely interlocked. All the plants were covered by a net, excepting one of each form. First, of the long-styled flowers, twelve were homomorphically fertilized by their own-form pollen, taken in every case from a separate plant; and not one flower set a seed-capsule: twelve other flowers were heteromorphically fertilized by pollen from short-styled flowers; and they set nine pods, each including on an average seven good seeds: as before, ten seeds is the maximum possible production. Secondly, of the short-styled flowers, twelve were homomorphically fertilized by own-form pollen, and they yielded one capsule, including only three good seeds; twelve other flowers were heteromorphically fertilized by pollen of long-styled flowers, and these produced nine capsules, but one was bad; the eight good capsules contained on an average exactly eight good seeds each.

The many flowers on the eleven long-styled plants under the net, which were not fertilized, produced only three capsules (including 8, 4, and 1 good seeds); whether, owing to the interlocking of the branches, these accidentally received pollen from the other form, I will not pretend to conjecture. The single long-styled plant which was uncovered, and grew close by the uncovered short-styled plant, produced five good pods; but it was a very poor and small plant.

The flowers borne on the thirteen short-styled plants under the net, which were not fertilized, produced twelve capsules (containing 5.6 seeds on average): as some of these capsules were very fine, and five were borne on one twig, I suspect that they had been visited by some minute insect which had accidentally got under the net and had carried pollen from the other form. The one uncovered short-styled plant yielded exactly the same number of capsules, namely, twelve.

From these facts we have some evidence, as in the case of *L. grandiflorum,* that the short-styled plants are in a very slight degree more fertile with their own pollen than are the long-styled plants. And we have the clearest evidence, from the result of the forty-eight flowers artificially fertilized, that the stigmas of each form require pollen from the stamens of corresponding height produced by the opposite form.

In contrast with the case of *L. grandiflorum,* it is a singular fact that the pollen-grains of both forms of *L. perenne* when placed on their own-form stigmas, though not causing fertility, yet emit their tubes; and these tubes I found, after an interval of eighteen hours, had penetrated the stigmatic tissue, but to what depth I did not ascertain. In this case the inaction of the pollen-grains on their own stigmas must be due either to the tubes not reaching the ovules, or reaching them and not efficiently acting on them. In the case of *Lythrum Salicaria*,[4] which I hope at some future time to lay before the Society, there are three distinct forms, each of which produces two kinds of pollen; but neither pollen, when placed on its own stigma, causes fertility, except occasionally and in a very moderate degree; yet the pollen-tubes in each case freely penetrate the stigmatic tissue.

The plants of *L. perenne* and *L. grandiflorum* grew, as stated, with their branches interlocked, and with scores of flowers of the two forms close together; they were covered by an open net, through which the wind, when high, passed; and such minute insects as *Thrips* could not, of course, be excluded; yet we have seen that the utmost possible amount of accidental fertilization on seventeen long-styled plants in the one case, and on eleven plants in the other case, was the production, in each, of three poor capsules; so that we may infer that, when the proper insects are excluded, the wind does hardly anything in the way of carrying pollen from plant to plant. I allude to this fact because botanists, in speaking of the fertilization of plants or of the production of hybrids, often refer to the wind or to insects as if the alternative were indifferent. This view, according to my experience, is entirely erroneous. When the wind is the agent in carrying pollen, either from one separated sex to the other, or from hermaphrodite to hermaphrodite (which latter case seems to be almost equally important for the ultimate welfare of the species, though occurring perhaps only at long intervals of time), we can recognize structure as manifestly adapted to the action of the wind as to that of insects when they are the carriers. We see adaptation to the wind in the incoherence of the pollen, in the inordinate quantity produced (as in the Coniferae, Spinage, &c.), in the dangling anthers well fitted to shake out the pollen, in the absence or small size of the perianth or in the protrusion of the stigmas at the period of fertilization, in the flowers being produced before they are hidden by the leaves, in the stigmas being downy or plumose (as in the Gramineae, Docks, and other plants) so as to secure the chance-blown grains. In plants which are fertilized by the wind, the flowers do not secrete nectar, their pollen is too incoherent to be easily collected by insects, they have not bright-coloured corollas to serve as guides, and they are not, as far as I have seen, visited by insects. When insects are the agents of fertilization (and this is incomparably the more frequent case both with plants having separated sexes and with hermaphrodites), the wind plays no part, but we see an endless number of adaptations to ensure the safe transport of the pollen by the living workers. We can recognize these adaptations most easily in irregular flowers; but they do not the less occur in perfectly regular flowers, of which those of *Linum* offer an instance, as I will almost immediately endeavour to show.

I have already alluded to the rotation of each separate stigma in the long-styled form alone of *Linum perenne.* In the other species examined by me, and in both forms when the species are dimorphic, the stigmatic surfaces face the centre of the flower, and the furrowed backs of the stigmas, to which the styles are attached, face the circumference. This is the case, in the bud, with the stigmas of the long-styled flowers of *L. perenne.* But by the time the flower in this form has expanded, the five stigmas, by the torsion of that part of the style which lies beneath the stigma, twist round and face the circumference. I should state that the five stigmas do not always perfectly turn round, two or three often facing only obliquely towards the circumference. My observations were made during October; and it is not improbable that earlier in the season the torsion would have been more perfect; for after two or three cold and wet days the movement was very incomplete. The flowers should be examined shortly after their expansion; for their duration is brief, and, as soon as they begin to wither, the styles become spirally twisted together, and the original position of the parts is lost.

He who will compare the structure of the whole flower in both forms of *L. perenne* and *grandiflorum,* and, I may add, of *L. flavum,* will, I think, entertain no doubt about the meaning of this torsion of the styles in the one form alone of *L. perenne,* as well as the meaning of the divergence of the stigmas in the short-styled forms of all three species. It is absolutely necessary, as we now know, that insects should reciprocally carry pollen from the flowers of the one form to those of the other. Insects are attracted by five drops of nectar, secreted exteriorly at the base of the stamens, so that to reach these drops they must insert their proboscides outside the ring of broad filaments, between them and the petals. In the short-styled form of the above three species, the stigmas face the axis of the flower; and had the styles retained their original upright and central position, not only would the stigmas have presented their backs to insects as they sucked the flowers, but they would have been separated from them by the ring of broad filaments, and could never have been fertilized. As it is, the styles diverge greatly and pass out between the filaments. The stigmas, being short, lie within the tube of the corolla; and their papillous faces, after the divergence of the styles, being turned upwards are necessarily brushed by every entering insect, and thus receive the required pollen.

In the long-styled form of *L. grandiflorum,* the parallel anthers and stigmas, slightly diverging from the axis of the flower, project only a little above the tube of the somewhat concave corolla; and they stand directly over the open space leading to the drops of nectar. Consequently when insects visit the flowers of either form (for the stamens in this species occupy the same position in both forms), they will get their proboscides well dusted with the coherent pollen. As soon as the insect inserts its proboscis to a little depth into the flower of the long-styled form, it will necessarily leave pollen on the faces and margins of the long stigmas; and as soon as the insect inserts its proboscis to a rather greater depth into the short-styled flowers, it will leave pollen on their upturned stigmatic surfaces. Thus the stigmas of both forms will indifferently receive the pollen of both forms; but we know that the pollen alone of the opposite form will produce any effect and cause fertilization.

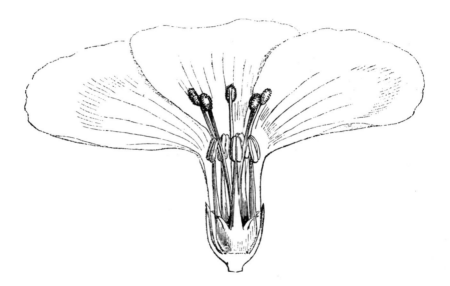

Fig. 1. Long-styled form of *L. perenne*, var. *Austriacum*, with the petals and calyx removed on the near side.

In the case of *L. perenne*, affairs are arranged a little more perfectly; for the stamens in the two forms stand at different heights, and pollen will adhere to different parts of an insect's body, and will generally be brushed off by the stigmas of corresponding height, to which stigmas each kind of pollen is adapted. In this species, the corolla is flatter, and in the one form the stigmas and in the other form the anthers stand at some height above the mouth of the corolla.[5] These longer stigmas and longer stamens do not diverge greatly; hence insects, especially rather small ones, will not insert their proboscides between the stigmas or between the anthers, but will strike against them, at nearly right angles, with the backs of their head or thorax. Now, in the long-styled flowers of *L. perenne,* if each stigma had not rotated on its axis, insects in visiting them would have struck their heads against the backs of the stigmas; as it is, they strike against the papillous fronts of the stigmas, and, their heads being already charged with the proper coherent pollen from the stamens of corresponding height borne by the flowers of the other form, fertilization is perfectly effected.

Thus we can understand the meaning of the torsion of the styles in the long-styled flowers alone, as well as their divergence in the short-styled flowers.

One other point is worth a passing notice. In botanical works many flowers are said to be fertilized in the bud. This rests solely, as far as I can discover, on the anthers opening in the bud; no evidence is adduced that the stigma is at this period mature, or that, if then penetrated by pollen-tubes, it is not subsequently, after the expansion of the flower, acted on by pollen brought from other flowers. In the case of *Cephalanthera grandiflora* I have shown[6] by experiment that insufficient precocious self-fertilization, together with subsequent full fertilization, is the regular course of events. The belief that flowers of any plant are habitually fertilized in the bud, or are perpetually self-fertilized, is a most effectual bar to really understanding their structure. I am far from wishing to say that some flowers, in certain seasons, are not fertilized in the bud: I have reason to believe that some flowers are frequently fertilized without expanding; but my observations lead me to disbelieve that this is ever the invariable course with all the flowers of any species whatever. As it is difficult to prove without troublesome experiments the falsity of the belief of regular fertilization in the bud, I here notice this subject. An estimable and laborious observer,[7] resting his belief on the usual kind of evidence, states that in *L. Austriacum* (which is dimorphic and is considered by Planchon as a variety of *L. perenne*) the anthers open the evening before the expansion of the flowers, and that the long-styled stigmas are then almost always fertilized. He asks whether this precocious fertilization in the several species of *Linum* and in other plants is not one cause of the short duration of their flowers. Now we know positively that, so far from *Linum perenne* being fertilized by its own pollen in the bud, its own pollen is as powerless on the stigma as so much inorganic dust.

Linum flavum. —To recur to our more immediate subject, in the long-styled form of this species the pistil is nearly twice as long as in the short-styled form; and the stigmas are longer with the papillae coarser. In the short-styled form the stigmas diverge and pass out between the filaments. The stamens in the two forms differ in height, and, what is singular, the anthers of the longer stamens are shorter; so that in the short-styled form both stigmas and anthers are shorter than in the other form. The pollen of the two forms does not differ. I have not been able to try any experiments on this species; but a careful observer, Mr. W. C. Crocker, intends proving their reciprocal fertility next summer. As this plant is propagated by cuttings, I have generally found that all the plants in the same garden belong to the same form. On inquiry I have never heard of its seeding in this country; but to anyone wishing to raise seedlings, in all probability the path is now open, namely, by carrying pollen from one form to the other.

I have now shown that three species of *Linum* are dimorphic, besides several races of *L. perenne*, esteemed by some botanists to be distinct species, such as *L. montanum*, *L. Sibiricum*, and *L. Austriacum*. According to Vaucher,[8] *L. Gallicum*, *L. maritimum*, and *L. strictum* are in the same manner dimorphic, as likewise is, according to Planchon,[9] *L. salsoloides*. This latter botanist is the only one who seems to have been struck with the importance of the subject; and he acutely asks whether this dimorphism has not some influence on the manner of fertilization. We thus know of seven dimorphic species of *Linum*; but as this structure has been overlooked in such common garden-flowers as *L. grandiflorum* and *L. flavum*, it is probably of frequent occurrence.

All the species, however, are certainly not thus characterized. I have examined many specimens of *L. catharticum*, and found in all that the stamens and stigmas were of nearly equal height and the same in all the plants. So, again, I looked, near Torquay, at many flowers of the wild *L. usitatissimum* or *angustifolium* (I know not which), and there was no trace of dimorphism. Again, I raised 111 plants from seed sent me from Kew, incorrectly named *L. Austriacum*; the plants were tall and straight, having a rather different aspect from the wild species seen at Torquay, with extremely fugacious blue flowers: in all these plants the stigmas stood on a level with the anthers or projected a very little above them. I protected the flowers from insects; but every one of the 111 plants produced plenty of seed. I mention this fact because it had occurred to me that possibly a species might be dimorphic in function, though not in structure.

Lastly, *Linum Lewisii*, which is ranked by Planchon as a variety of *L. perenne*, but which, now that we know the meaning of reciprocal dimorphism, surely deserves specific honours, must not be passed over. According to Planchon,[10] the same plant bears some flowers with anthers and stigmas of the same height, and others with styles either longer or shorter than the stamens; so that the same individual plant is trimorphic. This, as far as I know, is a unique case. From analogy we may pretty safely predict the function of the three kinds of flowers: those with stigmas and anthers of the same height will be self-fertile; those with these organs of unequal height will require reciprocal fertilization. A plant of *L. grandiflorum* or of the other dimorphic species, growing by itself, could no more perpetuate its race than could one sex of a dioecious plant, nor could any number of plants without the aid of insects. A single plant of *Linum Lewisii*, on the other hand, in all probability could propagate itself, even if no insects were present, as probably sometimes occurs in its Arctic home. If insects visited the plant, the flowers which were dimorphic would be fertile one with another or with those on any neighbouring plant. Thus the plant would receive the advantage of a cross. That this is an advantage, and is one great end gained by reciprocal dimorphism, I can entertain no doubt. That in some cases this dimorphism may be a step towards a complete separation of the sexes, I will not dispute; but good reasons could be assigned to show that there is no necessary connexion between reciprocal dimorphism and a tendency to dioecious structure. Although good is gained by the inevitable crossing of the dimorphic flowers, yet numerous other analogous facts lead me to conclude that some other quite unknown law of nature is here dimly indicated to us.

1. [Read 5 February 1863.] *Journal of the Proceedings of the Linnean Society (Botany)* 7 (1864): 69–83.†

2. *Linum;* common flax belongs to this group. This article was reprinted with substantial deletions, additions, and editorial changes in *The Different Forms of Flowers on Plants of the Same Species* (London: Murray, 1877, pp. 81–101).†

3. See p. 45, "On the Two Forms, or Dimorphic Condition, in the Species of *Primula,* and on Their Remarkable Sexual Relations."†

4. Purple loosestrife.†

5. I neglected to get drawings made from fresh flowers of the two forms. Mr. Fitch has made the above sketch of a long-styled flower from dried specimens and published engravings: his well-known skill ensures accuracy in the proportional size of the parts; and I believe their relative position is true.

6. Fertilization of Orchids, p. 108.

7. Études sur la Géograph. Bot., par Prof. H. Lecoq, 1856, tom. v. p. 325.

8. Hist. Physiolog. des Plantes d'Europe, 1841, tom. i. p. 401.

9. Hooker's London Journ. of Botany, 1848, vol. vii. p. 174.

10. Hooker's London Journ. of Botany, 1848, vol. vii. p. 175. It is not improbable that the allied genus *Hugonia* is dimorphic; for (p. 525) one species is described "staminibus exsertis;" another has "stamina 5, majora, stylos longe superantia;" and another is furnished "stylis staminibus longioribus."

♣ On the Sexual Relations of the
Three Forms of *Lythrum salicaria*[1]

Some of the species of *Lythrum* offer in their manner of fertilization a more remarkable case than can, perhaps, be found in any other plant or animal.[2] In *Lythrum salicaria* three plainly different forms occur: each of these is an hermaphrodite, each is distinct in its female organs from the other two forms, and each is furnished with two sets of stamens or males differing from each other in appearance and function. Altogether there are three females and three sets of males, all as distinct from each other as if they belonged to different species; and if smaller functional differences are considered, there are five distinct sets of males. Two of the three hermaphrodites must coexist, and the pollen be carried by insects reciprocally from one to the other, in order that either of the two should be fully fertile; but unless all three forms coexist, there will be waste of two sets of stamens, and the organization of the species, as a whole, will be imperfect. On the other hand, when all three hermaphrodites coexist, and the pollen is carried from one to the other, the scheme is perfect; there is no waste of pollen and no false co-adaptation. In short, nature has ordained a most complex marriage-arrangement, namely a triple union between three hermaphrodites,—each hermaphrodite being in its female organ quite distinct from the other two hermaphrodites and partially distinct in its male organs, and each furnished with two sets of males.

The three forms may be conveniently called, from the unequal lengths of their pistils, the *long-styled, mid-styled,* and *short-styled.* Their existence and differences were first observed by Vaucher,[3] and subsequently more carefully by Wirtgen; but, not being guided by any theory, neither author perceived some of the most curious points of difference. I will first briefly describe the three forms by the aid of the accompanying accurate diagram, which shows the flowers, six times magnified, in their natural position, with their petals and the near side of the calyx removed.

Long-styled Form.—This can at once be recognized by the length of the pistil, which is (including the ovarium) fully one-third longer than that of the mid-styled, and more than thrice as long as that of the short-styled form. It is so disproportionately long, compared with the flower, that it projects in the bud through the unfolded petals. It stands out considerably beyond the longer stamens; its terminal portion depends a little, but the stigma itself is slightly upturned: the globular stigma is considerably larger than that of the other two forms. The six longer stamens project about two-thirds of the length of the pistil, and

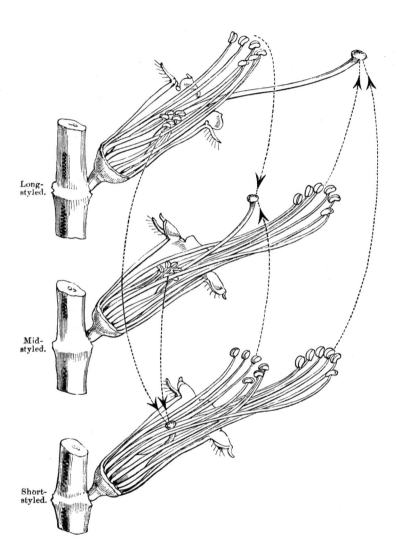

Long-
styled.

Mid-
styled.

Short-
styled.

Fig. 1. Diagrams of the flowers of the three forms of *Lythrum salicaria*, in their natural position, with the petals removed and with the near side of the calyx cut away: enlarged six times. The dotted lines with the arrows show which pollen must be applied to each stigma to cause full fertility.

correspond in length with the pistil of the mid-styled form. The correspondence with the pistil in length in this and the two following cases is generally very close; the difference, where there is any, being usually in a slight excess of length in the stamens. The six shorter stamens (each of which alternates with a longer one) lie concealed within the calyx; their ends are upturned, and they are graduated in length, so as to form a triple row—both which characters are here much more marked than with the longer stamens, which vary in these respects. The anthers of the shorter stamens are smaller than those of the longer stamens. Knowing that the pollen differs greatly in the longer and shorter stamens of the two other forms, I carefully compared that of the two sets of stamens in this form: in both the pollen-grains are yellow, but they are a little larger in the longer than in the shorter stamens. The difference is slight, so that I convinced myself of its reality only by putting two small heaps close together under the compound microscope, and I found I could always (with one exception) distinguish them: I then showed the specimens to two other persons, and they likewise distinguished the two kinds and pointed out which was the largest. The capsules of this form contain, on an average, 93 seeds: how this average was obtained will presently be explained. I repeatedly observed that the seed, when cleaned, seemed larger than that from the mid-styled or short-styled forms; consequently I placed 100 long-styled seeds in a good balance, and by the double method of weighing found that they equalled 121 seeds of the mid-styled and 142 of the short-styled; or, in short, that five long-styled seeds equalled six mid-styled and seven short-styled seeds. These slight differences in the weight of the seed, and, as we shall soon see, in the average number produced, are worth recording, as they characterize not mere varieties but coexisting forms of the same species.

Mid-styled Form.—The pistil occupies the position represented in the diagram, with its extremity considerably, but in a variable degree, upturned; the stigma is seated between the anthers of the long and the short stamens. The six longer stamens correspond in length with the pistil of the long-styled form; their filaments are coloured bright pink; the anthers are dark-coloured, but from containing bright green pollen and from their early dehiscence they appear emerald-green. Hence the general appearance of these stamens is remarkably dissimilar from that of the longer stamens of the long-styled form. The six shorter stamens, enclosed within the calyx, resemble in all respects the shorter stamens of the long-styled form, and both correspond in length with the short pistil of the short-styled form. The green pollen-grains of the longer stamens are plainly larger than the yellow pollen-grains of the shorter anthers: this fact was conspicuous in several camera-lucida drawings made for me by my son, Mr. W. E. Darwin. There is some variability in size, but 12/7000 of an inch may be taken as about the average diameter of the green pollen-grains when distended with water, and 9/7000 as the diameter of the yellow grains of the shorter stamens; so that the difference in diameter is in about the proportion of four to three. The capsules contain, on an average, 132 seeds; but, perhaps, as we shall see, this is rather too high an average. The seeds themselves are smaller than those of the long-styled form.

Short-styled Form.—The pistil is here very short, not one-third of the length of that of the long-styled form. It is enclosed within the calyx, which, differently from in the other two forms, does not enclose any anthers. The end of the pistil is generally bent upwards at right angles. The six longer stamens, with their pink filaments and green pollen, resemble in size of the grains and in all respects the longer stamens of the mid-styled form, and both correspond in length with the long-styled pistil. The six shorter stamens, with their uncoloured filaments and yellow pollen, resemble in size of the grains and in all respects the longer stamens of the long-styled form, and both correspond in length with the mid-styled pistil. The capsules contain fewer seeds on an average than in either of the preceding forms, namely 83.5, and they are considerably smaller in size. In this latter respect, but not in number, there is a gradation parallel to that of the length of the pistil, the long-styled having the largest, the mid-styled the next in size, and the short-styled the smallest seed.

From this description we see that there are three distinct female organs, or rather females as they are borne on distinct individuals, differing in the length and curvature of the style, in the size of the stigma, and in the number and size of the seed. In the three forms, taken together, there are thirty-six stamens or males, and these can be divided into three sets of a dozen each, differing from each other in length, curvature, and colour of the filaments, in the size of the anthers, and especially in the colour and diameter of the pollen-grains. Each of the three forms bears half-a-dozen of one kind of stamens and half-a-dozen of another kind, but not all three kinds. The three kinds correspond in length with the three pistils: the correspondence is always between half the stamens borne by two forms with the pistil of a third form. These remarks apply to the structure, and not, as yet, to the functions, of the reproductive organs.

I ascertained the average number of seed by counting them in eight fine selected capsules taken from plants of the three forms growing wild, and the result was, as we have seen, for the long-styled (neglecting decimals) 93, mid-styled 132, and short-styled 83. I should not have trusted this result, but I had a number of plants in my garden which, from their youth, did not yield the full complement of seed, but they were of exactly the same age and grew under exactly the same conditions, and were freely visited by bees. I took six fine capsules from each, and found the average to be for the long-styled 80, for the mid-styled 97, and for the short-styled 61. Lastly, I made numerous artificial unions, and, as may be seen in the following Tables, these gave in the long-styled an average of 90 seeds, in the mid-styled 117, and in the short-styled 71. So that we have good concurrent evidence of the different average production of seed by the three forms. To show that the artificial fertilizations, presently to be described, produced their full effect and may be trusted, I may state that one mid-styled capsule yielded 151 good seeds, which is the exact number of the finest wild capsule examined by me. Artificially fertilized short- and long-styled capsules actually produced a greater number of seeds than I have found in wild plants, but then I did not examine many of the latter. This Lythrum, I may add, offers a remarkable instance, how profoundly ignorant we are of the life-conditions of each species: naturally it grows "in wet ditches, watery places, and especially on the banks of streams," and though it produces so many minute seeds, it never spreads on the adjoining land; yet, planted in my garden, on clayey soil lying over the chalk, and which is so dry that a rush cannot be found, it thrives luxuriantly, grows to above six feet in height, produces self-sown seedlings, and (which is a severer test) is fully as fertile as in a state of nature. Nevertheless it would be almost a miracle to find this plant spontaneously growing on such land as my garden, though under its native climate.

According to Vaucher and Wirtgen, the three forms coexist in all parts of Europe. Some friends gathered for me in North Wales a number of twigs from separate plants growing near each other, and then classified them. My son did the same in Hampshire, and here is the result:—

	Long-styled	Mid-styled	Short-styled	Total
North Wales	95	97	72	264
Hampshire	53	38	38	129
Total	148	135	110	393

If twice or thrice the number had been collected, probably the three forms would have been found nearly equal; I infer this from considering the above figures, and from my son telling me that if he had collected in another spot, he felt sure that the mid-styled plants would have been in excess. I several times sowed small parcels of seed, and raised all three forms; but I neglected to record the parent form, except in one instance, in which I raised from short-styled seed twelve plants, of which only one turned out long-styled, four mid-styled, and seven short-styled.

Insects are necessary for the fertilization of this Lythrum. During two years I kept two plants of each form protected, and in the autumn they presented a remarkable contrast in appearance with the adjoining uncovered plants, which were densely covered with capsules. In 1863 a protected long-styled plant produced only five poor capsules; two mid-styled plants produced the same number; and two short-styled plants between them produced only one: these capsules contained very few seed; yet the plants were fully productive when artificially fertilized under the net. In a state of nature the flowers are incessantly visited for their nectar by hive- and humble-bees and various Diptera. The nectar is secreted all round the base of the ovarium; but a passage is formed along the upper and inner side of the calyx by the lateral deflection (not represented in the diagram) of the basal portions of the filaments; so that insects invariably alight on the upper side of the flowers, on the projecting stamens and pistil, and insert their probosces along the upper inner margin of the calyx. We can now see why the ends of the stamens with their anthers, and the ends of the pistils with their stigma, are a little upturned, in order that they may brush against the lower hairy surfaces of the insects' bodies. The short stamens which lie enclosed within the calyx of the long- and mid-styled forms can be touched only by the proboscis and the narrow chin of the sucking bee; hence they have their ends more upturned, and they are graduated in length, so as to fall into a narrow file, three deep, sure to be raked by the thin intruding proboscis. The anthers of the longer stamens stand laterally further apart and are more nearly of the same length, for they have to brush against the whole breadth of the insect's body. I may here incidentally remark, that in very many flowers the pistil, or the stamens, or both, are rectangularly bent to one side of the flower: this bending may be permanent, as with *Lythrum* and many others, or may be effected (as in *Dictamnus fraxinella*[4] and many others) by a temporary movement which occurs in the stamens when the anthers dehisce, and in the pistil when the stigma is mature; but these two movements are by no means always contemporaneous in the same flower. Now I have found no exception to the rule, that when the stamens and pistil are bent, the bending is exactly to that side of the flower which secretes nectar (even though there be a rudimentary nectary of large size on the opposite side, as in some species of *Corydalis*[5]); or, when nectar is secreted on all sides, to that side where the structure of the flowers allows the easiest access to it, as in *Lythrum*, Papilionaceous flowers, and many others. The rule consequently is that when the pistil and stamens are bent, the stigma and anthers are brought into the pathway towards the nectary. There are a few cases which seem to be exceptions, but they are not so in truth: for instance, in the Gloriosa lily, the stigma of the grotesque and rectangularly bent pistil is brought, not into the pathway from the open air towards the nectar-secreting recesses of the flower, but into the circular route from one nectary to the other; in *Scrophularia aquatica* the pistil is bent downwards from the mouth of the flower, but it thus strikes the pollen-dusted breasts of the wasps which habitually visit these ill-scented blooms. In the above rule we see one more instance of the supreme dominating power of insects over all the minor structural details of flowers, especially of those which have irregular corollas. Flowers which are fertilized by the wind must of course be excepted, but I do not know of a single instance of an irregular flower which is fertilized or crossed by this means.

I have delayed too long on these points, but I must allude to one other. We have seen that the three pistils of different lengths have each two half-dozen sets of stamens of corresponding length. When bees suck the flowers, the longest stamens, bearing the green pollen, rub against the abdomen and the interior sides of the posterior legs, as does likewise the stigma of the long-styled form. The stamens of middle length and the stigma of the mid-styled form rub against the under side of the thorax and between the front pair of legs. The shortest stamens and the stigma of the short styled form must rub against the proboscis and chin; for the bees in sucking insert only the front of their heads into the calyx. On catching bees, I observed much green pollen on the inner sides of the hind legs and on the abdomen, and much yellow pollen on the under side of the thorax. There was also pollen on the chin, and, it may be presumed, on the proboscis, but this was difficult to observe. I had, however, independent proof that pollen is carried on the proboscis; for in a protected short-styled plant (which produced only two capsules) one small branch was accidentally left during many days pressing against the fine net, and bees were seen inserting their probosces through the meshes, and in consequence numerous capsules were formed on this one small branch. From these several facts it follows that insects would chiefly carry to the stigma of each form pollen from the stamens of corresponding length; and we shall presently see the importance of this adaptation. It must not, however, be supposed that the bees do not get more or less dusted all over with the several kinds of pollen; they certainly do, as could be seen with the green pollen from the longest stamens. Moreover, a case will presently be given of a long-styled plant which grew absolutely by itself, and produced an abundance of capsules, which must have been fertilized by its own two kinds of pollen; but these capsules contained a very poor average of seed. Hence insects, and chiefly bees, act both as general carriers of pollen, and as special carriers of the right kind.[6]

Variability. —Before passing on to more important topics, I must say a few words on this head. Wirtgen remarks[7] on the variability in the branching of the stem, in the length of the bracteae, size of the petals, and in several other respects. The plants now growing in my garden have their leaves arranged oppositely, alternately, and in whorls of three, and differ greatly in shape. The stems of the plants bearing leaves in whorls are hexagonal; those of the other plants are quadrangular. But we are concerned only with the reproductive organs: the upward bending of the pistil is variable, and in a remarkable degree in the short-styled form, in which it is sometimes straight, sometimes slightly curved, but generally upturned at right angles. The stigma of the long-styled pistil frequently has longer papillae or is rougher than that of the mid-styled, and this than that of the short-styled form; but this character, though fixed and uniform with the two forms of *Primula,* is here variable, and I have seen mid-styled stigmas rougher than those of the long-styled. The degree to which the longer and middle stamens are graduated in length and are upturned at their ends is variable; sometimes all are equal. The colour of the green pollen in the long stamens is variable,[8] and is sometimes pale greenish yellow; in one short-styled plant it was almost white. The grains vary a little in size: I examined one short-styled plant with the grains above the average size; and I have seen a long-styled plant with undistinguishable grains from the longer and shorter anthers. We have here considerable fluctuations of character; and if any of these slight structural differences were of direct service to the plant, or were correlated with useful functional differences, we can perceive that the species is just in that state in which natural selection might readily do much for its modification.

To return to our proper subject—we see that there are three kinds of females and three kinds of males, each kind of the latter being borne by half-dozens on two of the three forms. It remains to discover whether these several sexes or sexual organs differ from each other in function. Nothing brings more prominently forward the complexity of the reproductive system of this extraordinary plant, than the necessity, in order to ascertain the above fact, of artificially making eighteen distinct unions. Thus the long-styled form had to be fertilized with pollen from its own two distinct kinds of anthers, from the two in the mid-styled, and from the two in the short-styled form. The same process had to be repeated with both the mid- and short-styled forms. It might have been thought sufficient to have tried on each stigma the green pollen, for instance, from either the mid- or short-styled longer stamens, and not from both; but the result proves that this would have been insufficient, and that it was necessary to try all six kinds of pollen on each stigma. As in artificial fertilizations there will always be some failures, it would have been advisable to have repeated each of the eighteen unions a score of times;

but the labour would have been too great; as it was, I made 223 artificial unions; *i.e.*, I fertilized, on an average, above a dozen flowers in the eighteen different methods. Each flower was castrated; the adjoining buds had to be removed, that the marking-thread, wool, &c. might be safely secured; and after each fertilization the stigma had to be examined with a lens to see that there was sufficient pollen. Plants of all three forms were protected during two years by large nets on a framework; two plants were used during one or both years, in order to avoid any individual peculiarity in any one plant. As soon as the flowers withered, the nets were removed; and in the autumn the capsules were daily inspected; when the seeds were ripe they were counted under the microscope. I have given these details that confidence may be placed in the following Tables, and as some excuse for two blunders which, I believe, I made. These blunders are referred to, with their probable causes, in two notes to the Tables; the erroneous numbers, however, are entered in the Tables, that it may not be supposed that I have in any one instance tampered with the results.

A few words explanatory of the three Tables must be given. Each is devoted to one form, and is divided into six compartments. The two upper ones in each table give the produce of good seed from the application of pollen from the two sets of stamens which correspond in length with the pistil of that form. The two next lower compartments show the result of pollen from the other two sets of stamens, which do not correspond in length with the pistil, and which are borne by the same two forms. The two lowest compartments show the result of the application of each form's own two kinds of pollen. The term "own pollen," used here and in the Tables, does not mean pollen from the flower to be fertilized—for this was never used—but from another flower on the same plant, or more commonly from a distinct plant of the same form. In the result given, "0" generally means that no capsule was produced, or that the capsule contained no good seed. In some part of each row of figures in each compartment, a short horizontal line may be seen; the unions above this line were made in 1862, and below it in 1863. It is of importance to observe this, as it shows that the same general result ensued in two successive years; but more especially because 1863 was a very hot and dry season, and the plants had occasionally to be watered. This did not prevent the full complement of seed being produced from the more fertile unions; but it rendered the less fertile unions even more sterile than they otherwise would have been. I have seen striking instances of this same fact in making homomorphic and heteromorphic unions in *Primula*[9]; and it is well known that the conditions of life must be highly favourable to give any chance of producing hybrids from species which cross with difficulty.

Table I   Long-styled Form

I. 13 flowers fertilized by the longer stamens of the mid-styled. *These stamens equal in length the pistil of the long-styled.* Product of good seed in each capsule.		II. 13 flowers fertilized by the longer stamens of the short-styled. *These stamens equal in length the pistil of the long-styled.* Product of good seed in each capsule.	
36	53	159	104
81	0	43	119
0	0	96 poor seed.	96
0	0	103	99
0	0	0	131
—	0	0	116
45		—	
41		114	

38 per cent. of these flowers yielded capsules. Each capsule contained, on an average, 51.2 seed.	84 per cent. of these flowers yielded capsules. Each capsule contained, on an average, 107.3 seed.

III. 14 flowers fertilized by the short stamens of the mid-styled.		IV. 12 flowers fertilized by the shorter stamens of the short-styled.	
3	0	20	0
0	0	0	0
0	0	0	0
0	0	0	0
0	0	—	0
—	0	0	0
0	0	0	
0			

Too sterile for any average.	Too sterile for any average.

V. 15 flowers fertilized by *own* longer stamens.		VI. 15 flowers fertilized by *own* shorter stamens.	
2	—	4	—
10	0	8	0
23	0	4	0
0	0	0	0
0	0	0	0
0	0	0	0
0	0	0	0

Too sterile for any average.	Too sterile for any average.

I fertilized a considerable number of flowers with pollen, taken by a camel's-hair brush, from both the long and short stamens of their own (long-styled) form; but I did not examine with a lens (as I did in the cases in the Tables) whether sufficient pollen had been placed on the stigma: only 5 capsules were produced, and these yielded on an average 14.5 seed. In 1863 I tried a much better experiment: a long-styled plant was grown by itself, miles away from any other plant, so that its stigmas could have received only the two kinds of pollen proper to this form. The flowers were incessantly visited by bees, so that the stigmas must have received on the most favourable days, and at the most favourable hours, successive applications of pollen: all who have crossed plants know that this highly favours fertilization. This plant produced an abundant crop of capsules; I took by chance 20, and these (excluding one poor one) contained seed as below: —

20	20	35	21	19
26	24	12	23	10
7	30	27	29	13
20	12	29	19	35

This gives an average of 21.5 seed per capsule; and as we know that this form, when standing near plants of the other two forms and fertilized by insects, produces an average of 93.1 seed per capsule, we see that the long-styled form fertilized by its own two pollens yields only between one-fourth and one-fifth of the full number of seed. I have spoken as if this plant had received both its own kinds of pollen, and this is, of course, possible; but, from the enclosed position of the shorter stamens, it is much more probable that the stigma received almost exclusively the pollen from its own longer stamens.

Table II   Mid-styled Form

I. 12 flowers fertilized by the longer stamens of the long-styled. *These stamens equal in length the pistil of the mid-styled.* Product of good seed in each capsule.		II. 12 flowers fertilized by the shorter stamens of the short-styled. *These stamens equal in length the pistil of the mid-styled.* Product of good seed in each capsule.	
138	122	112	109
149	50	130	143
147	151	143	124
109	119	100	145
133	138	33	12
144	0	—	141
—		104	

92 per cent. of the flowers (probably 100 per cent.) yielded capsules. Each capsule contained, on an average, 127.3 seed.	100 per cent. of the flowers yielded capsules. Each capsule contained, on average, 108.0 seed; or, excluding capsules with less that 20 seed, the average is 116.7 seed.

III. 13 flowers fertilized by the short stamens of the long-styled.

83	12
0	19 } seed small
0	85 } and poor
—	0
44	0
44	0
45	0

54 per cent. of the flowers yielded capsules. Each capsule contained, on an average, 47.4 seed; or, excluding capsules with less than 20 seed, the average is 60.2 seed.

IV. 15 flowers fertilized by the longer stamens of the short-styled.

130	86
115	113
14	29
6	17
2	113
9	79
—	128
132	0

93 per cent. of the flowers yielded capsules. Each capsule contained, on an average, 69.5 seed; or, excluding capsules with less than 20 seed, the average is 102.8.

V. 12 flowers ferlilized by *own* longer stamens.

92	0
9	0
63	0
—	0
136?[10]	0
0	0
0	

Excluding the capsule with 136 seed, 25 per cent. of the flowers yielded capsules, and each capsule contained, on an average, 54.6 seed; or, excluding capsules with less than 20 seed, the average is 77.5.

VI. 12 flowers fertilized by *own* shorter stamens.

0	0
0	0
0	0
—	0
0	0
0	0
0	

0 per cent. of the flowers yielded capsules.

I fertilized a considerable number of flowers with pollen, taken by a camel's-hair brush, from both the long and short stamens of their own (short-styled) form; but I did not examine with a lens (as I did in the cases in the Tables) whether sufficient pollen had been placed on the stigma: only 5 capsules were produced, and these yielded, on an average, 11.0 seed.

Table III   Short-styled Form

I. 12 flowers fertilized by the shorter stamens of the long-styled. *These stamens equal in length the pistil of the short-styled.*		II. 13 flowers fertilized by the shorter stamens of the mid-styled. *These stamens equal in length the pistil of the short-styled.*	
69	56	93	69
61	88	77	69
88	112	48	53
66	111	43	9
0	62	0	0
0	100	0	0
—		—	0

83 per cent. of the flowers yielded capsules. Each capsule contained, on an average, 81.3 seed.

61 per cent. of the flowers yielded capsules. Each capsule contained, on an average, 64.6 seed.

III. 10 flowers fertilized by the longer stamens of the long-styled.		IV. 10 flowers fertilized by the longer stamens of the mid-styled.	
0	14	0	0
0	0	0	0
0	0	0	0
0	0	0	0
—	0	—	0
23		0	

Too sterile for any average.

Too sterile for any average.

V. 10 flowers fertilized by *own* longer stamens.		VI. 10 flowers fertilized by *own* shorter stamens.	
0	0	64?[11]	0
0	0	0	0
0	0	0	0
—	0	—	0
0	0	21	0
0		9	

Too sterile for any average.

Too sterile for any average.

I fertilized a number of flowers without particular care with their own two pollens, but they did not produce a single capsule; the position of the stigma within the calyx renders the fertilization without some care difficult.

Summary of the Three Preceding Tables

Long-styled Form.—Twenty-six flowers fertilized by the stamens of corresponding length, borne by the mid- and short-styled forms, yielded 61.5 per cent. of capsules, which contained, on an average, 89.7 seed.

Twenty-six flowers fertilized by the other and shorter stamens of the mid- and short-styled forms yielded only two very poor capsules.

Thirty flowers fertilized by this form's own two sets of stamens yielded only eight very poor capsules; but flowers well fertilized by bees by one or both of their own kinds of pollen produced numerous capsules containing, on an average, 21.5 seed.

Short-styled Form.—Twenty-five flowers fertilized by the stamens of corresponding length, borne by the long- and mid-styled forms, yielded 72 per cent. of capsules, which (excluding one capsule with only nine seeds) contained, on an average, 70.8 seed.

Twenty flowers fertilized by the longer stamens of the long- and mid-styled forms yielded only two very poor capsules.

Twenty flowers fertilized by both their own two sets of stamens yielded only two poor (or perhaps three) capsules.

Mid-styled Form.—Twenty-four flowers fertilized by the stamens of corresponding length, borne by the long- and short-styled forms, yielded 96 (probably 100) per cent. of capsules, which contained (excluding one capsule with 12 seed), on an average, 117.2 seed.

Fifteen flowers fertilized by the longer stamens of the short-styled form yielded 93 per cent. of capsules, which (excluding four capsules with less than 20 seed) contained, on an average, 102.8 seed.

Thirteen flowers fertilized by the shorter stamens of the long-styled form yielded 54 per cent. of capsules, which capsules (excluding one with 19 seed) contained, on an average, 60.2 seed.

Twelve flowers fertilized by own longer stamens yielded 25 per cent. of capsules, which (excluding one with 9 seed) contained, on an average, 77.5 seed.

Twelve flowers fertilized by own shorter stamens yielded not a single capsule.

Considering the three Tables and this summary, we may safely draw the following conclusions. First, that, as in structure so in function, there are three females or female organs: this is manifest; for when all three receive the very same pollen, they are acted on most differently. So conversely with the thirty-six stamens, we know that they consist of three separate sets of a dozen each, differing in various respects; and in function the pollen of these three sets when applied to one and the same stigma acts most differently, as a glance at the Tables proves. But we shall presently see that the action of the pollen of the whole dozen longest and of the whole dozen shortest stamens is not identical.

Secondly, we see that only the longest stamens fully fertilize the longest pistil, the middle stamens the middle pistil, and the shortest stamens the shortest pistil. And now we can comprehend the meaning of the almost exact correspondence in length between the pistil of each form and the two half-dozen sets of stamens borne by the two other forms; for the stigma of each form is thus rubbed against the same spot of the insect's body, which becomes most charged with the proper pollen. In all three forms, the female organ is but feebly, or not at all, acted on by its own two kinds of pollen. In my papers on the dimorphism of *Primula* and *Linum*, I used the terms "heteromorphic" for the fully fertile unions between the female element of the one form and the male element of the other, and "homomorphic" for the less fertile or quite sterile unions between the female and male elements of the same form. The principle involved in these terms holds good with *Lythrum*, but is insufficient; for though in each of the three forms the fertile unions are all *heteromorphic*, the appropriate pollen coming from the stamens of corresponding length borne by the other two forms, and though the *homomorphic* unions of the females with their own two sets of males are always more or less sterile, there remain in each case two other sterile unions, not included in these two terms. Hence it will be found convenient to designate the two unions of each female with the two sets of stamens of corresponding length, which are fully fertile, as *legitimate unions*, and the four other, more or less sterile, unions of each female with the four other sets of stamens as *illegitimate unions*. Consequently, of the eighteen possible unions between the three forms, six are legitimate and twelve are illegitimate.

Another and curious conclusion cannot be considered as proved, but is rendered highly probable, by the Tables. The unions of the pistils and stamens of equal length are alone fully fertile. Now with the several illegitimate unions it will be found that the greater the inequality in length between the pistil and stamens, the greater the sterility of the result. There is no exception to this rule. Thus, with the long-styled form, its own shorter stamens are far less equal in length to the pistil than its own longer stamens; and the capsules fertilized by the pollen of the shorter stamens yielded fewer seeds: the same comparative result follows from the use of the pollen of the shorter stamens of the mid-styled form, which are much shorter than the shorter stamens of the short-styled (see diagram), and therefore less equal in length to the long-styled pistil. We shall see exactly the same result if we look to the four illegitimate unions under the mid- and short-styled forms. Certainly the difference in sterility in these several cases is very slight, but the sterility always increases with the increasing inequality of length between the pistil and the stamens which are used. Therefore I believe in the above rule; but a vast number of artificial unions would be requisite to prove it. If the rule be true, we must look at it as an incidental and useless result of the gradational changes through which this species has passed in arriving at its present condition. On the other hand, the correspondence in length between the pistil of each form and those stamens which alone give full fertility is clearly of service to the species, and is probably the result of direct adaptation.

Some of the illegitimate unions yielded, as may be seen in the Tables, during neither year a single seed; but, judging from the case of the long-styled plant, it is probable, if such unions could be effected repeatedly under the most favourable conditions, some few seeds would be produced. Anyhow, I can state that in all the eighteen possible unions the pollen-tubes penetrated, after eighteen hours, the stigma. I have reason to believe that the offspring from the illegitimate unions present some singular characteristics; but until my observations on this head are repeated, I must be silent. At first I thought that perhaps two kinds of pollen placed together on the same stigma would give more fertility than any one kind; but we have seen that this is not the case with each form's own two kinds of pollen; nor is it probable in any case, as I occasionally got, by the use of single kinds of pollen, fully as many seed as I have seen in a capsule naturally fertilized. Moreover the proper pollen from a single anther is more than sufficient to fully fertilize each stigma; hence, in this as in so many other cases, at least twelve times as much of each kind of pollen is produced as is necessary to ensure full fertilization. From the dusted condition of the whole body of those bees which I caught on these flowers, it is probable that some pollen of all kinds is deposited on each stigma; but there can hardly be a doubt that the pollen of the stamens of corresponding length will be prepotent and will wholly obliterate any effect from the other kinds of pollen, even if previously deposited on the stigma. I infer this partly from the fact ascertained by Gärtner that each species' own pollen is so prepotent over that of any other species, that if put on the stigma many hours subsequently, it will entirely obliterate the action of the foreign pollen. But I draw the above inference especially from the following experiment: I fertilized homomorphically or illegitimately some long-styled Cowslip flowers (*Primula veris*) with their own pollen, and exactly twenty-four hours subsequently I fertilized these same stigmas heteromorphically or legitimately with pollen from a short-styled dark-red Polyanthus. I must premise that I have raised many seedlings from crossed Cowslips and Polyanthus, and know their peculiar appearance; and I further know, by the test of the fertility of the mongrels *inter se*, and with both parent forms, that the Polyanthus is a variety of the Cowslip, and not of the Primrose (*P. vulgaris*) as some authors have supposed. Now from the long-styled Cowslip twice fertilized in the manner explained, I raised twenty-nine seedlings, and every one of them had flowers coloured more or less red; so that the heteromorphic Polyanthus-pollen wholly obliterated the influence of the homomorphic pure Cowslip-pollen, which had been placed on the stigmas twenty-four hours previously, and not a single pure Cowslip was produced.

The last conclusion which may be deduced from the Tables, even from a glance at them, is that the mid-styled form differs from both the others in its much higher capacity for fertilization. Not only did the twenty-four flowers fertilized by the stamens of corresponding lengths, all, or all but one, yield capsules rich in seed; but of the other four illegitimate unions, that by the longer stamens of the short-styled form was highly fertile, though less than in the two legitimate unions, and that by the short stamens of the long-styled form was fertile to a considerable degree; the two unions with this form's own pollen were sterile, but in different degrees. So that the mid-styled form, when fertilized by the six kinds of pollen, evinces five different grades of fertility. By comparing compartments 3 and 6 in Table II. we learn a remarkable fact, namely, that though the pollen from the short stamens of the long-styled and from this form's own (mid-styled) short stamens, used in these two unions, is identical in all respects, yet that its action is widely different; in the one case above half the fertilized flowers yielded capsules containing a fair number of seed; in the other case not one single capsule was produced. So, again, the green, large-grained pollen from the long stamens of the short-styled and from this form's own (mid-styled) long stamens is identical in all respects, but its action, as may be seen in compartments 4 and 5, is widely different. In both these cases the difference in action is so plain that it cannot be mistaken, but it can be corroborated. If we look to Table III., to the legitimate action of the short stamens of the long- and mid-styled forms on the pistil of the short-styled form, we again see a similar but slighter difference, the pollen of the short stamens of the mid-styled form yielding a smaller average of seed during the two years of 1862 and 1863 than that from the short stamens of the long-styled form. Again, if we look to Table I., to the legitimate action of the green pollen of the two sets of long stamens, we shall find exactly the same result, viz. that the pollen of the long stamens of the mid-styled form yielded during both years fewer seeds than that from the long stamens from the short-styled form. Hence it is certain that the two kinds of pollen produced by the mid-styled form are less potent than the similar pollens produced by the corresponding stamens of the two other forms.

When we see that the capsules of the mid-styled form yield a considerably larger average number of seed than those of the other two forms, —when we see how surely the flowers are fertilized in the legitimate unions, and how much more productive the illegitimate unions are than those of the other two forms, we are led to consider the mid-styled form as eminently feminine in its nature. And although it is impossible to consider as rudimentary or aborted the two perfectly developed sets of stamens of the mid-styled form which produce an abundance of perfectly well-developed pollen, yet we can hardly avoid connecting, as balanced, the higher efficiency of the female organ with the lesser potency of the two mid-styled pollens.

Finally, it is proved by the Tables that *Lythrum salicaria* habitually produces or consists of three females different in structure and widely different in function; that it produces or consists of three sets of males widely different in structure and function; and that two of the three sets of males are subdivided into subgroups of half a dozen each, differing in a marked manner in potency, so that regularly five kinds of pollen are elaborated by this one species of *Lythrum*.

Lythrum Graefferi.—I must now say a few words about some of the other species of the genus. I have examined numerous dried flowers of *L. Graefferi*, each from a separate plant, kindly sent me from Kew. This species, like *L. salicaria*, is trimorphic, and the three forms apparently occur in about equal numbers. In the long-styled form the pistil projects about one-third of the length of the calyx beyond its mouth, and is therefore shorter than in *L. salicaria*; the globose and hirsute stigma is larger than that of the other two forms; the longer stamens, which are graduated in length, have their anthers standing just above and just beneath the mouth of the calyx; the half-dozen shorter stamens rise rather above the middle of the calyx. In the mid-styled form the stigma projects just above the mouth of the calyx, and stands almost on a level with the longer stamens of the previous form; its own longer stamens project well above the mouth of the calyx and stand a little above the level of the stigma of the long-styled form; the shorter stamens correspond in all respects with the shorter ones in the previous form. In the short-styled form the stigma of the pistil is nearly on a level with the anthers of the shorter stamens in the two preceding forms; and the longer stamens correspond with the longer stamens of the mid-styled form, and the shorter stamens with the longer stamens of the long-styled form. In short, there is a close general correspondence in structure between this species and *L. salicaria*, but with some differences in the proportional lengths of the parts. Nevertheless the fact of each of the three pistils having two sets of stamens, borne by the two other forms, of corresponding lengths, comes out conspicuously. In the mid-styled form the distended pollen-grains from the longer stamens had nearly double the diameter of those from the shorter stamens; so that there is a greater difference in this respect than in *L. salicaria*. In the long-styled form, also, the difference in diameter between the pollen-grains of the longer and shorter stamens was plainer than in *L. salicaria*. These comparisons, however, must be received with caution, as they were made on specimens long kept in a dried condition.

Lythrum thymifolia.—This form, according to Vaucher,[12] is dimorphic like *Primula*, and therefore presents only two forms. I received two dried flowers from Kew, which presented two forms: in the one form the stigma projected far beyond the calyx, in the other it was included within the calyx; in this latter form the style was only one-fourth of the length of the style of the other form. There are only six stamens; these are somewhat graduated in length, and in the short-styled form the anthers stand a little above the stigma, but yet the stamens by no means equal in length the pistil of the long-styled form; in the long-styled form the stamens are rather shorter than in the other form. These six stamens alternate with the petals, and correspond homologically with the longer stamens of *L. salicaria* and *L. Graefferi*. As there are only six stamens, it is scarcely possible that this species can be trimorphic.

Lythrum hyssopifolia.—This species is said by Vaucher, but I believe erroneously, to be dimorphic. I have examined dried flowers from twenty-two separate plants from various localities, kindly sent to me by Mr. Hewett C. Watson, Prof. Babington, and others. These were all essentially alike. Hence the species cannot be dimorphic. The pistil varies somewhat in length, but when unusually long the stamens are likewise generally long; in the bud the stamens are short: perhaps these circumstances deceived Vaucher. There are from six to nine stamens, graduated in length; the stamens which are variable in being present or absent correspond with the six shorter stamens of *L. salicaria* and with the six which are absent in *L. thymifolia*. The stigma is included within the calyx, and stands in the midst of the anthers, and would generally be fertilized by them; but as the stigma and anthers are upturned, and as, according to Vaucher, there is a passage left in the upper side of the flower to the nectary, there can hardly be a doubt that the flowers are visited by insects, which would occasionally bring pollen from other flowers of the same or of any adjoining plant, as surely as occurs with the short-styled *L. salicaria*, of which the pistil and corresponding stamens closely resemble those of *L. hyssopifolia*. According to Vaucher and Lecoq,[13] this species, which is an annual, generally grows almost solitarily, whereas the three preceding species are social; and this alone would almost have convinced me that *L. hyssopifolia* cannot be dimorphic, as such plants cannot habitually live by themselves any better than one sex of a dioecious species.

Nesaea verticillata.[14] —I raised a number of plants from seed sent me by Professor Asa Gray, and they presented three forms. These differed from each other in the proportional lengths of their organs of fructification and in all respects in very nearly the same way as the three forms of *Lythrum Graefferi.* The green pollen-grains from the longest stamens, measured along their greater axis and not distended with water, were 13/7000 of an inch in length; those from the stamens of middle length 9–10/7000, and those from the shortest stamens 8–9/7000 of an inch.

We have seen that the genus *Lythrum* affords trimorphic, dimorphic, and monomorphic species.

The inquiry naturally arises, why do these species differ so remarkably in their sexual relations? of what service can reciprocal dimorphism or trimorphism be to certain species, whilst other species of the same genus present, like the great majority of plants, only one form? I have elsewhere given too briefly[15] the general grounds of my belief that with all organic beings distinct individuals at least occasionally cross together, and reciprocal dimorphism is plainly one most efficient means for ensuring this result. This result would appear to be one of high importance, for with dimorphic plants it is ensured at the risk of occasional sterility; not only is the pollen of each plant useless or nearly useless to that individual, but so is the pollen of all the plants of the same form, that is, of half the total number of individual plants. In that extensive class of plants called by C. K. Sprengel dichogams, in which the pollen of each flower is shed before its own stigma is ready, or in which the stigma (though this case occurs more rarely) is mature before the flower's own pollen is ready sterility can hardly fail to be the occasional result; and it would be the inevitable result with both dichogamous and reciprocally dimorphic flowers unless pollen were carried by insects (and in some few species by the wind) from one flower or plant to the other. As with reciprocal dimorphism so with dichogamy, within the same genus some of the species are and some are not thus characterized. Again, in the same genus, as in that of *Trifolium,* some species absolutely require insect-aid to produce seed, others are fertile without any such aid; now when insects are requisite for fertilization, pollen will generally be carried from one flower to the other. We thus see, by means of reciprocal dimorphism, of dichogamy, and of insect-aid, that some species require, or at least receive, incessant crosses with other individuals of the same species; whereas other species of the same genera can be, and probably are often fertilized during long periods by the pollen of their own flowers. Why this wide difference in the frequency of crosses should occur we are profoundly ignorant. I will only further remark on this head, that it would be a great mistake to suppose that many flowers, which are neither reciprocally dimorphic nor dichogamous, nor require insect-aid for their fertilization, nor show any particular adaptation in their structure for the visits of insects, are not habitually crossed with the pollen of other individuals; this occurs, for instance, habitually with cabbages, radishes, and onions, which nevertheless are perfectly fertile (as I know by trial) with their own pollen without aid of any kind.

But it may be further asked, granting that reciprocal dimorphism is of service by ensuring at each generation a cross (but I am far from pretending that it may not have some additional unknown signification), why did not dimorphism suffice for *L. salicaria* and *Graefferi*? why were they rendered reciprocally trimorphic, entailing such complicated sexual relations? We cannot answer, except perhaps so far:—if we suppose two plants of the *L. salicaria* to grow by themselves, then if the species were dimorphic it would only be an equal chance in favour of the two turning out different forms and consequently both being fertile; but as the species is trimorphic and each form can fertilize the two other forms, it is two to one in favour of the two turning out different forms and being consequently both fertile. We thus see how reciprocal trimorphism must be an advantage; and probably it would be more advantageous to this Lythrum, which commonly grows in almost a single row along the banks of streams, than it would be to Primroses or Cowslips which have neighbours on all sides. But even if trimorphism effected no good beyond that gained by dimorphism, we ought not to feel much surprised at its occurrence, for we continually see throughout nature the same end gained by the most complicated as well as by the most simple means: to give one instance:—in many dioecious plants pollen is carried from the male to the female by the wind, which is perhaps the simplest method conceivable, or by the adherence of the grains to the hairy bodies of insects, which is a method only a little less simple; but in *Catasetum* the conveyance is effected by the most complex machinery; for in this orchid we have sensitive horns which when touched cause a membrane to rupture, and this sets free certain springs by which the pollen-masses are shot forth like an arrow, and they adhere to the insect's body by a peculiar viscid matter, and then by the breaking of an elastic thread of the right strength the pollen is left sticking to the stigma of the female plant. The complexity of the means used in this and in many other cases, in fact depends on all the previous stages through which the species has passed, and on the successive adaptations of each part during each stage to changed conditions of life.

As some authors consider reciprocal dimorphism to be the first step toward dioeciousness, the difficulty of understanding how a trimorphic plant like *Lythrum salicaria* could become dioecious should be noticed; and as dimorphism and trimorphism are so closely allied, it is not probable that either state is necessarily in any way related to a separation of the sexes—though it may occasionally lead to this end. As far as *Lythrum salicaria* is concerned, the one tendency which we can discover is towards the abortion of the two sets of stamens in the mid-styled form. This tendency is evinced by its pollen, though abundant and apparently good, yielding a smaller percentage of seed than does the pollen of the corresponding stamens in the other two forms; and this fact is in itself curious, and shows by what insensibly graduated steps nature moves. If this tendency were carried out the mid-styled form would become a female, depending for its fertilization on two sets of stamens in the long- and short-styled forms; and these two forms would reciprocally fertilize each other like the two forms of *Primula* or *Linum*; but there would be no approach to a dioecious condition.

As the case of the trimorphic species of *Lythrum* is so complicated, and as it is easier to perceive the relations of the sexes in the animal than in the vegetable kingdom, it may be worth while to give, before concluding, a somewhat elaborate simile. We may take the case of a species of Ant, and suppose all the individuals invariably to live in three kinds of communities; in the first, a large-sized female (not to specify other differences) living with six middle-sized and six small-sized males; in the second, a middle-sized female with six large- and six small-sized males; and in the third community, a small-sized female with six large- and six middle-sized males. Each one of these three females, though enabled to unite with any male, would be nearly sterile with her own two sets of males, and likewise with two other sets of males living in the other two communities; for she would be fully fertile only when paired with a male of her own size. Hence the thirty-six males, distributed by half-dozens in the three communities, would be divided into three sets of a dozen each; and these sets, as well as the three females, would differ from each other sexually in exactly the same manner as distinct species of the same genus. Moreover the two sets of males living in the community of the extraordinarily fertile middle-sized female would be less potent sexually than the males of corresponding size in the two other communities. Lastly, we should find that from the eggs laid by each of the three females, all three sorts of females and all three sorts of males were habitually reared—proving to demonstration that all belonged to one and the same species.

To appreciate fully this remarkable case of the reciprocally trimorphic species of *Lythrum*, we may take a glance at the two great kingdoms of nature and search for anything analogous. With animals we have the most astonishing diversity of structure in the so-called cases of alternate generation, but as such animals have not arrived at maturity, they are not properly comparable with the forms of *Lythrum*. With mature animals we have extreme differences in structure in the two sexes; we have in some of the lower animals males, females, and hermaphrodites of the same species; we have the somewhat more curious case of certain Cirripedes which are hermaphrodites, but are sexually aided by whole clusters of what I have called complemental males; we have, as Mr. Wallace has lately shown, the females of certain Lepidoptera existing under three distinct forms; but in none of these cases is there any reason to suspect that there is more than one female or one male sexual element. With certain insects, as with Ants, in which there exist, besides males and females, two or three castes of workers, we have a slightly nearer approach to our case, for the workers are so far sexually affected as to have been rendered sterile. With plants, at least with phanerogamic plants, we have not that wonderful series of successive developmental forms so common with animals; nor could this be expected, as plants are fixed to one spot from their birth, and must be adapted throughout life to the same conditions. With plants we have sexual differences in structure, but apparently less strongly marked than with animals, from causes which are in part intelligible, such as there being no sexual selection; again, we have that class of dimorphic flowers so ably discussed recently by Hugo von Mohl, in which some of the flowers are minute, imperfectly developed, and necessarily self-fertile, whilst others are perfect and capable of crossing with other flowers of the same species; but in these several cases we have no reason to suspect that there is more than one female or one male sexual element. When we come to the class of reciprocally dimorphic plants, such as *Primula, Linum,* &c., we first meet with two masculine and two feminine sexes. But these cases, which seemed only a short time since so strange, now sink almost into insignificance before that of the trimorphic species of *Lythrum.*

Naturalists are so much accustomed to behold great diversities of structure associated with the two sexes, that they feel no surprise at the fact; but differences in sexual nature have been thought to be the very touchstone of specific distinction. We now see that such sexual differences—the greater or less power of fertilizing and being fertilized—may characterize and keep separate the coexisting individuals of the same species, in the same manner as they characterize and have kept separate those groups of individuals, produced from common parents during the lapse of ages or in different regions, which we rank and denominate as distinct species.

1. [Read 16 June 1864.] *Journal of the Proceedings of the Linnean Society (Botany)* 8 (1865): 169–96.†

2. See also *The Different Forms of Flowers on Plants of the Same Species* (London: Murray, 1877, pp. 137–67). where edited portions of this article are reprinted.†

3. Hist. Phys. des Plantes d'Europe, tom. ii., 1841, p. 371. Wirtgen, "Ueber *Lythrum salicaria* und dessen Formen," Verhand. des naturhist. Vereins der preuss. Rheinl., 5. Jahrgang, 1848, S. 7.

4. The gas plant.†

5. Large genus of herbs having irregular flowers; includes Dutchman's breeches.†

6. In my paper on the two forms of *Primula* (Journal Proc. Linn. Soc. 1862, p. 85) I stated that I had only occasionally seen humble-bees sucking the flowers of the Cowslip (*P. veris*). Since then I have had some beds in my garden containing nearly 706 plants, and these were incessantly visited by *Bombus hortorum* and *B. muscorum*. I caught some of these bees, and I found (as I had anticipated in my paper, p. 86) that a vast majority of the pollen-grains which adhered to the base of the proboscis were large-sized and had come from the long stamens of the short-styled form, and were thus placed ready to fertilize the stigma of the long-styled form. On the other hand, on the middle, and near the tip of the proboscis, a very large proportion of the pollen-grains were of the small size, and had come from the short stamens of the long-styled form. My son caught, also, a moth (*Cucullia verbasci*) hovering over the bed, and I found on its proboscis a similar distribution of the two kinds of pollen-grains. I give these facts as a further illustration of the importance of the relative lengths of the stamens and pistil.

7. Verhand. des naturhist. Vereins, 5. Jahrgang, 1848, S. 11, 13.

8. *Lagerstroemia Indica*, one of the Lythraceae, is strangely variable in its stamens—I presume in part due to its growth in a hothouse. The most perfect flowers produced with me five very long stamens with thick flesh-coloured filaments and green pollen, and from nineteen to twenty-nine short stamens with yellow pollen; but many flowers produced only one, two, three, or four long stamens with green pollen, which in some of the anthers was wholly replaced by yellow pollen; one anther offered the singular case of half, or one cell being filled with bright green, and the other cell with bright yellow pollen. One petal had a furrow near its base, which contained pollen. According to analogy with *Lythrum*, this species would produce three forms; if so, the above plant was a mid-styled form: it was quite sterile with its own two kinds of pollen.

9. In the spring of 1862 I crossed forty Cowslip flowers (*P. veris*) heteromorphically and homomorphically. The plants were accidentally exposed in the greenhouse to too hot a sun, and a number of umbels perished. Some, however, remained in moderately good health, and on these there were twelve flowers which had been fertilized heteromorphically and eleven which had been fertilized homomorphically. The twelve heteromorphic unions yielded seven fine capsules, containing on an average 57.3 good seed. Now mark the difference: the eleven homomorphic unions yielded only two capsules, of which one contained 39 seeds, but so poor, that I do not suppose one would have germinated, and the other only 17 fairly good seed. It would be superfluous to give any more details on this experiment, or on some which I made at the same time on *P. Sinensis*, after the appearance of Mr. John Scott's admirable paper on the various dimorphic species of *Primula*, in which he confirms my former results, and adds many original and valuable observations. Dr. Hildebrand has also (Botanische Zeitung, 1864, Jan. 1, S. 3) confirmed my general results with respect to *P. Sinensis*, and has corrected an error into which in some unaccountable manner I fell, namely, that the pollen-grains from the long- and short-styled forms were of the same size. Dr. Hildebrand has added a series of new and important

experiments, for he fertilized homomorphically a number of flowers with pollen from the same form, and likewise from the same individual flower. These latter he found were thus rendered rather more sterile. This experiment, I believe, has never been systematically tried before.

10. I have hardly any doubt that this result of 136 seed is due to a gross error. The flowers to be fertilized by their own longer stamens were first marked by "white thread," and those by the longer stamens of the long-styled form by "white silk;" a flower fertilized in the latter manner would have yielded about 136 seed, and it may be observed that one such pod is missing, viz., at the bottom of compartment 1. Therefore I have hardly any doubt that I fertilized a flower marked with "white thread," as if it had been marked with "white silk." With respect to the capsule which yielded 92 seed, in the same column with that which yielded 136, I do not know what to think. I endeavoured to prevent pollen dropping from an upper to any lower flower, and I tried to remember to wipe the pincers carefully after each fertilization; but in making eighteen different crosses, sometimes on windy days, and pestered by bees and flies buzzing about, some few errors could hardly be avoided. One day I had to keep a third man by me all the time to prevent the bees visiting the uncovered plants, for in a few seconds' time they might have done irreparable mischief. It was also extremely difficult to exclude minute Diptera from the net. In 1862 I made the great mistake of placing a mid-styled and long-styled under the same huge net: in 1863 I avoided this error.

11. I suspect that, by mistake, I fertilized this flower with the pollen of the shorter stamens of the long-styled form, and it would then have yielded about 64 seed. Flowers to be thus fertilized were marked with black silk; those with the pollen of the shorter stamens of the short-styled with black thread; and thus, I suspect, the mistake arose.

12. Hist. Phys. des Plantes d'Europe, tom. ii. (1841) pp. 369, 371.

13. Géograph. Bot. de l'Europe, tom. vi. (1857) p. 157.

14. Lythraceae (includes *Lythrum*).†

15. 'Origin of Species,' 3rd edit., p. 101. Hugo von Mohl has recently (Bot. Zeitung, 1863, S. 309, 321), in a most interesting paper, advanced the case of the minute, imperfectly developed, closed and self-fertile flowers borne by *Viola*, *Oxalis, Impatiens, Campanula*, &c., as an argument against my doctrine that no species is self-fertilized for perpetuity. I may state that in the spring of 1862 I examined some of these flowers, and saw, though less thoroughly, all that H. von Mohl has so well described. I can add only one remark, which I believe is correct, that in *V. canina* there is an open channel for the pollen-tubes from the extremity of the stigma to the ovarium; for I gently pressed a minute bubble of air repeatedly backwards and forwards from end to end. Though the imperfectly developed and the perfect flowers are so different in structure, it is a rather curious case of correlation, that in the double purple Violet (*V. odorata*) the minute imperfect flowers are double to the very core, so that a section appears like the head of a cabbage when cut through. There can be, as von Mohl asserts, no doubt that these flowers are always self-fertilized; they are moreover specially adapted for this end, as may be seen in the remarkable difference in the shape of the pistil in *V. canina* (and in a less degree in *V. hirta* and the single *V. odorata*) as compared with that of the perfect flower; and in the pollen-tubes which proceed from the grains within the anthers in *V. canina*, and from within the lower anthers of *Oxalis acetosella*, having the wonderful power of directing their course to the stigma. If these plants had produced the minute closed flowers alone, the proof would have been perfect that they could never have crossed with

other individuals. I am aware that in some of these cases it has been stated that the perfect flowers never produce any seed; as far as *Amphicarpoea* is concerned, I hear from Professor Asa Gray that the Petaliferous flowers certainly sometimes yield seed. The completely enclosed flowers of that curious grass, the *Leersia oryzoides,* as described by M. Duval-Jouve (Bull. Soc. Bot. de France, tom. x. 1863, p. 194), apparently offer the best case of perpetual self-fertilization; for when perfect flowers are protruded from the culms, they are, as far as is yet known, always sterile. In a number of plants kept by me in pots in water, not one single perfect flower has protruded, but the enclosed flowers produced plenty of seed. Without wishing to throw any doubt on M. Duval-Jouve's excellent observations, I may add that with the enclosed flowers borne by my plants, the act of fertilization, that is, the penetration of the stigma by the pollen-tubes, took place in the air and not in fluid within the glumes. With the exception of the *Leersia,* as the case now stands, I cannot see how the production of the small, imperfect flowers invalidates my doctrine that no species is perpetually self-fertilized, more than the multiplication of many plants by bulbs, stolons, &c. As I observe that the production of seed by the perfect flowers of *Viola* is spoken of as something capricious and accidental, I may state that, although it varies much in different years, it depends exclusively on the visits of bees; I ascertained this by marking many flowers thus visited, and finding that they produced capsules, and by covering up many flowers which (excepting a few that I artificially fertilized) did not, when thus protected, produce a single capsule. After bees have visited these flowers, the pollen may be seen scattered on the papillae and on the stigma itself, and they can hardly fail thus to cross distinct individuals. These remarks apply to *V. canina, hirta,* and *odorata;* with *V. tricolor* the case is somewhat different; but I must not enlarge any more on this subject. The production by so many plants of perfect and expanded, as well as of imperfect and closed flowers, seems to me to throw much light on many points; it shows how extraordinarily little pollen is necessary for full fertilization, for I ascertained with *V. canina* that the perfect and imperfect flowers (the latter producing so few pollen-grains) yielded the same average number of seeds; it shows us that fertilization can be perfected in closed flowers; it shows us that large, highly coloured petals, perfume, and the secretion of nectar are by no means indispensable for this act, even in those species which properly possess these characters. It seems to me that the necessity of an occasional cross with a distinct individual of the same species explains the universal presence of at least some expanded flowers, at the expense of injury from rain and the loss of much pollen by innumerable pollen-robbing insects; it explains the enormous superfluity of pollen from its liability to loss from these causes and during conveyance from flower to flower; it explains the use of a gaily coloured corolla, perfume, and nectar, namely, to attract insects, except in those comparatively few cases in which wind is the agent, and in these the last-named attributes are deficient.

ᴧ Partial Change of Sex in Unisexual Flowers[1]

Will any of your botanical readers have the kindness to inform me, whether in those monoecious or dioecious plants, in which the flowers are widely different, it has ever been observed that half the flower, or only a segment of it, has been of one sex and the other half or segment of the opposite sex; in the same manner as so frequently occurs with insects?

1. *Gardeners' Chronicle and Agricultural Gazette,* no. 6, 10 February 1866, p. 127.†

◚ Self-fertilization[1]

It is an astonishing fact that self-fertilization should not have been an habitual occurrence. It apparently demonstrates to us that there must be something injurious in the process. Nature thus tells us, in the most emphatic manner, that she abhors perpetual self-fertilization.

1. *Hardwicke's Science-Gossip: An Illustrated Medium of Interchange and Gossip for Students and Lovers of Nature,* 1866. P. 114. Extracted from Charles Darwin, *On the Various Contrivances by which British and Foreign Orchids Are Fertilised by Insects, and on the Good Effects of Intercrossing* (London: Murray, 1862, p. 359).†

◚ Oxalis Bowei[1]

I should be much obliged to any one who will be so kind as to look at his flowers of this Oxalis,[2] and observe where the summits of the branching stigmas stand with respect to the two sets of anthers. In all my plants the stigmas stand close beneath the lower anthers; but I have good reason to believe that two other forms exist—one with the stigmas standing above both sets of anthers, and the other with the stigmas between the two sets. If any one has flowers in either of these latter states, that is long-styled or mid-styled, I should be grateful if he would send me a few rather young flowers wrapped up in tin-foil or oil-silk; for I should thus be enabled to fertilize my own flowers and obtain seed.

1. *Gardeners' Chronicle and Agricultural Gazette,* no. 32, 11 August 1866, p. 756.†
2. Wood sorrel.†

◚ Cross-fertilising Papilionaceous Flowers[1]

All who have tried have found much difficulty in crossing papilionaceous flowers. Several years ago, Dr. Herbert remarked to me that with the exception of Erythrina[2] no hybrids had been made in this great family. Gärtner crossed 36 flowers of different varieties of the common Pea, and he did not get a single pod perfectly developed and with the full complement of seed; he crossed 10 flowers of Kidney Beans, and did not get a single pod. Some years ago I crossed the varieties of the Sweet Pea, and many more flowers dropped off unimpregnated than were fertilised. The difficulty arises from the anthers opening at so early an age that they must be removed long before the flower expands. After the operation the immature stigma is liable to exposure to the air; and it is difficult to judge when to apply the pollen. Moreover there is some reason to suspect that the stigma requires successive applications of pollen. To show the difficulty of fertilising papilionaceous flowers, I may mention that I lately removed all the pollen that I could with a soft brush from six recently expanded flowers of Lupinus pilosus protected from the visits of insects, and then applied pollen from a distinct individual of the same species. Although in this case there was no operation at an early age, yet five flowers out of the six dropped off unimpregnated. Had these flowers remained untouched, all, judging from the others, probably would have set, and the only difference would have been that their stigmas would have been surrounded by a mass of pollen as long as the flowers continued in bloom. This case is worth mentioning as showing how erroneous the belief is that fertilisation usually takes place in unopened flowers, in which the pollen is shed at an early age. These trials on the Lupines, and others formerly on Sweet Peas, led me to try the following plan. I rolled up thin paper into a cylinder, rather thinner than a knitting needle. I then tied a thread tight round, and cut off the cylinder beneath the thread, so that a little pipe closed at one end or cap, about the fifth of an inch in length, was left. This was easily filled with pollen from the keel-petal of any desired variety, and could then be placed on the pistil and secured below the stigma by being tied with a thread. I then castrated four flower-buds of the Sweet Pea, and placed on the young stigmas caps filled with pollen from another variety, and four fine pods were soon formed. I also fertilised eight castrated flowers or two species of Lupins with pollen from distinct plants of the same species, but from these I have got only four pods. I may add, that as an experiment I filled one of the little caps with pollen of Lathyrus grandiflorus and placed it on the stigma of a Sweet Pea (Lathyrus odoratus), and to my great surprise, considering how distinct these species are, a fine pod has been formed. I am certain no pollen could have been left in the flower of the Sweet Pea, as the anthers were removed whilst quite immature; and if these hybrid seeds grow, a curious hybrid will be produced. I should not have thought this plan of fertilising papilionaceous flowers worth mentioning had it not been applicable in all cases in which early castration is necessary, and likewise in certain cases mentioned by Gärtner, in which the stigma requires, or is benefited by, successive applications of pollen. In all such cases some trouble would be saved and certainty gained by the use of the little caps filled with the desired kind of pollen.

1. *Gardeners' Chronicle and Agricultural Gazette,* no. 32, 11 August 1866, p. 756.†

2. Tropical shrubs or trees; coral trees.†

⚓ [Note on the Common Broom][1]

In the Broom, if the flowers be protected from insects, the parts (stamen and pistil) do not spring out, and scarcely any pods are produced. In a flower lately expanded, when a bee alights on the keel, the shorter stamens alone are ejected, and they dust the abdomen of the insect. When the flower is a day or two older, if a bee alights on the keel, the pistil and longer stamens spring violently out, and the hairs on the pistil deposit plenty of pollen on the bee's back, against which the stigma is rubbed. When the bee flies away, the pistil curls still more, and the stigmatic surface becomes up-turned, and stands close to the protruded anthers of the shorter stamens. We have seen that the bee gets dusted in its abdomen from the shorter stamens of the younger flowers; and this pollen will be left on the up-turned stigma of the curled pistil of the older flowers. Thus both the upper and lower surface of the bee gets dusted with pollen, which will be transferred to the stigma at two different periods.

1. [Read 19 April 1866.] In George Henslow, "Note on the Structure of *Indigofera,* as Apparently Offering Facilities for the Intercrossing of Distinct Flowers," *Journal of the Linnean Society (Botany)* 9 (1867): 355–58.†

⚓ Fertilisation of Cypripediums[1]

As the sexes of Orchids form a subject of considerable interest, I beg to forward you the accompanying specimens of Cypripedium insigne.[2] Of this I have several plants, all however originally derived from the same piece, but in spite of numerous attempts, I have uniformly failed to fertilise the flowers. The seed-vessel swells and the flower fades as usual, but no seed is produced. It appears to me that my plant produces a male flower only, and is not hermaphrodite. Have any others of your correspondents made a similar observation? I enclose a flower of Cypripedium insigne and two barren seed-vessels, to which the pollen of C. barbatum and C. venustum was applied this year. To prove that the pollen masses of the plant in question are good, I send also a seed-vessel of C. barbatum, fertilised with the pollen of one of the same flowers of C. insigne, and which is full of seeds. *A. D. B.*

The specimens forwarded appeared on examination to be perfectly formed as regards their stamens and pistils, but perfectly destitute of ovules. On forwarding them to Mr. Darwin, that gentleman kindly favoured us with the following remarks. EDS.:—From the remarkable fact lately ascertained by Dr. Hildebrand, that with many Orchids the ovules do not become developed until many weeks or even months have elapsed after the pollen-tubes have penetrated the stigma, it is not a little difficult to ascertain whether any Orchis is exclusively a male plant, that is, whether the female organs have aborted. Of course there is no difficulty in ascertaining the rudimentary condition of the pollen, and so ascertaining that a plant is a female. The explanation of the sterility of the seed-capsules in the Cypripediums sent to me I have little doubt lies in the circumstance of their having been fertilised by pollen taken from the same plant or seedling. I now know of a long series of cases in which various Orchids are absolutely sterile when impregnated by their own pollen (proved, however, to be in itself effective), but which can be easily impregnated by pollen taken from other individuals of the same species, or from distinct species. These facts strike me as most remarkable under a physiological point of view, and they point to the necessity of an occasional or regular union between distinct individuals of the same species.

1. *Gardeners' Chronicle and Agricultural Gazette,* no. 14, 6 April 1867, p. 350.†
2. The first paragraph of this article is an inquiry written to the editor of the *Gardeners' Chronicle* by "A.D.B." and forwarded to Darwin for his reply.†

⚓ [Inquiry about Proportional Number of Males and Females Born to Domestic Animals]¹

I should be very much obliged to you or to any of your readers, if they would have the great kindness to refer me to any observations which may have been published on the proportional number of males and females born to our various domestic animals, such as cattle, sheep, horses, dogs, poultry, ducks, &c. I presume that this point has often been attended to, but I am at a loss where to search, and should be grateful for any reference or for any unpublished facts.

1. *Gardeners' Chronicle and Agricultural Gazette,* no. 7, 15 February 1868, p. 160.†

← Queries about Expression for Anthropological Inquiry[1]

1. Is astonishment expressed by the eyes and mouth being opened wide, and by the eyebrows being raised?

2. Does shame excite a blush when the color of the skin allows it to be visible?

3. When a man is indignant or defiant does he frown, hold his body and head erect, square his shoulders, and clench his fists?

4. When considering deeply on any subject, or trying to understand any puzzle, does he frown or wrinkle the skin beneath the lower eyelids?

5. When in low spirits, are the corners of the mouth depressed, and the inner corner or angle of the eyebrows raised by that muscle which the French call the "grief muscle?"

6. When in good spirits do the eyes sparkle, with the skin around and under them a little wrinkled, and with the corners of the mouth a little drawn back?

7. When a man sneers or snarls at another, is the corner of the upper lip over the canine teeth raised on the side facing the man whom he addresses?

8. Can a dogged or obstinate expression be recognized, which is chiefly shown by the mouth being firmly closed, a lowering brow, and a slight frown?

9. Is contempt expressed by a slight protrusion of the lips and turning up of the nose, with a slight expiration?

10. Is disgust shown by the lower lip being turned down, the upper lip slightly raised, with a sudden expiration something like incipient vomiting?

11. Is extreme fear expressed in the same general manner as with Europeans?

12. Is laughter ever carried to such an extreme as to bring tears into the eyes?

13. When a man wishes to show that he cannot prevent something being done, or cannot himself do something, does he shrug his shoulders, turn inwards his elbows, extend outwards his hands, and open the palms?

14. Do the children, when sulky, pout, or greatly protrude the lips?

15. Can guilty, or sly, or jealous expressions be recognized? though I know not how these can be defined.

16. As a sign to keep silent, is a gentle hiss uttered?

17. Is the head nodded vertically in affirmation and shaken laterally in negation?

Observations on natives who have had little communication with

Europeans would be, of course, the most valuable, though those made on any natives would be of much interest.

General remarks on expression are of comparatively little value. A definite description of the countenance under any emotion or frame of mind would possess much more value.

An answer to any *single* one of the foregoing questions would be gratefully accepted.

Memory is so deceptive on subjects like these that I hope it may not be trusted to.

1. *Annual Report of the Board of Regents of the Smithsonian Institution . . . for the Year 1867.* Senate Mis. doc. no. 86, p. 324, 1868.†

✦ Hedgehogs[1]

As in the August and September numbers, you have published an account of hedgehogs apparently carrying away pears and crabs sticking on their spines, you may think the following statement worth insertion as a further corroboration. I have received this account in a letter dated August 5, 1867, from Mr. Swinhoe at Amoy:—"Mr. Gisbert, the Spanish Consul at Amoy, informs me that when he was an engineer on the roads in Spain some years ago, he was fond of shooting and roaming about the country. He states that in the Sierra Morena, a strawberry-tree (Arbutus unedo?) was very abundant, and bore large quantities of red, fruit-like, fine, large, red strawberries. These gave quite a glow to the woods. The district in the mountain chain he refers to, is on the divisional line between the provinces of Seville and Badajos. Under these trees hedgehogs occurred innumerable, and fed on the fruit, which the Spaniards call Madrône. Mr. Gisbert has often seen an Erizo (hedgehog) trotting along with at least a dozen of these strawberries sticking on its spines. He supposes that the hedgehogs were carrying the fruit to their holes to eat in quiet and security, and that to procure them they must have rolled themselves on the fruit which was scattered in great abundance all over the ground beneath the trees."

1. *Hardwicke's Science-Gossip: An Illustrated Medium of Interchange and Gossip for Students and Lovers of Nature,* 1868. P. 280.†

✦ The Formation of Mould by Worms[1]

As Mr. Fish asks me in so obliging a manner whether I continue of the same opinion as formerly in regard to the efficiency of worms in bringing up within their intestines fine soil from below, I must answer in the affirmative. I have made no more actual measurements, but I have watched during the last 25 years the gradual, and at last complete, disappearance of innumerable large flints on the surface of a field with very poor soil after it had been laid down as pasture. I have also purposely covered a few yards square of a grass-field with fine chalk, so as to observe the worms burrowing up through it, and leaving their castings on the surface, which were soon spread out by the rain. The Regent's Park in early autumn is a capital place to observe the wonderful amount of work effected under favourable circumstances by worms, even in the course of a week or two. My observations in Staffordshire were chiefly made on poor, sandy grass-land, and I think that Mr. Fish will find that the proportion by weight or measure of carbon in poor soil is but small, and that the decay of the Grass will account for but a small proportion of the matter successively deposited on the surface. Except when peat or peaty soil is forming, the carbon compounds seem soon to be decomposed and disappear. Judging from the quick rate at which I have proved that the surface becomes covered with fine soil, if the mere decay of the Grass were as effective as Mr. Fish thinks, many feet in thickness would be formed in the course of a few centuries—a result which would be as surprising as delightful to the dwellers on poor land, or indeed on any land, which is never overflowed by mud-bearing water. In ordinary soils the worms do not burrow down to great depths, consequently fine vegetable soil is not accumulated to any inordinate thickness.

1. *Gardeners' Chronicle and Agricultural Gazette,* no. 20, 15 May 1869, p. 530.†

✎ Notes on the Fertilization of Orchids[1]

Having drawn up some notes for a French translation of my work 'On the various contrivances by which British and Foreign Orchids are Fertilized by Insects' (1862), it has appeared to me that these notes would be worth publishing in English. I have thus been able to bring up the literature of the subject to the present day, by giving references to, together with very brief abstracts of, all the papers published since my work appeared. These papers contain, on the one hand, corrections of some serious errors into which I had fallen, and, on the other hand, confirmations of many of my statements. I have also been able to add, from my own observations and those of others, a few new facts of interest. A heading is given to each note, which will show the nature of the correction or addition, without any reference to my book; but I have added in a parenthesis the page to which the note ought to be appended.

Orchis or *Anacamptis pyramidalis* (p. 20).—The late Prof. Treviranus has confirmed (Botanische Zeitung, 1863, p. 241) my observations on this remarkable species; but he differs from me in one or two minor points.

On the Kinds of Insects which Habitually Visit and Fertilize Some of the Common British Species of Orchis (p. 35).—I believe that it may be safely predicated that orchids with very long nectaries, such as the *Anacamptis, Gymnadenia,* and *Platanthera,* are habitually fertilized by Lepidoptera, whilst those with only moderately long nectaries are fertilized by bees and Diptera—in short, that the length of the nectary is correlated with that of the proboscis of the insect which visits the plant. I have now seen *Orchis morio* fertilized by various kinds of bees, namely:—by the hive-bee (*Apis mellifica*), to some of which from ten to sixteen pollen-masses were attached; by *Bombus muscorum,* with several pollen-masses attached to the bare surface close above the mandibles; by *Eucera longicornis,* with eleven pollen-masses attached to its head; and by *Osmia rufa.* These bees, and the other Hymenoptera mentioned throughout these notes, have been named for me by our highest authority, Mr. Frederick Smith, of the British Museum. The Diptera have been named by Mr. F. Walker, of the same establishment. In Northern Germany, Dr. H. Müller of Lippstadt found pollen-masses of *Orchis morio* attached to *Bombus silvarum, lapidarius, confusus,* and *pratorum.* The same excellent observer found the pollen-masses of *Orchis latifolia* attached to a *Bombus;* but this orchis is also frequented by Diptera. A friend watched for me *Orchis mascula,* and saw several flowers visited by a *Bombus,* apparently *B. muscorum;* but it is surprising how seldom any insect can be seen visiting this common species. With respect to *Orchis maculata,* my son, Mr. George Darwin, has clearly made out the manner of its fertilization. He saw many specimens of a fly (*Empis livida*) inserting their proboscides into the nectary; and subsequently I saw the same occurrence. He brought home six specimens of this *Empis,* with pollinia attached to their spherical eyes, on a level with the bases of the antennae. The pollinia had undergone the movement of depression, and stood a little above and parallel to the proboscis: hence they were in a position excellently adapted to strike the stigma. Six pollinia were thus attached to one specimen, and three to another. My son also saw another and smaller species (*Empis pennipes*) inserting its proboscis into the nectary; but this species did not act so well or so regularly as the other in fertilizing the flowers. One specimen of this latter *Empis* had five pollinia, and a second had three pollinia, attached to the dorsal surface of the convex thorax.

On Nectar Being Secreted and Contained between the Outer and Inner Membranes of the Nectary in Several Species of Orchis (p. 51).—I have repeated my observations on the nectaries of some of our common species, and especially on those of *Orchis morio, at the time when various bees were continually visiting* the flowers; but I could never see the minutest drop of nectar within the nectary. Each bee remained a considerable time with its proboscis in constant movement whilst inserted into the nectary. I observed the same fact with *Empis* in the case of *Orchis maculata;* and in this orchis I could occasionally detect minute brown specks, where punctures had been made. Hence the view suggested by me that insects puncture the inner lining of the nectary and suck the fluid contained between the two coats may be safely accepted. I have said in my work that this hypothesis was a bold one, as no instance was known of Lepidoptera penetrating with their delicate proboscides any membrane; but I now hear from Mr. R. Trimen that at the Cape of Good Hope moths and butterflies do much injury to peaches and plums by penetrating the skin, in parts which have not been in the least broken.

Since the Appearance of my Work, the Following Observations Have Been Published on Other Species of Orchis *and on Certain Allied Forms* (p. 53).—Mr. J. Traherne Moggridge has given (Journ. Linn. Soc. vol. viii. Botany, 1865, p. 256) a very interesting account of the structure and manner of fertilization of *Orchis* or *Aceras longibracteata*. Both pollinia, as in *Anacamptis pyramidalis*, are attached to the same viscid disk; but, differently from those in that species, after being removed from the anther-cases, they first converge and then undergo the movement of depression. But the most interesting peculiarity in this species is that insects suck nectar out of minute open cells in the honeycombed surface of the labellum. Mr. Moggridge saw this plant fertilized by a large bee, the *Xylocopa violacea*. He adds some observations on *Orchis hircina*, and describes the structure and manner of fertilization of *Serapias cordigera* by another bee, viz. the *Ceratina albilabris*. In this *Serapias* both pollinia are attached to the same viscid disk; when first withdrawn, they are bent backwards, but soon afterwards move forwards and downwards in the usual manner. As the stigmatic cavity is narrow, the pollinia are guided into it by two guiding plates.

Mr. Moggridge sent me from Northern Italy living plants of *Orchis* or *Neotinea intacta*, together with excellent drawings and a full account of the structure of the flower. He informed me that this species is remarkable for producing seed without the aid of insects; and I ascertained that when insects were carefully excluded, almost all the flowers produced capsules. Their fertilization follows from the pollen being extremely incoherent, and spontaneously falling on the stigma. Nevertheless a short nectary is present, the pollinia possess small viscid disks, and all the parts are so arranged that, if insects were to visit the flowers, the pollen-masses would probably be removed and then carried to another flower, but not so effectually as with most other orchids. We shall hereafter find a few other cases of orchids which have structural peculiarities adapted both for self-fertilization and for crossing. I may here also refer to a paper by Mr. R. Trimen (Journ. Linn. Soc. vol. vii. Botany, 1863, p. 144) on the beautiful *Disa grandiflora* of the Cape of Good Hope. This orchid presents several remarkable characteristics, one of these being that the pollinia do not spontaneously undergo any movement of depression, the weight of the pollen-masses sufficing to bend the caudicle into the proper curvature for the act of fertilization. Another peculiarity is that the posterior sepal secretes nectar, and is developed into a spur-like nectary. Mr. Trimen informs me that he has seen a Dipterous insect, allied to *Bombylius*, frequenting the flowers. I may add that Mr. Trimen has sent me descriptions and specimens of various other South-African orchids, which confirm the general conclusions at which I have arrived in my work.

On the Movement of the Pollinia of Ophrys muscifera (p. 56).—Mr. T. H. Farrer, who has lately been attending to the fertilization of various plants, has convinced me that I have erred, and that the pollinia of this *Ophrys* do undergo a movement of depression. Hence my remarks on the correlation of the various parts of the flower are to a certain extent invalidated; but there can be no doubt that the naturally bent caudicle plays an important part in placing the pollen-mass in a proper position for striking the stigma. I have continued occasionally to watch the flowers of this species, but have never succeeded in seeing insects visit them; but I have been led to suspect that they puncture or gnaw the small lustrous prominences beneath the viscid disks, which, I may add, are likewise present in several allied species. I have observed very minute punctures on these prominences, but I could not decide whether these had been made by insects or whether superficial cells had spontaneously burst.

Ophrys aranifera (p. 63).—F. Delpino states (Fecondazione nelle Piante &c., Firenze, 1867, p. 19) that he has examined in Italy thousands of specimens of this *Ophrys*, and that it seldom produces capsules. It does not secrete any nectar. Although he never saw an insect on the flowers (excepting once a green locust), nevertheless they are fertilized by insects; for he found pollen on the stigmas of some flowers, which had their own pollinia still within the anther-cases. The pollinia never spontaneously fall out. He appears to think that I infer that this *Ophrys* fertilizes itself, which is an error.

Ophrys apifera (p. 71).—Prof. Treviranus at first doubted (Botanische Zeitung, 1862, p. 11) the accuracy of my account of this *Ophrys*, and of the differences between it and *O. arachnites*; but he has subsequently (Bot. Zeit. 1863, p. 241) fully confirmed all that I have stated.

Ophrys arachnites (p. 72).—I have now examined several additional living specimens of this *Ophrys*, and can confirm my statement that the pollinia do not fall out of the anther-cases, even when the spikes are strongly shaken; nor do they fall out when the spikes are kept standing in water for a week. Mr. J. Moggridge has made (Journ. Linn. Soc., Bot. vol. viii. 1865, p. 258) a remarkable observation on *O. scolopax*, which is closely allied to *O. arachnites*,—namely, that at Mentone it never exhibits any tendency to self-fertilization, whilst at Cannes all the flowers fertilize themselves, owing to a slight modification in the curvature of the anther, which causes the pollinia to fall out. This botanist has given, in his 'Flora of Mentone,'[2] a full description, with excellent figures, of *O. scolopax, arachnites, aranifera*, and *apifera*; and he believes, from the number of intermediate forms, that they must all be ranked as varieties of a single species, and that their differences are intimately connected with their period of flowering. It does not appear that these forms in England, judging from their distribution, are liable to pass into each other, within any moderate or observable period of time.

On the Fertilization of Herminium monorchis (p. 74).—My son, Mr. George Darwin, has fully observed the manner of fertilization of this minute and rare orchis. It differs from that of any other genus known to me. He saw the flowers entered by various minute insects, and brought home no less than twenty-seven specimens with pollinia (generally with only one, but sometimes with two) attached to them. These insects consisted of minute Hymenoptera (of which *Tetrastichus diaphantus* was the commonest), of Diptera and Coleoptera, the latter being *Malthodes brevicollis*. The one indispensable point appears to be that the insect should be of very minute size, the largest being only the 1/20 of an inch in length. It is an extraordinary fact that in all the specimens the pollinia were attached to the same peculiar spot, namely, to the outer side of one of the two front legs, to the projection formed by the articulation of the femur with the coxa. In one instance alone a pollinium was attached to the outside of the femur a little beneath the articulation. The cause of this peculiar manner of attachment is sufficiently clear: the middle part of the labellum stands so close to the anther and stigma, that insects always enter the flower at one corner, between the margin of the labellum and one of the upper petals; they also almost always crawl in with their backs turned directly or obliquely towards the labellum. My son saw several which had begun to crawl into the flower in a different position; but they came out and changed their position. Thus, standing in either corner of the flower, with their backs turned towards the labellum, they inserted their heads and fore legs into the short nectary, which is seated between the two widely separated viscid disks. I ascertained that they stand in this position by finding three dead insects, which had been permanently glued to the disks. Whilst sucking the nectar, which occupies about two or three minutes, the projecting joint of the femur stands under the large helmet-like viscid disk on either side; and when the insect retreats, the disk exactly fits on, and is glued to, the prominent joint. The movement of depression in the caudicle then takes place, and the mass of pollen-grains projects just beyond the tibia; so that the insect, when entering another flower, can hardly fail to fertilize the stigma, which is situated directly beneath the disk on either side. I know of hardly any other case in which the whole structure of the flower is more beautifully correlated than in the *Herminium* for a most peculiar manner of fertilization.

On the Movement of the Pollinia in Peristylus viridis (p. 76).—Mr. T. H. Farrer informs me that the pollinia certainly undergo a movement of depression, but that this does not take place until twenty or thirty minutes have elapsed after their removal from the anther-cases. This length of time probably accounts for my oversight. He asserts that, after the movement of depression, the pollinia become much better adapted to strike the stigmatic surface. He suggests that insects may take a long time to lick up the nectar from the two naked spots on the labellum, and through the narrow slit-like opening into the nectary—and that during this time the pollinium becomes firmly attached, by the slow hardening of the viscid matter, to the insect's body, so as to be subsequently ready to fertilize another flower when visited by the same insect.

On the Lepidoptera which Fertilize the Gymnadenia conopsea, *and on the Divergence of the Pollinia* (p. 82).—Mr. George Darwin went at night to a bank where this species grows plentifully, and soon caught

Plusia chrysitis with six pollinia, *P. gamma* with three, *Anaitis plagiata* with five, and *Triphoena pronuba* with seven pollinia attached to their proboscides. I may add that he caught the first-named moth, bearing the pollinia of this orchis, in my flower-garden, although more than a quarter of a mile distant from any spot where the plant grows. I state in my work that I do not understand the cause of the divergence of the pollinia so that they are enabled to strike the lateral stigmatic surfaces; but the explanation is simple. The upper margin of the nectary is arched, being formed on one side by the disk of one pollinium, and on the other side by the other disk. Now if a moth inserts its proboscis obliquely, and there are no guiding-ridges by which, as in *Anacamptis pyramidalis*, a moth is compelled to insert its proboscis directly in front, or if a bristle be inserted obliquely one pollinium alone is removed. In this case the pollinium becomes attached a little on one side of the bristle or proboscis; and its extremity, after the vertical movement of depression, occupies a proper position for striking the lateral stigma on the same side.

On the Gymnadenia tridentata *of North America* (p. 83).—Prof. Asa Gray has published (American Journal of Science, vol. xxxiv. 1862, p. 426, and footnote p. 260; and vol. xxxvi, 1863, p. 293) some interesting notes on the *Gymnadenia tridentata*. The anther opens in the bud, and some of the pollen invariably falls on the naked cellular tip of the rostellum; and this part, strange to say, is penetrated by the pollen-tubes, so that the flowers are self-fertilized. Nevertheless "all the arrangements for the removal of the pollinia by insects (including the movement of depression) are as perfect as in the species which depend upon insect aid." Hence there can be little doubt that this species is occasionally crossed.

Habenaria or Platanthera bifolia (p. 88).—According to Dr. H. Müller, of Lippstadt, *Pl. bifolia* of English authors is the *Pl. solstitalis of* Boenninghausen; and he fully agrees with me that it must be ranked as specifically distinct from *Pl. chlorantha*. Dr. Müller states that this latter species is connected by a series of gradations with another form which in Germany is called *Pl. bifolia*. He gives a very full and valuable account of the variability of these species of *Platanthera* and of their structure in relation to their manner of fertilization. (See Verhandl. d. Nat. Verein. Jahrg. xxv. III. Folge, v. Bd. pp. 36–38.)

American Species of Platanthera (p. 91).—Prof. Asa Gray has described (American Journal of Science, vol. xxxiv. 1862, pp. 143, 259, & 424, and vol. xxxvi. 1863, p. 292) the structure of ten American species of *Platanthera*. Most of these resemble in their manner of fertilization the two British species described by me; but some of them, in which the viscid disks do not stand far apart, have curious contrivances, such as a channelled labellum, lateral shields, &c., compelling moths to insert their proboscides directly in front. *Pl. Hookeri*, on the other hand (*ibid.* vol. xxxiv. 1862, p. 143), differs in a very interesting manner: the two viscid disks stand widely separated from each other; consequently a moth, unless of gigantic size, would be able to suck the copious nectar without touching either disk; but this risk is avoided in the following manner:— The central line of the stigma is prominent, and the labellum, instead of hanging down, as in most of the other species, is curved upwards, so that the front of the flower is made somewhat tubular and is divided into two halves. Thus a moth is compelled to go to one or the other side, and its face will almost certainly be brought into contact with one of the disks. The drum of the pollinium, when removed, contracts in the same manner as I have described under *Pl. chlorantha*. Prof. Gray has seen a butterfly from Canada with the pollinia of this species attached to each eye. In the case of *Platanthera flava* (American Journal of Science, vol. xxxvi. 1863, p. 292), moths are compelled in a different manner to enter the nectary on one side. A narrow but strong protuberance, rising from the base of the labellum, projects upwards and backwards, so as almost to touch the column; thus the moth, being forced to go to either side, is almost sure to withdraw one of the viscid disks. In the allied and wonderful *Bonatea speciosa* of the Cape of Good Hope there is a similar contrivance for the same purpose.

Platanthera hyperborea and *dilatata* have been regarded by some botanists as varieties of the same species; and Prof. Asa Gray says (Amer. Journ. of Science, vol. xxxiv. 1862, pp. 259 & 425) that he has often been tempted to come to the same conclusion; but now, on closer examination, he finds, besides other characters, a remarkable physiological difference, namely, that *Pl. dilatata*, like its congeners, requires insect aid and cannot fertilize itself; whilst in *Pl. hyperborea* the pollen-masses commonly fall out of the anther-cells whilst the flower is very young or in bud, and thus the stigma is self-fertilized. Nevertheless the various structures adapted for crossing are still present.

Fertilization of Epipactis palustris (p. 102).—My son, Mr. W. E. Darwin, has carefully observed for me this plant in the Isle of Wight. Hive-bees seem to be the chief agents in fertilization; for he saw about a score of flowers visited by these insects, many of which had pollen-masses attached to their foreheads, just above the mandibles. I had supposed that insects crawled into the flowers; but hive-bees are too large to do this; they always clung, whilst sucking the nectar, to the distal and hinged half of the labellum, which was thus pressed downwards. Owing to this part being elastic and tending to spring up, the bees, as they left the flowers, seemed to fly rather upwards; and this would favour, in the manner explained by me, the complete withdrawal of the pollen-masses, quite as well as an insect crawling out of the flower in an upward direction. Perhaps, however, this upward movement may not be so necessary as I had supposed; for, judging from the point at which the pollen-masses were attached to the bees, the back part of the head would press against, and thus lift up, the blunt, solid, upper end of the anther, thus freeing the pollen-masses.

Various other insects besides hive-bees visit this *Epipactis*. My son saw several large flies (*Sarcophaga carnosa*) haunting the flowers; but they did not enter in so neat and regular a manner as the hive-bees; nevertheless two had pollen-masses attached to their foreheads. Several smaller flies (*Coelopa frigida*) were also seen entering and leaving the flowers, with pollen-masses adhering rather irregularly to the dorsal surface of the thorax. Three or four distinct kinds of Hymenoptera (one of small size being *Crabro brevis*) likewise visited the flowers; and three of these Hymenoptera had pollen-masses attached to their backs. Other still more minute Diptera, Coleoptera, and ants were seen sucking the nectar; but these insects appeared to be too small to transport the pollen-masses. It is remarkable that some of the foregoing insects should visit these flowers; for Mr. F. Walker informs me that the *Sarcophaga* frequents decaying animal matter, and the *Coelopa* haunts seaweed, occasionally settling on flowers; the *Crabro* also, as I hear from Mr. F. Smith, collects small beetles (*Halticoe*) for provisioning its nest. It is equally remarkable, seeing how many kinds of insects visit this *Epipactis*, that, although my son watched for some hours on three occasions hundreds of plants, not a single humble-bee alighted on a flower, though many were flying about. In a footnote I have given the results of experiments made by Mr. More,[3] by cutting off the distal and hinged half of the labellum, in order to ascertain how far this part is important. He has now repeated the experiment on nine additional flowers: of these, three did not produce seed-capsules; but this may have been accidental. Of six capsules which were produced, two contained about as many seeds as the capsules of unmutilated flowers on the same plant; but four capsules contained much fewer seeds. The seeds themselves were well-formed. These experiments, as far as they go, support the view that the distal part of the labellum plays an important part in leading insects to enter and leave the flower in a proper manner for fertilization.

Fertilization of Epipactis latifolia (p. 104).—Although this orchis is not common in the vicinity of Down, by a fortunate chance several plants sprang up in a gravel walk close to my house, so that I have been able to observe them during several years, and have thus discovered how they are fertilized. Although hive-bees and humble-bees of many kinds were constantly flying over the plants, I never saw a bee or any Dipterous insect visit the flowers; whilst, on the other hand, I repeatedly observed each year the common wasp (*Vespa sylvestris*) sucking the nectar out of the open cup-shaped labellum. I thus saw the act of fertilization effected by the pollen-masses being removed and carried on the foreheads of the wasps to other flowers. Mr. Oxenden also informs me that a large bed of *E. purpurata* (which is considered by some botanists a distinct species, and by others a variety) was frequented by "swarms of wasps." It is very remarkable that the sweet nectar of this *Epipactis* should not be attractive to any kind of bee. If wasps were to become extinct in any district, so would the *Epipactis latifolia*.

Dr. H. Müller of Lippstadt has published (Verhandl. d. Nat. Ver. Jahrg. xxv. III. Folge, v. Bd. pp. 7–36) some very important observations on the differences in structure and in the manner of fertilization, as well as on the connecting gradations, between *Epipactis rubiginosa, microphylla,* and *viridiflora*. The latter species is highly remarkable by the absence of a rostellum, and by being regularly self-fertilized. This latter circumstance follows from the incoherent pollen of the lower part of the pollen-masses emitting, whilst still within the anther-cells, pollen-tubes, which penetrate the stigma; and this occurred even in the bud state. This species, however, is probably visited by insects, and occasionally crossed; for the labellum contains nectar. *E. microphylla* is equally remarkable, by being intermediate in structure between *E. latifolia,* which is always fertilized by the aid of insects, and *E. viridiflora*, which does not necessarily require any such aid. The whole of this memoir by Dr. H. Müller deserves to be attentively studied.

Cephalanthera grandiflora (p. 108).—During the year 1862, the flowers of this orchis appeared to have been visited much less frequently by insects than during the previous years; for the masses of pollen were seldom broken down. Although I have repeatedly examined the flowers, I have never seen a trace of nectar; but some appearances lead me to suspect that the ridges within the base of the labellum are attractive to insects, and are gnawed by them, as in the case of many Vandeae and other exotic orchids.

Goodyera repens (p. 114).—Mr. R. B. Thomson informs me that in the north of Scotland he saw many humble-bees visiting the flowers and removing the pollen-masses, which were attached to their proboscides. The bee sent was *Bombus pratorum*. This species grows also in the

United States; and Prof. Gray (Amer. Journ. of Science, vol. xxxiv. 1862, p. 427) confirms my account of its structure and manner of fertilization, which is likewise applicable to another and very distinct species, namely, *Goodyera pubescens.* Prof. Gray states that the passage into the flower, which is at first very narrow, becomes, as I suspected, more open during its older state. Prof. Gray believes, however, that it is the column, and not the labellum, which changes its position.

Spiranthes autumnalis (p. 123).—As in the case of the *Goodyera,* Prof. Gray feels confident that it is the column which moves from the labellum as the flower grows older, and not, as I had supposed, the labellum which moves from the column. He adds that this change of position, which plays so important a part in the fertilization of the flower, "is so striking that we wonder how we overlooked it" (Amer. Journ. of Science, vol. xxxiv. p. 427).

On the Rostellum of Listera ovata *Not Exploding Spontaneously* (p. 149).—I have covered up some additional plants, and found that the rostellum lost its power of explosion in about four days, the viscid matter then turning brown within the loculi of the rostellum. The weather at the time was unusually hot, and this may have hastened the process. After the four days had elapsed, the pollen had become very incoherent and some had fallen on the two corners, or even over the whole surface, of the stigma, which was penetrated by the pollen-tubes. Hence, if insects should fail to remove the pollinia by causing the explosion of the rostellum, this orchid certainly seems capable of occasional self-fertilization. But the scattering of the incoherent pollen was largely aided by, and perhaps wholly depended on, the presence of *Thrips*—insects so minute that they could not be excluded by any net.

Listera cordata (p. 152).—Prof. Dickie has been so good as to observe the flowers on living plants. He informs me that, when the pollen is mature, the crest of the rostellum is directed towards the labellum, and that, as soon as touched, the viscid matter explodes, the pollinia becoming attached to the touching object; after the explosion, the rostellum bends downwards and spreads out, thus protecting the virgin stigmatic surface; subsequently the rostellum rises and exposes the stigma; so that everything here goes on as I have described under *Listera ovata.* The flowers are frequented by minute Diptera and Hymenoptera.

On the Self-fertilization of Neottia nidus-avis, *and on the Rostellum Not Exploding Spontaneously* (p. 153).—I covered up with a net several

plants, and after four days found that the rostellum had not spontaneously exploded, and had already almost lost this power. The pollen had
become incoherent, and in all the flowers much had fallen on the
stigmatic surfaces, which were penetrated by pollen-tubes. The spreading
of the pollen seemed to be in part caused by the presence of *Thrips*, many
of which minute insects were crawling about dusted all over with pollen.
The covered-up plants produced plenty of capsules, but these were much
smaller and contained much fewer seeds than the capsules produced by
the adjoining uncovered plants. I may here add that I detected on the
crest of the rostellum some minute rough points, which seemed *particularly* sensitive in causing the rostellum to explode.

Dr. H. Müller, of Lippstadt, informs me that he has seen Diptera
sucking the nectar and removing the pollinia of this plant.

On the Self-fertilization of Certain Epidendreae (p. 166).—Dr. Crüger
says (Journ. Linn. Soc. vol. viii. Botany, 1864, p. 131) that "we have in
Trinidad three plants belonging to the Epidendreae (a *Schomburgkia*,
Cattleya, and *Epidendron*) which rarely open their flowers, and are
invariably impregnated when they do open them. In these cases it is
easily seen that the pollen-masses have been acted on by the stigmatic
fluid, and that the pollen-tubes descend from the pollen-masses *in situ*
down into the ovarian canal." Mr. Anderson, a skilful cultivator of
orchids in Scotland, informs me (see also 'Cottage Gardener,' 1863, p.
206) that with him the flowers of *Dendrobium cretaceum* never expand,
and yet produce capsules with plenty of seed, which, when examined by
me, was found to be perfectly good. These orchids make a near approach
to those dimorphic plants (as *Oxalis*, *Ononis*, and *Viola*) which habitually produce open and perfect, as well as closed and imperfect flowers.

On the Slow Movement of the Pollinia in Oncidium (p. 189).—Mr.
Charles Wright, in a letter to Prof. Asa Gray, states that he observed in
Cuba a pollinium on an *Oncidium* attached to a *Bombus*, and he
concluded at first that I was completely mistaken about the movement of
depression; but after several hours the pollinium moved into the proper
position for fertilizing the flower.

Manner of Fertilization of Various Exotic Orchids (p. 189).—I may here
remark that Delpino (Fecondazione nelle Piante, Firenze, 1867, p. 19)
says he has examined flowers of *Vanda*, *Epidendron*, *Phaius*, *Oncidium*,
and *Dendrobium*, and confirms my general statements. The late Prof.

Bronn, in his German translation of this work (1862, p. 221), gives a description of the structure and manner of fertilization of *Stanhopea devoniensis*.

Sexes of Acropera *Not Separated* (p. 206).—I have committed a great error about this genus, in supposing that the sexes were separate. Mr. J. Scott, of the Royal Botanic Garden of Edinburgh, soon convinced me that it was an hermaphrodite, by sending me capsules containing good seed, which he had obtained by fertilizing some flowers with pollen from the same plant. He succeeded in doing this by cutting open the stigmatic chamber, and inserting the pollen-masses. My error arose from my ignorance of the remarkable fact that, as shown by Dr. Hildebrand (Botanische Zeitung, 1863, Oct. 30 *et seq.*, and Aug. 4, 1865), in many orchids the ovules are not developed until several weeks or even months after the pollen-tubes have penetrated the stigma. No doubt if I had examined the ovaria of *Acropera* some time after the flowers had withered, I should have found well-developed ovules. In many exotic orchids besides *Acropera* (namely, in *Gongora, Cirrhoea, Acineta, Stanhopea*, &c.), the entrance into the stigmatic chamber is so narrow that the pollen-masses cannot be inserted without the greatest difficulty. How fertilization is effected in these cases is not yet known. That insects are the agents there can be no doubt; for Dr. Crüger saw a bee (*Euglossa*) with a pollinium of a *Stanhopea* attached to its back; and bees of the same genus continually visit *Gongora*. Fritz Müller has observed, in the case of *Cirrhoea* (Bot. Zeitung, Sept. 1868, p. 630), that if one end of the pollen-mass be inserted into the narrow entrance of the stigmatic chamber, this part, from being bathed by the stigmatic fluid, swells, and the whole pollen-mass is thus gradually drawn into the stigmatic entrance. But, from observations which I have made on *Acropera* and *Stanhopea* in my own hot-house, I suspect that, with many of these orchids, the pedicel with the narrow end of the pollinium, and not the broad end, is ordinarily inserted into the stigmatic chamber. By thus placing the pollinium, I have occasionally succeeded in fertilizing some of these orchids, and have obtained seed-capsules.

Structure and Fertilization of the Vandeae &c. *of Brazil* (p. 210).—Fritz Müller has sent me many letters containing an astonishing number of new and curious observations on the structure and manner of cross-fertilization of various orchids inhabiting South Brazil. I much regret that I have not here space or time to give an abstract of his many discoveries, which support the general conclusions given in my work; but I hope that he will some day be induced to publish a full account of his observations.

Fertilization of Catasetum (p. 211).—It have been highly satisfactory to me that my observations and predictive conclusions in regard to *Catasetum* have been fully confirmed by the late Dr. Crüger, the Director of the Botanic Gardens of Trinidad, in letters to me and in his paper in the 'Journal of the Linnean Society' (vol. viii. Bot. 1864, p. 127). He sent me specimens of the bees, belonging to three species of *Euglossa*, which he saw gnawing the inside of the labellum. The pollinia, when ejected, become attached to, and lie flat on, the backs of the bees, on the hairy surface of the thorax. Dr. Crüger has also proved that I was correct in asserting that the sexes of *Catasetum* are separate, for he fertilized female flowers with pollen from the male plants; and Fritz Müller effected the same thing with *Catasetum mentosum* in South Brazil. Nevertheless, from two accounts which I have received, it appears that *Catasetum tridentatum*, though a male plant, occasionally produces seed-capsules; but every botanist knows that this occasionally occurs with the males of other dioecious plants. Fritz Müller has given (Botanische Zeitung, Sept. 1868, p. 630) a most interesting account, agreeing with mine, of the state of the minute pollinia in the female plant: the anther never opens, and the pollen-masses are not attached to the viscid disks, so that they cannot be removed by any natural means. The pollen-grains, as so generally occurs with rudimentary organs, are extremely variable in size and shape. Nevertheless the grains of the rudimentary pollen-masses belonging to the female plant, when applied (which can never naturally occur) to the stigmatic surface, emitted their pollen-tubes! This appears to me a very curious instance of the slow and gradual manner in which structures are modified; for the female pollen-masses, included within an anther which never opens, are seen still partially to retain their former powers and function.

Mormodes luxatum (p. 265).—I have now examined another species of *Mormodes*, the rare *M. luxatum*, and I find that the chief points of structure, and the action of the different parts, including the sensitiveness of the filament, are the same as in *M. ignea*. The cup of the labellum, however, is much larger, and is not pressed down firmly on the filament on the summit of the column. This cup probably serves to attract insects, and, as in *Catasetum*, is gnawed by them. The flowers are asymmetrical to an extraordinary degree, the right-hand and left-hand sides differing much in shape.

Cycnoches ventricosum (p. 265).—The plant described in my work as a second species of *Mormodes* proves to be *Cycnoches ventricosum*. I first received from Mr. Veitch some flower-buds, from which the section (fig.

xxx.) was taken; but subsequently he sent me some perfect flowers. The yellowish-green petals and sepals are reflexed; the thick labellum is singularly shaped, with its upper surface convex, like a shallow basin turned upside down. The thin column is of extraordinary length, and arches like the neck of a swan over the labellum; so that the whole flower presents a very singular appearance. In the section of the flower, given in my work, we see the elastic pedicel of the pollinium bowed, as in *Catasetum* or *Mormodes;* but at the period of growth represented in the figure the pedicel was still united to the rostellum, the future line of separation being shown by a layer of hyaline tissue indistinct towards the upper end of the disk. The disk is cut of gigantic size, and its lower end is produced into a great fringed curtain, which hangs in front of the stigmatic chamber. The viscid matter of the disk sets hard very quickly, and changes colour. The disk adheres to any object with surprising strength. The anther is very different in shape from that of *Catasetum* or *Mormodes,* and apparently would retain the pollen-masses with greater force. A part of the filament of the anther, lying between two little leaf-like appendages, is sensitive; and when this part is touched, the pollinium is swung upwards, as in *Mormodes,* and with sufficient force, if no object stands in the way, to throw it to the distance of an inch. An insect of large size alights probably on the labellum, for the sake of gnawing the convex surface, or perhaps on the extremity of the arched and depending column, and then, by touching the sensitive point, causes the ejection of the pollen-masses, which are affixed to its body and thus transported to another flower or plant.

Fertilization of the Arethuseae (p. 269).—*Epipogium Gmelini* has been the subject of an admirable memoir (Ueber den Blüthenbau, &c., Göttingen, 1866) by Dr. P. Rohrbach, who has shown how the flowers are fertilized by *Bombus lucorum.* With respect to another genus belonging to this same tribe, namely *Pogonia,* Dr. Scudder of the United States has described (Proc. Boston Nat. Hist. Soc. vol. ix. 1863, p. 182) the manner in which it is fertilized by the aid of insects.

Cypripedium (p. 274).—Prof. Asa Gray, after examining several American species of *Cypripedium,* wrote to me (see also Amer. Journ. of Science, vol. xxxiv. 1862, p. 427) that he was convinced that I was in error, and that the flowers are fertilized by small insects entering the labellum through the large opening on the upper surface, and crawling out by one of the two small orifices close to either anther and the stigma. Accordingly I caught a very small bee which seemed of about the right size, namely the *Andrena parvula* (and this by a strange chance proved, as we shall presently see, to be the right genus), and placed it in the labellum through the upper large opening. The bee vainly endeavoured to crawl out again the same way, but always fell backwards, owing to the margins being inflected. The labellum thus acts like one of those conical traps with the edges turned inwards, which are sold to catch beetles and cockroaches in the London kitchens. Ultimately the little bee forced its way out through one of the small orifices close to one of the anthers, and was found when caught to be smeared with the glutinous pollen. I then again put the same bee into the labellum; and again it crawled out through one of the small orifices. I repeated the operation five times, always with the same result. I then cut away the labellum, so as to examine the stigma, and found it well smeared over with pollen. Delpino (Fecondazione &c. 1867, p. 20) with much sagacity foresaw that some insect would be discovered to act in the manner just described; for he argued that if an insect were to insert its proboscis, as I had supposed, from the outside through one of the small orifices close to one of the anthers, the stigma would be fertilized by the plant's own pollen; and in this he did not believe, from having confidence in what I have often insisted on—namely, that all the contrivances for fertilization are arranged so that the stigma shall receive pollen from a distinct flower or plant. But these speculations are now all superfluous; for, owing to the admirable observations of Dr. H. Müller, of Lippstadt (verh. d. Nat. Ver. Jahrg. xxv. III. Folge, v. Bd. p. 1), we actually know that *Cypripedium calceolus* in a state of nature is fertilized by two species of *Andrena*, in the manner above supposed.

On the Relation between the More or Less Viscid Condition of the Pollen and Stigma in Cypripedium (p. 276).—The relation between the state of the pollen and stigma, which I have pointed out in my work, is strongly confirmed by Prof. Gray's statement (Amer. Journ. of Science, vol. xxxiv. 1862, p. 428), namely, that in *C. acaule* the pollen is much more granular or less viscid than in other American species of the genus, and in this species alone the stigma is slightly concave and viscid! Dr. Gray adds that in most of the species the broad stigma presents another remarkable peculiarity, "in being closely beset with minute, rigid, sharp-pointed papillae, all directed forwards, which are excellently adapted to brush off the pollen from an insect's head or back."

The Use of the Copious Fluid Contained within the Labellum of Coryanthes (p. 278).—The *Coryanthes macrantha* is perhaps the most wonderful of all known orchids, even more wonderful in structure and function than *Catasetum*. Its manner of fertilization has been described by Dr. Crüger in the 'Journal of the Linnean Society' (vol. viii. Bot. 1864, p. 130), and in letters to me. He sent me bees, belonging to the genus

Euglossa, which he saw at work. The fluid in the bucket formed by the basal part of the labellum is not nectar and does not attract insects, but serves, by wetting their wings, to prevent them from crawling out except through the small passages close to the anther and stigma. Thus the secretion of fluid in this orchis serves exactly the same end as the inflected margins of the labellum in *Cypripedium.*

On the Evidence that Insects Visit Many Exotic Orchids in Order to Gnaw Parts of the Labellum, and Not for the Sake of Nectar (p. 284).—It has been highly satisfactory to me that this hypothesis has been fully confirmed. In the West Indies, Dr. Crüger witnessed humble-bees of the genus *Euglossa* gnawing the labellum of *Catasetum, Coryanthes, Gongora,* and *Stanhopea;* and Fritz Müller has repeatedly found, in South Brazil, the prominences on the labellum of *Oncidium* gnawed. We are thus enabled to understand the meaning of the various extraordinary crests and projections on the labellum of various exotic orchids; for they invariably stand in such a position that insects, whilst gnawing them, will be almost sure to touch the viscid disks of the pollinia, and thus remove them.

Bonatea speciosa (p. 305).—The manner of fertilization of this extraordinary orchis has now been fully described by Mr. R. Trimen in the 'Journal of the Linnean Society' (vol. ix. Bot. 1865, p. 156). A projection rising from the base of the labellum is one of its most remarkable peculiarities, as an insect is thus compelled to insert its proboscis on one side, and thus to touch one of the two widely separated and projecting viscid disks. Mr. J. P. Mansel Weale has also published (*ibid.* vol. x. 1869, p. 470) analogous observations on a second species, viz. *Bonatea Darwinii.* Mr. Weale caught a skipper-butterfly (*Pyrgus elmo*) quite embarrassed by the number of pollinia belonging to this orchis which adhered to its sternum. I do not know of any other case in which the pollinia adhere to the sternum of a Lepidopterous insect.

On the Nature of the Contraction which Causes the Pollinia, after Their Removal from the Anther, to Change Their Position (p. 338).—In *Orchis hircina,* I clearly saw, under the microscope, the whole front of the viscid disk become depressed as the two pollinia together underwent the movement of depression.

Number of Seeds (p. 344).—The number of seeds produced by *Orchis maculata,* as given in my work, is small in comparison with that produced by some foreign species. I have shown (Variation of Animals and Plants under Domestication, vol. ii. 1868, p. 379), on the authority of Mr. Scott, that a single capsule of *Acropera* contained 371,250 seeds; and the species produces so many flowers and racemes, that a single plant probably sometimes produces as many as 74 millions of seeds in the course of a single year. Fritz Müller carefully estimated, by weighing, the number of seeds in a single capsule of a *Maxillaria* in South Brazil, and found the number 1,756,440. The same plant sometimes produces half-a-dozen capsules.

Number of Pollen-Grains (p. 355).—I have endeavoured to estimate the number of pollen-grains produced by a single flower of *Orchis mascula.* There are two pollen-masses; in one of these I counted 153 packets of pollen; each packet contains, as far as I could count, by carefully breaking it up under the microscope, nearly 100 compound grains; and each compound grain is formed of four grains. By multiplying these figures together, the product for a single flower is about 120,000 pollen-grains. Now we have seen that in the allied *O. maculata* a single capsule produced about 6,200 seeds; so that there are nearly twenty pollen-grains for each ovule or seed. As a single flower of a *Maxillaria* produced 1,756,000 seeds, it would produce, according to the above ratio, nearly 34 million pollen-grains, each of which, no doubt, includes the elements for the reproduction of every single character in the mature plant!

Enumeration of the Orchideae *which, as at Present Known, Habitually Fertilize Themselves* (p. 358).—We have now seen that self-fertilization habitually occurs, in a more or less perfect manner, in one of the species of *Ophrys*, of *Neotinea, Gymnadenia, Platanthera, Epipactis, Cephalan-thera, Neottia*, and in those *Epidendreae* and in *Dendrobium* which often produce flowers that never expand. No doubt other cases will hereafter be discovered. Self-fertilization seems to be more perfectly secured in *Ophrys apifera* and in *Neotinea intacta* than in the other species. But it deserves especial notice that in all these orchids structures are still present, not in a rudimentary condition, which are manifestly adapted for the transport by insects of the pollen-masses from one flower to another. As I have elsewhere remarked, some plants, both indigenous and naturalized, rarely or never bear flowers, or, if they do bear flowers, these never produce seed. But no one doubts that it is a general law of nature that phanerogamic plants should produce flowers, and that these flowers should produce seed. When they fail to do this, we believe that such plants would perform their proper functions under different conditions, or that they formerly did so and will do so again. On analogical grounds I believe that the few orchids which do not now intercross, either did formerly intercross (the means for effecting this being still retained) or that they will do so at some future period under different conditions, unless, indeed, they become extinct from the evil effects of long-continued close interbreeding.

1. *Annals and Magazine of Natural History, including Zoology, Botany, and Geology*, 4th ser., 4 (1869): 141–59.†

2. John Traherne Moggridge, *Contributions to the Flora of Mentone and to a Winter Flora of the Riviera* (London: Reeve, 1871).†

3. See Darwin's *The Various Contrivances by which Orchids are Fertilised by Insects*, 2d ed. (London: Murray, 1888, pp. 98–99).†

☙ Origin of Species[1]

I am much obliged to your Correspondent[2] of June 5 for having pointed out a great error in my 'Origin of Species,'[3] on the possible rate of increase of the elephant. I inquired from the late Dr. Falconer with respect to the age of breeding, &c., and understated the data obtained from him, with the intention, vain as it has proved, of not exaggerating the result. Finding that the calculation was difficult, I applied to a good arithmetician; but he did not know any formula by which a result could easily be obtained; and he now informs me that I then applied to some Cambridge mathematician. Who this was I cannot remember, and therefore cannot find out how the error arose. From the many familiar instances of rapid geometrical increase, I confess that, if the answer had been thirty or sixty million elephants, I should not have felt much surprise; but I ought not to have relied so implicitly on my mathematical friend. I have misled your Correspondent by using language which implies that the elephant produces a pair of young at each birth; but the calculation by this assumption is rendered easier and the result but little different. A friend has extended your Correspondent's calculation to a further period of years. Commencing with a pair of elephants, at the age of thirty, and assuming that they would in each generation survive ten years after the last period of breeding—namely, when ninety years old—there would be, after a period of 750 to 760 years (instead of after 500 years, as I stated in 'The Origin of Species'), considerably more than fifteen million elephants alive, namely, 18,803,080. At the next succeeding period of 780 to 790 years there would be alive no less than 34,584,256 elephants.

1. *Athenaeum. Journal of Literature, Science, and the Fine Arts*, no. 2174, 26 June 1869, p. 861.†

2. Ponderer, "Darwin's Elephants," *Athenaeum. Journal of Literature, Science, and the Fine Arts*, no. 2171, 5 June 1869, p. 772.†

3. In the *Origin*, 1859, p. 64, Darwin indicated that a pair of elephants would have 15,000,000 descendants after five centuries assuming each pair lived 100 years and produced three pair of offspring, that is, two babies every thirty years. "Ponderer," giving the terms of a progression series, said that after seventeen generations, there would be 85,524 elephants alive.†

Origin of Species[1]

I have received a letter from Germany on the increase of the elephant, in which a learned Professor arrives at a totally different result from that of Mr. Garbett,[2] both of which differ from that of your Correspondent "Ponderer." Hence you may perhaps think it worth while to publish a rule by which my son, Mr. George Darwin, finds that the product for any number of generations may easily be calculated:—

"The supposition is that each pair of elephants begins to breed when aged 30, breeds at 60, and again, for the last time, at 90, and dies when aged 100, bringing forth a pair at each birth. We start, then, in the year 0 with a pair of elephants, aged 30. They produce a pair in the year 0, a pair in the year 30, a pair in the year 60, and die in the year 70. In the year 60, then, there will be the following pairs alive, viz.: one aged 90, one aged 60, two aged 30, four aged 0. The last three sets are the only ones which will breed in the year 90. At each breeding a pair produces a pair, so that the number of pairs produced in the year 90 will be the sum of the three numbers 1, 2, 4, *i.e.* 7. Henceforward, at each period, there will be sets of pairs, aged 30, 60, 90 respectively, which breed. These sets will consist of the pairs born at the three preceding periods respectively. Thus the number of pairs born at any period will be the sum of the three preceding numbers in the series, which gives the number of births at each period; and because the first three terms of this series are 1, 2, 4, therefore the series is 1, 2, 4, 7, 13, 24, 44, &c. These are the numbers given by 'Ponderer.' At any period, the whole number of pairs of elephants consists of the young elephants together with the three sets of parents; but since the sum of the three sets of parents is equal in number to the number of young ones, therefore the whole number of pairs is twice the number of young ones, and therefore the whole number of elephants at this period (and for ten years onwards) is four times the corresponding number in the series. In order to obtain the general term of the series, it is necessary to solve an easy equation by the Calculus of Finite Differences."[3]

1. *Athenaeum. Journal of Literature, Science, and the Fine Arts*, no. 2177, 17 July 1869, p. 82.†

2. Edward L. Garbett, "Origin of Species," *Athenaeum. Journal of Literature, Science, and the Fine Arts*, no. 2175, 3 July 1869, pp. 18–19. Garbett's answer was 2,400,000 elephants after five centuries, and 50,000,000 after six centuries.†

3. See also Robert Stauffer, *Charles Darwin's Natural Selection* (Cambridge: Cambridge University Press, 1975), p. 177. Darwin, in writing the 1856–58 manuscript of his *Big Species Book* said that a pair of elephants living for ninety years and producing two offspring every thirty years would have 5,111,514 descendants in five hundred years; if eight were produced by parents during their lifetimes, the number of descendants would be above 15,000,000. In the Cambridge University Library, Charles Darwin's Manuscripts (vol. 46.1, nos. 35 and 36), on two sheets of paper, are additional computations of the elephant problem. On one sheet is the same progression series given by the "Ponderer," and by George. The correct answer of 5,111,514 descendants is given. On the second sheet are figures based on four sets of young (a pair per set) being produced by parents. Under these conditons 15,111,870 offspring would be alive after twenty-five generations. Thus, when writing the *Origin of Species* in 1858–59, Darwin seems inadvertently to have copied the conditions of the problem from one sheet, and the answer from the second. In the last (sixth) edition of the *Origin* (London: Murray, 1872), p. 51, Darwin said that there would be nearly nineteen million elephants alive after 740–750 years (twenty-five generations). Thus, Darwin's 1872 answer was the same as that given in the 26 June 1869 *Athenaeum* article. Dr. Hugh E. Stelson, Professor Emeritus of Mathematics, Michigan State University, has kindly worked out the "easy equation by the calculus of Finite Differences," and computed, according to Darwin's 1859 *Origin* condition, that after twenty-five generations there would be 5,111,520 descendants. He obtained 5,111,514 elephants by the Fibonacci progression series given by the "Ponderer" and by George Darwin. See also Martin Gardiner, "Mathematical Games: The Multiple Fascinations of the Fibonacci Sequence," *Scientific American* 220 (1969): 116–20.†

🐦 Pangenesis: Mr. Darwin's Reply to Professor Delpino[1]

I could say something in answer to most of Delpino's ingenious criticisms,[2] but I will confine myself to one point; remarking, however, that I cannot see the force of his objection to the belief that the gemmules have the power of self-division. The analogy of the multiplication within the body of an infected person of the contagious atoms of small-pox or scarlet-fever still seems to me fair. The criticism which at first struck me as much the most forcible, relates to the re-growth of an amputated limb or other organ. I have assumed, from what we know of the ordinary laws of growth, that gemmules become developed only when united with the nascent or very young cells which precede them in the due order of successive development. Now, Delpino remarks that when the limb of a mature salamander is cut off, nascent cells would not exist on the stump, but only mature ones; consequently, as he urges, the gemmules, according to the hypothesis, could not be there developed and form a new limb.

But have we any reason for assuming that with animals the same cells or organic units endure throughout life and are not replaced by new cells? All physiologists admit that the whole frame is being constantly renovated. The bones, which it might be thought would be least capable of renewal, undergo before maturity great changes in form and size and in the diameter of the medullary canal; even after maturity their shape does not remain the same. If, then, it be admitted that the tissues throughout the body are constantly being renovated by means of the old cells giving birth through proliferation or division to new cells, the difficulty of the gemmules being developed at any point at which a limb may be cut off, disappears; for some nascent cells would exist there; and we must bear in mind that gemmules may possibly become developed in union with cells which are not strictly the proper ones, as shown in the extreme case of nails occasionally growing on the stumps of the amputated fingers of man. It is probable that the renovation of the tissues by the formation of new cells becomes less and less in old age, and so does the power of regrowth. The curious fact that insects which live but a short time after their final metamorphosis, have singularly little power of regrowth, may be partly explained by the deficiency in their tissues of nascent cells.

In the case of plants, the cells composing the tissues endure for life, and are not renewed. The woody cells in the trunk of a tree originally existed as delicate cells in the young shoot. Now, it is remarkable, considering how low plants stand in the scale of life, what little power of re-growth most of their organs or parts possess, not withstanding their high vitality. Cut off a young shoot, and the next bud below will form a new shoot; cut off an old stem, and hundreds of adventitious buds will be formed. No one, I believe, ever saw a mutilated leaf repaired in the same manner as the limb of a salamander; yet on the cut margins of certain leaves innumerable buds will be quickly developed. In the bark, on the other hand, new cells must be continually forming, for the outer layers are continually being thrown off, and bark can certainly reproduce itself on a decorticated surface (see Professor Oliver in *Transactions of Tyneside Club*, vol. iii. 1855, p. 67), from an isolated point not connected with the surrounding uninjured bark; so that this case is fairly analogous with that of the re-growth of an amputated limb.

I will add only one other remark. Delpino insists that, according to the hypothesis, the same cells must throw off gemmules at many successive periods of their development. But I can see no such necessity. Certain epidermic cells, for instance, form horn; but their conversion into this substance is apparently due to the chemical nature of the contents of the cells; and of the changes consequent on the absorption of certain elements. An atom or gemmule thrown off at an early period from one of these cells would, when properly nourished, first form a cell like the parent cell, and ultimately be converted into horn, without the necessity of throwing off successive gemmules. As, however, a cell is a complex structure, with its investing membrane, nucleus, and nucleolus, a gemmule, as Mr. G. H. Lewes has remarked in his interesting discussion on this subject (*Fortnightly Review*, Nov. 1, 1868, p. 508), must, perhaps, be a compound one, so as to reproduce all the parts. The attack by Delpino on the weak point of the hypothesis, namely, that it requires the support of several subordinate hypotheses, is perfectly just, though perhaps pushed to an extreme. But I can speak from recent experience, that he who has to consider complex cases of inheritance, as limited either separately or conjointly by sex, age, and season, with the inherited characters themselves and the form of inheritance liable to change from crossing and variability, will be able to disentangle the phenomena much more clearly, if he admits for the time our hypothesis with all its imperfections. He will then have fixed in his mind that transmission and development are quite distinct phenomena, —the gemmules being thrown off from all parts of the organization, and transmitted from both parents to both sexes at the earliest age, their development alone depending on the nature of the nascent tissues of the individual, whether permanently or temporarily modified by sex, age, season of the year, or other conditions.

1. *Scientific Opinion: A Weekly Record of Scientific Progress at Home & Abroad* 2 (1869): 426.†

2. Federico Delpino, "On the Darwinian Theory of Pangenesis," *Scientific Opinion* ..., 2 (1869): 365–67, 391–93, 407–8, transl. from *Rivista Contemporanea Nazionale Italiana*.†

◄ The Fertilisation of Winter-Flowering Plants[1]

Will you permit me to add a few words to Mr. Bennett's letter, published at p. 58 of your last number?[2] I did not cover up the *Lamium*[3] with a bell-glass, but with what is called by ladies, "net." During the last twenty years I have followed this plan, and have fertilised thousands of flowers thus covered up, but have never perceived that their fertility was in the least injured. I make this statement in case anyone should be induced to use a bell-glass, which I believe to be injurious from the moisture of the contained air. Nevertheless, I have occasionally placed flowers, which grew high up, within small wide-mouthed bottles, and have obtained good seed from them. With respect to the *Vinca*, I suppose that Mr. Bennett intended to express that pollen had actually fallen, without the aid of insects, on the stigmatic surface, and had emitted tubes. As far as the mere opening of the anthers in the bud is concerned, I feel convinced from repeated observations that this is a most fallacious indication of self-fertilisation. As Mr. Bennett asks about the fertilisation of Grasses, I may add that Signor Delpino,[4] of Florence, will soon publish some novel and very curious observations on this subject, of which he has given me an account in a letter, and which I am glad to say are far from being opposed to the very general law that distinct individual plants must be occasionally crossed.

1. *Nature. A Weekly Illustrated Journal of Science*, vol. 1, 18 November 1869, p. 85.[†]
2. Alfred W. Bennett, "Fertilisation of Winter-Flowering Plants," *Nature*, vol. 1, 11 November 1870, p. 58.[†]
3. *Lamium* (white-lead nettle) of the Labiatae.[†]
4. Federico Delpino. See various botanical papers: *Royal Society of London Catalogue of Scientific Papers* 7 (1877): 514.[†]

⚓ Note on the Habits of the Pampas Woodpecker (*Colaptes campestris*)[1]

In the last of Mr. Hudson's valuable articles on the Ornithology of Buenos Ayres,[2] he remarks, with respect to my observations on the *Colaptes campestris*, that it is not possible for a naturalist "to know much of a species from seeing perhaps one or two individuals in the course of a rapid ride across the Pampas." My observations were made in Banda Oriental, on the northern bank of the Plata, where, thirty-seven years ago, this bird was common; and during my successive visits, especially near Maldonado, I repeatedly saw many specimens living on the open and undulating plains, at the distance of many miles from a tree. I was confirmed in my belief, that these birds do not frequent trees, by the beaks of some which I shot being muddy, by their tails being but little abraded, and by their alighting on posts or branches of trees (where such grew) horizontally and crosswise, in the manner of ordinary birds, though, as I have stated, they sometimes alighted vertically. When I wrote these notes, I knew nothing of the works of Azara, who lived for many years in Paraguay, and is generally esteemed as an accurate observer. Now Azara calls this bird the Woodpecker of the plains, and remarks that the name is highly appropriate[3]; for, as he asserts, it never visits woods, or climbs up trees, or searches for insects under the bark.[4] He describes its manner of feeding on the open ground, and of alighting, sometimes horizontally and sometimes vertically, on trunks, rocks, &c., exactly as I have done. He states that the legs are longer than those of other species of Woodpeckers. The beak, however, is not so straight and strong, nor the tail-feathers so stiff, as in the typical members of the group. Therefore this species appears to have been to a slight extent

modified, in accordance with its less arboreal habits. Azara further states
that it builds its nest in holes, excavated in old mud walls or in the banks
of streams. I may add that the *Colaptes pitius*, which in Chile represents
the Pampas species, likewise frequents dry stony hills, where only a few
bushes or trees grow, and may be continually seen feeding on the
ground. According to Molina, this *Colaptes* also builds its nest in holes in
banks.

Mr. Hudson, on the other hand, states that near Buenos Ayres, where
there are some woods, the *Colaptes campestris* climbs trees and bores
into the bark like other Woodpeckers. He says, "it is sometimes found
several miles distant from any trees. This, however, is rare, and it is on
such occasions always apparently on its way to some tree in the distance.
It here builds its nest in holes in trees." I have not the least doubt that
Mr. Hudson's account is perfectly accurate, and that I have committed
an error in stating that this species never climbs trees. But is it not
possible that this bird may have somewhat different habits in different
districts, and that I may not be quite so inaccurate as Mr. Hudson
supposes? I cannot doubt, from what I saw in Banda Oriental, that this
species there habitually frequents the open plains, and lives exclusively
on the food thus obtained. Still less can I doubt the account given by
Azara of its general habits of life, and of its manner of nidification.
Finally, I trust that Mr. Hudson is mistaken when he says that any one
acquainted with the habits of this bird might be induced to believe that I
"had purposely wrested the truth in order to prove" my theory. He
exonerates me from this charge; but I should be loath to think that there
are many naturalists who, without any evidence, would accuse a fellow
worker of telling a deliberate falsehood to prove his theory.

1. *Proceedings of the Scientific Meetings of the Zoological Society of London
for the Year 1870*, 1870. Pp. 705–6.†
2. P.Z.S. 1870, p. 158.
3. Darwin meant to say "inappropriate."†
4. Apunt. ii. p. 311 (1802).

↰ Fertilisation of Leschenaultia[1]

As "F.W.B." inquires, in your number of August 26,[2] about the seeding
of Leschenaultia,[3] I will give my small experience. During 1860 and 1862,
I was led to make some observations on the fertilisation of L. formosa
and biloba, from having read that with these flowers self-fertilisation was
an inevitable contingency; and this, from what I had seen during many
years, seemed to me highly improbable. I found, as "F.W.B." states,
that before the flower expands, the anthers open and the pollen is shed.
This occurs in a considerable number of plants, as in most Leguminosae,

Fumariaceae, &c.; but it can be clearly shown that this by no means necessarily leads to self-fertilisation. In Leschenaultia the pollen, when shed, is neatly collected in a cup-shaped indusium, the mouth of which is at first widely open, but soon closes. Thus far I can follow "F.W.B.;" but he will, I think, find, on further examination, that the pollen must, in order that the flower should be fertilised, be subsequently removed from the indusium, and then placed on an exterior stigmatic surface. This no doubt is effected by insects, tempted to visit the flowers by the copious supply of nectar. On the outside of the indusium there is a viscid surface, and when on two occasions I placed some pollen-grains on the surface, I found, after an interval of about 20 hours, that it was deeply penetrated by numerous pollen-tubes. I was so much surprised at this position of the stigma, that I asked Dr. Hooker to dissect some flowers, which he did with care, and he confirmed my conclusion with respect to L. formosa. He also examined two other species, and found no trace of a stigma within the indusium. I should here add that Mr. Bentham[4] has subsequently described the structure of the parts in this genus, but I cannot at the present moment lay my hand on his paper. When the flower is fully expanded the lips of the indusium fit closely, and cannot be very easily opened. If, however, a finely-pointed, small camel-hair brush be held parallel to the pistil, and be gently inserted into the flower, so as to imitate the entry of an insect, the tip of the brush, by pressing against the slightly projecting lower lip of the indusium, opens it; and some of the hairs enter and become smeared with pollen. If the same brush be now successively inserted into several flowers, pollen-grains will be found left on the exterior viscid stigma. During the early part of the summer I treated in this manner several flowers, but with no result. Towards the end of July, however, five flowers were thus treated, and the germens of all soon became much enlarged. Two of them, after a time, shanked off, but three remained on till the autumn, and each contained about 25 seeds. My plant produced hundreds of flowers during two or three summers, but the germens of none spontaneously swelled, with the exception of two growing close together, which I imagined had been visited by some insect. These two produced some seeds, but fewer in number than in the above case. All the seeds were in external appearance good, but when sown they did not germinate. The flowers were necessarily fertilised with pollen from the same plant, but it would have been incomparably better if pollen from a distinct seedling plant could have been employed. This would have been all the more advisable, as the late Mr. Drummond, of Swan River, in Australia, to whom I wrote, asking him to observe in the proper season what insects visited the Leschenaultias, informed me that the species growing there in a state of Nature very rarely produced seed. It appears at first sight a surprising circumstance that in this genus and in some allied genera, the pollen, whilst the flowers are still in bud, should be scooped out of the anthers, in which it might have remained ready for use, and then be immediately enclosed in a specially contrived receptacle, from which it has afterwards to be removed, so as to be placed on the stigma. But he who believes in the principle of gradual evolution, and looks at each structure as the summing up of a long series of adaptations to past and changing conditions—each successive modification being retained as far as that is possible through the force of inheritance—will not feel surprise at the above complex and apparently superfluous arrangement, or the other still more complex arrangements, though they may all serve for one and the same general purpose. Any one desiring to learn how diversified are the means for preventing self-fertilisation, even within the limits of the same family of plants, should study Mr. Bentham's short but extremely curious paper, just published (in the Journal of the Linnean Society), on the styles of the Australian Proteaceae.[5] I cannot resist specifying one of the remarkable contrivances described by Mr. Bentham. In Synaphea the upper anther does not subserve its proper function of producing pollen, but has been converted into a short broad strap, firmly fixed to the edge of the stigmatic disc. By this means the stigma is held in such a position that it cannot receive pollen from the fertile anthers of the same flower; or, as Mr. Bentham puts the case, "the stigma thus held by the eunuch

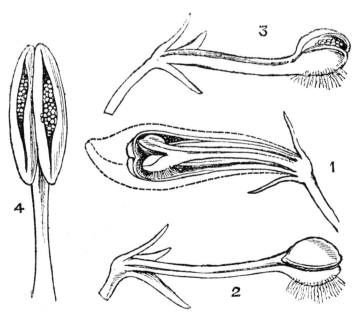

Fig. 1. *Leschenaultia formosa.*

(i.e., the barren anther) is safe from all pollution from her brother anthers, and is preserved intact from [for] any pollen that may be inserted . . . by insects or other agencies."[6]

1. *Gardeners' Chronicle and Agricultural Gazette*, no. 36, 9 September 1871, p. 1166. See also, "Cross-breeding in Plants: Fertilisation of Leschenaultia formosa," p. 42.†
2. "F. W. B.," "Fertilisation of Leschenaultia formosa," *Gardeners' Chronicle and Agricultural Gazette*, no. 34, 26 August 1871, p. 1103.†
3. *Leschenaultia:* Australian herbs or shrubs of the family Goodeniaceae, order Campanulales.†
4. George Bentham, "Note on the Stigmatic Apparatus of Goodenovieae," *Journal of the Linnean Society (Botany)* 10 (1869): 203–6.†
5. George Bentham, "Notes on the Styles of Australian *Proteaceae*," *Journal of the Linnean Society (Botany)* 13 (1873): 58–64.†
6. Ibid., p. 64. The original in Bentham reads, "intact for any pollen. . . ."†

⚓ Pangenesis[1]

In a paper, read March 30, 1871, before the Royal Society, and just published in the Proceedings, Mr. Galton[2] gives the results of his interesting experiments on the inter-transfusion of the blood of distinct varieties of rabbits. These experiments were undertaken to test whether there was any truth in my provisional hypothesis of Pangenesis. Mr. Galton, in recapitulating "the cardinal points," says that the gemmules are supposed "to swarm in the blood." He enlarges on this head, and remarks, "Under Mr. Darwin's theory, the gemmules in each individual must, therefore, be looked upon as entozoa of his blood," &c. Now, in the chapter on Pangenesis in my "Variation of Animals and Plants under Domestication," I have not said one word about the blood, or about any fluid proper to any circulating system. It is, indeed, obvious that the presence of gemmules in the blood can form no necessary part of my hypothesis; for I refer in illustration of it to the lowest animals, such as the Protozoa, which do not possess blood or any vessels; and I refer to plants in which the fluid, when present in the vessels, cannot be considered as true blood. The fundamental laws of growth, reproduction, inheritance, &c., are so closely similar throughout the whole organic kingdom, that the means by which the gemmules (assuming for the moment their existence) are diffused through the body, would probably be the same in all beings; therefore the means can hardly be diffusion through the blood. Nevertheless, when I first heard of Mr. Galton's experiments, I did not sufficiently reflect on the subject, and saw not the difficulty of believing in the presence of gemmules in the blood. I have said (Variation, &c., vol. ii., p. 379) that "the gemmules in each organism must be thoroughly diffused; nor does this seem improbable, considering their minuteness, and the steady circulation of fluids throughout the body." But when I used these latter words and other similar ones, I presume that I was thinking of the diffusion of the gemmules through the tissues, or from cell to cell, independently of the presence of vessels,—as in the remarkable experiments by Dr. Bence Jones,[3] in which chemical elements absorbed by the stomach were detected in the course of some minutes in the crystalline lens of the eye; or again as in the repeated loss of colour and its recovery after a few days by the hair, in the singular case of a neuralgic lady recorded by Mr. Paget.[4] Nor can it be objected that the gemmules could not pass through tissues or cell-walls, for the contents of each pollen-grain have to pass through the coats, both of the pollen-tube and embryonic sack. I may add, with respect to the passage of fluids through membrane, that they pass from cell to cell in the absorbing hairs of the roots of living plants at a rate, as I have myself observed under the microscope, which is truly surprising.

When, therefore, Mr. Galton concludes from the fact that rabbits of one variety, with a large proportion of the blood of another variety in their veins, do not produce mongrelised offspring, that the hypothesis of Pangenesis is false, it seems to me that his conclusion is a little hasty. His words are, "I have now made experiments of transfusion and cross circulation on a large scale in rabbits, and have arrived at definite results, negativing, in my opinion, beyond all doubt the truth of the doctrine of Pangenesis." If Mr. Galton could have proved that the reproductive elements were contained in the blood of the higher animals, and were merely separated or collected by the reproductive glands, he would have made a most important physiological discovery. As it is, I think every one will admit that his experiments are extremely curious, and that he deserves the highest credit for his ingenuity and perseverance. But it does not appear to me that Pangenesis has, as yet, received its death blow; though, from presenting so many vulnerable points, its life is always in jeopardy; and this is my excuse for having said a few words in its defence.

1. *Nature. A Weekly Illustrated Journal of Science,* vol. 3, 27 April 1871, pp. 502–3.†

2. Francis Galton, "Experiments in Pangenesis, by Breeding from Rabbits of a Pure Variety, into Whose Circulation Blood Taken from Other Varieties Had Previously Been Largely Transfused," *Proceedings of the Royal Society of London* 19 (1871): 393–410.†

3. Henry Bence Jones, "On the Rapidity of the Passage of Crystalloid Substances into the Vascular and Non-vascular Textures of the Body," *Proceedings of the Royal Society of London* 14: (1865): 63–64, and "On the Rate of Passage of Crystalloids into and out of the Vascular and Non-vascular Textures of the Body," *Proceedings of the Royal Society of London* 14 (1865): 220–23.†

4. This reference could not be traced, but see G. E. Paget, "Instances of Remarkable Abnormalities in the Voluntary Muscles," *Transactions of the Philosophical Society of Cambridge* 10 (1864): 240–47.†

ᐂ A New View of Darwinism[1]

I am much obliged to Mr. Howorth for his courteous expressions towards me in the letter in your last number.[2] If he will be so good as to look at p. 111 and p. 148, vol. ii. of my "Variation of Animals and Plants under Domestication," he will find a good many facts and a discussion on the fertility and sterility of organisms from increased food and other causes. He will see my reasons for disagreeing with Mr. Doubleday,[3] whose work I carefully read many years ago.

1. *Nature. A Weekly Illustrated Journal of Science*, vol. 4, 6 July 1871, pp. 180–81.†
2. Henry H. Howorth, "A New View of Darwinism," *Nature*, vol. 4, 29 June 1871, pp. 161–62.†
3. Thomas Doubleday, *The True Law of Population Shewn to be Connected with the Food of the People* (London: Simpkin, Marshall, 1842).†

ᐂ A Letter from Mr. Darwin[1]

In our issue of June 24, of the present year, the following passage was contained in an editorial article:—

"Only yesterday we received from one of the greatest scientific men of England, whose name is famous throughout the entire civilized world, a private letter of which the following was the closing sentence:—'I have now read 'Truths for the Times,' and I admire them from my inmost heart; and I believe that I agree to every word.'"

We are now authorized by kind permission of the writer to say that the above extract is from a letter written by Mr. Charles Darwin. In another letter dated Nov. 16, Mr. Darwin says:—

"I have read again 'Truths for the Times,' and abide by my words as strictly true. If you still think fit to publish them, you had better perhaps omit 'I believe,' and add 'almost' to 'every word,' so that it will run—'and I agree to almost every word.' The points on which I doubtfully differ are unimportant; but it is better to be accurate. I should be much obliged if you would somehow prefer to word as an extract from a letter not originally intended for publication, or to this effect; as it seems to be somewhat conceited or arrogant otherwise to express my assent."

1. *Index*, vol. 2, 23 December 1871, p. 404.†

ᴧ   Bree on Darwinism[1]

Permit me to state—though the statement is almost superfluous—that Mr. Wallace,[2] in his review of Dr. Bree's work,[3] gives with perfect correctness what I intended to express, and what I believe was expressed clearly, with respect to the probable position of man in the early part of his pedigree. As I have not seen Dr. Bree's recent work, and as his letter is unintelligible to me, I cannot even conjecture how he has so completely mistaken my meaning: but, perhaps, no one who has read Mr. Wallace's article, or who has read a work formerly published by Dr. Bree on the same subject[4] as his recent one, will be surprised at any amount of misunderstanding on his part.

   1. *Nature. A Weekly Illustrated Journal of Science,* vol. 6, 8 August 1872, p. 279.†
   2. Alfred R. Wallace, "The Last Attack on Darwinism," *Nature,* vol. 6, 25 July 1872, pp. 237–93.†
   3. Charles Robert Bree, *An Exposition of Fallacies in the Hypothesis of Mr. Darwin* (London: Longmans, Green, 1872).†
   4. Charles Robert Bree, *Species Not Transmutable, nor the Result of Secondary Causes: Being a Critical Examination of Mr. Darwin's Work Entitled "Origin and Variation of Species"* (London: Groombridge [1860]).†

ᴧ   The Descent of Man[1]

The early progenitors of man were no doubt once covered with hair, both sexes having beards; their ears were pointed and capable of movement; and their bodies were provided with a tail, having the proper muscles. Their limbs and bodies were also acted on by many muscles which now only occasionally reappear, but are normally present in the Quandrumana.

   1. *Hardwicke's Science-Gossip: An Illustrated Medium of Interchange and Gossip for Students and Lovers of Nature,* 1872. P. 112.†

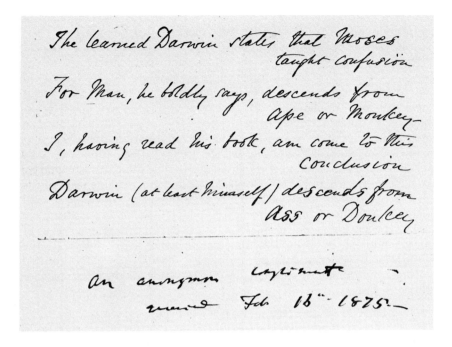

The learned Darwin states that Moses
                    taught confusion
For Man, he boldly says, descends from
                    ape or Monkey—
I, having read his book, am come to this
                    Conclusion
Darwin (at least himself) descends from
                    Ass or Donkey

An anonymous compliment   —.
                received Feb 16th 1875—

Fig. 1. The appended comment ("An anonymous compliment,—received Feb. 16th, 1875") is in Darwin's handwriting. Published with permission of the Syndics of the University Library, Cambridge.

⟡ Natural Selection[1]

Any one interested in the subject to which you allude at p. 42 of your last number,[2] namely, the relative importance in causing modifications of the body or mind, on the one hand of habit or of the direct action of external conditions, and on the other hand of natural or artificial selection, will find this subject briefly discussed in the second volume (pp. 301–315) of my "Variation of Animals and Plants under Domestication." I have there given a considerable body of facts, chiefly in relation to acclimatisation, which presents the greatest difficulty in the present question; and it may be inferred from these facts, firstly, that variations of a directly opposite nature, which would be liable either to preservation or elimination through natural selection, not rarely arise in organisms long exposed to similar conditions; and secondly, that habit, independently of selection, has often produced a marked effect. But it is most difficult, as I have insisted in many of my works, though in some cases possible, to discriminate between the results of the two processes. Both tend to concur, for the individuals which inherit in the strongest manner any useful habit will commonly be preserved.

Take, as an instance, the fur of quadrupeds, which grows thickest in the individuals living far north; now there is reason to believe that weather acts directly on the skin with its appendages, but it is extremely difficult to judge how much of the effect ought to be attributed to the direct action of a low temperature, and how much to the best protected individuals of many generations having survived during the severest winters. I have made many observations and collected many facts, showing the potent influence of habit and of the use or disuse of parts on organic beings; but there are numberless peculiarities of structure and of instinct (as in the case of sterile neuter insects) which cannot be thus accounted for. He would be a bold man who would attempt to explain by these means the origin of the exsertile claws and great canine teeth of the tiger; or of the horny lamellae on the beak of the duck, which are so well adapted for sifting water. Nor would anyone, I presume, even attempt to explain the development, for instance, of the beautifully plumed seeds of the dandelion, or of the endless contrivances which are necessary for the fertilisation of very many flowers by insects, through gradually acquired and inherited habit, or through the direct action of the external conditions of life.

1. *Spectator*, 18 January 1873, p. 76.†
2. "Dr. Carpenter on Mental Acquisitions and Inheritance," *Spectator*, 11 January 1873, pp. 42–44.†

⚓ Inherited Instinct[1]

The following letter seems to me so valuable, and the accuracy of the statements vouched for by so high an authority, that I have obtained permission from Dr. Huggins[2] to send it for publication. No one who has attended to animals either in a state of nature or domestication will doubt that many special fears, tastes, &c., which must have been acquired at a remote period, are now strictly inherited. This has been clearly proved to be the case by Mr. Spalding with chickens and turkeys just born, in his admirable article recently published in *Macmillan's Magazine*.[3] It is probable that most inherited or instinctive feelings were originally acquired by slow degrees through habit and the experience of their utility; for instance the fear of man, which as I showed many years ago, is gained very slowly by birds on oceanic islands. It is, however, almost certain that many of the most wonderful instincts have been acquired independently of habit, through the preservation of useful variations of pre-existing instincts. Other instincts may have arisen suddenly in an individual and then been transmitted to its offspring, independently both of selection and serviceable experience, though subsequently strengthened by habit. The tumbler-pigeon is a case in point, for no one would have thought of teaching a pigeon to turn head over heels in the air; and until some bird exhibited a tendency in this direction, there could have been no selection. In the following case we see a specialised feeling of antipathy transmitted through three generations of dogs, as well as to some collateral members of the same family, and which must have been acquired within a very recent period. Unfortunately it is not known how the feeling first arose in the grandfather of Dr. Huggins's dog. We may suspect that it was due to some ill-treatment; but it may have originated without any assignable cause, as with certain animals in the Zoological Gardens, which, as I am assured by Mr. Bartlett, have taken a strong hatred to him and others without any provocation. As far as it can be ascertained, the great-grandfather of Dr. Huggins's dog did not evince the feeling of antipathy, described in the following letter.

1. *Nature. A Weekly Illustrated Journal of Science*, vol. 7, 13 February 1873, p. 281.†
2. The letter of William Huggins' appended to Darwin's, gives an account of three generations of mastiffs which showed great fright when in the vicinity of a butcher's shop, or of a butcher.†
3. Douglas A. Spalding, "Instinct, with Original Observations on Young Animals," *MacMillan's Magazine*, 27 (February 1873): 282–83.†

➤ Perception in the Lower Animals[1]

As several persons seem interested in Mr. Wallace's[2] suggestion that animals find their way home by recognising the odour of the places which they have passed whilst shut up, you may perhaps think the following little fact worth giving. Many years ago I was on a mail-coach, and as soon as we came to a public-house, the coachman pulled up for the fraction of a second. He did so when we came to a second public-house, and I then asked him the reason. He pointed to the off-hand wheeler,[3] and said that she had been long completely blind, and she would stop at every place on the road at which she had before stopped. He had found by experience that less time was wasted by pulling up his team than by trying to drive her past the place, for she was contented with a momentary stop. After this I watched her, and it was evident that she knew exactly, before the coachman began to pull up the other horses, every public-house on the road, for she had at some time stopped at all. I think there can be little doubt that this mare recognised all these houses by her sense of smell. With respect to cats, so many cases have been recorded of their returning from a considerable distance to their homes, after having been carried away shut up in baskets, that I can hardly disbelieve them, though these stories are disbelieved by some persons. Now, as far as I have observed, cats do not possess a very acute sense of smell, and they seem to discover their prey by eyesight and by hearing. This leads me to mention another trifling fact: I sent a riding-horse by railway from Kent *via* Yarmouth, to Freshwater Bay, in the Isle of Wight. On the first day that I rode eastward, my horse, when I turned to go home, was very unwilling to return towards his stable, and he several times turned round. This led me to make repeated trials, and every time that I slackened the reins, he turned sharply round and began to trot to the eastward by a little north, which was nearly in the direction of his home in Kent. I had ridden this horse daily for several years, and he had never before behaved in this manner. My impression was that he somehow knew the direction whence he had been brought. I should state that the last stage from Yarmouth to Freshwater is almost due south, and along this road he had been ridden by my groom; but he never once showed any wish to return in this direction. I had purchased this horse several years before from a gentleman in my own neighbourhood, who had possessed him for a considerable time. Nevertheless it is possible, though far from probable, that the horse may have been born in the Isle of Wight. Even if we grant to animals a sense of the points of the compass, of which there is no evidence, how can we account, for instance, for the turtles which formerly congregated in multitudes, only at one season of the year, on the shores of the Isle of Ascension, finding their way to that speck of land in the midst of the great Atlantic Ocean?

1. *Nature. A Weekly Illustrated Journal of Science*, vol. 7, 13 March 1873, p. 360.†

2. Alfred R. Wallace, "Inherited Feeling," *Nature*, vol. 7, 20 February 1873, p. 303.†

3. The horse on the far side from the driver, and nearest the wheels.†

⟣ Origin of Certain Instincts[1]

The writer of the interesting article in Nature of March 20[2] doubts whether my belief "that many of the most wonderful instincts have been acquired, independently of habit, through the preservation of useful variations of pre-existing instincts," means more than "that in a great many instances we cannot conceive how the instincts originated." This in one sense is perfectly true, but what I wished to bring prominently forward was simply that in certain cases instincts had not been acquired through the experience of their utility, with continued practice during successive generations. I had in my mind the case of neuter insects, which never leave offspring to inherit the teachings of experience, and which are themselves the offspring of parents which possess quite different instincts. The Hive-bee is the best known instance, as neither the queen nor the drones construct cells, secrete wax, collect honey, &c. If this had been the sole case, it might have been maintained that the queens, like the fertile females of humble-bees, had in former ages worked like the present neuters, and had thus gradually acquired these instincts; and that they had ever afterwards transmitted them to their sterile offspring, though they themselves no longer practised such instincts. But there are several species of Hive-bees (*Apis*) of which the sterile workers have somewhat different habits and instincts, as shown by their combs. There are also many species of ants, the fertile females of which are believed not themselves to work, but to be served by the neuters, which capture and drag them to their nests; and the instincts of the neuters in the different species of the same genus are often different. All who believe in the principle of evolution will admit that with social insects the closely allied species of the same genus are descended from a single parent-form; and yet the sterile workers of the several species have somehow acquired different instincts. This case appeared to me so remarkable that I discussed it at some length in my "Origin of Species"[3]; but I do not expect that anyone who has less faith in natural selection than I have, will admit the explanation there given. Although he may explain in some other way, or leave unexplained, the development of the wondrous instincts possessed by the various sterile workers, he will, I think, be compelled to admit that they cannot have been acquired by the experience of one generation having been transmitted to a succeeding one. I should indeed be glad if anyone could show that there was some fallacy in this reasoning. It may be added that the possession of highly complex instincts, though not derived through conscious experience, does not at all preclude insects bringing into play their individual sagacity in modifying their work under new or peculiar circumstances; but such sagacity, as far as inheritance is concerned, as well as their instincts, can be modified or injured only by advantage being taken of variation in the minute brain of their parents, probably of their mothers.

The acquirement or development of certain reflex actions, in which muscles that cannot be influenced by the will are acted on, is a somewhat analogous case to that of the above class of instincts, as I have shown in my recently published book on Expression[4]; for consciousness, on which the sense of utility depends, cannot have come into play in the case of actions effected by involuntary muscles. The beautifully adapted movements of the iris, when the retina is stimulated by too much or too little light, is a case in point.

The writer of the article in referring to my words "the preservation of useful variations of pre-existing instincts" adds "the question is, whence these variations?" Nothing is more to be desired in natural history than that some one should be able to answer such a query. But as far as our present subject is concerned, the writer probably will admit that a multitude of variations have arisen, for instance in colour and in the character of the hair, feathers, horns, &c., which are quite independent of habit and of use in previous generations. It seems far from wonderful, considering the complex conditions to which the whole organisation is exposed during the successive stages of its development from the germ, that every part should be liable to occasional modifications: the wonder indeed is that any two individuals of the same species are at all closely alike. If this be admitted, why should not the brain, as well as all other parts of the body, sometimes vary in a slight degree, independently of useful experience and habit? Those physiologists, and there are many, who believe that a new mental characteristic cannot be transmitted to the child except through some modification of that material sub-stratum which proceeds from the parents, and from which the brain of the child is ultimately developed, will not doubt that any cause which affects its development may, and often will, modify the transmitted mental characters. With species in a state of nature such modifications or variations would commonly lead to the partial or complete loss of an instinct, or to its perversion; and the individual would suffer. But if under the then existing conditions any such mental variation was serviceable, it would be preserved and fixed, and would ultimately become common to all the members of the species.

The writer of the article also takes up the case of the tumbling of the pigeon, which habit, if seen in a wild bird, would certainly have been called instinctive; more especially if, as has been asserted, it aids these birds in escaping from hawks. He suggests that it "is a fancy instinct, an outlet for the overflowing activity of a creature whose wants are all provided for without any exertion on its part"; but even on this supposition there must have been some physical cause which induced the first tumbler to spend its overflowing activity in a manner unlike that of any other bird in the world. The behaviour of the ground-tumbler or Lotan of India, renders it highly probable that in this sub-breed the tumbling is due to some affection of the brain, which has been transmitted from before the year 1600 to the present day. It is necessary gently to shake these birds, or in the case of the Kalmi Lotan, to touch them on the neck with a wand, in order to make them begin rolling over backwards on the ground. This they continue to do with extraordinary rapidity, until they are utterly exhausted, or even, as some say, until they die, unless they are taken up, held in the hands, and soothed; and then they recover. It is well-known that certain lesions of the brain, or internal parasites, cause animals to turn incessantly round and round, either to the right or left, sometimes accompanied by a backward movement: and I have just read, through the kindness of Dr. Brunton, the account given by Mr. W. J. Moore (*Indian Medical Gazette,* Jan. and Feb. 1873) of the somewhat analogous result which followed from pricking the base of the brain of a pigeon with a needle. Birds thus treated roll over backwards in convulsions, in exactly the same manner as do the ground-tumblers; and the same effect is produced by giving them hydrocyanic acid with strychnine. One pigeon which had its brain thus pricked recovered perfectly, but continued ever afterwards to perform summersaults like a tumbler, though not belonging to any tumbling breed. The movement appears to be of the nature of a recurrent spasm or convulsion which throws the bird backwards, as in tetanus; it then recovers its balance, and is again thrown backwards. Whether this tendency originated from some accidental injury, or, as seems more probable, from some morbid affection of the brain, cannot be told; but at the present time the affection can hardly be called morbid in the case of common tumblers, as these birds are perfectly healthy and seem to enjoy performing their feats, or, as an old writer expresses it, "showing like footballs in the air." The habit apparently can be controlled to a certain extent by the will. But what more particularly concerns us is that it is strictly inherited. Young birds reared in an aviary which have never seen a pigeon tumble, take to it when first let free. The habit also varies much in degree in different individuals and in different sub-breeds; and it can be greatly augmented by continued selection, as seen in the house-tumblers, which can hardly rise more than a foot or two above the ground without going head over heels in the air. Fuller details on tumbler-pigeons, may be found in my "Variation of Animals under Domestication," vol. i. pp. 150, 209.

In conclusion, from the case of neuter insects, of certain reflex actions, and of movements such as those of the tumbler-pigeon, it seems to me in the highest degree probable that many instincts have originated from modifications or variations in the brain, which we in our ignorance most improperly call spontaneous or accidental; such variations having led, independently of experience and of habit, to changes in pre-existing instincts, or to quite new instincts, and these proving of service to the species, have been preserved and fixed, being, however, often strengthened or improved by subsequent habit.

With regard to the question of the means by which animals find their way home from a long distance, a striking account, in relation to man, will be found in the English translation of the Expedition to North Siberia, by Von Wrangell.[5] He there describes the wonderful manner in which the natives kept a true course towards a particular spot, whilst passing for a long distance through hummocky ice, with incessant changes of direction, and with no guide in the heavens or on the frozen sea. He states (but I quote only from memory of many years standing) that he, an experienced surveyor, and using a compass, failed to do that which these savages easily effected. Yet no one will suppose that they possessed any special sense which is quite absent in us. We must bear in mind that neither a compass, nor the north star, nor any other such sign, suffices to guide a man to a particular spot through an intricate country, or through hummocky ice, when many deviations from a straight course are inevitable, unless the deviations are allowed for, or a sort of "dead reckoning" is kept. All men are able to do this in a greater or less degree, and the natives of Siberia apparently to a wonderful extent, though probably in an unconscious manner. This is effected chiefly, no doubt, by eyesight, but partly, perhaps, by the sense of muscular movement, in the same manner as a man with his eyes blinded can proceed (and some men much better than others) for a short distance in a nearly straight line, or turn at right angles, or back again. The manner in which the sense of direction is sometimes suddenly disarranged in very old and feeble persons and the feeling of strong distress which, as I know, has been experienced by persons when they have suddenly found out that they have been proceeding in a wholly unexpected and wrong direction, leads to the suspicion that some part of the brain is specialised for the function of direction. Whether animals may not possess the faculty of keeping a dead reckoning of their course in a much more perfect degree than can man; or whether this faculty may not come into play on the commencement of a journey when an animal is shut up in a basket, I will not attempt to discuss, as I have not sufficient data.

I am tempted to add one other case, but here again I am forced to quote from memory, as I have not my books at hand. Audubon kept a pinioned wild goose in confinement, and when the period of migration arrived, it became extremely restless, like all other migratory birds under similar circumstances; and at last it escaped. The poor creature then immediately began its long journey on foot, but its sense of direction seemed to have been perverted, for instead of travelling due southward, it proceeded in exactly the wrong direction, due northward.

1. *Nature. A Weekly Illustrated Journal of Science*, vol. 7, 3 April 1873, pp. 417–18.†

2. "Perception and Instinct in Lower Animals," *Nature*, vol. 7, 20 March 1873, pp. 377–78.†

3. *Origin*, 1859, pp. 235–42.†

4. *The Expression of the Emotions in Man and Animals*, 1872. Pp. 35–42.†

5. Ferdinand Petrovich Vrangel', *Narrative of an Expedition to the Polar Sea, in the Years 1820, 1821, 1822, & 1823* . . ., ed. Major Edward Sabine (London: Madden, 1840).†

⚔ Habits of Ants[1]

Some months ago (vol. vii. p. 443) I sent you an extract from a letter from Mr. Hague,[2] a geologist residing in California, who gave me a very curious account of the terrifying effect on the other ants of the sight of a few which he had killed on one of their paths. Mr. Traherne Moggridge saw this account in Nature, and wrote to me that he had heard from a gentleman who had lived in Australia that merely drawing a finger across the path deters ants from crossing the line.

Mr. Moggridge tried this experiment with some ants at Mentone with similar effects. I therefore sent the letter to Mr. Hague, and asked him to observe whether his ants were alarmed by the smell left by the finger, or were really terrified by the sight of their dead and dying comrades. The case appears curious, as I believe no one has ever observed an invertebrate animal realising danger by seeing the corpses of a fellow species. It is indeed very doubtful whether the higher animals can draw any such inferences from the sight; but I believe that everyone who has had experience in trapping animals is convinced that individuals who have never been caught learn that a trap is dangerous by seeing others caught.

Here follows Mr. Hague's letter, fully confirming his former statement.[3]

1. *Nature. A Weekly Illustrated Journal of Science*, vol. 8, 24 July 1873, p. 244.†
2. James D. Hague, "Perception in Ants," *Nature*, vol. 7, 10 April 1873, pp. 443–44.†
3. In summary, Hague reported that the taint of the hand led the ants to detour the area, and dead ants excited in them actions suggesting fright, and led to their avoiding the spot.†

⚔ On the Males and Complemental Males of Certain Cirripedes, and on Rudimentary Structures[1]

I beg permission to make a few remarks bearing on Prof. Wyville Thomson's interesting account of the rudimentary males of *Scalpellum regium*, in your number of August 28th.[2] Since I described in 1851, the males and complemental males of certain cirripedes,[3] I have been most anxious that some competent naturalist should re-examine them; more especially as a German, without apparently having taken the trouble to look at any specimens, has spoken of my description as a fantastic dream. That the males of an animal should be attached to the female, should be very much smaller than, and differ greatly in structure from her, is nothing new or strange. Nevertheless, the difference between the males and the hermaphrodites of *Scalpellum vulgare* is so great, that when I first roughly dissected the former, even the suspicion that they belonged to the class of cirripedes did not cross my mind. These males are half as large as the head of a small pin; whereas the hermaphrodites are from an inch to an inch and a quarter in length. They consist of little more than a mere sack, containing the male reproductive organs, with rudiments of only four of the valves; there is no mouth or alimentary canal, but there exists a rudimentary thorax with rudimentary cirri, and these apparently serve to protect the orifice of the sack from the intrusion of enemies. The males of Alcippe and Cryptophialus are even more rudimentary; of the seventeen segments which ought to be fully developed, together with their appendages, only three remain, and these are imperfectly developed; the other fourteen segments are represented by a mere slight projection bearing the probosci-formed penis. This latter organ, on the other hand, is so enormously developed in Cryptophialus, that when fully extended it must have been between eight and nine times the length of the animal! There is another curious point about these little males, viz., the great difference between those belonging to the several species of the same genus Scalpellum: some are manifestly pedunculated cirripedes, differing by characters which in an independent creature would be considered as of only generic value; whereas others do not offer a single character by which they can be recognised as cirripedes, with the exception of the cast-off prehensile, larval antennae, preserved by being buried in the natural cement at the point of attachment. But the fact which has interested me most is the existence of what I have called Complemental Males, from their being attached not to females, but to hermaphrodites; the latter having male organs perfect, although not so largely developed as in ordinary cirripedes. We must turn to the vegetable kingdom for anything analogous to this; for, as is well known, certain plants present hermaphrodite and male individuals, the latter aiding in the cross-fertilisation of the former. The males and complemental males in some of the species of three out of the four very distinct genera in which I have described their occurrence, are, as already stated, extremely minute, and, as they cannot feed, are short-lived. They are developed like other cirripedes, from larvae, furnished with well-developed natatory legs, eyes of great size and complex prehensile antennae; by these organs they are enabled to find, cling to, and ultimately to become cemented to the hermaphrodite or female. The male larvae, after casting their skins and being as fully developed as they ever will be, perform their masculine function, and then perish. At the next breeding season they are succeeded by a fresh crop of these annual males. In Scalpellum vulgare I have found as many as ten males attached to the orifice of the sack of a single hermaphrodite; and in Alcippe, fourteen males attached to a single female.

He who admits the principle of evolution will naturally inquire why and how these minute rudimentary males, and especially the complemental males, have been developed. It is of course impossible to give any definite answer, but a few remarks may be hazarded on this subject. In my "Variation under Domestication," I have given reasons for the belief that it is an extremely general, though apparently not quite universal law, that organisms occasionally intercross, and that great benefit is derived therefrom. I have been laboriously experimenting on this subject for the last six or seven years, and I may add, that with plants there cannot be the least doubt that great vigour is thus gained; and the results indicate that the good depends on the crossed individuals having been exposed to slightly different conditions of life. Now as cirripedes are always attached to some object, and as they are commonly hermaphrodites, their intercrossing appears, at first sight, impossible, except by the chance carriage of the spermatic fluid by the currents of the sea, like pollen by the wind; but it is not probable that this can often happen, as the act of impregnation takes place within the well-enclosed sack. As, however, these animals possess a probosci-formed penis capable of great elongation, two closely attached hermaphrodites could reciprocally fertilise each other. This, as I have elsewhere proved, does sometimes, perhaps often, actually occur. Hence perhaps it arises, that most cirripedes are attached in clusters. The curious Anelasma, which lives buried in the skin of sharks in the northern seas, is said always to live in pairs. Whilst reflecting how far cirripedes usually adhered to their support in clusters, the case of the genus Acasta occurred to me, in which all the species are embedded in sponges, generally at some little distance from each other; I then turned to my description of the animal, and found it stated, that in several of the species the probosci-formed penis is "remarkably long;" and this I think can hardly be an accidental coincidence. With respect to the habits of the genera which are provided with true males or complemental males:—all the species of Scalpellum, excepting one, are specially modified for attachment to the delicate branches of corallines; the one species of Ibla, about which I know anything, lives attached, generally two or three together, to the peduncle of another cirripede, viz. a Pollicipes; Alcippe and Cryptophialus are embedded in small cavities which they excavate in shells. No doubt in all these cases two or more full-grown individuals might become attached close together to the same support; and this sometimes occurs with *Scalpellum vulgare*, but the individuals in such groups are apt to be distorted and to have their peduncles twisted. There would be much difficulty in two or more individuals of Alcippe and Cryptophialus living embedded in the same cavity. Moreover, it might well happen that sufficient food would not be brought by the currents of the sea to several individuals of these species living close together. Nevertheless in all these cases it would be a manifest advantage to the species, if two individuals could live and flourish close together, so as occasionally to intercross. Now if certain individuals were reduced in size and transmitted this character, they could readily be attached to the other and larger individuals; and as the process of reduction was continued, the smaller individuals would be enabled to adhere closer and closer to the orifice of the sack, or, as actually occurs with some species of Scalpellum and with Ibla, within the sack of the larger individual; and thus the act of fertilisation would be safely effected. It is generally admitted that a division of physiological labour is an advantage to all organisms; accordingly, a separation of the sexes would be so to cirripedes, that is if this could be effected with full security for the propagation of the species. How in any case a tendency to a separation of the sexes first arises, we do not know; but we can plainly see that if it occurred in the present case, the smaller individuals would almost necessarily become males, as there would be much less expenditure of organic matter in the production of the spermatic fluid than of ova. Indeed with *Scalpellum vulgare* the whole body of the male is smaller than a single one of the many ova produced by the hermaphrodite. The other and larger individuals would on the same principle either remain hermaphrodites, but with their masculine organs more or less reduced, or would be converted into females. At any rate, whether these views are correct or not, we see at the present time within the genus Scalpellum a graduated series: first on the masculine side, from an animal which is obviously a pedunculated cirripede with well-proportioned valves, to a mere sack enclosing the male organs, either with the merest rudiments of valves, or entirely destitute of them; and secondly on the feminine side, we have either true females, or hermaphrodites with the male organs perfect, yet greatly reduced.

With respect to the means by which so many of the most important organs in numerous animals and plants have been greatly reduced in size and rendered rudimentary, or have been quite obliterated, we may attribute much to the inherited effects of the disuse of parts. But this would not apply to certain parts, for instance to the calcareous valves of male cirripedes which cannot be said to be actively used. Before I read Mr. Mivart's[4] acute criticisms on this subject, I thought that the principle of the economy of growth would account for the continued reduction and final obliteration of parts; and I still think, that during the earlier periods of reduction the process would be thus greatly aided. But if we consider, for instance, the rudimentary pistils or stamens of many plants, it seems incredible that the reduction and final obliteration of a minute papilla, formed of mere cellular tissue, could be of any service to the species. The following conjectural remarks are made solely in the hope of calling the attention of naturalists to this subject. It is known from the researches of Quetelet[5] on the height of man, that the number of individuals who exceed the average height by a given quantity is the same as the number of those who are shorter than the average by the same quantity; so that men may be grouped symmetrically about the average with reference to their height. I may add, to make this clearer, that there exists the same number of men between three and four inches above the average height, as there are below it. So it is with the circumference of their chests; and we may presume that this is the usual law of variation in all the parts of every species under ordinary conditions of life. That almost every part of the body is capable of independent variation we have good reason to believe, for it is this which gives rise to the individual differences characteristic of all species. Now it does not seem improbable that with a species under unfavourable conditions, when, during many generations, or in certain areas, it is pressed for food and exists in scanty numbers, that all or most of its parts should tend to vary in a greater number of individuals towards diminution than towards increment of size; so that the grouping would be no longer symmetrical with reference to the average size of any organ under consideration. In this case the individuals which were born with parts diminished in size and efficiency, on which the welfare of the species depended, would be eliminated; those individuals alone surviving in the long run which possessed such parts of the proper size. But the survival of none would be affected by the greater or less diminution of parts already reduced in size and functionally useless. We have assumed that under the above stated unfavourable conditions a larger number of individuals are born with any particular part or organ diminished in size, than are born with it increased to the same relative degree; and as these individuals, having their already reduced and useless parts still more diminished by variation under poor conditions, would not be eliminated, they would intercross with the many individuals having the part of nearly average size, and with the few having it of increased size. The result of such intercrossing would be, in the course of time, the steady diminution and ultimate disappearance of all such useless parts. No doubt the process would take place with excessive slowness; but this result agrees perfectly with what we see in nature; for the number of forms possessing the merest traces of various organs is immense. I repeat that I have ventured to make these hypothetical remarks solely for the sake of calling attention to this subject.

1. *Nature. A Weekly Illustrated Journal of Science*, vol. 8, 25 September 1873, pp. 431–32.[†]

2. Wyville Thomson, "Notes from the Challenger," *Nature*, vol. 8, 28 August 1873, pp. 347–49.†

3. *A Monograph on the Sub-Class Cirripedia, with Figures of All the Species* (London: Ray Society, 1851).†

4. St. George Mivart, *On the Genesis of Species* (London: Macmillan, 1871).†

5. Lambert A. J. Quetelet, *A Treatise on Man and the Development of His Faculties* (Edinburgh: Chambers, 1842).†

◄ Recent Researches on Termites and Honey-Bees[1]

The accompanying letter,[2] just received from Fritz Müller, in Southern Brazil, is so interesting that it appears to me well worth publishing in Nature. His discovery of the two sexually mature forms of Termites, and of their habits, is now published in Germany[3]; nevertheless few Englishmen will have as yet seen the account.

In the German paper he justly compares, as far as function is concerned, the winged males and females of the one form, and the wingless males and females of the second form, with those plants which produce flowers of two forms, serving different ends, of which so excellent an account has lately appeared in Nature by his brother, Hermann Müller.[4]

The facts, also, given by Fritz Müller with respect to the stingless bees of Brazil will surprise and interest entomologists.

1. *Nature. A Weekly Illustrated Journal of Science*, vol. 9, 19 February 1874, pp. 308–9.†

2. Fritz Müller's long letter, which gives detailed accounts of the habits of certain termites and stingless honeybees, is omitted here.†

3. Fritz Müller, "Beitrage zur kenntniss der Termiten," *Jenaische Zirtschrift fur Medicin- und Naturwissenschaft*, etc. 7 (1873): 333–58, 451–63.†

4. Hermann Müller, "On the Fertilisation of Flowers by Insects and the Reciprocal Adaptations of Both, *Nature* 8 (1873): 187–89, 205–6, 433–35; 9 (1874): 44–46, 164–66.†

◄ Fertilisation of the Fumariaceae[1]

I beg permission to make a few remarks on Mr. J. Traherne Moggridge's statement (Nature, vol. ix. p. 423) that the flowers of *Fumaria capreolata*[2] are at first pale or nearly white, and only attain their brightest colouring, becoming even crimson, after the ovaries are set. He then adds:—"If the reverse had been the case there is little doubt that we should have regarded the bright colouring as specially adapted to attract insects." But does Mr. Moggridge know that these flowers are visited chiefly by diurnal insects? It has often been observed that flowers which are visited by moths are commonly white or very pale; but if they are odoriferous, they may be of any tint, even very dark or green. If therefore the flowers of the above Fumaria are visited by moths, it would be an injury to the plant had the flowers been from the first of a fine crimson. I have often seen bees sucking the flowers of the fumariaceous genera, *Corydalis, Dielytra,* and *Adlumia;* but many years ago I watched perseveringly the flowers of *Fumaria officinalis* and *parviflora,* and never saw them visited by a single insect; and I concluded from reasons which I will not here give (as I cannot find my original notes), that they were frequented during the night by small moths. Insects are not necessary for the fertilisation of *Fumaria officinalis;* for I covered up a plant, and it produced as many seeds as an uncovered one which grew near. On the other hand, with some species of *Corydalis,* the aid of insects is indispensable. With respect to the flowers of *F. capreolata* becoming brighter coloured as they grow old, we see the same thing in some hawthorns, and with the double rocket in our gardens. But is it surprising that this should sometimes occur with flowers, seeing that the leaves of a multitude of plants assume, as they become oxygenised, the most splendid tints during the autumn?

1. *Nature. A Weekly Illustrated Journal of Science,* vol. 9, 16 April 1874, p. 460.†
2. Fumaria: many are climbing plants with watery juice.†

☙ Flowers of the Primrose
Destroyed by Birds[1]

For above twenty years I have observed every spring in my shrubberies and in the neighbouring woods, that a large number of the flowers of the primrose are cut off, and lie strewn on the ground close round the plants. So it is sometimes with the flowers of the cowslip and polyanthus, when they are borne on short stalks. This year the devastation has been greater than ever; and in a little wood not far from my house many hundred flowers have been destroyed, and some clumps have been completely denuded. For reasons presently to be given, I have no doubt that this is done by birds; and as I once saw some green-finches flying away from some primroses, I suspect that this is the enemy. The object of the birds in thus cutting off the flowers long perplexed me. As we have little water hereabouts, I at one time thought that it was done in order to squeeze the juice out of the stalks; but I have since observed that they are as frequently cut during very rainy, as during dry weather. One of my sons then suggested that the object was to get the nectar of the flowers; and I have no doubt that this is the right explanation. On a hasty glance it appears as if the foot-stalk had been cut through; but on close inspection, it will invariably be found that the extreme base of the calyx and the young ovary are left attached to the foot-stalk. And if the cut-off ends of the flowers be examined, it will be seen that they do not fit the narrow cut-off ends of the calyx, which remains attached to the stalk. A piece of the calyx between one and two-tenths of an inch in length, has generally been cut clean away; and these little bits of the calyx can often be found on the ground; but sometimes they remain hanging by a few fibres to the upper part of the calyx of the detached flowers. Now no animal that I can think of, except a bird, could make two almost parallel clean cuts, transversely across the calyx of a flower. The part which is cut off contains within the narrow tube of the corolla the nectar; and the pressure of the bird's beak would force this out at both the cut-off ends. I have never heard of any bird in Europe feeding on nectar; though there are many that do so in the tropical parts of the New and Old Worlds, and which are believed to aid in the cross-fertilisation of the species. In such cases both the bird and the plant would profit. But with the primrose it is an unmitigated evil, and might well lead to its extermination; for in the wood above alluded to many hundred flowers have been destroyed this season, and cannot produce a single seed. My object in this com-munication to Nature is to ask your correspondents in England and abroad to observe whether the primroses there suffer, and to state the result, whether negative or affirmative, adding whether primroses are abundant in each district. I cannot remember having formerly seen anything of the kind in the midland counties of England. If the habit of cutting off the flowers should prove, as seems probable, to be general, we must look at it as inherited or instinctive; for it is unlikely that each bird should have discovered during its individual life-time the exact spot where the nectar lies concealed within the tube of the corolla, and should have learnt to bite off the flowers so skilfully that a minute portion of the calyx is always left attached to the foot-stalk. If, on the other hand, the evil is confined to this part of Kent, it will be a curious case of a new habit or instinct arising in this primrose-decked land.

1. *Nature. A Weekly Illustrated Journal of Science*, vol. 9, 23 April 1874, p. 482.†

➘ Flowers of the Primrose Destroyed by Birds[1]

I hope that you will permit me to make a few final remarks on the destruction of primrose flowers by birds. But first I must return my best thanks to your correspondents,[2] as well as to some gentlemen who have written direct to me, and to whom I have not had time to send separate answers. Secondly, I must plead guilty to the high crime of inaccuracy. As the stalks from which the flowers had been cut were shrivelled, I mistook, in a manner now inexplicable to me, the base of the ruptured or removed ovarium for the summit; a remnant of the shrivelled placenta being mistaken for the base of the pistil. I have now looked more carefully, and find that on twelve stalks only three had any remnant of the ovarium left. I have also examined sixteen bits of the calyx which had been cut off by a caged bullfinch, presently to be noticed, and in fifteen of these not only had the ovarium been torn into fragments or quite destroyed, but all the ovules had been devoured, excepting sometimes one or two. In several cases the calyx had been split open longitudinally. The ovarium was in the same state in thirteen small portions of the calyx lying on the ground near a wild cowslip plant. It is therefore clear that the ovules are the chief attraction; but the birds in removing by pressure the ovules could not fail to squeeze out the nectar at the open end, as occurred when I squeezed similar bits between my fingers. The birds thus get a dainty morsel, namely, young ovules with sweet sauce. I still think that the nectar is, in part, the attraction, as caged bullfinches and canary birds much like sugar; but more especially because Mr. C. J. Monro has sent me some flowers from a cherry-tree near Barnet, which during several years has been attacked; and he finds many of the flowers, both those on the tree and on the ground, with rather large ragged holes in the calyx, like, but much larger than, those often made by humble bees when they rob flowers in an illegitimate manner. Now the inside of the flower of the cherry, round the ovarium, is bedewed (if protected from the visits of insects) with drops of nectar, which sometimes collect so as almost to fill up the bottom of the flower. In the case of the cherry I cannot doubt that this is the attraction, for I examined the ovarium of ten flowers, and although they had all been scored by the bird's beak, and in four instances punctured, the ovule had in no case been devoured.

To return to the primroses: from the accounts received, it seems that the flowers are cut off in the manner described by me, near Preston in Lancashire, in North Hampshire, Devonshire, and Ireland, as well as in Kent. In several other places, not worth specifying, where primroses are abundant, they have not been thus attacked; and this may possibly be due to the proper enemy, namely, as I now suspect, the bullfinch, not being a common bird. In my former letter I remarked that if the habit of cutting off the flowers proved to be a widely extended one, we should have to consider it as inherited or instinctive; as it is not likely that each bird should discover during its individual lifetime the exact spot where the nectar, and, as I must now add, the ovules, lie concealed, or should learn to bite off the flower so skilfully at the proper point. That the habit is instinctive, Prof. Frankland has given me interesting evidence. When he read my letter he happened to have in the room a bunch of cowslip flowers and a caged bullfinch, to whom he immediately gave some of the flowers, and afterwards many primrose flowers. The latter were cut off in exactly the same manner, and quite as neatly, as by the wild birds near here. I know that this is the case by having examined the cut-off portions. The bird worked so quickly that he easily destroyed twenty flowers in three minutes; a single wild pair would therefore cause great havoc. Prof. Frankland informs me that his bird pressed the cut-off portions of the calyx in its beak, and gradually worked them out on one side, and then dropped them. Thus the ovules were removed, and the nectar necessarily squeezed out. A canary bird to whom some cowslip and primrose flowers were given attacked all parts indiscriminately, and ate up the corolla, calyx, and stalks. A lady also informs me that her canary and siskin always attack primrose and cowslip flowers, if kept in the same room. They generally first make a ragged hole through the calyx opposite the ovarium, and remove the ovules, as I found to be the case with flowers which were sent to me; but the ovules had not been so well removed as by the bullfinch, and the nectar could not be obtained by this method of attack.

But now comes the interesting point: the caged bullfinch just referred to was caught in 1872 near Ventnor, in the Isle of Wight, soon after it had left the nest, by which time the primroses would have been out of flower, and since then, as I hear from Prof. Frankland, it had never seen a primrose or cowslip flower. Nevertheless, as soon as this bird, now nearly two years old, saw these flowers, some machinery in its brain was set into action, which instantly told it in an unerring manner how and where to bite off and press the flowers, so as to gain the hidden prize. We are reminded by this little fact of Mr. Spalding's[3] admirable observations on the instinctive actions of chickens when their eyes were uncovered, after having been blind-folded from the moment of being hatched.

Prof. Frankland seems to have been much struck with the behaviour of his bullfinch, and remarks in his letter that "it had all the precision of a chemical reaction; the result of putting a primrose within its reach can be almost as certainly predicted as that of putting a plate of iron into a solution of sulphate of copper."

P.S. —This letter was printed before I saw your last number, and I am glad to find that some of my statements are confirmed, more especially with respect to bullfinches. During the last fortnight not one primrose has been attacked in the little wood where shortly before there was such havoc. I imagined that the pair of bullfinches, which I saw there earlier in the season, had wandered away; but yesterday evening (May 10) it occurred to me that the flowers produced late in the season might fail to secrete nectar, or that the recent cold weather might have produced this effect. Accordingly, in the afternoon I gathered fifteen flowers from as many distinct plants, and kept them in water in my room for seventeen hours. Earlier in the season I treated some flowers in this same manner, and found the tube of the corolla full of nectar; but now only one of the flowers contained a very small quantity of nectar, another showing a mere trace of it. And the flowers being no longer cut off by the birds supports my belief that the nectar is one chief attraction to them; the ovules without the sauce not being worth the gathering. I may add that as the primrose is a dimorphic plant, these non-nectariferous flowers would be sterile, for they would not be visited by insects.

1. *Nature. A Weekly Illustrated Journal of Science,* vol. 10, 14 May 1874, pp. 24–25.†

2. Results of the observations of ten correspondents were reported in *Nature,* vol. 10, 7 May 1874, pp. 6–7, and of seven correspondents in *Nature,* vol. 9, 30 April 1874, p. 509.†

3. D. A. Spalding, "On Instinct," *Nature,* vol. 6, 10 October 1872, pp. 485–86.†

[A Communication on Irritability of *Pinguicula*][1]

Most of us remember the use that Paley[2] made of the watch as an evidence of design, and of necessity of a designer. Twenty or thirty years ago this doctrine suffered by injudicious illustration, and a new school arose deriving its chief inspiration from Goethe. Modifications in form were set down as variations from an ideal pattern or type, and adaptations to special ends, though admitted in some cases, were discredited in others. Not the least service which Mr. Darwin has rendered to science has been the demonstration that many adaptations formerly supposed either to be of trifling moment or purposeless illustrations of a particular preordained pattern, are really adaptations to special purposes, or, at least, are the relics of traces of former adaptation of this kind. While some naturalists have been counting spots and measuring scales, splitting hairs 'twixt south and south-west sides, disputing whether there are two or twenty species of Brambles, or referring every little bump to a theoretical typical form, Mr. Darwin has been quietly and steadily setting to work to show the purpose and meaning of various organs and rudimentary structures. In this manner he has made clear the use and purport of many parts and variations in plants, the study of which was before to a large extent barren in results. In thus affording a rational and intelligible explanation of many struc-

tures and phenomena, Mr. Darwin has not only advanced physiological
science to a high degree, and infected others with the desire so far as their
means and abilities are concerned to do likewise, but he has placed a
most effective weapon in the hands of those who, like Paley, attach very
high importance to the study of Natural Theology. Our pages of late
years have teemed with illustrations of adaptations of structure to
function, especially with regard to the fertilisation of flowers by insects.
Only lately, through the kindness of Dr. Asa Gray,[3] we have had
occasion to lay before our readers the curious arrangements by which
Droseras and Sarracenias obtain some at least of their nourishment by
entrapping and digesting insects. Dr. Sanderson[4] has shown us how the
movement of the leaves of Venus' Fly-trap Dionaea is accompanied by
electrical phenomena, as in the case of the muscles of animals. One of the
most curious illustrations yet made known, showing the relation of
structural form to definite purpose in the economy of the plant, is that
laid before the Scientific Committee on Wednesday last by Mr. Darwin.
Mr. Darwin's researches are not yet fully completed, and at some future
time he will give a fuller account of his researches, meanwhile no reader
will fail to see the exceeding interest of the phenomena we now proceed
to relate: —

"The leaves of Pinguicula vulgaris,[5] according to Mr. Darwin, possess
a power of digesting animal matter similar to that shown by the Sundews
(Drosera). Albumen, fibrin, meat or cartilage induce a secretion from the
glands of the upper surface of the leaf, and their secretion becomes feebly
acid (but not so much so as that of Drosera). Their secretion is
reabsorbed, and causes an aggregation of the protoplasm in the cells of
the glands, such as had been observed in other similar cases. Before
excitement the glands were seen to be filled with a homogeneous pale
greenish fluid; after the aggregation of the protoplasm it can be seen to
move. When a row of insects or of Cabbage seeds are placed near the
margin of a leaf (or when a single insect is placed at one point,) the whole
margin (or one point) becomes curled considerably over in two or three
hours; the apex of the leaf will not turn over towards the base. Small
fragments of glass also cause a similar movement, but to a much less
degree. The inflexed margin pours forth a secretion which envelopes the
flies or seeds, but pieces of glass cause no, or hardly any, increase of secretion. But here comes a puzzle: If the flies or fly be removed, the margin of
the leaf turns back in less than twenty-four hours; but it does so also when
a row of flies and Cabbage seeds are left adhering; so that the use or
meaning of the inflexion is at present quite a puzzle."

We must await the publication in full of Mr. Darwin's researches before
we can say more on the subject. Meantime, as many of our readers will
speedily be hieing northwards to the moorlands, where Pinguicula

grows, and where Drosera is abundant, we would fain hope that some of them will be enabled to watch the plants in question, and ascertain what insects are entrapped, and under what circumstances.

1. *Gardeners' Chronicle. A Weekly Illustrated Journal of Horticulture and Allied Subjects*, n.s., vol. 2, 4 July 1874, p. 15.†

2. William Paley, *Natural Theology: Or Evidences of the Existence and Attitudes of the Diety, Collected from the Appearances of Nature*, 10th ed. (London: Faulder, 1805).†

3. Asa Gray, "Sarracenias as Fly-catchers," *American Journal of Science* 7 (1874): 440–42.†

4. J. Burdon Sanderson, "On the Electrical Phenomena which Accompany the Contraction of the Leaf of Dionaea Muscipula," *Report of the British Association* 43 (1873): 133, and "Note on the Electrical Phenomena which Accompany Irritation of the Leaf of Dionaea Muscipula," *Proceedings of the Royal Society of London* 21 (1873): 495–96.†

5. *Pinguicula:* butterworts.†

◣ Cherry Blossoms[1]

In the last number of Nature (vol. xiv., p. 10), Mr. Pryor states that the flowers of the wild cherry are bitten off in large numbers in much the same manner as I formerly described in the case of the primrose. Some days ago I observed many cherry blossoms in this state, and to-day I saw some actually falling. I approached stealthily so as to discover what bird was at work, and behold it was a squirrel. There could be no doubt about it for the squirrel was low in the tree and actually had a blossom between its teeth. It is none the less true that birds likewise bite the flowers of the cherry tree.

1. *Nature. A Weekly Illustrated Journal of Science*, vol. 14, 11 May 1876, p. 28.†

◣ Holly Berries[1]

Several of your correspondents have noticed the scarcity of Holly-berries in different parts of the country, and the same thing may be observed to a remarkable extent in this neighbourhood. Your correspondents account for the fact by spring frosts, but it must be remembered how hardy a plant the Holly is, being found in Norway as far north as the 62d degree of north latitude (Lecoq *Géographie Botanique*, vii., p. 370), another explanation seems to me more probable. Bees of all kinds were in this neighbourhood extraordinarily rare during the spring. I can state this positively, as I wished to observe a particular point in their behavior in sucking the common red Clover; and, therefore, often visited the fields where this plant was growing; but I could see very few bees. I was so much struck by this fact that I examined several meadows abounding with flowers of all kinds, but bees were everywhere rare. Reflecting, in the course of the summer, on this extraordinary scarcity, it occurred to me that this part of England would be temporarily in the same predicament as New Zealand before the introduction of hive bees, when the Clovers (which, as I know by trial, require the aid of bees for perfect fertilisation) would not set seed. By an odd chance I received the very next morning a letter from a stranger in Kent, asking me if I could assign any reason for the seed-crop of Clover having largely failed in his neighbourhood, though the plants looked vigorous and healthy. Now the Holly is a dioecious plant, and during the last forty years I have looked at many flowers in different districts, and have never found an hermaphrodite. Bees are the chief transporters of pollen from the male to the female tree, and the latter will produce but few berries if bees are scarce. In my *Origin of Species* I state that, having found a female tree exactly 60 yards from a male tree, I put the stigmas of twenty flowers, taken from different branches, under the microscope, and on all, without exception, there were a few pollen-grains, and on some a profusion. As the wind had set for several days from the female to the male tree, the pollen could not thus have been carried. The weather had been cold and boisterous, and therefore not favourable; nevertheless every female flower which I examined had been effectually fertilised by the bees, which I saw at work, and which had flown from tree to tree in search of nectar. Therefore, as I believe, we cannot decorate our Christmas hearths with the scarlet berries of the Holly, because bees were rare during the spring; but what caused their rarity I do not in the least know.

1. *Gardeners' Chronicle. A Weekly Illustrated Journal of Horticulture and Allied Subjects*, n.s., vol. 7, 6 January 1877, p. 19.†

The Scarcity of Holly Berries and Bees[1]

I beg a little space in your journal to confess my error with respect to the cause of the scarcity of Holly berries. I have been convinced of this by the two communications in your last number, by a statement in the *Garden* by Mr. Fish,[2] and by some private letters which I have received. It appears that several causes in combination have led to this scarcity; but I still think that the rarity of bees of all kinds in this neighbourhood during the spring, of which fact I feel assured, may have played a part, though a quite subordinate one.

1. *Gardeners' Chronicle. A Weekly Illustrated Journal of Horticulture and Allied Subjects*, n.s., vol. 7, 20 January 1877, p. 83.†

2. D. T. Fish, "Scarcity of Holly Berries," *The Garden*, vol. 11, 13 January 1877, p. 40.†

❧ Fertilisation of Plants[1]

In the last number of the *Gardeners' Chronicle* (p. 203) Mr. Henslow[2] quotes my words, that "the seeds from which the self-fertilised plants of the third generation (of Petunia) were raised were not well ripened." The word *self-fertilised* is a misprint for *crossed*, as he would have seen if he had looked to the full account of my experiments given at p. 191, where I say, "The sole conjecture which I can form is that the *crossed* seeds had not been sufficiently ripened, &c."[3] But I have no right to expect a critic to take so much trouble, and I am much obliged to him for having led me to detect this unfortunate misprint. Mr. Henslow then goes on to say that "Mr. Darwin also accounts for the greater growth of the eighth generation of Ipomoea from their having been raised from unhealthy seeds." He ought, I think, to have added that the greater growth of the self-fertilised plants was confined to the early part of their lives, and that they were ultimately beaten in height by the crossed plants in the ratio of one hundred to eighty-five. It was this anomalous manner of growth which led me to compare these plants with those of Iberis which were raised from seeds not well ripened. I have long been convinced that controversy is a mere waste of time; I will, therefore, not make any other remarks on Mr. Henslow's criticisms, though I think that I could answer them satisfactorily. I hope that any reader who is interested in the subject will not take Mr. Henslow's interpretation of my statements without consulting my book.

1. *Gardeners' Chronicle. A Weekly Illustrated Journal of Horticulture and Allied Subjects*, n.s., 24 February 1877, p. 246.†

2. George Henslow, "Fertilisation of Plants," *Gardeners' Chronicle*, n.s., 17 February 1877, pp. 203–4.†

3. *The Effects of Cross and Self Fertilisation in the Vegetable Kingdom* (London: Murray, 1876).†

❧ A Biographical Sketch of an Infant[1]

M. Taine's very interesting account of the mental development of an infant, translated in the last number of Mind (p. 252),[2] has led me to look over a diary which I kept thirty-seven years ago with respect to one of my own infants. I had excellent opportunities for close observation, and wrote down at once whatever was observed. My chief object was expression, and my notes were used in my book on this subject; but as I attended to some other points, my observations may possibly possess some little interest in comparison with those by M. Taine, and with others which hereafter no doubt will be made. I feel sure, from what I have seen with my own infants, that the period of development of the several faculties will be found to differ considerably in different infants.

During the first seven days various reflex actions, namely sneezing, hickuping, yawning, stretching, and of course sucking and screaming, were well performed by my infant. On the seventh day, I touched the naked sole of his foot with a bit of paper, and he jerked it away, curling at the same time his toes, like a much older child when tickled. The perfection of these reflex movements shows that the extreme imperfection of the voluntary ones is not due to the state of the muscles or of the coordinating centres, but to that of the seat of the will. At this time, though so early, it seemed clear to me that a warm soft hand applied to his face excited a wish to suck. This must be considered as a reflex or an instinctive action, for it is impossible to believe that experience and association with the touch of his mother's breast could so soon have come into play. During the first fortnight he often started on hearing any sudden sound, and blinked his eyes. The same fact was observed with some of my other infants within the first fortnight. Once, when he was 66 days old, I happened to sneeze, and he started violently, frowned, looked frightened, and cried rather badly: for an hour afterwards he was in a state which would be called nervous in an older person, for every slight noise made him start. A few days before this same date, he first started at an object suddenly seen; but for a long time afterwards sounds made him start and wink his eyes much more frequently than did sight; thus when 114 days old, I shook a paste-board box with comfits in it near his face and he started, whilst the same box when empty or any other object shaken as near or much nearer to his face produced no effect. We may infer from these several facts that the winking of the eyes, which manifestly serves to protect them, had not been acquired through experience. Although so sensitive to sound in a general way, he was not able even when 124 days old easily to recognise whence a sound proceeded, so as to direct his eyes to the source.

With respect to vision,—his eyes were fixed on a candle as early as the 9th day, and up to the 45th day nothing else seemed thus to fix them; but on the 49th day his attention was attracted by a bright-coloured tassel, as was shown by his eyes becoming fixed and the movements of his arms ceasing. It was surprising how slowly he acquired the power of following with his eyes an object if swinging at all rapidly; for he could not do this well when seven and a half months old. At the age of 32 days he perceived his mother's bosom when three or four inches from it, as was shown by the protrusion of his lips and his eyes becoming fixed; but I much doubt whether this had any connection with vision; he certainly had not touched the bosom. Whether he was guided through smell or the sensation of warmth or through association with the position in which he was held, I do not at all know.

The movements of his limbs and body were for a long time vague and purposeless, and usually performed in a jerking manner; but there was one exception to this rule, namely, that from a very early period, certainly long before he was 40 days old, he could move his hands to his own mouth. When 77 days old, he took the sucking bottle (with which he was partly fed) in his right hand, whether he was held on the left or right arm of his nurse, and he would not take it in his left hand until a week later although I tried to make him do so; so that the right hand was a week in advance of the left. Yet this infant afterwards proved to be left-handed, the tendency being no doubt inherited—his grandfather, mother, and a brother having been or being left-handed. When between 80 and 90 days old, he drew all sorts of objects into this mouth, and in two or three weeks' time could do this with some skill; but he often first touched his nose with the object and then dragged it down into his mouth. After grasping my finger and drawing it to his mouth, his own hand prevented him from sucking it; but on the 114th day, after acting in this manner, he slipped his own hand down so that he could get the end of my finger into his mouth. This action was repeated several times, and evidently was not a chance but a rational one. The intentional movements of the hands and arms were thus much in advance of those of the body and legs, though the purposeless movements of the latter were from a very early period usually alternate as in the act of walking. When four months old, he often looked intently at his own hands and other objects close to him, and in doing so the eyes were turned much inwards, so that he often squinted frightfully. In a fortnight after this time (*i.e.* 132 days old) I observed that if an object was brought as near to his face as his own hands were, he tried to seize it, but often failed; and he did not try to do so in regard to more distant objects. I think there can be little doubt that the convergence of his eyes gave him the clue and excited him to move his arms. Although this infant thus began to use his hands at an early period, he showed no special aptitude in this respect, for when he was 2 years and 4 months old, he held pencils, pens, and other objects far less neatly and efficiently than did his sister who was then only 14 months old, and who showed great inherent aptitude in handling anything.

Anger. —It was difficult to decide at how early an age anger was felt; on his eighth day he frowned and wrinkled the skin round his eyes before a crying fit, but this may have been due to pain or distress, and not to anger. When about ten weeks old, he was given some rather cold milk and he kept a slight frown on his forehead all the time that he was sucking, so that he looked like a grown-up person made cross from being compelled to do something which he did not like. When nearly four months old, and perhaps much earlier, there could be no doubt, from the manner in which the blood gushed into his whole face and scalp, that he easily got into a violent passion. A small cause sufficed; thus, when a little over seven months old, he screamed with rage because a lemon slipped away and he could not seize it with his hands. When eleven months old, if a wrong plaything was given him, he would push it away and beat it; I presume that the beating was an instinctive sign of anger, like the snapping of the jaws by a young crocodile just out of the egg, and not that he imagined he could hurt the plaything. When two years and three months old, he became a great adept at throwing books or sticks, &c., at anyone who offended him; and so it was with some of my other sons. On the other hand, I could never see a trace of such aptitude in my infant daughters; and this makes me think that a tendency to throw objects is inherited by boys.

Fear. —This feeling probably is one of the earliest which is experienced by infants, as shown by their starting at any sudden sound when only a few weeks old, followed by crying. Before the present one was 4½ months old I had been accustomed to make close to him many strange and loud noises, which were all taken as excellent jokes, but at this period I one day made a loud snoring noise which I had never done before; he instantly looked grave and then burst out crying. Two or three days afterwards, I made through forgetfulness the same noise with the same result. About the same time (*viz.* on the 137th day) I approached with my back towards him and then stood motionless: he looked very grave and much surprised, and would soon have cried, had I not turned round; then his face instantly relaxed into a smile. It is well known how intensely older children suffer from vague and undefined fears, as from the dark, or in passing an obscure corner in a large hall, &c. I may give as an instance that I took the child in question, when 2¼ years old, to the Zoological Gardens, and he enjoyed looking at all the animals which were like those that he knew, such as deer, antelopes &c., and all the birds, even the ostriches, but was much alarmed at the various larger animals in cages. He often said afterwards that he wished to go again, but not to see "beasts in houses"; and we could in no manner account for this fear. May we not suspect that the vague but very real fears of children, which are quite independent of experience, are the inherited effects of real dangers and abject superstitions during ancient savage times? It is quite conformable with what we know of the transmission of formerly well-developed characters, that they should appear at an early period of life, and afterwards disappear.

Pleasurable Sensations.—It may be presumed that infants feel pleasure whilst sucking, and the expression of their swimming eyes seems to show that this is the case. This infant smiled when 45 days, a second infant when 46 days old; and these were true smiles, indicative of pleasure, for their eyes brightened and eyelids slightly closed. The smiles arose chiefly when looking at their mother, and were therefore probably of mental origin; but this infant often smiled then, and for some time afterwards, from some inward pleasurable feeling, for nothing was happening which could have in any way excited or amused him. When 110 days old he was exceedingly amused by a pinafore being thrown over his face and then suddenly withdrawn; and so he was when I suddenly uncovered my own face and approached his. He then uttered a little noise which was an incipient laugh. Here surprise was the chief cause of the amusement, as is the case to a large extent with the wit of grown-up persons. I believe that for three or four weeks before the time when he was amused by a face being suddenly uncovered, he received a little pinch on his nose and cheeks as a good joke. I was at first surprised at humour being appreciated by an infant only a little above three months old, but we should remember how very early puppies and kittens begin to play. When four months old, he showed in an unmistakable manner that he liked to hear the pianoforte played; so that here apparently was the earliest sign of an aesthetic feeling, unless the attraction of bright colours, which was exhibited much earlier, may be so considered.

Affection.—This probably arose very early in life, if we may judge by his smiling at those who had charge of him when under two months old; though I had no distinct evidence of his distinguishing and recognising anyone, until he was nearly four months old. When nearly five months old, he plainly showed his wish to go to his nurse. But he did not spontaneously exhibit affection by overt acts until a little above a year old, namely, by kissing several times his nurse who had been absent for a short time. With respect to the allied feeling of sympathy, this was clearly shown at 6 months and 11 days by his melancholy face, with the corners of his mouth well depressed, when his nurse pretended to cry. Jealousy was plainly exhibited when I fondled a large doll, and when I weighed his infant sister, he being then $15\frac{1}{2}$ months old. Seeing how

strong a feeling jealousy is in dogs, it would probably be exhibited by
infants at an earlier age than that just specified, if they were tried in a
fitting manner.

Association of Ideas, Reason, &c.—The first action which exhibited, as
far as I observed, a kind of practical reasoning, has already been noticed,
namely, the slipping his hand down my finger so as to get the end of it
into his mouth; and this happened on the 114th day. When four and a
half months old, he repeatedly smiled at my image and his own in a
mirror, and no doubt mistook them for real objects; but he showed sense
in being evidently surprised at my voice coming from behind him. Like
all infants he much enjoyed thus looking at himself, and in less than two
months perfectly understood that it was an image; for if I made quite
silently any odd grimace, he would suddenly turn round to look at me.
He was, however, puzzled at the age of seven months, when being out of
doors he saw me on the inside of a large plate-glass window, and seemed
in doubt whether or not it was an image. Another of my infants, a little
girl, when exactly a year old, was not nearly so acute, and seemed quite
perplexed at the image of a person in a mirror approaching her from
behind. The higher apes which I tried with a small looking-glass behaved
differently; they placed their hands behind the glass, and in doing so
showed their sense, but far from taking pleasure in looking at themselves
they got angry and would look no more.

When five months old, associated ideas arising independently of any
instruction became fixed in his mind; thus as soon as his hat and cloak
were put on, he was very cross if he was not immediately taken out of
doors. When exactly seven months old, he made the great step of
associating his nurse with her name, so that if I called it out he would
look round for her. Another infant used to amuse himself by shaking his
head laterally: we praised and imitated him, saying "Shake your head";
and when he was seven months old, he would sometimes do so on being
told without any other guide. During the next four months the former
infant associated many things and actions with words; thus when asked
for a kiss he would protrude his lips and keep still,—would shake his
head and say in a scolding voice "Ah" to the coal-box or a little spilt
water, &c., which he had been taught to consider as dirty. I may add that
when a few days under nine months old he associated his own name with
his image in the looking-glass, and when called by name would turn
towards the glass even when at some distance from it. When a few days
over nine months, he learnt spontaneously that a hand or other object
causing a shadow to fall on the wall in front of him was to be looked for
behind. Whilst under a year old, it was sufficient to repeat two or three
times at intervals any short sentence to fix firmly in his mind some

associated idea. In the infant described by M. Taine (pp. 254–256) the age at which ideas readily became associated seems to have been considerably later, unless indeed the earlier cases were overlooked. The facility with which associated ideas due to instruction and others spontaneously arising were acquired, seemed to me by far the most strongly marked of all the distinctions between the mind of an infant and that of the cleverest full-grown dog that I have ever known. What a contrast does the mind of an infant present to that of the pike, described by Professor Möbius,[3] who during three whole months dashed and stunned himself against a glass partition which separated him from some minnows; and when, after at last learning that he could not attack them with impunity, he was placed in the aquarium with these same minnows, then in a persistent and senseless manner he would not attack them!

Curiosity, as M. Taine remarks, is displayed at an early age by infants, and is highly important in the development of their minds; but I made no special observation on this head. Imitation likewise comes into play. When our infant was only four months old I thought that he tried to imitate sounds; but I may have deceived myself, for I was not thoroughly convinced that he did so until he was ten months old. At the age of 11½ months he could readily imitate all sorts of actions, such as shaking his head and saying "Ah" to any dirty object, or by carefully and slowly putting his forefinger in the middle of the palm of his other hand, to the childish rhyme of "Pat it and pat it and mark it with T". It was amusing to behold his pleased expression after successfully performing any such accomplishment.

I do not know whether it is worth mentioning, as showing something about the strength of memory in a young child, that this one when 3 years and 23 days old on being shown an engraving of his grandfather, whom he had not seen for exactly six months, instantly recognised him and mentioned a whole string of events which had occurred whilst visiting him, and which certainly had never been mentioned in the interval.

Moral Sense. —The first sign of moral sense was noticed at the age of nearly 13 months. I said "Doddy (his nickname) won't give poor papa a kiss,—naughty Doddy". These words, without doubt, made him feel slightly uncomfortable; and at last when I had returned to my chair, he protruded his lips as a sign that he was ready to kiss me; and he then shook his hand in an angry manner until I came and received his kiss. Nearly the same little scene recurred in a few days, and the reconciliation seemed to give him so much satisfaction, that several times afterwards he pretended to be angry and slapped me, and then insisted on giving me a kiss. So that here we have a touch of the dramatic art, which is so strongly pronounced in most young children. About this time it became easy to work on his feelings and make him do whatever was wanted. When 2 years and 3 months old, he gave his last bit of gingerbread to his little sister, and then cried out with high self-approbation "Oh kind Doddy, kind Doddy". Two months later, he became extremely sensitive to ridicule, and was so suspicious that he often thought people who were laughing and talking together were laughing at him. A little later (2 years and 7½ months old) I met him coming out of the dining room with his eyes unnaturally bright, and an odd unnatural or affected manner, so that I went into the room to see who was there, and found that he had been taking pounded sugar, which he had been told not to do. As he had never been in any way punished, his odd manner certainly was not due to fear, and I suppose it was pleasurable excitement struggling with conscience. A fortnight afterwards, I met him coming out of the same room, and he was eyeing his pinafore which he had carefully rolled up; and again his manner was so odd that I determined to see what was within his pinafore, notwithstanding that he said there was nothing and repeatedly commanded me to "go away," and I found it stained with pickle-juice; so that here was carefully planned deceit. As this child was educated solely by working on his good feelings, he soon became as truthful, open, and tender, as anyone could desire.

Unconsciousness, Shyness.—No one can have attended to very young children without being struck at the unabashed manner in which they fixedly stare without blinking their eyes at a new face; an old person can look in this manner only at an animal or inanimate object. This, I believe, is the result of young children not thinking in the least about themselves, and therefore not being in the least shy, though they are sometimes afraid of strangers. I saw the first symptom of shyness in my child when nearly two years and three months old: this was shown towards myself, after an absence of ten days from home, chiefly by his eyes being kept slightly averted from mine; but he soon came and sat on my knee and kissed me, and all trace of shyness disappeared.

Means of Communication.—The noise of crying or rather of squalling, as no tears are shed for a long time, is of course uttered in an instinctive manner, but serves to show that there is suffering. After a time the sound differs according to the cause, such as hunger or pain. This was noticed when this infant was eleven weeks old, and I believe at an earlier age in another infant. Moreover, he appeared soon to learn to begin crying voluntarily, or to wrinkle his face in the manner proper to the occasion, so as to show that he wanted something. When 46 days old, he first made little noises without any meaning to please himself, and these soon became varied. An incipient laugh was observed on the 113th day, but much earlier in another infant. At this date I thought, as already remarked, that he began to try to imitate sounds, as he certainly did at a considerably later period. When five and a half months old, he uttered an articulate sound "da" but without any meaning attached to it. When a little over a year old, he used gestures to explain his wishes; to give a simple instance, he picked up a bit of paper and giving it to me pointed to the fire, as he had often seen and liked to see paper burnt. At exactly the age of a year, he made the great step of inventing a word for food, namely, *mum*, but what led him to it I did not discover. And now instead of beginning to cry when he was hungry, he used this word in a demonstrative manner or as a verb, implying "Give me food". This word therefore corresponds with *ham* as used by M. Taine's infant at the later age of 14 months. But he also used *mum* as a substantive of wide signification; thus he called sugar *shu-mum*, and a little later after he had learned the word "black," he called liquorice *black-shu-mum*, —black-sugar-food.

I was particularly struck with the fact that when asking for food by the word *mum* he gave to it (I will copy the words written down at the time) "a most strongly marked interrogatory sound at the end". He also gave to "Ah," which he chiefly used at first when recognising any person or his own image in a mirror, an exclamatory sound, such as we employ when surprised. I remark in my notes that the use of these intonations seemed to have arisen instinctively, and I regret that more observations were not made on this subject. I record, however, in my notes that at a rather later period, when between 18 and 21 months old, he modulated his voice in refusing peremptorily to do anything by a defiant whine, so as to express "That I won't"; and again his humph of assent expressed "Yes, to be sure". M. Taine also insists strongly on the highly expressive tones of the sounds made by his infant before she had learnt to speak. The interrogatory sound which my child gave to the word *mum* when asking for food is especially curious; for if anyone will use a single word or a short sentence in this manner, he will find that the musical pitch of his voice rises considerably at the close. I did not then see that this fact bears on the view which I have elsewhere maintained that before man used articulate language, he uttered notes in a true musical scale as does the anthropoid ape Hylobates.

Finally, the wants of an infant are at first made intelligible by instinctive cries, which after a time are modified in part unconsciously, and in part, as I believe, voluntarily as a means of communication,—by the unconscious expression of the features,—by gestures and in a marked manner by different intonations,—lastly by words of a general nature invented by himself, then of a more precise nature imitated from those which he hears; and these latter are acquired at a wonderfully quick rate. An infant understands to a certain extent, and as I believe at a very early period, the meaning or feelings of those who tend him, by the expression of their features. There can hardly be a doubt about this with respect to smiling; and it seemed to me that the infant whose biography I have here given understood a compassionate expression at a little over five months old. When 6 months and 11 days old he certainly showed sympathy with his nurse on her pretending to cry. When pleased after performing some new accomplishment, being then almost a year old, he evidently studied the expression of those around him. It was probably due to differences of expression and not merely of the form of the features that certain faces clearly pleased him much more than others, even at so early an age as a little over six months. Before he was a year old, he understood intonations and gestures, as well as several words and short sentences. He understood one word, namely, his nurse's name, exactly five months before he invented his first word *mum;* and this is what might have been expected, as we know that the lower animals easily learn to understand spoken words.

1. *Mind. Quarterly Review of Psychology and Philosophy* 2(1877): 285–94. Also, Howard E. Gruber and Paul H. Barrett, *Darwin on Man* (New York: Dutton, 1974, pp. 464–74).†

2. M. Taine, "On the Acquisition of Language by Children," *Mind. A Quarterly Review of Psychology and Philosophy* 2 (1877): 252–59.†

3. *Die Bewegungen der Thiere, &c.*, 1873, p. 11.

Testimonial to Mr. Darwin.
Evolution in the Netherlands
[Including a Letter from
Charles Darwin][1]

On the sixty-eighth birthday of your great countryman, Mr. Charles Darwin, an album with 217 photographs of his admirers in the Netherlands, among whom are eighty-one Doctors and twenty-one University Professors, was presented to him. To the album was joined a letter, of which you will find a copy here inclosed, with the answer of Mr. Darwin.

I suppose you will like to give to both letters a place in your very estimable journal, and therefore I have the honour to forward them to you.

Sir.—In the early part of the present century there resided in Amsterdam a physician, Dr. J. E. Doornik, who, in 1816, took his departure for Java, and passed the remainder of his life for the greater part in India. His name, though little known elsewhere than in the Netherlands, yet well deserves to be held in remembrance, since he occupies an honourable place among the pioneers of the theory of development. Among his numerous publications on natural philosophy, with a view to this, are worthy of mention his "Wijsgeerig-natuurkundig onderzoek aangaande den vorspronkelijken mensch en de vorspronkelijke stammen van deszelfs geslacht" ("Philosophic Researches concerning Original Man and the Origin of his Species"), and his treatise, "Over het begrip van levenskracht uit een geologisch oogpunt beschouwd" ("On the Idea of Vitality considered from a Geological Point of View"). The first already appeared in 1808; the latter, though written about the same time, was published in 1816, together with other papers more or less similar in tendency, under the title of "Wijsgeerig-natuurkundige verhandelingen" ("Treatises on the Philosophy of Natural History"). In these publications we recognise Doornik as a decided advocate of the theory that the various modifications in which life was revealed in consecutive times originated each from the other. He already occupies the point of vantage on which, shortly afterwards, Lamarck, with reference to the animal kingdom, and in his wake, Prévost and Lyell, with respect to the geological history of our globe, have taken their stand.

Yet the seeds scattered by Dr. Doornik did not take root in fertile soil. It is true that a Groningen professor, G. Bakker, combated at great length some of his arguments regarding the origin of man; it attracted but little public attention, and they soon passed into oblivion.

A generation had passed away ere the theory of evolution began to attract more attention in the Netherlands. The impulse was given by the appearance of the well-known work, "Vestiges of the Natural History of Creation," of which a Dutch translation was published in 1849 by Dr. T. H. van den Brock, Professor of Chemistry at the Military Medical College in Utrecht, with an introductory preface by the celebrated chemist, Prof. G. T. Mulder, as well known in England as elsewhere. This work excited a lively controversy, but its opponents were more numerous than its partisans. Remarkably enough, it found more favour with the general public, and especially with some theologians of liberal principles, than with the representatives of the natural sciences. The majority of zoologists and botanists of any celebrity in the Netherlands looked upon the writer's opinions as a chimera, and speculated on the weaker points rather than on the merits of the work. Notwithstanding, this presented no obstacle to a comparative success, and in 1854, even a third edition of the translation was published, enriched by the translator with numerous annotations.

Among the few Dutch *savants* to recognise the light which the theory of development spreads over creation, must be mentioned two Utrecht professors, viz., F. C. Donders and P. Harting. The former, in his inaugural address pronounced in 1848, "De Harmonie van het dierlijk leven, de openbaring van wetten" ("The Harmony of Animal Life, the Revelation of Laws"), expressed his opinion that, in the gradual change of form consequent upon change of circumstances, may lie the cause of the origin of differences which we are now wont to designate as species. The latter, in the winter of 1856, delivered a series of lectures before a mixed audience, on "The History of Creation," which he published the following year under the title of "Voorwereldlijke Scheppingen" ("Ante-mundane Creations"), with a diffuse supplement devoted to a critical consideration of the theory of development. Though herein he came to a standstill with a "non liquet," yet it cannot be denied that there gleamed through it his prepossession in favour of a theory which several years later his famed and learned colleague, J. van der Hoeven, Professor at Leyden, making a well-known French writer's words his own, was accustomed to signalise as an explanation, "de l'inconnu par l'impossible."

In 1858 your illustrious countryman, Sir Charles Lyell was staying for a few days in Utrecht. In the course of conversations with this distinguished *savant* on the theory of development, for which Lyell himself, at least in his writings, had shown himself no pleader, the learned of this country were first made observant of what had been and what was being done in that direction in England. He attracted attention to the treatise of Wallace in the Journal of the Linnean Society, and related how his friend Darwin had been occupied for years in an earnest study of this subject, and that ere long a work would appear from his pen, which, in his opinion, would make a considerable impression. From these conversations it was evident that Lyell himself was wavering. In the following edition of his "Principles of Geology," he declared himself, as we know, a partisan of the hypothesis of development, and Prof. Harting speedily followed in the same track. In his "Algemeene Dierkunde" ("General Zoology"), published in 1862, he was able to declare himself with full conviction a partisan of this hypothesis. Also another famous *savant*, Miquel, Professor of Botany at Utrecht, who had previously declared himself an opponent of the Theory of Development, became a convert to it in his later years, for although this is not expressed in his published writings, it was clearly manifest in his private conversation and in his lectures. To what must this conversion be attributed? With Harting and Miquel, as well as with Lyell and so many others in every country of

Europe, this was the fruit produced by the study of your "Origin of Species," published in 1859, which first furnished one vast basis for the theory of development. That work, translated into Dutch by Dr. F. C. Winkler, now conservator of the Geological, Mineralogical, and Paleontological collections in "Feyler's Foundation" at Haarlem excited great and general interest. It is true that a theory, striking so keenly and so deep at the roots of existing opinions and prejudices, could not be expected at once to meet with general approbation. Many even amongst naturalists offered vehement opposition. Prof. J. van der Hoeven, bred up as he was in the school of Cuvier, endeavoured to administer an antidote for what he regarded as a baneful poison by translating into our tongue Hopkins' well-known article in *Fraser's Magazine.*[2] However, neither this production nor the professor's influence over his students could withstand the current, especially when, after his death, the German zoologist, Prof. Emil Selenka, now Professor of Zoology at Erlangen, was appointed at Leyden. A decided advocate of your theory, he awakened in the younger zoologists a lively enthusiasm, and founded a school in which the conviction survives that the theory of development is the key to the explanation of the History of Creation.

In Utrecht, Prof. Harting, with convictions more and more decided, was busy in the same direction; and Selenka's successor in Leyden, Prof. C. K. Hoffmann, did not remain in the rear. Other names, among which are Groningen and Amsterdam professors, might here be cited. By the translation of your "Descent of Man" and "The Expressions of the Emotions in Man and Animals," with copious explanatory notes and by various original papers and translations treating on your theory, Dr. Hartogh Heys van Zouteveen has also largely contributed to the more general spread of your opinions in the Netherlands.

To testify how generally they are held in esteem among the younger zoologists and botanists, and more and more obtain among professors of analogous branches in this country, we might refer to a multitude of less important papers and articles in the periodicals.

This, however, we deem superfluous, since by offering for your acceptance an album, containing the portraits of a number of professional and amateur naturalists in the Netherlands, we offer a convincing proof of our estimation of your indefatigable endeavours in the promotion of science and our admiration of you, Sir, as the cynosure in this untrodden path. We recognise with pleasure Dr. Hartogh Heys van Zouteveen as the primary mover of such a demonstration of our homage. The execution, however, devolved upon the directors of the "Netherland Zoological Society," who reasoned that, with the presentation of this unpretending mark of esteem, a few words on the History of the Theory of Development in the Netherlands would not be entirely unacceptable, the more so, since this historic sketch clearly shows that, albeit some ideas in that direction had already been suggested here, yet to you alone reverts the honour of having formed by your writings a school of zealous and convinced partisans of the theory of development.

Among the names in the accompanying list you will observe several professors of Natural History, Anatomy. and Physiology at the three Dutch Universities, the "Athenaeum Illustre" of Amsterdam, and the Polytechnical Academy of Delft, the Conservators of the Zoological Museums, the Directors of the Zoological Gardens, and several lecturers on zoology and botany at the High Burghal Schools.

Accept, then, Sir, on your sixty-ninth birthday, this testimony of regard and esteem, not for any value it can have for you, but as a proof, which we are persuaded cannot but afford you some satisfaction, that the seeds by you so liberally strewn have also fallen on fertile soil in the Netherlands.

The following is Mr. Darwin's reply:—

Sir.—I received yesterday the magnificent present of the album, together with your letter. I hope that you will endeavour to find some means to express to the 217 distinguished observers and lovers of natural science, who have sent me their photographs, my gratitude for their extreme kindness. I feel deeply gratified by this gift, and I do not think that any testimonial more honourable to me could have been imagined. I am well aware that my books could never have been written, and would not have made any impression on the public mind, had not an immense amount of material been collected by a long series of admirable observers, and it is to them that honour is chiefly due.

I suppose that every worker at science occasionally feels depressed, and doubts whether what he has published has been worth the labour which it has cost him; but for the remaining years of my life, whenever I want cheering, I will look at the portraits of my distinguished co-workers in the field of science, and remember their generous sympathy. When I die the album will be a most precious bequest to my children. I must further express my obligation for the very interesting history contained in your letter of the progress of opinion in the Netherlands, with respect to evolution, the whole of which is quite new to me. I must again thank all my kind friends from my heart for their ever-memorable testimonial.

1. *Nature. A Weekly Illustrated Journal of Science*, vol. 15, 8 March 1877, pp. 410–12. The introduction to the article was written by P. Harting, Professor, University, Utrecht. The letter written to Darwin was sent by the Directors of the Netherlands Zoological Society, and signed by A. A. van Bemmelen, President, and H. T. Veth, Secretary.†

2. William Hopkins, "Physical Theories of the Phenomena of Life," *Fraser's*

Magazine, vol. 61, June 1860, pp. 739–52, and vol. 62, July 1860, pp. 74–90.†

◆◀ The Contractile Filaments of the Teasel[1]

The observations of my son Francis on the contractile filaments protruded from the glands of Dipsacus,[2] offer so new and remarkable a fact
in the physiology of plants, that any confirmation of them is valuable. I
hope therefore that you will publish the appended letter from Prof.
Cohn, of Breslau, whom every one will allow to be one of the highest
authorities in Europe on such a subject. Prof. Cohn's remarks were not
intended for publication, but he has kindly allowed me to lay them
before your readers.

Extract from Prof. Cohn's Letter

"Immediately after the receipt of your very kind letter of July 26 I went
to fetch Dipsacus, several species of which grow in our Botanic Garden;
and proceeding after your recommendations, I put transverse sections of
the cup-like bases of young leaves, or the epidermis of these parts carefully
removed from the green parenchyma, into distilled water. I thus had the
pleasure of witnessing with my own eyes this most curious discovery.
First I ascertained the anatomical structure of the pear-like glands which
are rather elegant and remarkable. From the basal cell rises the stalk-cell,
in the second story there are two cells, in the third four, and in the
uppermost series eight cuneiform cells converging to the centre. But you
may conceive how much I was surprised by seeing the filiform protuberances issuing from the apex of the glands; it was quite a perplexing
spectacle. The filaments are, in their refrangibility, very like the pseudopodia of some Rhizopods (*e.g.*, Arcella or Difflugia). I followed their
changes for some time, and remarked quite definitely, as I find described
in the paper of Mr. Francis Darwin how the protuberances slowly
lengthen out, crook themselves hooklike or winding, and get knobbed
either at the summit or midway; I saw the knobs or beads glide down the
thread, and at last be sucked into a globular mass adhering to the gland. I
saw the protuberances always rise between the septa of two or more
adjoining cells, but nearly as frequently between the *lateral* septa as on
the apical centre. Generally there were many protuberances on the same
gland, pressed forward out of different spots; sometimes I saw two
diverging branches proceed from the same point like a pair of compasses,
each behaving independently in its changes. But the most curious
appearance in these protuberances was a constant waving undulation

along their extension, sometimes slower and perceptible with difficulty, sometimes vigorous and quicker, but never ceasing; more delicate filaments appeared to me very like Vibrio, or the vibratory flagella of some Infusoria. Not finding a special description of the waving movements of the filaments in your son's paper, I asked some of my pupils if they saw anything remarkable in the filaments, without indicating what, but they all took the same impression as myself. The only facts I have not yet been able to witness of your son's discoveries are Figs. 6, 14, 15, and the moniliform contraction; nor have I yet found time to apply chemical reagents, of which your son has made such good use.

"Of course I am not able, after two days' inspection, to form a definite judgment about the true nature of the filiform protuberances. Putting aside the hypothesis of a parasitic Rhizopod, there are two probabilities which still balance in my mind, as clearly stated by your son. (1) The protuberances are secretions of some colloidal matter, absorbing water, but insoluble in it; the movements are physical (not vital ones), the elongation of the filaments depending upon the imbibition, their contraction on the withdrawal of water by different reagents. There are such substances, *e.g., myeline,* which shows rather similar changes in water. Please also to repeat the experiments I performed at the meeting of the British Association last year. Into a cylindrical glass containing soluble silicate of alkali (Wasserglas), diluted with half its amount of water, put a small piece of crystallised chloride of iron; from the fragment there rises a hollow reddish tube growing upwards and moving very quickly, like an Enteromorpha. But if you put into the diluted silicate some *protochloride* of iron (the latter is usually in the form of a powder, but may easily be brought by gentle pressure of the fingers into crumb-like masses), then from the lumps there arise innumerable filaments, very delicate and transparent, very like the glass threads of Hyalonema, which rise in fascicules vertically till they reach the surface of the fluid.

"But I cannot deny that the general impression produced by Dipsacus does not contradict the hypothesis that the changes of the filaments are the vital phenomena of protoplasmic pseudopodia.

"A French biologist (whose name I cannot just now remember) has proved many years ago (I think in an early number of the *Bull. de la Soc. Bot. de France*) that the water in the cups of Dipsacus is not a simple collection of rain in a gutter, but a secretion of the leaf bases. If this be truly the case, it is quite probable that the glands may have a special adaptation for this purpose. Indeed, I should not hesitate to agree with the vital theory, if there were any analogy known in plants. But further study of the phenomenon and the repetition of the chemical reactions which your son has already indicated, will, I hope, in a short time enable me to form a more decided judgment in this perplexing dilemma.

"In the meantime I am happy to congratulate Mr. Francis Darwin and yourself on account of the extraordinary discovery he has made, and the truly scientific paper in which he has elaborated it, and which has added a series of quite unexpected facts to the physiology of plants."

In a subsequent letter, Prof. Cohn describes what appear to him as thinned points or pores in the cell wall of the glands from which the filaments seem to be protruded. He also mentions the very curious fact which he has discovered, that by adding iodine to the detached epidermis of the leaf cups of Dipsacus the whole fluid contents of the epidermis cells turn blue like diluted starch paste, although no starch grains are met with in any epidermis cell except in the stomata.[3] He adds that the basal cell of the gland becomes blue, while the rest of it and the excreted globules are stained yellow.

I may add that I have heard from Prof. Hoffmann, of Giessen, that he formerly observed contractile filament of a somewhat similar nature on the annulus of *Agaricus muscarius*. He has described them in the *Botanische Zeitung*, 1853, and figured them, *ibid.*, 1859, tab. xi. Fig. 17.

1. *Nature. A Weekly Illustrated Journal of Science*, vol. 16, 23 August 1877, p. 339.†
2. Abstract published in *Proc.* Roy. Soc., 1877, No. 179; published in full in *Quarterly Journal of Microscopical Science*, July, 1877.
3. Prof. Cohn adds that the blue coloration of the epidermis by iodine occurs in the leaves of Ornithogalum.

⚫ Sexual Selection in Relation to Monkeys[1]

In the discussion on Sexual Selection in my "Descent of Man," no case interested and perplexed me so much as the brightly-coloured hinder ends and adjoining parts of certain monkeys. As these parts are more brightly coloured in one sex than the other, and as they become more brilliant during the season of love, I concluded that the colours had been gained as a sexual attraction. I was well aware that I thus laid myself open to ridicule; though in fact it is not more surprising that a monkey should display his bright-red hinder end than that a peacock should display his magnificent tail. I had, however, at that time no evidence of monkeys exhibiting this part of their bodies during their courtship; and such display in the case of birds affords the best evidence that the ornaments of the males are of service to them by attracting or exciting the females. I have lately read an article by Joh. von Fischer, of Gotha, published in *Der Zoologische Garten*, April, 1876,[2] on the expression of monkeys under various emotions, which is well worthy of study by any one interested in the subject, and which shows that the author is a careful

and acute observer. In this article there is an account of the behaviour of
a young male mandrill when he first beheld himself in a looking-glass,
and it is added, that after a time he turned round and presented his red
hinder end to the glass. Accordingly I wrote to Herr J. von Fischer to ask
what he supposed was the meaning of this strange action, and he has sent
me two long letters full of new and curious details, which will, I hope, be
hereafter published.[3] He says that he was himself at first perplexed by the
above action, and was thus led carefully to observe several individuals of
various other species of monkeys, which he has long kept in his house.
He finds that not only the mandrill (*Cynocephalus mormon*) but the drill
(*C. leucophaeus*) and three other kinds of baboons (*C. hamadryas,
sphinx,* and *babouin*) also *Cynopithecus niger,* and *Macacus rhesus* and
nemestrinus, turn this part of their bodies, which in all these species is
more or less brightly coloured, to him when they are pleased, and to
other persons as a sort of greeting. He took pains to cure a *Macacus
rhesus,* which he had kept for five years, of this indecorous habit, and at
last succeeded. These monkeys are particularly apt to act in this manner,
grinning at the same time, when first introduced to a new monkey, but
often also to their old monkey friends; and after this mutual display they
begin to play together. The young mandrill ceased spontaneously after a
time to act in this manner towards his master, von Fischer, but continued to do so towards persons who were strangers and to new monkeys. A young *Cynopithecus niger* never acted, excepting on one
occasion, in this way towards his master, but frequently towards
strangers, and continues to do so up to the present time. From these facts
von Fischer concludes that the monkeys which behaved in this manner
before a looking-glass (viz., the mandrill, drill, *Cynopithecus niger,
Macacus rhesus,* and *nemestrinus*) acted as if their reflection were a new
acquaintance. The mandrill and drill, which have their hinder ends
especially ornamented, display it even whilst quite young, more frequently and more ostentatiously than do the other kinds. Next in order
comes *Cynocephalus hamadryas,* whilst the other species act in this
manner seldomer. The individuals, however, of the same species, vary in
this respect, and some which were very shy never displayed their hinder
ends. It deserves especial attention that von Fischer has never seen any
species purposely exhibit the hinder part of its body, if not at all
coloured. This remark applies to many individuals of *Macacus cynomol-
gus* and *Cercocebus radiatus* (which is closely allied to *M. rhesus*), to
three species of Cercopithecus and several American monkeys. The habit
of turning the hinder ends as a greeting to an old friend or new
acquaintance, which seems to us so odd, is not really more so than the
habits of many savages, for instance that of rubbing their bellies with
their hands, or rubbing noses together. The habit with the mandrill and

drill seems to be instinctive or inherited, as it was followed by very young animals; but it is modified or guided, like so many other instincts, by observation, for von Fischer says that they take pains to make their display fully, and if made before two observers, they turn to him who seems to pay the most attention.

With respect to the origin of the habit, von Fischer remarks that his monkeys like to have their naked hinder ends patted or stroked, and that they then grunt with pleasure. They often also turn this part of their bodies to other monkeys to have bits of dirt picked off, and so no doubt it would be with respect to thorns. But the habit with adult animals is connected to a certain extent with sexual feelings, for von Fischer watched through a glass door a female *Cynopithecus niger,* and she during several days, "umdrehte und dem Männchen mit gurgelnden Tönen die stark geröthete Sitzfläche zeigte, was ich früher nie an diesem Thier bemerkt hatte. Beim Anblick dieses Gegenstandes erregte sich das Männchen sichtlich, denn es polterte heftig an den Stäben, ebenfalls gurgelnde Laute ausstossend." As all the monkeys which have the hinder parts of their bodies more or less bright coloured live, according to von Fischer, in open rocky places, he thinks that these colours serve to render one sex conspicuous at a distance to the other; but as monkeys are such gregarious animals, I should have thought that there was no need for the sexes to recognise each other at a distance. It seems to me more probable that the bright colours, whether on the face or hinder end, or, as in the mandrill, on both, serve as a sexual ornament and attraction. Anyhow, as we now know that monkeys have the habit of turning their hinder ends towards other monkeys, it ceases to be at all surprising that it should have been this part of their bodies which has been more or less decorated. The fact that it is only the monkeys thus characterised which, as far as at present known, act in this manner as a greeting towards other monkeys, renders it doubtful whether the habit was first acquired from some independent cause, and that afterwards the parts in question were coloured as a sexual ornament; or whether the colouring and the habit of turning round were first acquired through variation and sexual selection, and that afterwards the habit was retained as a sign of pleasure or as a greeting, through the principle of inherited association. This principle apparently comes into play on many occasions: thus it is generally admitted that the songs of birds serve mainly as an attraction during the season of love, and that the *leks,* or great congregations of the black grouse, are connected with their courtship; but the habit of singing has been retained by some birds when they feel happy, for instance by the common robin, and the habit of congregating has been retained by the black grouse, during other seasons of the year.

I beg leave to refer to one other point in relation to sexual selection. It has been objected that this form of selection, as far as the ornaments of the males are concerned, implies that all the females within the same district must possess and exercise exactly the same taste. It should, however, be observed in the first place, that although the range of variation of a species may be very large, it is by no means indefinite. I have elsewhere given a good instance of this fact in the pigeon,[4] of which there are at least a hundred varieties differing widely in their colours, and at least a score of varieties of the fowl differing in the same manner; but the range of colour in these two species is extremely distinct. Therefore the females of natural species cannot have an unlimited scope for their taste. In the second place, I presume that no supporter of the principle of sexual selection believes that the females select particular points of beauty in the males; they are merely excited or attracted in a greater degree by one male than by another, and this seems often to depend, especially with birds, on brilliant colouring. Even man, excepting perhaps an artist, does not analyse the slight differences in the features of the woman whom he may admire, on which her beauty depends. The male mandrill has not only the hinder end of his body, but his face gorgeously coloured and marked with oblique ridges, a yellow beard, and other ornaments. We may infer from what we see of the variation of animals under domestication, that the above several ornaments of the mandrill were gradually acquired by one individual varying a little in one way, and another individual in another way. The males which were the handsomest or the most attractive in any manner to the females would pair oftenest, and would leave rather more offspring than other males. The offspring of the former, although variously intercrossed, would either inherit the peculiarities of their fathers, or transmit an increased tendency to vary in the same manner. Consequently the whole body of males inhabiting the same country, would tend from the effects of constant intercrossing to become modified almost uniformly, but some-times a little more in one character and sometimes in another, though at an extremely slow rate; all ultimately being thus rendered more attractive to the females. The process is like that which I have called unconscious selection by man, and of which I have given several instances. In one country the inhabitants value a fleet or light dog or horse, and in another country a heavier and more powerful one; in neither country is there any selection of the individual animals with lighter or stronger bodies and limbs; nevertheless after a considerable lapse of time the individuals are found to have been modified in the desired manner almost uniformly, though differently in each country. In two absolutely distinct countries inhabited by the same species, the individuals of which can never during long ages have intermigrated and intercrossed, and where, moreover, the variations will probably not have been identically the same, sexual selection might cause the males to differ. Nor does the belief appear to me altogether fanciful that two sets of females, surrounded by a very different environment, would be apt to acquire somewhat different tastes with respect to form, sound, or colour. However this may be, I have given in my "Descent of Man" instances of closely-allied birds inhabiting distinct countries, of which the young and the females cannot be distinguished, whilst the adult males differ considerably, and this may be attributed with much probability to the action of sexual selection.[5]

1. *Nature. A Weekly Illustrated Journal of Science*, vol. 15, 2 November 1876, pp. 18–19.†
2. Johann von Fischer, "Aus dem Leben eines jungen Madril (Cynocephalus mormon): Seine Erkrankung und sein Tod," *Der Zoologische Garten* 17 (1876): 116–27, 174–79.†
3. Johann von Fischer, "Aus dem Leben eines Drill's (Cynocephalus leucophaeus)," *Der Zoologische Garten* 18 (1877): 73–97.†
4. *The Variation of Animals and Plants under Domestication*, 2 vols. (London: Murray, 1868), vol. 1, chap. 5, 6.†
5. *The Descent of Man, and Selection in Relation to Sex*, 2 vols. (London: Murray, 1871), chap. 13–16.†

◖ Fritz Müller on Flowers and Insects[1]

The enclosed letter[2] from that excellent observer, Fritz Müller, contains some miscellaneous observations on certain plants and insects of South Brazil, which are so new and curious that they will probably interest your naturalist readers. With respect to his case of bees getting their abdomens dusted with pollen while gnawing the glands of the calyx of one of the Malpighiaceae,[3] and thus effecting the cross-fertilisation of the flowers, I will remark that this case is closely analogous to that of Coronilla recorded by Mr. Farrer[4] in your journal some years ago, in which parts of the flowers have been greatly modified, so that bees may act as fertilisers while sucking the secretion on the outside of the calyx. The case is interesting in another way. My son Francis[5] has shown that the food-bodies of the Bull's-horn Acacia, which are consumed by the ants that protect the tree from its enemies (as described by Mr. Belt[6]), consist of modified glands; and he suggests that aboriginally the ants licked a secretion from the glands, but that at a subsequent period the glands were rendered more nutritious and attractive by the retention of the secretion and other changes, and that they were then devoured by the ants. But my son could advance no case of glands being thus gnawed or devoured by insects, and here we have an example.

With respect to *Solanum palinacanthum*, which bears two kinds of flowers on the same plant, one with a long style and large stigma, the other with a short style and small stigma, I think more evidence is requisite before this species can be considered as truly heterostyled, for I find that the pollen-grains from the two forms do not differ in diameter. Theoretically it would be a great anomaly if flowers on the same plant were functionally heterostyled, for this structure is evidently adapted to insure the cross-fertilisation of distinct plants. Is it not more probable that the case is merely one of the same plant bearing male flowers through partial abortion, together with the original hermaphrodite flowers? Fritz Müller justly expresses surprise at Mr. Leggett's suspicion that the difference in length of the pistil in the flowers of *Pontederia cordata*[7] of the United States is due to difference of age; but since the publication of my book[8] Mr. Leggett has fully admitted, in the *Bulletin* of the Torrey Botanical Club,[9] that this species is truly heterostyled and trimorphic. The last point on which I wish to remark is the difference between the males and females of certain butterflies in the neuration of the wings, and in the presence of tufts of peculiarly-formed scales. An American naturalist has recently advanced this case as one that cannot possibly be accounted for by sexual selection. Consequently, Fritz Müller's observations which have been published in full in a recent number of *Kosmos*,[10] are to me highly interesting, and in themselves highly remarkable.

1. *Nature. A Weekly Illustrated Journal of Science*, vol. 17, 29 November 1877, p. 78.†

2. The letter of Fritz Müller, which, because of its length is not reprinted here, contains descriptions of many kinds of flowers and various conditions related to their fertilization by insects. Müller also mentioned certain butterflies, the males of which have scent-producing scales, thought to be for sexual attraction of the females.†

3. Malpighiacaea: a family of tropical shrubs, including some ornamental climbing vines.†

4. T. H. Farrer, "Fertilisation of Papilionaceous Flowers: Coronilla," *Nature* 10 (1874): 169–70.†

5. Francis Darwin, "On the Glandular Bodies on Acacia sphaerocephala and Cecropia peltata, Serving as Food for Ants: With an Appendix on the Nectar-glands of the Common Brake Fern, Pteris aquilina," *Journal of the Linnean Society (Botany)* 15 (1877): 389–409.†

6. Thomas Belt, *The Naturalist in Nicaragua* (London: Murray, 1874, p. 218).†

7. Common pickerelweed, an aquatic plant.†

8. *The Different Forms of Flowers on Plants of the Same Species* (London: Murray, 1877, p. 252).†

9. William Henry Leggett, "[Notes on Structure, Dimophism,] Lepiduum Virginicum, L., . . . Pontederia cordata, L., *New York Botanical Club Bulletin* 1 (1870): 5–6; 2 (1871): 25–26; 6 (1875–79): 62–63, 163–64, 170–71, 179.†

10. Fritz Müller, "The Scent-scales of the Male Maracujá Butterflies," *Kosmos* 1 (1877): 391–95, transl. E. A. Elliott, in George B. Longstaff, *Butterfly-hunting in Many Lands* (London: Longmans, Green, 1912, pp. 655–59).†

❧ Growth under Difficulties[1]

The enclosed branch of Cotyledon (Echeveria stolonifera) was cut from a plant growing in my greenhouse, and was suspended on August 10 in my study, which is a dry room, and in which a fire burns most of the year. It has sent out two fine flowering stems which, from the position in which the branch was hung, have bent upwards (as may be seen in the figure). They have now (December 6) begun to flower. You will see that the plant has sent out a number of small roots. I may add that the specimen weighed on September 1 45.46 grammes, on December 6 36.94 grammes, so that its growth has continued in spite of a considerable loss from evaporation.

1. *Gardeners' Chronicle. A Weekly Illustrated Journal of Horticulture and Allied Subjects*, n.s., vol. 8, 29 December 1877, p. 805.†

Fig. 1. *Cotyledon (Echeveria) stolonifera.*

⚓ Transplantation of Shells[1]

It is well known that animals and plants inhabiting freshwater have, as a general rule, a very wide distribution; yet each river system, with all the pools and lakes in connection with it, seems completely cut off from every other system of the same country. Still more complete is the separation between the freshwaters of distinct continents or of islands; nevertheless they often possess freshwater species in common. In my "Origin of Species" I have suggested various means of transportal; but as few facts on this head are positively known, the case given in the adjoined letter of a living Unio, which had caught one of the toes of a duck's foot between its valves, and was secured in the act of being transported, seems to me well worth recording.

The following case will, I think prove of interest to you, as it corroborates your belief that freshwater shells are sometimes transplanted by the agency of aquatic birds.

In the sketch I have endeavoured to give you a correct idea of the way in which the shell was attached to the duck's foot.

It was given to me by Mr. H. L. Newcomb, who shot the bird, which was a blue-winged teal (*Querquedula discors*), while flying, near the Artichoke river at West Newbury, Mass., September 6, 1877. The shell, the common mussel, or clam (*Unio complanatus*), is a very abundant species, being found in nearly all the rivers and ponds of the Atlantic slope. How long the shell had been attached is only a matter of conjecture, but it had abraded the skin of the bird's toe, and left quite an impression. It was living when the bird was shot.

It would have undoubtedly been transplanted to some pond or river, perhaps miles from its original home, had the bird not been shot, and might then have propagated its kind.

1. *Nature. A Weekly Illustrated Journal of Science*, vol. 18, 30 May 1878, pp. 120–21. The letter to Darwin was written by Arthur H. Gray.†

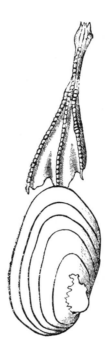

Fig. 1. Clam and duck's foot.

✒ Prefatory Letter: Flowers and
Their Unbidden Guests[1]

I am extremely glad to hear that you have undertaken to edit Kerner's work on *Flowers and their Unbidden Guests;* for it opens out a highly original and curious field of research. It is possible that some of Kerner's generalisations may hereafter require to be slightly modified; but I feel sure that every remark which he has made well deserves careful consideration. The beauty and poetry of flowers will not be at all lessened to the general observer, by his being led through Kerner's investigation to notice various small, and apparently quite unimportant, details of structure,—such as the presence of differently directed hairs, viscid glands, etc., which prevent the access of certain insects, and not of others. He will, I believe, come to the conclusion that flowers are not only delightful from their beauty and fragrance, but display most wonderful adaptations for various purposes. I cordially wish that your translation may find many readers, not so much for your sake as for theirs.

1. Pp. v–vi in A. Kerner, *Flowers and Their Unbidden Guests*, W. Ogle, trans., rev., ed. (London: Paul, 1878). Darwin's letter is addressed to Dr. Ogle.†

ᕈ Fritz Müller on a Frog Having Eggs on Its Back—on the Abortion of the Hairs on the Legs of Certain Caddis-Flies, &c.[1]

Several of the facts given in the following letter from Fritz Müller, especially those in the third paragraph, appear to me very interesting.[2] Many persons have felt much perplexed about the steps or means by which structures rendered useless under changed conditions of life, at first become reduced, and finally quite disappear. A more striking case of such disappearance has never been published than that here given by Fritz Müller. Several years ago some valuable letters on this subject by Mr. Romanes[3] (together with one by me[4]) were inserted in the columns of Nature. Since then various facts have often led me to speculate on the existence of some inherent tendency in every part of every organism to be gradually reduced and to disappear, unless in some manner prevented. But beyond this vague speculation I could never clearly see my way. As far, therefore, as I can judge, the explanation suggested by Fritz Müller well deserves the careful consideration of all those who are interested on such points, and may prove of widely extended application. Hardly anyone who has considered such cases as those of the stripes which occasionally appear on the legs and even bodies of horses and asses or of the development of certain muscles in man which are not proper to him, but are common in the Quadrumana—or again, of some peloric flowers—will doubt that characters lost for an almost endless number of generations, may suddenly reappear. In the case of natural species we are so much accustomed to apply the term reversion or atavism to the reappearance of a lost part that we are liable to forget that its disappearance may be equally due to this same cause.

As every modification, whether or not due to reversion, may be considered as a case of variation, the important law or conclusion arrived at by the mathematician Delboeuf,[5] may be here applied; and I will quote Mr. Murphy's[6] condensed statement ("Habit and Intelligence," 1879, p. 241) with respect to it: "If in any species a number of individuals, bearing a ratio not infinitely small to the entire number of births, are in every generation born with any particular variation which is neither beneficial nor injurious to its possessors, and if the effect of the variation is not counteracted by reversion, the proportion of the new variety to the original form will constantly increase until it approaches indefinitely near to equality." Now in the case advanced by Fritz Müller the cause of the variation is supposed to be atavism to a very remote progenitor, and this may have wholly prevailed over any tendency to atavism to more recent progenitors; and of such prevalence analogous instances could be given.

1. *Nature. A Weekly Illustrated Journal of Science*, vol. 19, 20 March 1879, pp. 462–63.†

2. In the letter, too long to be reproduced here, Fritz Müller said, "Thus there may even now exist in all caddis-flies an ancestral tendency [atavism] to the production of hairless feet in the pupae, which tendency in the common species is victoriously counteracted by natural selection, for any pupa, unable to swim, would be mercilessly drowned. But as soon as swimming is not required and the fringes consequently become useless, this ancestral tendency, not counterbalanced by natural selection, will prevail, and lead to the abortion of the fringes." Müller's figures of the frog, and the legs of caddis-fly pupae, are reproduced here.†

3. George Romanes, "Natural Selection and Dysteleology," *Nature. A Weekly Illustrated Journal of Science*, vol. 9, 12 March 1874, pp. 361–62, and "Rudimentary Organs," *Nature*, vol. 9, 9 April 1874, pp. 440–41.†

4. See p. 177, "On the Males and Complemental Males of Certain Cirripedes, and on Rudimentary Structures."†

5. J. Delboeuf, "Une Loi Mathématique Applicable à la Théorie du Transformisme," *Revue Scientifique de la France et de L'Étranger* 12 (1877): 669–79.†

6. Joseph John Murphy, *Habit and Intelligence: A Series of Essays on the Laws of Life and Mind* (London: Macmillan, 1879).†

Fig. 1. Frog with eggs on the back.

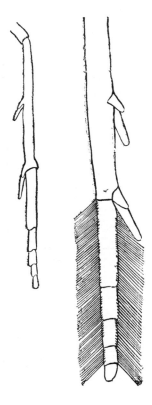

Fig. 2. Tibia and tarsus of the two pairs of legs of the pupa of a species of Leptoceridae, inhabiting Bromeliae.
Fig. 3. The same of a nearly allied species inhabiting rivulets.

☙ Rats and Water-Casks[1]

Mr. Nicols says, in Nature, vol. xix. p. 433:—

"A ship's carpenter told me that, in the old days, before the use of iron tanks on board ship became general, the rats used to attack the water-casks, cutting the stave so thin that they could suck the water through the wood without actually making a hole in it. If any one could substantiate this it would have an important bearing on the question under consideration."

Capt. Wickham, when First Lieutenant on board H.M.S. *Beagle*, told me that when he was a midshipman it was his duty, on one of the king's ships to see that certain vessels on deck were always kept full of water, in order to prevent the rats gnawing holes through the water casks, and that through such holes nearly all the water in a cask would leak away.

1. *Nature. A Weekly Illustrated Journal of Science*, vol. 19, 27 March 1879, p. 481.†

➴ Fertility of Hybrids from the Common and Chinese Goose[1]

In the "Origin of Species" I have given the case, on the excellent authority of Mr. Eyton, of hybrids from the common and Chinese goose (*Anser cygnoides*) being quite fertile *inter se;* and this is the most remarkable fact as yet recorded with respect to the fertility of hybrids, for many persons feel sceptical about the hare and the rabbit. I was therefore glad to have the opportunity of repeating the trial, through the kindness of the Rev. Dr. Goodacre, who gave me a brother and sister hybrid from the same hatch. A union between these birds was therefore a shade closer than that made by Mr. Eyton, who coupled a brother and sister from different hatches. As there were tame geese at a neighbouring farm-house, and as my birds were apt to wander, they were confined in a large cage; but we found out after a time that a daily visit to a pond (during which time they were watched) was indispensable for the fertilisation of the eggs. The result was that three birds were hatched from the first set of eggs; two others were fully formed, but did not succeed in breaking through the shell; and the remaining first-laid eggs were unfertilised. From a second lot of eggs two birds were hatched. I should have thought that this small number of only five birds reared alive indicated some degree of infertility in the parents, had not Mr. Eyton reared eight hybrids from one set of eggs. My small success may perhaps be attributed in part to the confinement of the parents and their very close relationship. The five hybrids, grandchildren of the pure parents, were extremely fine birds, and resembled in every detail their hybrid parents. It appeared superfluous to test the fertility of these hybrids with either pure species, as this had been done by Dr. Goodacre; and every possible gradation between them may be commonly seen, according to Mr. Blyth and Capt. Hutton in India, and occasionally in England.

The fact of these two species of geese breeding so freely together is remarkable from their distinctness, which has led some ornithologists to place them in separate genera or sub-genera. The Chinese goose differs conspicuously from the common goose in the knob at the base of the beak, which affects the shape of the skull; in the very long neck with a stripe of dark feathers running down it; in the number of the sacral vertebrae; in the proportions of the sternum[2]; markedly in the voice or "resonant trumpeting," and, according to Mr. Dixon,[3] in the period of incubation, though this has been denied by others. In the wild state the two species inhabit different regions.[4] I am aware that Dr. Goodacre is inclined to believe that *Anser cygnoides* is only a variety of the common goose raised under domestication. He shows that in all the above indicated characters, parallel or almost parallel variations have arisen with other animals under domestication. But it would, I believe, be quite impossible to find so many *concurrent and constant* points of difference as the above, between any two domesticated varieties of the same species. If these two species are classed as varieties, so might the horse and ass, or the hare and rabbit.

The fertility of the hybrids in the present case probably depends to a limited degree (1) on the reproductive power of all the Anatidae being very little affected by changed conditions, and (2) on both species having been long domesticated. For the view propounded by Pallas,[5] that domestication tends to eliminate the almost universal sterility of species when intercrossed, becomes the more probable the more we learn about the history and multiple origin of most of our domesticated animals. This view, in so far as it can be trusted, removes a difficulty in the acceptance of the descent-theory, for it shows that mutual sterility is no safe and immutable criterion of specific difference. We have, however, much better evidence on this head, in the fact of two individuals of the same form of heterostyled plants, which belong to the same species as certainly as do two individuals of any species, yielding when crossed fewer seeds than the normal number, and the plants raised from such seeds being, in the case of *Lythrum salicaria*, as sterile as are the most sterile hybrids.

1. *Nature. A Weekly Illustrated Journal of Science*, vol. 21, 1 January 1880, p. 207.†

2. Charlesworth's "Mag. of Nat. Hist.," vol. iv., new series, 1840, p. 90. T. C. Eyton, "Remarks on the Skeletons of the Common and Chinese Goose."

3. "Ornamental and Domestic Poultry," 1848, p. 85.

4. Dr. L. v. Schrenck's "Reisen und Forschungen im Amur-Land," B. i. p. 457.

5. Peter Simon Pallas, "Memoire sur la variation des animaux; première partie, lue à l'Assemblée publique du 19 Septembre, en presence de Msgr. le Prince Royal de Prusse," *Akademiia nauk SSSR. Acta academiae scientiarum imperialis Petropolitanae* 4 (1780): 69–102.†

◄ The Sexual Colours of Certain Butterflies[1]

Dr. Schulte, of Fürstenwalde, has called my attention to the beautiful colours which appear on all four wings of a butterfly, the *Diadema bolina*, when looked at from one point of view. The two sexes of this butterfly differ widely in colour. The wings of the male, when viewed from behind, are black with six marks of pure white, and they present an elegant appearance; but when viewed in front, in which position, as Dr. Schulte remarks, the male would be seen by the female when approaching her, the white marks are surrounded by a halo of beautiful blue. Mr. Butler, also showed me in the British Museum an analogous and more striking case in the genus Apatura, in which the sexes likewise differ in colour, and in the males the most magnificent green and blue tints are visible only to a person standing in front. Again with Ornithoptera[2] the hind wings of the male are in several species of a fine golden yellow, but only when viewed in front; this holds good with *O. magellanus* but here we have a partial exception, as was pointed out to me by Mr. Butler, for the hind wings when viewed from behind change from a golden tint into a pale iridescent blue. Whether this latter colour has any special meaning could be discovered only by some one observing the behaviour of the male in its native home. Butterflies when at rest close their wings, and their lower surfaces, which are often obscurely tinted, can then alone be seen; and this it is generally admitted, serves as a protection. But the males, when courting the females, alternately depress and raise their wings, thus displaying the brilliantly coloured upper surface; and it seems the natural inference that they act in this manner in order to charm or excite the females. In the cases above described this inference is rendered much more probable, as the full beauty of the male can be seen by the female only when he advances towards her. We are thus reminded of the elaborate and diversified manner in which the males of many birds, for instance the peacock, argus pheasant, &c., display their wonderful plumage to the greatest advantage before their unadorned friends.

The consideration of these cases leads me to add a few remarks on how far consciousness necessarily comes into play in the first acquirement of certain instincts, including sexual display; for as all the males of the same species behave in the same manner whilst courting the female, we may infer that the display is at least now instinctive. Most naturalists appear to believe that every instinct was at first consciously performed; but this seems to me an erroneous conclusion in many cases, though true in others. Birds, when variously excited, assume strange attitudes and ruffle their feathers; and if the erection of the feathers in some particular manner were advantageous to a male whilst courting the female, there does not seem to be any improbability in the offspring which inherited this action being favoured; and we know that odd tricks and new gestures performed unconsciously are often inherited by man.[3] We may take a different case (which I believe has been already advanced by some one), that of young ground birds which squat and hide themselves when in danger immediately after emerging from the egg; and here it seems hardly possible that the habit could have been consciously acquired just after birth without any experience. But if those young birds which remained motionless when frightened, were oftener preserved from beasts of prey than those which tried to escape, the habit of squatting might have been acquired without any consciousness on the part of the young birds. This reasoning applies with special force to some young wading and water birds, the old of which do not conceal themselves when in danger. Again a hen partridge when there is danger flies a short distance from her young ones and leaves them closely squatted; she then flutters along the ground as if crippled, in the wonderful manner which is familiar to almost every one; but differently from a really wounded bird, she makes herself conspicuous. Now it is more than doubtful whether any bird ever existed with sufficient intellect to think that if she imitated the actions of an injured bird she would draw away a dog or other enemy from her young ones; for this presupposes that she had observed such actions in an injured comrade and knew that they would tempt an enemy to pursuit. Many naturalists now admit that, for instance, the hinge of a shell has been formed by the preservation and inheritance of successive useful variations, the individuals with a somewhat better constructed shell being preserved in greater numbers than those with a less well constructed one; and why should not beneficial variations in the inherited actions of a partridge be preserved in like manner, without any thought or conscious intention on her part any more than on the part of the mullusc, the hinge of whose shell has been modified and improved independently of consciousness.

1. *Nature. A Weekly Illustrated Journal of Science*, vol. 21, 8 January 1880, p. 237.†

2. Large Malayan butterflies, females larger than males and less brightly colored.†

3. See "Darwin's M Notebook," in Howard E. Gruber and Paul H. Barrett, *Darwin on Man* (New York: Dutton, 1974, p. 266).†

◀ The Omori Shell Mounds[1]

I have received the enclosed letter from Prof. Morse,[2] with a request that I should forward it to you. I hope that it may be published, for the article in Nature[3] to which it refers seemed to me to do very scant justice to Prof. Morse's work. I refer more especially to the evidence adduced by him on cannibalism by the ancient inhabitants of Japan—on their platycnemic tibiae—on their degree of skill in ceramic art—and beyond all other points, on the changes in the molluscan fauna of the islands since the period in question.

It is a remarkable fact, which incidentally appears in Prof. Morse's memoir, that several Japanese gentlemen have already formed large collections of the shells of the Archipelago, and have zealously aided him in the investigation of the prehistoric mounds. This is a most encouraging omen of the future progress of science in Japan.

1. *Nature. A Weekly Illustrated Journal of Science*, vol. 21, 15 April 1880, p. 561.†
   2. E. S. Morse, in his accompanying letter (because of its length not reprinted here), refutes numerous complaints given in a review by F. V. Dickins of a previous memoir by Morse on shell-mounds of Omori. Morse accused Dickins of not having carefully read his memoir, and of not being familiar with the geography and paleontology of Japan.†
   3. Fredk. V. Dickins, "Pre-historic Man in Japan," *Nature*, vol. 21, 12 February 1880, p. 350.†

✦ Sir Wyville Thomson and Natural Selection[1]

I am sorry to find that Sir Wyville Thomson does not understand the principle of natural selection, as explained by Mr. Wallace and myself. If he had done so, he could not have written the following sentence in the Introduction to the Voyage of the *Challenger*[2]:—"The character of the abyssal fauna refuses to give the least support to the theory which refers the evolution of species to extreme variation guided only by natural selection." This is a standard of criticism not uncommonly reached by theologians and metaphysicians, when they write on scientific subjects, but is something new as coming from a naturalist. Prof. Huxley demurs to it in the last number of Nature[3]; but he does not touch on the expression of *extreme variation*, nor on that of evolution being guided *only* by natural selection. Can Sir Wyville Thomson name any one who has said that the evolution of species depends only on natural selection? As far as concerns myself, I believe that no one has brought forward so many observations on the effects of the use and disuse of parts, as I have done in my "Variation of Animals and Plants under Domestication"; and these observations were made for this special object. I have likewise there adduced a considerable body of facts, showing the direct action of external conditions on organisms; though no doubt since my books were published much as been learnt on this head. If Sir Wyville Thomson were to visit the yard of a breeder, and saw all his cattle or sheep almost absolutely true, that is, closely similar, he would exclaim: "Sir, I see here no extreme variation; nor can I find any support to the belief that you have followed the principle of selection in the breeding of your animals." From what I formerly saw of breeders, I have no doubt that the man thus rebuked would have smiled and said not a word. If he had afterwards told the story to other breeders, I greatly fear that they would have used emphatic but irreverent language about naturalists.

1. *Nature. A Weekly Illustrated Journal of Science*, vol. 23, 11 November 1880, p. 32.†

2. Charles Wyville Thomson, *The Voyage of H. M. S. Challenger, Zoology* (Edinburgh: Longmans, 1880, vol. 1, p. 50).†

3. T. H. Huxley, "The Coming of Age of the Origin of Species," *Nature*, vol. 22, 6 May 1880, pp. 1–4.†

⋏ Black Sheep[1]

The following extract of a letter from Mr. Sanderson of Chislehurst, who permits me to publish it, seems worth placing on record. It relates to the former frequent appearance of spotted or black sheep in the Australian flocks, as long as animals thus coloured were of use to man, although they were never, as far as Mr. Sanderson knows, separately bred from, and certainly not in his own case. On the other hand, as soon as coloured sheep ceased to be of use they were no longer allowed to grow up, and their numbers rapidly decreased. I have elsewhere assigned reasons for the belief that the occasional appearance of dark-coloured or piebald sheep is due to reversion to the primeval colouring of the species. This tendency to reversion appears to be most difficult quite to eradicate, and quickly to gain in strength if there is no selection. Mr. Sanderson writes:—"In the early days before fences were erected and when shepherds had charge of very large flocks (occasionally 4000 or 5000) it was important to have a few sheep easily noticed amongst the rest; and hence the value of a certain number of black or partly black sheep, so that coloured lambs were then carefully preserved. It was easy to count ten or a dozen such sheep in a flock, and when one was missing it was pretty safe to conclude that a good many had strayed with it, so that the shepherd really kept count of his flock by counting his speckled sheep. As fences were erected the flocks were made smaller, and the necessity for having these spotted sheep passed away. Their wool also being of small value the practice soon grew of killing them off as lambs, or so young that they had small chance of breeding, and it surprised me how at the end of my sheep-farming experience of about eight years the percentage of coloured lambs produced was so much smaller than at the beginning. As the quantity of coloured wool from Australia seems to have much diminished, the above experience would appear to be general."

1. *Nature. A Weekly Illustrated Journal of Science*, vol. 23, 30 December 1880, p. 193.†

⋏ Movements of Plants[1]

Fritz Müller, in a letter from St. Catharina, Brazil, dated January 9, has given me some remarkable facts about the movements of plants. He has observed striking instances of allied plants, which place their leaves vertically at night, by widely different movements; and this is of interest as supporting the conclusion at which my son Francis and I arrived, namely, that leaves go to sleep in order to escape the full effect of radiation. In the great family of the Gramineae the species in one genus alone, namely Strephium, are known to sleep, and this they do by the leaves moving vertically upwards; but Fritz Müller finds in a species of Olyra, a genus which in Endlicher's "Genera Plantarum"[2] immediately precedes Strephium, that the leaves bend vertically down at night.

Two species of Phyllanthus (Euphorbiaceae) grow as weeds near Fritz Müller's house; in one of them with erect branches the leaves bend so as to stand vertically up at night. In the other species with horizontal branches, the leaves move vertically down at night, rotating on their axes, in the same manner as do those of the Leguminous genus Cassia. Owing to this rotation, combined with the sinking movement, the upper surfaces of the opposite leaflets are brought into contact in a dependent position beneath the main petiole; and they are thus excellently protected from radiation, in the manner described by us. On the following morning the leaflets rotate in an opposite direction, whilst rising so as to resume the diurnal horizontal position with their upper surface exposed to the light. Now in some rare cases Fritz Müller has observed the extraordinary fact that three or four, or even almost all the leaflets on one side of a leaf of this Phyllanthus rise in the morning from their nocturnal vertically dependent position into a horizontal one, without rotating, and on the wrong side of the main petiole. These leaflets thus project horizontally with their upper surfaces directed towards the sky, but partly shaded by the leaflets proper to this side. I have never before heard of a plant appearing to make a mistake in its movements; and the mistake in this instance is a great one, for the leaflets move 90° in a direction opposite to the proper one. Fritz Müller adds that the tips of the horizontal branches of this Phyllanthus curl downwards at night, and thus the youngest leaves are still better protected from radiation.

The leaves of some plants, when brightly illuminated, direct their edges towards the light; and this remarkable movement I have called paraheliotropism. Fritz Müller informs me that the leaflets of the Phyllanthus just referred to, as well as those of some Brazilian Cassiae, "take an almost perfectly vertical position, when at noon, on a summer day, the sun is nearly in the zenith. To-day the leaflets, though continuing to be fully exposed to the sun, now at 3 p.m. have already returned to a nearly horizontal position." F. Müller doubts whether so strongly marked a case of paraheliotropism would ever be observed under the duller skies of England; and this doubt is probably correct, for the leaflets of *Cassia neglecta*, on the plants raised from seed formerly sent me by him, moved in this manner, but so slightly that I thought it prudent not to give the case. With several species of Hedychium,[3] a widely different paraheliotropic movement occurs, which may be compared with that of the leaflets of Oxalis and Averrhoa[4]; for "the lateral halves of the leaves, when exposed to bright sunshine, bend downwards, so that they meet beneath the leaf."

1. *Nature. A Weekly Illustrated Journal of Science*, vol. 23, 3 March 1881, p. 409.†
2. Stephano Endlicher, *Genera Plantarum Secundum Ordines Naturales Disposita* (Vienna: Beck, 1836–40).†
3. Zingiberaceae.†
4. Origin uncertain; probably native to the coastal forests of Brazil. See J. C. Willis, *A Dictionary of the Flowering Plants and Ferns*, 7th ed., rev. by H. K. Airy Shaw (Cambridge: Cambridge University Press, 1966).†

ᴧ Mr. Darwin on Vivisection
[A Letter to Frithiof Holmgren][1]

In answer to your courteous letter of April 7, I have no objection to express my opinion with respect to the right of experimenting on living animals. I use this latter expression as more correct and comprehensive than that of vivisection. You are at liberty to make any use of this letter which you may think fit, but if published I should wish the whole to appear. I have all my life been a strong advocate for humanity to animals, and have done what I could in my writings to enforce this duty. Several years ago, when the agitation against physiologists commenced in England, it was asserted that inhumanity was here practised, and useless suffering caused to animals; and I was led to think that it might be advisable to have an Act of Parliament on the subject. I then took an active part in trying to get a Bill passed, such as would have removed all just cause of complaint, and at the same time have left physiologists free to pursue their researches,—a Bill very different from the Act which has since been passed. It is right to add that the investigation of the matter by a Royal Commission proved that the accusations made against our English physiologists were false. From all that I have heard, however, I fear that in some parts of Europe little regard is paid to the sufferings of animals, and if this be the case, I should be glad to hear of legislation against inhumanity in any such country. On the other hand, I know that physiology cannot possibly progress except by means of experiments on living animals, and I feel the deepest conviction that he who retards the progress of physiology commits a crime against mankind. Any one who remembers, as I can, the state of this science half a century ago, must admit that it has made immense progress, and it is now progressing at an ever-increasing rate. What improvements in medical practice may be directly attributed to physiological research is a question which can be properly discussed only by those physiologists and medical practitioners who have studied the history of their subjects; but, as far as I can learn, the benefits are already great. However this may be, no one, unless he is grossly ignorant of what science has done for mankind, can entertain any doubt of the incalculable benefits which will hereafter be derived from physiology, not only by man, but by the lower animals. Look for instance at Pasteur's results in modifying the germs of the most malignant diseases, from which, as it so happens, animals will in the first place receive more relief than man. Let it be remembered how many lives and what a fearful amount of suffering have been saved by the knowledge gained of parasitic worms through the experiments of Virchow and others on living animals. In the future every one will be astonished at the ingratitude shown, at least in England, to these benefactors of mankind. As for myself, permit me to assure you that I honour, and shall always honour, every one who advances the noble science of physiology.

1. *British Medical Journal* 1 (1881): 660. Also, *Nature. A Weekly Illustrated Journal of Science*, vol. 23, 21 April 1881, p. 583, and Francis Darwin, ed., *Life and Letters of Charles Darwin*, 3 vols. (London: Murray, 1887), 3:205–6. Also, *Times*, 18 April 1881.†

ᐊ Mr. Darwin on Vivisection[1]

I do not wish to discuss the views expressed by Miss Cobbe in the letter which appeared in the *Times* of the 19th inst.; but as she asserts that I have "misinformed" my correspondent in Sweden in saying that "the investigation of the matter by a Royal Commission proved that the accusations made against our English physiologists were false," I will merely ask leave to refer to some other sentences from the Report of the Commission.

(1.) The sentence—"It is not to be doubted that inhumanity may be found in persons of very high position as physiologists," which Miss Cobbe quotes from page 17 of the report, and which, in her opinion, "can necessarily concern English physiologists alone and not foreigners," is immediately followed by the words "We have seen that it was so in Majendie." Majendie was a French physiologist who became notorious some half-century ago for his cruel experiments on living animals.

(2). The Commissioners, after speaking of the "general sentiment of humanity" prevailing in this country, say (p. 10):—

"This principle is accepted generally by the very highly educated men whose lives are devoted either to scientific investigation and education or to the mitigation or the removal of the sufferings of their fellow-creatures; though differences of degree in regard to its practical application will be easily discernible by those who study the evidence as it has been laid before us."

Again, according to the Commissioners (p. 10): —

"The secretary of the Royal Society for the Prevention of Cruelty to Animals, when asked whether the general tendency of the scientific world in this country is at variance with humanity, says he believes it to be very different, indeed, from that of foreign physiologists; and while giving it as the opinion of the Society that experiments are performed which are in their nature beyond any legitimate province of science, and that the pain which they inflict is pain which it is not justifiable to inflict even for the scientific object in view, he readily acknowledges that he does not know a single case of wanton cruelty, and that in general the English physiologists have used anaesthetics where they think they can do so with safety to the experiment."

1. *Times*, 22 April 1881. Also, Francis Darwin, ed., *Life and Letters of Charles Darwin*, 3 vols. (London: Murray, 1887), 3:207–8.†

◀◣ The Movements of Leaves[1]

Fritz Mueller has sent me some additional observations on the movements of leaves, when exposed to a bright light. Such movements seem to be as well developed and as diversified under the bright sun of Brazil, as are the well-known sleep or nyctitropic movements of plants in all parts of the world. This result has interested me much, as I long doubted whether paraheliotropic movements were common enough to deserve to be separately designated. It is a remarkable fact that in certain species these movements closely resemble the sleep movements of allied forms. Thus the leaflets of one of the Brazilian Cassiae assume when exposed to sunshine nearly the same position as those of the not distantly allied Haematoxylon when asleep, as shown in Fig. 153 of "The Movements of Plants." Whereas the leaflets of this Cassia sleep by moving down and rotating on their axes, in the same peculiar manner as in so many other species of the genus. Again, with the unnamed species of Phyllanthus, the leaves move forwards at night, so that their midribs then stand nearly parallel to the horizontal branches from which they spring; but when they are exposed to bright sunshine they rise up vertically, and their upper surfaces come into contact, as they are opposite. Now this is the position which the leaves of another species, namely *Phyllanthus compressus*, assume when they go to sleep at night. Fritz Müller states that the paraheliotropic movements of the leaves of a Mucuna, a large twining Papilionaceous plant, are strange and inexplicable; the leaflets sleep by hanging vertically down, but under bright sunshine the petiole rises vertically up, and the terminal leaflet rotates by means of its pulvinus through an angle of 180°, and thus its upper surface stands on the same side with the lower surfaces of the lateral leaflets. Fritz Müller adds, "I do not understand the meaning of this rotation of the terminal leaflet, as even without such a movement it would be apparently equally well protected against the rays of the sun. The leaflets, also, on many of the leaves on the same plant assume various other strange positions." With one species of Desmodium, presently to be mentioned as sleeping in a remarkable manner, the leaflets rise up vertically when exposed to bright sunshine, and the upper surfaces of the lateral leaflets are thus brought into contact. The leaves of *Bauhinia grandiflora* go to sleep at an unusually early hour in the evening, and in the manner described at p. 373 of "The Movements of Plants," namely, by the two halves of the same leaf rising up and coming into close contact: now the leaves of *Bauhinia Brasiliensis* do not sleep, as far as Fritz Müller has seen, but they are very sensitive to a bright light, and when thus exposed the two halves rise up and stand at 45° or upwards above the horizon.

Fritz Müller has sent me some cases, in addition to those given in my former letter of March 3,[2] of the leaves of closely-allied plants which assume a vertical position at night by widely different movements; and these cases are of interest as indicating that sleep-movements have been acquired for a special purpose. We have just seen that of two species of Bauhinia the leaves of one sleep conspiciously, while those of a second species apparently do not sleep at all. The leaves of *Euphorbia jacquiniae-flora* depend vertically at night, whereas those of a dwarfish Brazilian species rise vertically up at night. The leaves of this Euphorbia stand opposite one another—a position which is rather rare in the genus; and the rising movement may be of service to the plant, as the upper surfaces of the opposite leaves mutually protect one another by coming into contact. In the genus Sida the leaves of two species rise, while those of a third Brazilian species sink vertically down at night. Two species of Desmodium are common plants near Fritz Müller's house: in one the leaflets move simply downwards at night; but in the other not only do the three leaflets move vertically down, while the main petiole rises vertically up, as is likewise the case with *D. gyrans*, but in addition the lateral leaflets rotate so as to stand parallel with the terminal leaflet, behind which they are more or less completely hidden. This, as far as I have seen, is a new kind of nyctitropic movement; but it leads to a result common to several species, namely, that of packing the three leaflets closely together and placing them in a vertical position.

1. *Nature. A Weekly Illustrated Journal of Science*, vol. 23, 28 April 1881, pp. 603–4.†
2. See p. 224, "Movements of Plants."†

◄ Inheritance[1]

The tendency in any new character or modification to reappear in the offspring at the same age at which it first appeared in the parents or in one of the parents, is of so much importance in reference to the diversified characters proper to the larvae of many animals at successive ages, that almost any fresh instance is worth putting on record. I have given many such instances under the term of "inheritance at corresponding ages." No doubt the fact of variations being sometimes inherited at an earlier age than that at which they first appeared—a form of inheritance which has been called by some naturalists "accelerated inheritance"—is almost equally important, for, as was shown in the first edition of the "Origin of Species," all the leading facts of embryology can be explained by these two forms of inheritance, combined with the fact of many variations arising at a somewhat late stage of life. A good instance of inheritance at a corresponding age has lately been communicated to me by Mr. J. P. Bishop of Perry, Wyoming, N. Y., United States:—The hair of a gentleman of American birth (whose name I suppress) began to turn grey when he was twenty years old, and in the course of four or five years became perfectly white. He is now seventy-five years old, and retains plenty of hair on his head. His wife had dark hair, which, at the age of seventy, was only sprinkled with grey. They had four children, all daughters, now grown to womanhood. The eldest daughter began to turn grey at about twenty, and her hair at thirty was perfectly white. A second daughter began to be grey at the same age, and her hair is now almost white. The two remaining daughters have not inherited the peculiarity. Two of the maternal aunts of the father of these children "began to turn grey at an early age, so that by middle life their hair was white." Hence the gentleman in question spoke of the change of colour of his own hair as "a family peculiarity."

Mr. Bishop has also given me a case of inheritance of another kind, namely, of a peculiarity which arose, as it appears, from an injury, accompanied by a diseased state of the part. This latter fact seems to be an important element in all such cases, as I have elsewhere endeavoured to show. A gentleman, when a boy, had the skin of both thumbs badly cracked from exposure to cold, combined with some skin disease. His thumbs swelled greatly, and remained in this state for a long time. When they healed they were misshapen, and the nails ever afterwards were singularly narrow, short, and thick. This gentleman had four children, of whom the eldest, Sarah, had both her thumbs and nails like her father's; the third child, also a daughter, had one thumb similarly deformed. The two other children, a boy and a girl, were normal. The daughter, Sarah, had four children, of whom the eldest and the third, both daughters, had their two thumbs deformed; the other two children, a boy and a girl, were normal. The great-grandchildren of this gentleman were all normal. Mr. Bishop believes that the old gentleman was correct in attributing the state of his thumbs to cold aided by skin disease, and he positively asserted that his thumbs were not originally misshapen, and there was no record of any previous inherited tendency of the kind in his family. He had six brothers and sisters, who lived to have families, some of them very large families, and in none was there any trace of deformity in their thumbs.

Several more or less closely analogous cases have been recorded; but until within a recent period every one naturally felt much doubt whether the effects of a mutilation or injury were ever really inherited, as accidental coincidences would almost certainly occasionally occur. The subject, however, now wears a totally different aspect, since Dr. Brown-Séquard's[2] famous experiments proving that guinea-pigs of the next generation were affected by operations on certain nerves. Mr. Eugène Dupuy of San Francisco, California, has likewise found, as he informs me, that with these animals "lesions of nerve-trunks are almost invariably transmitted." For instance, "the effects of sections of the cervical sympathetic on the eyes are reproduced in the young, also epilepsy (as described by my eminent friend and master, Dr. Brown-Séquard) when induced by lesions of the sciatic nerve." Mr. Dupuy has communicated to me a still more remarkable case of the transmitted effects on the brain from an injury to a nerve; but I do not feel at liberty to give this case, as Mr. Dupuy intends to pursue his researches, and will, as I hope, publish the results.

1. *Nature. A Weekly Illustrated Journal of Science*, vol. 24, 21 July 1881, p. 257.†

2. E. Brown-Séquard, "Hereditary Transmission of an Epileptiform Affection Accidently Produced," *Proceedings of the Royal Society of London* 10 (1860): 297–98.†

◀ Leaves Injured at Night by Free Radiation[1]

Fritz Müller, in a letter to me from Sta. Catherina in Brazil, dated August 9, supports the view which I have advanced with respect to leaves placing themselves in a vertical position at night, during their so-called sleep, in order to escape being chilled and injured by radiation into the open sky. He says: "We have had last week some rather cold nights (2° to 3° C. at sunrise), and these have given me a new confirmation of your view on the meaning of the nyctitropic movements of plants. Near my house there are some Pandanus trees,[2] about a dozen years old; the youngest terminal leaves stand upright, whereas the older ones are bent down so as to expose their upper surfaces to the sky. These young leaves, though of course the most tender, are still as fresh and green as before; on the contrary, the older ones have suffered from the cold, and have become quite yellowish. Again, the leaves of *Oxalis sepium* were observed by me to sleep in a very imperfect manner during the summer, even after the most sunny days; but now, in winter, every leaflet hangs down in a perpendicular position during the whole night." It is a new fact to me that leaves should sleep in a more or less perfect manner at different seasons of the year.

1. *Nature. A Weekly Illustrated Journal of Science*, vol. 24, 15 September 1881, p. 459.†
2. Marsh or coastal plants of the Old World tropics, with aerial roots; screw pine; often grown for decorative purposes.†

[A Letter to Mrs. Emily Talbot on the Mental and Bodily Development of Infants][1]

Does the education of the parents, for instance, influence the mental powers of their children at any age, either at a very early or somewhat more advanced stage? This could perhaps be learned by schoolmasters or mistresses, if a large number of children were first classed according to age and their mental attainments, and afterwards in accordance with the education of their parents, as far as this could be discovered. As observation is one of the earliest faculties developed in young children, and as this power would probably be exercised in an equal degree by the children of educated and uneducated persons, it seems not impossible that any transmitted effect from education would be displayed only at a somewhat advanced age. It would be desirable to test statistically, in a similar manner, the truth of the often-repeated statement that coloured children at first learn as quickly as white children, but that they afterwards fall off in progress. If it could be proved that education acts not only on the individual, but by transmission on the race, this would be a great encouragement to all working on this all-important subject. It is well known that children sometimes exhibit at a very early age strong special tastes, for which no cause can be assigned, although occasionally they may be accounted for by reversion to the taste or occupation of some progenitor; and it would be interesting to learn how far such early tastes are persistent and influence the future career of the individual. In some instances such tastes die away without apparently leaving any after effect; but it would be desirable to know how far this is commonly the case, as we should then know whether it were important to direct, as far as this is possible, the early tastes of our children. It may be more beneficial that a child should follow energetically some pursuit, of however trifling a nature, and thus acquire perseverance, than that he should be turned from it, because of no future advantage to him. I will mention one other small point of inquiry in relation to very young children, which may possibly prove important with respect to the origin of language,[2] but it could be investigated only by persons possessing an accurate musical ear: children, even before they can articulate, express some of their feelings and desires by noises uttered in different notes. For instance, they make an interrogative noise, and others of assent and dissent in different tones, and it would, I think, be worth while to ascertain whether there is any uniformity in different children in the pitch of their voices under various frames of mind.

1. *Nature. A Weekly Illustrated Journal of Science*, vol. 24, 13 October 1881, p. 565.† Also, Francis Darwin and A. C. Seward, eds., *More Letters of Charles Darwin*, 2 vols. (London: Murray, 1903) 2:54–55.†
2. See Darwin's "N Notebook," p. 31, and Darwin's "Old and Useless Notes," in Howard E. Gruber and Paul H. Barrett, *Darwin on Man* (New York: Dutton, 1974, pp. 336, 382–83).†

⚘ [Extracts from Two Letters: On Glacial Drift][1]

The origin of these gravels[2] has always been a difficult question, but a suggestion which Mr. Darwin some years ago (1876) did me the honour to communicate gives what appears to be the true explanation of the somewhat puzzling phenomena. Having since had an opportunity of testing the value of the suggestion referred to, I have found it extremely helpful, and believe that my co-workers will agree with me in this opinion. Mr. Darwin, after remarking that his observations were made near Southampton, writes as follows:—"I need say nothing about the character of the drift there (which includes Palaeolithic celts), for you have described its essential features in a few words (*Great Ice Age*, p. 506).[3] It covers the whole country, even plain-like surfaces, almost irrespective of the present outline of the land. The coarse stratification has sometimes been disturbed; and I find that you allude to 'the larger stones often standing on end,' which is the point that struck me so much. Not only moderately-sized angular stones but small oval pebbles often stand vertically up, in a manner which I have never seen in ordinary gravel-beds. This fact reminded me of what occurs in my own neighbourhood in the stiff red clay, full of unworn flints, over the chalk, which is no doubt the residue left undissolved by rain-water. In this clay flints as long and as thin as my arm often stand perpendicularly up, and I have been told by the tank-diggers that it is their 'natural position'! I presume that this position may safely be attributed to the differential movement of parts of the red clay, as it subsided very slowly from the dissolution of the underlying chalk, so that the flints arrange themselves in the lines of least resistance. The similar but less-strongly marked arrangement of the stones in the drift near Southampton makes me suspect that it also must have slowly subsided, and the notion has crossed my mind that during the commencement and height of the Glacial Period great beds of frozen snow accumulated over Southern England, and that during the summer gravel and stones were washed from the higher land over its surface, and in superficial channels. The larger streams may have cut right through the frozen snow, and deposited gravel in lines at the bottom. But at each succeeding autumn, when the running-water failed, I imagine that the lines of drainage would have been filled up with blown snow, afterwards congealed; and that owing to the great surface-accumulations of snow it would be a mere chance whether the drainage, together with gravel and sand, would follow the same lines during the next summer. Thus, as I apprehend, alternate layers of frozen snow and drift in sheets and lines would ultimately have covered the country to a great thickness, with lines of drift probably deposited in various directions at the bottom by the larger streams. As the climate became warmer the lower beds of frozen snow would have melted with extreme slowness, and during this movement the elongated pebbles would have arranged themselves more or less vertically. The drift would also have been deposited almost irrespective of the outline of the underlying land. When I viewed the country I could not persuade myself that any flood, however great, could have deposited such coarse gravel over the almost level platforms between the valleys."

Mr. Darwin writes me again recently to say that subsequent observations near Southampton and elsewhere have only tended to strengthen him in his conclusion. Referring to the structure of his own neighbourhood (Beckingham, Kent), he says the chalk-platform slopes gently down from the edge of the escarpment (which is about 800 feet in height) towards the north, where it disappears below the Tertiary strata. "The beds of the large and broad valleys, and only of these, are covered with an immense mass of closely-packed, broken, and angular flints, in which mass remains of the musk-sheep and woolly elephant have been found. This great accumulation of unworn flints must therefore have been made when the climate was cold, and I believe it can be accounted for by the large valleys having been filled up to a great depth during a large part of the year with drifted frozen snow, over which rubbish from the upper parts of the platforms was washed by the summer rains and torrents, sometimes along one line and sometimes along another, or in channels cut through the snow all along the main course of the broad valleys."

1. Pp. 141–42 in James Geikie, *Prehistoric Europe: A Geologic Sketch* (London: Stanford, 1881). Also, Francis Darwin, ed., *Life and Letters of Charles Darwin*, 3 vols. (London: Murray, 1887) 3:213–15.†

2. Geikie has reference to gravel of the Pleistocene or Glacial Age.†

3. James Geikie, *The Great Ice Age and its Relation to the Antiquity of Man* (London: Isbister, 1874).†

← Mr. Charles Darwin and the Defence of Science[1]

I saw in some paper that there would perhaps be a subscription to pay Dr. Ferrier's legal expenses in the late absurd and wicked prosecution.[2] As I live so retired, I might not hear of the subscription, and I should regret beyond measure not to have the pleasure and the honour of showing my sympathy and admiration of Dr. Ferrier's researches . . .

1. *British Medical Journal* 2 (1881): 917. Also, Francis Darwin and A. C. Seward, eds., *More Letters of Charles Darwin*, 2 vols. (London: Murray, 1903) 2:437. This letter by Darwin was addressed to Dr. Lauder Brunton.†

2. For a detailed discussion of the incident, see Francis Darwin and A. C. Seward, eds., *More Letters of Charles Darwin*, 2 vols. (London: Murray, 1903) 2:437–41. In brief, Dr. Ferrier was charged for an infringment of the Vivisection Act, and the British Medical Association supported the defense of Dr. Ferrier.

← The Parasitic Habits of Molothrus[1]

In the "Origin of Species" I adopted the view maintained by some writers, that the cuckoo lays her eggs in other birds' nests, owing to her habit of laying them at intervals of two or three days; for it could hardly fail to be disadvantageous to her, more especially as she has to migrate at a very early period, to have young birds of different ages and eggs all together in the same nest. Nevertheless this occurs with the non-parasitic North American cuckoo. If it has not been for this latter case, it might have been argued that the habit of the common cuckoo to lay her eggs at much longer intervals of time than do most other birds, was an adaptation to give her time to search for foster-parents. The Rhea or South American ostrich is believed likewise to lay her eggs at intervals of two or three days, and several hens deposit their eggs in the same nest on which the male sits; so that one hen may almost be said to be parasitic on another hen. These facts formerly made me very curious to learn how the several species of Molothrus,[2] which are parasitic on other birds in very varying degrees, laid their eggs; and I have just received a letter from Mr. W. Nation, dated Lima, September 22, 1881, giving me information on this head. He says that he has there kept in confinement for a long time *Molothrus perpurascens*, and has likewise observed its habits in a state of nature. It is a resident species of Western Peru, and lays its eggs exclusively in the nests of a sparrow (*Zonotrichia*), starling (*Sturnella bellicosa*), and a pipit (*Aenthus chiz*). He then proceeds: "The eggs of the sparrow are very much like those of the Molothrus in size and colour. The eggs of the starling are larger and somewhat different in colour; while the eggs of the pipit are very different both in size and colour. Generally one egg of the Molothrus is found in a nest, but I have found as many as six. The young Molothrus does not always eject its foster-brothers; for I have seen a young one nearly fully feathered in a nest with two young starlings. I have also found two young birds of the Molothrus nearly fully feathered in the nest of a starling; but in this instance the young starlings had been ejected from the nest." He then states that he had long kept in confinement a male and female of this species of Molothrus, which are now six years old. The hen began to lay at the age of two years, and has laid each time six eggs, which is the number laid by Icterus,[3] a near ally of Molothrus. The dates on which the eggs were laid this year are as follows:—February 1, 6, 11, 16, 21, and 26; so that there was an interval of exactly four clear days between the laying of each egg. Later in the season she laid six additional eggs, but at much longer intervals and irregularly, viz. on March 8, April 6 and 13, May 1, 16, and 21. These interesting facts, observed by Mr. Nation in relation to a bird so widely distinct from the cuckoo as is the Molothrus, strongly support the conclusion that there is some close connection between parasitism and the laying of eggs at considerable intervals of time. Mr. Nation adds that in the genus Molothrus, out of every three young birds he has invariably found two to be males; whereas with Sturnella, which lays only three eggs, two of the young birds are, without any exception, females.

1. *Nature. A Weekly Illustrated Journal of Science*, vol. 25, 17 November 1881, pp. 51–52.†
2. Cowbirds.†
3. Orioles.†

The Action of Carbonate of Ammonia on the Roots of Certain Plants[1]

Many years ago I observed the fact that when the roots of *Euphorbia Peplus* were placed in a solution of carbonate of ammonia a cloud of fine granules was deposited in less than a minute, and was seen travelling from the tip up the root from cell to cell.[2] The subject seemed to me worthy of further investigation. Plants of the same *Euphorbia* were therefore dug up together with a ball of earth, and having been left for a short time in water, the roots were washed clean. Some of the finer transparent rootlets were then examined, and sections were made of the thicker roots, generally by my son Francis, who has aided me in many ways. All the cells were found to be colourless and destitute of any solid matter, the laticiferous ducts being here excluded from consideration. These roots, after being left for a few minutes or for several hours in solutions of different strengths, viz. from 1 to 7 parts of the carbonate to 1000 of water, presented a wonderfully changed appearance. A solution of only 1 part to 10,000 of water sufficed in the course of 24 hours to produce the same result. In well-developed cases the longitudinal rows of cells close to the tip of the root, with the exception of those forming the extreme apex, were filled with brown granular matter, and were thus rendered opaque. Long-continued immersion in water produced no such effect. The granular masses were square in outline, like the cells in which they were contained; but they often became rounded after a day or two; and this was apparently due to the contraction of the protoplasmic utricle. Above the dark-brown cells, which form a transverse zone close to the tip, and which apparently corresponds with the zone of quickest growth, the roots, as seen under a high power, are longitudinally striped with darker and lighter brown. The darker tint is due to the presence of innumerable rounded granules of brownish matter; and the cells containing them are arranged in longitudinal rows, while other longitudinal rows are destitute of granules. In a few instances the rows differed slightly in tint, and yet no granules could be seen in the darker cells; and I suppose that this was owing to their being too minute to be visible. Occasionally, in the upper parts of the roots, the granules became confluent, and formed one or two small rounded masses of hyaline brown matter. The striped appearance sometimes extended from the tips of the finest rootlets close up to the stem of the plant.

On a casual inspection it would be said that the longitudinal rows of brownish and of almost colourless exterior cells regularly alternated with one another; but on closer examination, two or three adjoining rows of cells were often seen to contain granules, and in other places two or three ordinary rows contained only colourless fluid. In one instance many adjoining longitudinal rows contained granules; but the tendency to alternation was even here well shown, as the alternate rows differed in tint from including a greater or less number of granules. High up the roots the alternations often quite failed, as all the exterior cells contained granules. If a longitudinal row of cells with granules is traced up a rootlet, it is seen to be soon interrupted by one or more colourless cells;

but I have traced as many as 18 cells in a row all containing granules. So, again, a longitudinal row of colourless cells changes after a time into one with granular matter. As a root thickens upwards, some of the longitudinal rows of cells divide into two rows; and a row containing granules may divide into two such rows, or into one with and another without granules; and so it is with dividing rows of colourless cells. I could not perceive the least difference in shape or size, or in any other character, between the cells of the same rank which contained and those which were destitute of granules.

Near the tip of the root it is the exterior cells which become charged, after immersion in the solution, with brown granular matter; and this often holds good with the cells of the root-cap. Higher up the root, the layer of cells formed by the alternating longitudinal rows with and without granules is sometimes bounded externally by a layer of empty cells, which, I suppose, had by some means been emptied of their contents, and were ready to be exfoliated. Besides the exterior cells with and without granules, many separate cells in the parenchyma at different depths from the surface, and all or several of the elongated endoderm-cells surrounding the central vascular bundle, are more or less filled with granular matter, none of which cells contained any solid matter before the roots were immersed in the solution.

I should have felt little surprise at the effect produced by the solution if all the cells of the same nature (for instance, if all the exterior cells or all the parenchyma-cells) had been equally affected. The strong tendency to alternation in the exterior cells is more especially remarkable. There is also another remarkable fact with respect to these latter cells, namely, that those containing the granules do not give rise to root-hairs, as these arise exclusively from the colourless and apparently empty cells. In longitudinal sections of one root, 62 hairs were traced down to such colourless cells; and I was not able to find a single one arising from a cell which contained granules. But I shall have hereafter to return to this subject.

With respect to the rate at which the granular matter is deposited, if a rootlet is placed under a cover-glass and irrigated with a few drops of the solution, some deposition occurs before the slide can be transferred to the microscope and the focus adjusted. A thin rootlet was therefore arranged for observation, and a drop of the solution (7 to 1000) placed on the edge of the cover-glass, and in 20 seconds the cells near the tip became slightly clouded. Another thin rootlet was placed with the tip projecting beyond the cover-glass, and the focus was adjusted to a point at a distance of .07 inch from the tip, on which a drop of the solution was then placed, and the cells at the above distance became cloudy in 2 m. 30 sec.

Various other solutions, beside that of carbonate of ammonia, caused the deposition of granules in the same cells as in the foregoing cases. This occurred conspicuously with a solution of 4 parts of phosphate of ammonia to 1000 water; but the action was not so rapid as with the carbonate. The same remarks are applicable to nitrate of ammonia. A solution of one part of fuchsine, which contains nitrogen, to 50,000 of water distinctly acted. A solution of 2.5 parts of pure carbonate of soda to 1000 water caused, after 24 hours, the cells close to the tip to become very brown from being charged with fine granular matter; and higher up the rootlets, longitudinal rows of cells, either containing coarse granules or pale-brown fluid without any distinguishable granules, alternated with rows of colourless cells. Lastly, roots immersed for only one hour in a watch-glass of water, to which two drops of a 1-per-cent. solution of osmic acid had been added, presented an extraordinary appearance; for the exterior cells in alternate rows, some parenchyma, and most of the endoderm-cells contained much almost black granular matter.

The granules precipitated through the action of carbonate of ammonia are never afterwards, as far as I could judge, redissolved. Roots still attached to living plants were immersed in solutions of 1 part of the carbonate to 500, to 2000, and to 4000 parts of water, and granular matter was deposited in the cells in the usual manner. The roots were then left in damp peat or in water, with the stems and leaves exposed to the air and light, for various periods between 2 and 15 days. The roots were then reexamined at different times, and granules were found in almost every instance in the cells. But it should be noticed that though the plants themselves looked healthy, the finer roots were flaccid, and sometimes showed evident signs of decay; so that it was manifest that they had been much injured by the treatment to which they had been subjected, probably by their immersion in the solution.

With respect to the nature of the granules, I can say but little. They were not dissolved by long-continued immersion in alcohol or in acetic acid, or by irrigation with sulphuric ether. They were not dissolved by a 10-per-cent. solution of common salt, which was tried at the suggestion of Mr. Vines, who has found that this solution dissolves aleurone-grains either partially or completely. When sections or rootlets containing *freshly deposited* granules were left for a day or two in glycerine and water, these were sometimes broken up, so as to be no longer visible, and the cell-sap in this case acquired a brownish tint. When sections or thin rootlets were heated for a short time in a moderately strong solution of caustic potash, and afterwards left in it for a day or two, the granules were dissolved; whereas the hyaline globules in the laticiferous ducts were not dissolved. From these several facts I suppose that the granules are of the nature of protein.

After roots had been left for 2 or 3 minutes in water heated to a temperature of 210°–212° F., and were then placed in a strong solution of the carbonate of ammonia, no granular matter was deposited; and this seems to indicate that the action is a vital one. On the other hand, granules were often deposited in the cells, even the loose cells, of the root-cap, and it is very doubtful whether these could be alive. I may add that these root-cap cells were coloured, by a weak solution of fuchsine, of a brighter pink than those in other parts of the rootlets.

Other Euphorbiaceous Plants.—The exterior cells of the roots of *Euphorbia amygdaloides* were much less acted on (Nov. 16) by a solution of carbonate of ammonia than those of *E. Peplus*. Here and there two and three cells in a row contained brownish granules, and these abounded in the elongated endoderm-cells. Nearly the same remarks are applicable to *E. myrsinites*, though in most specimens the cells with granules were still rarer. The roots of two fleshy species, *E. rhipsaloides* and *ornithopus*, did not appear to be at all affected by the solution.

Turning now to other Euphorbiaceous genera, the roots of *Poinsettia pulcherrima, Manihot Glaziovi, Croton oblongifolium,* and *Hevea Spruciana* were not affected. Nor were those of *Mercurialis perennis*, as far as the exterior cells are concerned; but here and there a single cell in the parenchyma became blue; but these cells were not carefully examined.[3] Judging from the cases presently to be given, they probably contained granules which had been precipitated by the ammonia solution.

On the other hand, the roots of *Phylanthus compressus* were conspicuously acted on by an immersion of 21 hours in a solution of 4 parts of the carbonate to 1000 of water, though in a somewhat different manner from those of *Euphorbia Peplus*. In parts the exterior cells in many adjoining longitudinal rows contained brownish granules; while in other parts at no great distance many adjoining rows were colourless and empty—that is, contained no solid matter. For instance, in one place 13 longitudinal rows with granules ran alongside one another, then came a single row of empty cells, and then at least 9 rows with granules. In another place there were 13 adjoining rows of cells all empty. When one of these rows was followed up or down the root for some distance, it changed its character, either becoming or ceasing to be granular, and then resuming its former character. Close to the tips of the roots all the longitudinal rows of cells contained brownish matter; but this matter in several instances consisted of small dark-brown spheres, due apparently to the aggregation of granules. The endoderm-cells round the vascular bundle contained either similar spheres or granular matter.

As many adjoining rows of cells on the surface of the roots of this plant had the same character, an excellent opportunity was afforded for observing the relation of the root-hairs to the cells; and in several dissected roots it was manifest that, as a general rule, the hairs rose exclusively from the colourless empty cells; whereas none arose from those containing granules. Twice, however, partial exceptions to this rule were observed: in one case the exterior walls of two adjoining cells, and in another case those of four adjoining cells, projected, so that they formed short blunt papillae which included granules; and these papillae exactly resembled nascent root-hairs. It is not, however, certain that they would ever have become fully developed.

All the exterior cells close to the tip of the root in this case and in many others contained matter which was acted on by carbonate of ammonia; and I was led by various appearances to suppose at one time that this matter remained in all the higher cells until it was consumed in some of them by the formation of the root-hairs. These consequently would arise exclusively from cells in which no granules would be deposited when they were acted on by the solution. In opposition to this supposition is the fact, first, that root-hairs could be seen beginning to be developed from empty cells; and, secondly, that very many cells which were empty apparently had never produced root-hairs. Nor does this notion throw the least light on single cells in the parenchyma and on many cells, though not all, in the endoderm containing granular matter.

With another Euphorbiaceous plant, *Coelebogyne ilicifolia*, the immersion for 20 hours of its roots, or of thin sections of the roots, in a solution of 4 parts of carbonate of ammonia to 1000 parts of water produced a singular effect; for many separate cells in the parenchyma and those in the endoderm surrounding the vascular bundle assumed a pale or dark blue, and sometimes a greenish colour. As far as I could judge, both the granules within these cells and the cell-sap became thus coloured. Irrigation with sulphuric ether did not affect the colour, though the many oil-globules in the cells were dissolved.

The foregoing observations on the Euphorbiaceae led me to experiment on the roots of some other plants belonging to various families. At one time I erroneously imagined that there was some relation between the deposition of granules in certain cells and the presence of laticiferous ducts, and consequently an undue number of plants with milky juice were selected for observation. A solution of carbonate of ammonia produced no obvious effect on the roots of a small majority of the plants which were tried; but on several a slight, and on others a marked, effect was produced. I should state that when the exterior appearance of a root did not indicate any action, sections were rarely made; so that the interior cells were not examined. No obvious effect was produced with the following plants: —*Argemone grandiflora, Brassica oleracea, Vicia* sativa, Trifolium repens, Vinca rosea, Hoya campanulata, Stapelia hamata, Schubertia graveolens, Carica Papaya, Opuntia boliviensis, Cucurbita ovifera, a Begonia, Beta vulgaris, Taxus baccata, Cycas pectinata, Phalaris canariensis, a common pasture-grass, Lemna, and two species of Allium. It may perhaps be worth notice that the radicles, but not the hypocotyls, of seedlings of Beta vulgaris were completely killed by an immersion for 20 hours in solutions of either 4 or of only 2 parts of the carbonate to 1000 of water; and this occurred with no other plant which was tried.

With the following plants the solution produced some slight effect. The roots of a fern, Nephrodium molle, were immersed for 20 hours in a solution of 4 to 1000; and this caused the deposition of some brown granular matter in the cells near their tips; and more or less confluent globules could be seen in the underlying parenchyma-cells. So it was with an unnamed greenhouse species of fern; and in this case the almost loose cells of the root-cap contained brown granules. The roots of a Ranunculus (R. acris?) similarly treated exhibited near their tips brown granular matter. The tips also of the roots of Dipsacus sylvestris became, under similar treatment, almost black; and higher up the roots, here and there a single parenchyma-cell was coloured pale blue. This occurred in one instance when a rootlet was looked at 35 minutes after irrigation with the solution. Several roots of Apium graveolens were left for 20 and 24 hours in solutions of 4 and 7 to 1000; and in some cases brownish granules, more or less aggregated together, were deposited in some of the exterior cells, and a few of the deeper cells in the parenchyma were coloured blue. The tips of the roots of Pastinaca sativa turned dark brown by a similar immersion; but this was due to the formation of orange-brown balls of matter near the vascular bundle; higher up the roots there were no granules in the exterior cells. The tips of the roots of Lamium purpureum, after an immersion of 18 hours in a solution of 4 to 1000, were rendered brown, and the cells contained innumerable pale-coloured hyaline globules. The older roots of Leontodon Taraxacum and of a Sonchus had their tips turned brown by the solution. With Lactuca sativa the tips were rendered opaque; but much granular matter was not deposited except in that of one rather thick leading root, and here short longitudinal rows of cells containing dark-brown granular matter alternated with rows of colourless cells; the almost loose cells of the root-cap likewise contained brown granules. In the several following cases a much more strongly marked effect was produced by the solution.

Urtica. —This plant, the common nettle, shall be first considered, as it is distantly allied to the Euphorbiaceae, though the roots are not so much affected as in succeeding cases. Several roots were left for 27 hours in a solution of the carbonate (4 to 1000). In one of them the exterior cells were plainly tinted of a brown colour in many longitudinal rows, but they contained no visible granules; and these rows regularly alternated with others formed of colourless cells. In another part of this same root all the exterior cells were coloured dark brown, and contained visible granules, which were generally collected into heaps at one end of the cell, or were fused together in some instances into small brown spheres. In a second, rather thick root, there was a space in which all the exterior cells had become brown; but at no great distance rows of brown and colourless cells regularly alternated. In a third, rather thick, and in a fourth, thin root the alternation was extremely regular. Near the tip of a fifth (thin) rootlet two rows of a brown colour ran alongside one another in many places; but when these and other single rows were traced up the root, they changed into colourless rows, and afterwards reassumed their former character. Whenever the root-hairs were traced down to their bases, they were seen to arise from colourless cells. Neither granules nor brown fluid were observed in the parenchyma-cells nor in those surrounding the vascular bundle.

Some roots which had been left in water for several days were longitudinally striped with very faint brown lines; and one cell was observed which included granules; so that plain water produces some effect. These same roots, after being irrigated with a solution of 7 to 1000, were left for 24 hours; and now the longitudinal rows of brown cells had become much darker, and presented a much stronger contrast with the colourless cells. Several of the brown cells moreover included granules, which here and there were aggregated into small dark-brown rounded masses.

Drosera, Dionaea, and *Drosophyllum.*—The roots of the plants belonging to these three closely allied genera are strongly acted on by a solution of carbonate of ammonia. In the case of a young plant of the *Dionaea,* all the exterior cells of the roots, after immersion for 24 hours in a solution of 4 to 1000, contained almost black or orange, or nearly colourless spheres and rounded masses of translucent matter, which were not present in the fresh roots. In this case, therefore, the exterior cells did not differ in alternate rows. Near the extremity of one of these roots many separate cells in the parenchyma, as seen in transverse sections, contained similar translucent spheres, but generally of an orange colour or colourless. The cells surrounding the vascular bundle abounded with much smaller dark-coloured spheres.

Three main or leading roots of *Drosophyllum lusitanicum* were cut off and examined before being immersed in the solution, and no aggregated masses could be seen in them. Two were left for 22 hours in a solution of

4 to 1000, and they presented an extraordinarily changed appearance; for the exterior cells in many rows from the tips to the cut-off ends of the roots included either one large, or, more commonly, several spherical or oval, or columnar masses of brown translucent matter. The columnar masses had sinuous outlines, and appeared to have been formed by the confluence of several small spheres. The loose, or almost loose, oval cells composing the root-cap included similar brown spheres; and this fact deserves attention. Two rows of cells containing the just-described masses often ran up the root alongside one another; and sometimes there were three or four such adjacent rows. These alternated with others which were colourless, and contained either no solid matter, or rarely a few minute pale spheres. These roots were carefully examined; and all the many root-hairs arose from the colourless rows of cells, except in some few cases in which the cells on both sides abounded to an unusual degree with aggregated masses; and here root-hairs arose from cells including a very few minute spheres.

In longitudinal sections of the above roots, the cells in the parenchyma at different depths from the surface were seen to include spheres, but many of them were of small size and pale-coloured. There was no marked increase in the amount of aggregated matter in the cells closely surrounding the vascular bundle, as is so often the case with other plants.

The third cut-off root was placed under the microscope, and was irrigated with a solution of 7 to 1000. After 13 minutes very small translucent granules could be seen in many of the cells; and after 35 minutes several cells near the cut-off end contained moderately large spheres of translucent matter. But I suppose that the solution was too strong; for the granules disappeared after about 45 minutes, except close to the tip; and the higher parts of the root no longer presented a striped appearance. Nevertheless the large spherical, oval, and oddly shaped masses in the cells near the cut-off end remained perfect, and they were watched for the next 2¼ hours. During this time they slowly changed their shapes, but not afterwards, though observed for nearly 24 hours. For instance, two spheres in one cell became confluent and formed an oval mass; two other spheres ran together and formed a dumbbell-shaped body, which ultimately changed into a sphere; and, lastly, an irregular mass first became oval, then united itself with another oval mass, and both together became spherical.

Saxifraga umbrosa.—This plant, from its affinity to the Droseraceae, was cursorily observed. Many of the exterior cells of roots which had been immersed for 19 hours in a solution of 4 to 1000 were filled with brown granular matter. Only two or three cells in a longitudinal row were thus filled; but sometimes four or five such short rows were grouped together; and these groups alternated with rows of colourless cells.

Sarracenia purpurea.—Two rootlets were left in water for 24 hours, but they presented no granules or aggregated masses. They were then irrigated with a solution of 7 to 1000, and in 20 minutes pale-brown aggregated masses could be distinctly seen near their tips. Two other, almost colourless, rootlets were left for 1 hour 10 minutes in the same solution; and now all the exterior cells contained brown granular matter, but much darker in some cells than in others. Some of the cells contained, besides the granules, oval and occasionally spherical masses of transparent, almost colourless matter, which apparently did not change their shapes. The cells round the central vascular bundle included similarly shaped masses, but of a yellowish-brown colour. These roots and others were left for 24 hours in the solution of 7 to 1000, and their tips were now blackened. Some of the exterior cells, more especially those of the thicker roots, were filled with orange instead of brown granules; while other cells contained oval, spherical, or oddly shaped masses of orange, instead of almost colourless or pale-brown translucent matter. Some of these masses consisted of an aggregation of small, partially confluent spheres of different tints of orange. In transverse sections it could be seen that the two exterior layers of cells and those surrounding the vascular bundle contained the above-described masses, while the more central parenchyma-cells abounded with grains of starch. A solution of 4 parts of the carbonate to 1000 of water sufficed to produce similar effects.

The root-hairs, after immersion in the solution, were not so transparent as is commonly the case, from including very fine granular matter, and from their shrunken protoplasmic lining being of a yellowish colour. The roots themselves were also usually opaque. Consequently the root-hairs were not easily traced down to their bases. They were distributed very unequally, being quite absent from the browner parts of the roots, while present on the parts which had remained pale-coloured. Notwithstanding this latter fact, it is very doubtful whether the rule of root-hairs arising almost exclusively from cells destitute of solid matter here holds good.

Pelargonium zonale.—A fresh root was examined, and the cells contained no granules. It was then irrigated with a solution of 7 to 1000, and in about 15 minutes granules could be distinctly seen in the exterior cells in alternate rows. Two other rootlets, after being left in water for 48 hours, were not at all affected. They were then irrigated with the same solution and reexamined after 24 hours; and now the exterior cells in rows, as well as those surrounding the vascular bundle, abounded with granular matter. Other roots were left for 48 hours in a solution of 4 to 1000; and the cells near their tips were so packed with dark-brown granular matter as to be blackened. Higher up the roots, the granules were pale brown, translucent, irregularly rounded, and often more or less confluent. In some dark-coloured rootlets the cells included a few small spheres of dark brown matter instead of granules. Usually the cells containing the granules formed single longitudinal rows, which alternated with rows of colourless cells. But occasionally several adjoining rows included granules; thus in one place two adjacent rows of cells with granules were succeeded by an empty row; this by two alternations of granules and empty rows; then came two adjoining rows with granules, an empty row, and three adjoining granular rows. In another place an empty row was succeeded by five adjoining rows with granules; these by an empty row; this by three adjoining rows with granules, and this by an empty row.

After many casual observations, in which all the root-hairs appeared to arise from cells destitute of granules, this was found to be the case with 50 hairs which were traced down to their bases. With one problematical exception, not a single hair could be found which arose from a cell containing granules. In this one exceptional case, a hair seemed to spring from the transverse wall separating two cells; but with a good light and under a high power, the wall apparently consisted of two walls, separated by an excessively narrow clear space, as if a cell had here failed to be fully developed.

The solution likewise caused the precipitation of granules in the elongated cells surrounding the vascular bundle, and in some tubes or ducts within the bundle. The solution apparently does not act on cells which have been killed. The ends of a root were torn open, so that the vascular bundle was fully exposed; the root was then left for 24 hours in a strong solution of 7 to 1000, and no granules were deposited in the exposed cells round the vascular bundle; but by tearing open fresh parts of the same roots, these cells were found full of granules.

The granules were not dissolved by immersion for 24 hours in alcohol; but they were dissolved by a cold solution of caustic potash. The dissolution, however, took place very slowly; for though on two occasions the granules wholly, or almost wholly, disappeared after an immersion of 20 hours, yet with a thicker root they were not dissolved, though rendered browner, by an immersion for this length of time; but they finally disappeared after 18 additional hours in a fresh solution of the potash. In the cells round the vascular bundle, from which the granules had been dissolved by the potash, matter resembling oil-globules in appearance remained.

Lastly, two drops of a 1-per-cent. solution of osmic acid were added to

½ oz. of distilled water, and some roots were left in this fluid for 20 hours. They were affected in very different degrees. Some were only a little discoloured; and in such roots a single exterior cell here and there contained either blackish granules or small black spheres. Other roots were much blackened; and in these longitudinal rows of dark brown or blackened cells plainly alternated with colourless rows. The cells surrounding the vascular bundle and many of the parenchyma-cells also contained blackened granules. Hence it is probable that carbonate of ammonia likewise acts on some of the parenchyma-cells; but if so, the fact was overlooked, or accidentally not recorded, in my notes.

Oxalis Acetosella.—Roots were first examined, and then placed in a solution of 7 to 1000. Some slight degree of aggregation was seen in a few minutes. After 30 minutes all the cells near the tips contained rounded accumulations of granules. Higher up in one of the roots, single cells, or from two to five cells in a row, were filled with minute hyaline globules. In some places these had become confluent, so that they formed larger globules having a sinuous outline. The cells underlying the exterior layer likewise contained extremely fine granular matter. Still higher up the same root there were considerable spaces in which none of the cells contained granules. But again higher up, the granules reappeared. The root-hairs were numerous; but not one was seen which arose from a cell containing granules.

Roots of *Oxalis sepium, corniculata,* and of a greenhouse species with small yellow flowers were immersed in a solution of 7 to 1000, and granular matter was deposited in the layer of cells underlying the exterior layer. This occurred in the case of *O. sepium* in 20 minutes. With *O. corniculata* the cells with granules were isolated—that is, did not form rows; and the granules were either brown or of a bluish-green colour. In the case of *Oxalis (Biophytum) sensitiva,* the exterior cells of the roots, after immersion for 44 hours in the same strong solution, were not much affected; but some of the deeper parenchyma-cells contained dark-brown translucent spheres, and the elongated cells round the vascular bundle were almost filled with granular matter.

Fragaria (Garden Var. of the Common Strawberry).—Some white, almost transparent roots from a runner were examined (Dec. 12), and the cells contained no solid matter, except starch-grains. They were then irrigated with a solution of 7 to 1000; and in from 10 to 15 minutes they became very opaque, especially near their tips. After being left a little time longer in the solution, longitudinal sections were made. The cells forming the exterior layer contained no solid matter, but the walls had become brown. There was much brown, finely granular matter in many of the parenchyma-cells at different depths from the surface; and these formed interrupted longitudinal rows, which alternated in the same zone with rows of empty colourless cells. Almost all the endoderm-cells likewise contained granules. In the parenchyma the cells which included much granular matter contained no starch-grains; while those abounding with starch-grains contained only a few or no granules. The fact was best seen after the sections had been irrigated with a solution of iodine; and they then presented a very remarkable appearance, considering how homogeneous they had been before being treated with the ammonia and iodine; for the fine granular matter was rendered still browner and the starch-grains of a beautiful blue. These roots were left for a week in diluted alcohol, and the granules were not dissolved.

Not a single root-hair could be found on these roots. A rooted stolon was therefore dug up and potted on Dec. 12th; it was then forced forwards in the hot-house, and afterwards kept very dry. When examined on Jan. 3rd the roots were found clothed with innumerable root-hairs; and they were then left for 23 hours in the solution of 7 to 1000. Sections of the thicker roots presented exactly the same appearances as described above; and the exterior cells, from which the root-hairs arose, were destitute of granules. The thinner roots differed somewhat in appearance, as the parenchyma-cells did not contain any fine granules, but in their places small, spherical, or oval, or irregularly-shaped masses or filaments of brown translucent matter, resembling a highly viscid fluid. There were also in these cells other still smaller colourless spheres. The cells, however, close to the tip of the root were filled with brown granular matter.

Solanum (*capsicastrum* ?, var. Empress).—Roots, after an immersion of 20½ hours in a solution of 4 to 1000, were split longitudinally and examined, but with no great care. The exterior cells did not appear to have been affected; but some of the parenchyma-cells close beneath the exterior cells contained minute aggregated masses of brown, opaque, or sometimes hyaline granules. Moreover many, but by no means all, of the elongated cells surrounding the vascular bundle included dark-brown fine granular matter. Three roots which had been left in water for the same length of time, viz. 20½ hours, were similarly examined, but their cells presented none of the above appearances.

Primula acaulis.—Several roots were left (Dec. 22) for 18 hours in a solution of 4 to 1000, and they were all much affected, except some of the thinnest rootlets. Many of the exterior cells contained granules within the shrunken protoplasmic utricle, which had contracted into one, two, or even three, oval or spherical bags, lying within the same cell. The rows of cells containing the granules showed some tendency to alternate with rows of empty cells. The granules were rendered orange-brown by iodine. The innumerable root-hairs all arose from the empty cells; and I saw only two partial exceptions, in which the outer walls of cells containing granules were produced into short papillae, as in the formerly described case of *Phyllanthus*, and these resembled nascent root-hairs. Within one of these papillae, granules surrounded by the shrunken utricle could be seen. In the parenchyma single cells were seen containing minute hyaline globules, which were colourless or pale or dark blue, or occasionally greenish or yellowish. Many of the endoderm-cells likewise contained more or less confluent hyaline globules; but these were colourless, and larger than those in the parenchyma. They resembled starch-grains so closely that they were tried with iodine, but were not coloured blue. Roots which had been kept for 48 hours in water exhibited none of the coloured or colourless globules; but these appeared when the roots were afterwards immersed for 24 hours in the ammonia solution.

Although it is certain that granules were deposited in the exterior cells in the case just described, yet in four other roots, after an immersion of 24 hours in the solution, no granules could be seen in any of the exterior cells. Some of the parenchyma-cells, however, were of a fine blue colour, and contained many globules or granules, but no starch-grains, while others contained starch-grains as well as some few globules.

Cyclamen persicum. —Sections taken from roots of this plant which had been immersed in a solution of carbonate of ammonia presented an extraordinary different appearance from those of fresh roots. All the cells in the latter appeared empty, excepting those of the endoderm, which sometimes included a few very fine pale-coloured granules, unlike those in the same cells after immersion. Thick and thin roots were left for 22 hours in a solution of 7 to 1000, and the cells forming the exterior layer were filled over considerable spaces with green granules, while over other spaces they were empty. The granular and empty cells did not form regular alternate rows, as occurs in so many other plants; yet, as we shall presently see, there is occasionally some degree of alternation. The exterior cells with the green granules were so numerous in certain cases, that roots which had been pale brown before immersion were afterwards distinctly green. The green granules sometimes became aggregated into spherical, or oval, or elongated masses having a sinuous outline; and some of these are shown within the root-hairs in fig. 2. Many of the cells of the parenchyma, either standing separately or two or three in a row (as shown in fig. 1), contain similar green, or sometimes brownish, granules. Almost all the narrow elongated cells of the endoderm (*b*, fig. 1) likewise contain these granules, with merely here and there an empty cell. Although both kinds of cells often appear as if gorged with the granules, yet these really form only a layer adhering to the inside of the protoplasmic utricle, as could be seen when cells had been cut through. With some thick fleshy roots, after an immersion for 42 hours (and thick roots require a long immersion for the full effect to be produced) the green granules in the parenchyma-cells had become completely confluent, and now formed spheres of transparent green matter of considerable size.

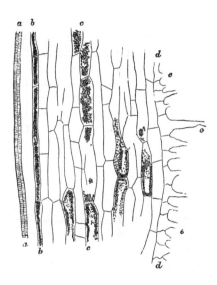

Fig. 1. Longitudinal section of root of *Cyclamen persicum* after immersion in a solution of carbonate of ammonia, and deposition in some of the cells of granules. *a*, part of vascular bundle; *b*, endoderm-cells; *c*, parenchyma-cells; *d*. exterior cells of the root, bearing root-hairs; *e*, with their tips cut off. Drawing made by aid of a camera, magnified 260 times, but here reduced to two thirds of original scale.

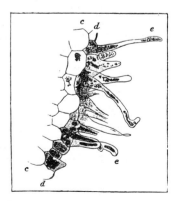

Fig. 2. Transverse section of another part of the same root, magnified as before, showing the exterior cells, *d*, together with the root-hairs, *e*, here containing granules.

The granules are not dissolved, nor is their colour discharged by sulphuric ether. Acetic acid instantly changes the green into a dull orange tint. The granules are not dissolved by alcohol. Their precipitation by the ammonia solution seems to depend on the life of the cell; for some transverse sections were examined and found colourless, as well as destitute of granules. They were then irrigated with a solution of 7 to 1000, and reexamined after 22 hours; and only a very few cells in two out of the five sections showed any trace of colour, which, oddly enough, was blue instead of green. The few coloured cells occurred exclusively in the thickest parts of the sections, where the central ones would obviously have had the best chance of keeping alive for some time. In these coloured cells a little very fine granular matter could be distinguished.

On most of the roots root-hairs were extremely numerous, and they generally arose from cells destitute of granules; yet in many places whole groups of cells abounding with granules gave rise to well-developed root-hairs. Therefore the rule which holds good with so many plants, namely, that root-hairs arise exclusively from colourless cells destitute of granules, here quite breaks down. The granules extend from the cells into the hairs which spring from them, as is shown in fig. 2; and they here sometimes become confluent, forming rounded or elongated masses of transparent green matter. This matter within the tips of some of the hairs seemed to pass into a brownish fluid. It was repeatedly observed that where many hairs rose close together from cells containing the green granules, the tips of the hairs were glued together by cakes or masses of orange-coloured translucent tough matter. This matter could be seen, under favourable circumstances, to consist either of very thin homogeneous sheets or of aggregated granules. It was not acted on by an immersion of two hours in absolute alcohol or in sulphuric ether. The smaller globules were either dissolved or destroyed by sulphuric acid, while others were rendered highly transparent. The formation of this orange-coloured matter is independent of the previous action of ammonia; and I have noticed similar matter attached to the rootlets of many other plants. It is probably formed by the softening or liquefaction of the outer surface of the walls of the hairs, and the subsequent consolidation of the matter thus produced.[4] Nevertheless some appearances led me to suspect that the brownish fluid which was seen within the tips of the hairs enclosing the green granules may perhaps exude through the walls, and ultimately form the cakes of orange matter.

A few other solutions were tried. Roots were left for from 20 to 43 hours in a solution of 7 parts of pure carbonate of soda to 1000 of water, and in no case were granules deposited in the exterior cells; but some of these cells in longitudinal rows became brown; these alternated with rows of colourless cells. In one instance several of these cells included oval or spherical masses of an apparently tenacious fluid of a brown tint. Single cells in the parenchyma likewise became brown; others were dotted, like a mezzotinto engraving, with barely distinguishable granules, which, however, in other cells were plainly visible; and, lastly, a few of these cells included spherical or oval masses of the same nature as those just mentioned in the exterior cells. Most or all of the endoderm-cells either contained a homogeneous brown fluid, or they appeared, from including excessively fine granules, like a mezzotinto engraving. In no case were any of the cells coloured green.

Some roots were immersed for from 20 to 44 hours in a solution of carbonate of potash of 7 to 1000; and these were affected in nearly the same manner as those in the soda solution. In the exterior cells, however, more granules were deposited; and these were oftener aggregated together, forming transparent orange-coloured spheres. The cells containing the granules or spheres were of a brown colour, and were arranged in longitudinal rows which alternated with rows of colourless cells. There were fewer granules in the parenchyma-cells than in the roots which had been subjected to the soda solution; and there were none in the endoderm-cells, even in roots which had been left immersed for 44 hours. A solution of phosphate of ammonia (4 to 1000) produced no effect on the roots after 43 hours' immersion.

Concluding Remarks. —The most remarkable conclusion which follows from the foregoing observations is that, in the roots of various plants, cells appearing quite similar and of the same homologous nature yet differ greatly in their contents, as shown by the action on them of certain solutions. Thus, of the exterior cells, one, two, or more adjacent longitudinal rows are often affected; and these alternate with rows in which no effect has been produced. Hence such roots present a longitudinally striped appearance. Single cells in the parenchyma, or occasionally two or three in a row, are in like manner affected; and so it is with the endoderm-cells, though it is rare when all are affected. The difference in aspect between sections of roots before and after their immersion in a proper solution is sometimes extra-ordinarily great. Of all the solutions tried, that of carbonate of ammonia acts most quickly, indeed almost instantaneously; and in all cases the action travels up the root from cell to cell with remarkable rapidity. With *Euphorbia Peplus* a solution of 1 part of the carbonate to 10,000 of water acted, though not very quickly.

When the action is very slight, the fluid contents of the cells are merely rendered pale brown. Nevertheless, judging from the gradations which could be observed, the brown tint is probably due to the presence of invisibly minute granules. More commonly distinctly visible granules are deposited, and these, in the case of *Cyclamen persicum*, adhered to the inner surface of the protoplasmic utricle; and this probably is the case with other plants. From granules we are led on to globules more or less confluent, and thence to spherical or oval or oddly shaped masses of translucent matter. These were coloured pale or dark blue or green in seven of the genera experimented on; but usually they are brownish. The granules or globules are not acted on, except as far as colour is concerned, by alcohol, sulphuric ether, a solution of iodine, or acetic acid; but they are slowly dissolved by caustic potash. It has been shown in a previous paper that in the leaves of certain plants carbonate of ammonia first causes the deposition of granules from the cell-sap, which aggregate together, and that matter is afterwards withdrawn from the protoplasmic utricle which likewise undergoes aggregation. Something of the same kind apparently occurs in roots, judging from the occasional difference in colour of the aggregated masses within the same cell, and more especially from what has been described as occurring in the root-cells of *Sarracenia* and *Pelargonium*.

Other solutions besides that of carbonate of ammonia induce nearly, but not quite, the same effects. Phosphate of ammonia acted more slowly than the carbonate on the roots of *Euphorbia Peplus*, and not at all on those of *Cyclamen*. With this latter plant and with the *Euphorbia* carbonate of soda was efficient, but in a less degree than the carbonate of ammonia. In one trial which was made, carbonate of potash acted on the exterior cells, but hardly at all on those of the parenchyma and endoderm. An extremely weak solution of osmic acid was highly potent, and the deposited granules were blackened. This acid is poisonous; but it must not be supposed that the mere death of a cell induces deposition. This is far from holding good; so that, judging from several trials, cells which have been killed are not acted on even by carbonate of ammonia, which is the most efficient of all known agents.

I have not sufficient data to judge how generally roots are acted on by the carbonate of ammonia in the manner described. Those of 49 genera, many of which belong to widely separated families, were tried. The roots of 15 were conspicuously acted on, those of 11 in a slight degree, making together 26 genera; while those of the remaining 23 genera were not affected, at least in any plain manner. But it should be stated that sections of all these latter roots were not made, so that the cells of the parenchyma and endoderm were not examined. We may therefore suspect that if various other reagents had been tried, and if sections had been made of all, some effect would have been observed in a larger proportional number of cases than actually occurred. I have elsewhere shown that the contents of the glandular hairs and of the epidermic and other cells of the leaves undergo aggregation in a considerable number of plants when they are acted on by carbonate of ammonia; and the roots of these same plants are especially liable to be affected in the same manner. We see this in 7 out of the 15 genera, which had their roots conspicuously affected coming under both heads.

The question naturally arises, what is the meaning of matter being precipitated by a solution of carbonate of ammonia and of some other substances in certain cells and not in other cells of the same homologous nature? The fact of granules and spherical masses being formed within the loose exfoliating cells of the root-cap, as was observed in several instances, and conspicuously in that of *Drosophyllum*, apparently indicates that such matter is no longer of any use to the plant, and is of the nature of an excretion. It does not, however, follow that all the aggregated matter within the root-cells is of this nature, though the greater part may be; and we know that in the filaments of *Spirogyra* not only are granules deposited from the cell-sap which aggregate into spheres, but that the spiral chlorophyll-bands also contract into spherical or oval masses. The view that the granules consist of excreted matter is supported, to a certain extent, by their not being redissolved, as far as I could judge, in the roots of living plants of *Euphorbia Peplus*; and in this respect they differ in a marked manner from the aggregated matter in the leaves of *Drosera* and its allies. A larger amount of granular matter is deposited close to the tip of the root than elsewhere; and it might have been expected that where growth with the accompanying chemical changes was most rapid, there the largest amount of excreted matter would accumulate. It also deserves notice that there exists some degree of antagonism between the presence of these granules and of starch-grains in the same cells. On the other hand, it must be admitted that no excretion in the vegetable kingdom, as far as is at present known, remains dissolved in the cell-sap, or, as in the present cases, is precipitated only through the action of certain reagents.

On the view here suggested the exterior cells in many rows, some parenchyma-cells, and many or most of the endoderm-cells serve as receptacles for useless matter. It will, however, at first appear highly improbable that so many cells should serve for such a purpose. But this objection has no great weight; for in certain cases a surprising number of cells may be found which, instead of containing chlorophyll-grains like the surrounding cells, are filled with crystalline masses of carbonate of lime and other earthy salts which are never redissolved. Many isolated cells or rows of cells likewise contain gummy, resinous, or oily secretions and other substances, which, it is believed, are of "no further use in the changes connected with nutrition or growth."[5] We thus see that useless or excreted matter is commonly collected in separate cells; and we thus get a clue, on the view here suggested, for understanding why the deposited granules and spherical masses are found in isolated cells or rows of cells, and not in the other cells of the same homologous nature; and this is the circumstance which, as lately remarked, at first surprised me most.

In the roots of plants the endoderm-cells commonly separate those of the parenchyma from the vascular bundle. Very little is known about their use or functions; so that every particular deserves notice. They resemble the exterior cells in their walls partly consisting of corky or cuticularized matter[6]; and we have here seen that they likewise resemble the exterior cells by serving as receptacles for the deposited granular matter, which, in accordance with our view, must be excreted from the inner parenchyma-cells or from the vascular bundle.

The fact of the granules being deposited in the exterior cells in one, two, or more adjacent longitudinal rows, which alternate with rows destitute of granules, is the more remarkable, as close to the tip of the root all the exterior cells are commonly gorged with granular matter. It appears, therefore, that matter of some kind must have passed laterally from those rows which do not contain granular matter, after being acted on by the ammonia, into the adjoining rows. Why the useless matter should not pass out of the root through the outer walls of the cells, probably depends on the thickness and cuticular nature of the outer walls.

Pfeffer states that root-hairs are developed on the gemmae, and apparently on the thallus, of *Marchantia polymorpha* from superficial cells which, even before the growth of the hairs, do not contain starch- or chlorophyll-grains; although these bodies are present together with matter of an unknown nature in the adjacent superficial cells. He has observed a nearly similar case with the roots of *Hydrocharis*.[7] No one else seems to have even suspected that root-hairs were not developed indifferently from any or all of the exterior cells. But it has now been shown that with many plants, with only one marked exception, namely that of *Cyclamen*, the root-hairs arise exclusively from cells in which granular matter has not been deposited after the action of certain solutions. This relation between the presence of hairs and the contents of the cells cannot be accounted for by matter, which would have been deposited if the roots had been subjected to a proper solution, having been consumed in the formation of the hairs; and this notion is wholly inapplicable to the cases described by Pfeffer. May we believe that cells filled with effete matter become unfitted for absorbing or transmitting water with the necessary salts, and do not therefore develop root-hairs? Or is the absence of hairs from the cells which contain the deposited matter due merely to the advantage which is commonly derived from a physiological division of labour? This and many other questions about the cells, in which granules or larger masses of translucent matter are deposited after certain solutions have been absorbed, cannot at present be answered. But I hope that some one better fitted than I am, from possessing much more chemical and histological knowledge, may be induced to investigate the whole subject.

1. [Read 16 March 1882.] *Journal of the Linnean Society (Botany)* 19 (1882): 239–61.†
2. 'Insectivorous Plants,' 1875, p. 64. The subject was at that time, 22 years ago, only casually investigated; and I believe that I erred greatly about *Lemna* unless, indeed, some different species was then observed, or that the season of the year makes a great difference in the behaviour of the roots, which is not probable.
3. The rhizomes and buried parts of the stems of this plant are white; but after immersion for a day in the ammonia solution they became in parts either pale or rich blue. This change of colour occasionally occurred in parts exposed to the air which had not been subjected to the solution. As a similar change occurs in certain cells in the roots of various plants after their immersion in the solution, I asked Mr. Sorby to be so kind as to examine the rhizomes and underground stems of the *Mercurialis*. He informs me that he does not understand the change of colour; but he was unable to spare time for a full examination. He found that when the rhizomes and stems were boiled in alcohol, they yielded matter which was soluble in water, and which appeared to pass so rapidly into a brown substance with curious shades of green, that the real change was hidden. On the whole, the appearances differed a good deal from those observed by him in the case of blue flowers.
4. See some remarks on this liquefaction of the outer surface of root-hairs by my son Francis and myself in 'The Power of Movement in Plants,' 1880, p. 69.
5. Sachs, 'Text-Book of Botany' (Engl. transl.), 1875, p. 113. Also De Bary, 'Vergleichende Anatomie,' pp. 142–143. When odoriferous oils or other strongly tasting or poisonous substances are deposited in cells, and are thus thrown out of the active life of the plant, there is reason to believe that they are by no means useless to it, but indirectly serve as a protection against insects and other enemies.
6. On the nature of endoderm-cells, see De Bary, 'Vergleichende Anatomie,' 1877, p. 129.
7. 'Arbeiten des botan. Instituts in Würzburg,' Band i. p. 79.

◂ The Action of Carbonate of Ammonia on Chlorophyll-Bodies[1]

In my 'Insectivorous Plants' I have described, under the term of aggregation, a phenomenon which has excited the surprise of all who have beheld it.[2] It is best exhibited in the tentacles or so-called glandular hairs of *Drosera*, when a minute particle of any solid substance, or a drop of almost any nitrogenous fluid, is placed on a gland. Under favourable circumstances the transparent purple fluid in the cells nearest

to the gland becomes in a few seconds or minutes slightly turbid. Soon
minute granules can be distinguished under a high power, which quickly
coalesce or grow larger; and for many hours afterwards oval or
globular, or curiously-shaped masses of a purple colour and of considerable size may be observed sending out processes or filaments, dividing,
coalescing, and redividing in the most singular manner, until finally one
or two solid spheres are formed which remain motionless. The moving
masses include vacuoles which change their appearance. (I append here
three figures of aggregated masses copied from my son Francis's paper,[3]
showing the forms assumed.) After aggregation has been partially
effected, the layer of protoplasm lining the walls of the cells may be seen
with singular clearness flowing in great waves; and my son observed
similarly flowing threads of protoplasm which connected together the
grains of chlorophyll. After a time the minute colourless particles which
are imbedded in the flowing protoplasm are drawn towards and unite
with the aggregated masses; so that the protoplasm on the walls being
now rendered quite transparent is no longer visible, though some is still
present, and still flows, as may be inferred from the occasional transport

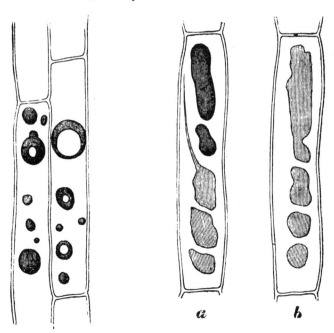

Fig. 1. Cells in a tentacle of *Drosera rotundifolia*, showing aggregated masses
after the action of carbonate of ammonia. Some of the masses with vacuoles.
Fig. 2. Aggregated masses undergoing redissolution. *b*, same cell as *a*, but masses
drawn at a later period.

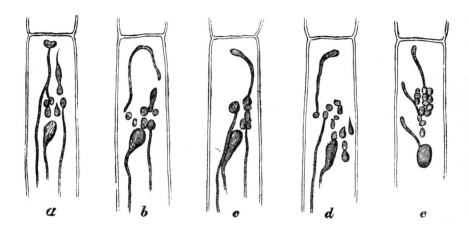

Fig. 3. The same cell drawn at successive short intervals of time, showing the aggregated masses produced by an infusion of raw meat. The changes of form occurred so rapidly that it was impossible to copy the appearance of the *whole* cell at a given moment.

of particles in the cell-sap. The granules withdrawn from the walls, together probably with some matter derived from the flowing proto-plasm and from the cell-sap, often form a colourless, or very pale purple, well-defined layer of considerable thickness, which surrounds the pre-viously aggregated and now generally spherical dark-purple masses. The surrounding layers or zones consist of solid matter, more brittle than the central parts of the aggregated masses, as could be seen when they were crushed beneath a cover-glass. It may be added that there is no *à priori* improbability in some of the protoplasm being withdrawn, together with the imbedded granules, from the walls; for the whole of the protoplasm within the hairs of *Tradescantia* contracts, when subjected to great cold, into several spheres, and these, when warmed again, spread themselves out over the walls.[4]

The process of aggregation commences in the gland which is stimu-lated, and slowly travels down the whole length of the tentacle, and even into the disk of the leaf, but very much more slowly than the impulse which causes the basal part of the tentacle to bend inwards. It is a more interesting fact that when the glands on the disk are stimulated, they transmit some influence to the glands of the surrounding tentacles, which undergo throughout their whole length the process of aggregation, although they themselves have not been directly stimulated; and this process may be compared with a reflex action in the nervous system of an animal. After a few days the solid aggregated masses are redissolved. The process of redissolution commences in the cells at the bases of the tentacles and travels slowly upwards; therefore in a reversed direction to that of aggregation. Considering that the aggregated masses are solid enough to be broken into fragments, their prompt redissolution is a surprising fact; and we are led to suspect that some ferment must be generated in the disk of the leaf, and be transmitted up the tentacles. The double process of aggregation and of redissolution takes place every time that a leaf of *Drosera* catches an insect.

Aggregation is a vital process—that is, it cannot occur in cells after their death. This was shown by waving leaves[5] for a few minutes in water at a temperature of 65.5° C. (150° F.), or even at a somewhat lower temperature, and then immersing them in a rather strong solution of carbonate of ammonia, which does not cause in this case any aggregation, although the most powerful of all known agents. If a tentacle is slightly crushed, so that many of the cells are ruptured, though they still retain much of their purple fluid contents, no aggregation occurs in them when they are similarly immersed, notwithstanding that in closely adjoining cells which have not been killed, as could be seen by the protoplasm still flowing round the walls, aggregation ensued. So that the process is quite arrested by the death of a cell, and it is much delayed if a leaf, before being immersed in the solution, is kept for some time in carbonic acid; and this agrees with the well-known fact that protoplasm retains its activity only as long as it is in an oxygenated condition. When tentacles, including recently aggregated masses, are suddenly killed or much injured by being dipped into hot water, or by being irrigated with alcohol, acetic acid, or a solution of iodine, the aggregated masses suddenly disintegrate and disappear, leaving only a little fine granular matter; but this disintegration does not occur with the more solid masses which have been aggregated for some time.

From the several foregoing considerations, from the aggregated masses being of an albuminoid nature (as shown by the tests employed by my son Francis, and as is admitted by Pfeffer[6]), and from their incessant, long-continued amoeba-like movements, I formerly concluded that not only these masses, but that the minute globules which first appear in the cell-sap consist, *at least in part*, of living and spontaneously moving protoplasm. And I feel compelled to adhere to my original conclusion, notwithstanding that such high authorities as Cohn and Pfeffer believe that the aggregated masses consist merely of condensed cell-sap. The movements of the masses, I presume, are considered by these botanists to be of the same nature as those curious ones described by Beneke as occurring in myelin when immersed in water and in a solution of sugar.[7]

From the doubts thus thrown upon my original conclusion, it seemed to me advisable to observe the action of carbonate of ammonia on grains of chlorophyll, as it is generally admitted that these consist of modified protoplasm. The grains not only change their positions under certain circumstances, which may be due merely to the movements of the streaming protoplasm in which they are imbedded, but they likewise have the power of changing their shapes, as has been recently proved by Stahl.[8] They are also capable of self-division.[9] Now, if it can be shown that a solution of carbonate of ammonia tends to cause the grains of living chlorophyll to become confluent one with another and with previously aggregated masses, this fact would support the conclusion that the aggregated masses consist, at least in part, of living protoplasm, to which their incessant movements may be attributed. And it is the object of the present paper to show that chlorophyll-bodies are thus acted on in certain cases by carbonate of ammonia. The fact by itself possesses some little interest, independently of the light which it throws on the remarkable phenomenon of aggregation.

Dionaea muscipula.—The effects of carbonate of ammonia are best shown in the case of young, small, and thin leaves produced by starved plants, as these are quickly penetrated by the solution. Transverse sections of such leaves and of others were made before they had been immersed[10]; and the cells, including those of the epidermis, could easily be seen to be packed with grains of chlorophyll. It is, however, necessary to avoid examining a leaf which has ever caught an insect; for in this case many of the cells will be found filled with yellowish matter instead of with chlorophyll-grains. Several leaves were left for different lengths of time in solutions of different strengths; but it will suffice to describe a few cases. A small thin leaf was immersed for 24 hours in a solution of 7 parts of the carbonate to 1000 of water, and transverse sections were then examined. The cells near the margin of the leaf, throughout its whole thickness, did not now exhibit a single chlorophyll-grain, but in their place masses of transparent yellowish-green matter of the most diversified shapes. They resembled those of *Drosera* shown at fig. 3, if we suppose several of them to be pressed lightly together. Some of the masses in the same cell were connected by extremely fine threads. Spheres of more solid matter were sometimes included within the oddly-shaped greenish masses. The contrast in appearance between these sections and those taken from one corner of the same leaf before it had been immersed was wonderfully great. The sections were then clarified by being left for some time in alcohol, but not a grain of chlorophyll could be seen; whereas the fresh slices similarly clarified exhibited with the utmost plainness the now colourless grains. The oddly-shaped green masses exhibited none of the movements so conspicuous in the case of

Drosera; but this could hardly have been expected after the injury caused by slicing; and the leaves are much too opaque to be examined without the aid of sections. Some other sections from the same immersed leaf presented a rather different appearance, as they contained much extremely fine granular green matter, which became pale brown after being kept in alcohol. No chlorophyll-grains could be seen in any of these sections. After adding iodine (dissolved in water with iodide of potassium), many particles of starch became visible by being coloured blue; but none were present in the first described section. Some of the larger rounded aggregated masses were coated with blue particles. Others were quite free of such particles, and were coloured by the iodine bright orange.

A superficial slice was taken from a fresh leaf, showing the upper epidermic and glandular surface, and all the cells abounded with large grains of chlorophyll. But with a leaf which had been immersed for 24 hours in a solution of carbonate of ammonia (7 to 1000), a similar section presented a wonderfully different aspect; no chlorophyll-grains could be seen. Some of the cells contained one or two transparent yellowish spheres, which, it could hardly be doubted, had been formed by the fusion of previously-existing chlorophyll-grains. Other cells contained very fine brownish granular matter, and this apparently had been deposited from the cell-sap with its colour changed. This granular matter was generally aggregated into one or two either separate or more or less confluent spherical balls, having a rough surface. Sometimes a dark-brown granular sphere was surrounded by a zone of paler granular matter. In other cases brown granular spheres lay in the centre of transparent yellow spheres. In one case a sphere of this latter kind, with two others consisting exclusively of the yellowish transparent matter, were observed in the same cell. In other cases the brown balls were surrounded merely by an extremely narrow border of transparent matter. It appears that in these cases the granular matter had first been deposited, and then had become more or less aggregated into balls; and that afterwards the yellowish transparent matter, formed by the fusion of the modified chlorophyll-grains, had aggregated either round the granular matter or into independent spherical and oddly-shaped masses.

Transverse sections of other immersed leaves presented various appearances. In one cell a central transparent sphere was surrounded by a halo of brown granular matter, and this again by a zone of the transparent matter, and such matter quite filled some adjoining cells. In the cells of another leaf there were, throughout its whole thickness, yellow, greenish, orange, pale or very dark-brown spheres. Some of these latter spheres had a dark centre, which was so hard that it was cracked by pressure, and the line of separation from the surrounding zone of paler matter was distinct. Two brown spheres were in one case included within the same transparent sphere. Gradations seemed to show that the opaque granular matter ultimately passed into dark-coloured transparent matter. In these same sections there were some colourless or yellowish highly-transparent small spheres, which, I believe, were merely much swollen chlorophyll-grains. One, two, or more of such grains, while still partly retaining their outlines, sometimes clung to the darker granular spheres. When there were only one or two of them thus clinging, they assumed the shapes of half- or quarter-moons. It appeared as if such swollen grains when completely confluent had often given rise to the pale zones surrounding the granular spheres. The pale zones were rendered still more transparent by acetic acid; and on one occasion they quite disappeared, after being left in the acid for 24 hours; but whether the matter was dissolved or had merely disintegrated was not ascertained. This acid produces the same effect on recently aggregated pale-coloured or almost colourless matter in the tentacles of *Drosera*.

In one leaf a good many unaltered chlorophyll-grains could still be distinguished in some of the cells; and this occurred more frequently in the thickest part of the leaf, near the midrib, than elsewhere. In one section the chlorophyll-grains had run together, and formed in some of the cells narrow green rims round all four walls. In many sections, more especially in those in which the process of aggregation had not been carried very far, there was much extremely fine granular matter, which did not resemble smashed or disintegrated chlorophyll-grains, such as may often be seen in sections of ordinary leaves. This granular matter occasionally passed into excessively minute, transparent, more or less confluent globules.

Judging from these several appearances, we may conclude that carbonate of ammonia first acts on the cell-sap, producing a granular deposit of a pale brownish colour, and that this tends to aggregate into balls; that afterwards the grains of chlorophyll are acted on, some swelling up and becoming completely confluent, so that no trace of their original structure is left, and others breaking up into extremely fine greenish granular matter, which appears likewise to undergo aggregation. The final result is the formation of balls of brown, and sometimes reddish, granular matter, often surrounded by zones, more or less thick, of yellowish or greenish, or almost colourless transparent matter. Or, again, spheres, ovals, and oddly-shaped masses are formed, consisting exclusively of this transparent yellowish-green matter. As soon as the process of aggregation has been thoroughly carried out, not a grain of chlorophyll can be seen.

Drosera rotundifolia.—It is advisable to select for observation pale reddish leaves, as the dark-red ones are too opaque; and the process of aggregation does not go on well in the small completely green leaves which may sometimes be found. The tentacles, which are merely delicate prolongations of the leaf, are from their transparency well fitted for observation. In sections of the disks of fresh leaves, the cells of the epidermis are seen to abound with grains of chlorophyll, as well as those of the underlying parenchyma. The bases of the exterior tentacles and the part immediately beneath the glands are generally coloured pale green from the presence of chlorophyll-grains in the parenchyma; and some occur throughout the whole length of the longer tentacles, but are not easily seen on account of the purple cell-sap. Sometimes the epidermal cells of the longer tentacles include chlorophyll-grains; but this is rather a rare event. The footstalks of the short tentacles on the disk are bright green, and invariably abound with grains of chlorophyll.

A pale leaf, in which the basal cells of the exterior tentacles contained numerous grains of chlorophyll, was left for 24 hours in a solution of only 2 parts of the carbonate to 1000 of water; and now innumerable greenish spheres, resembling oil in appearance, were present in these cells, and the ordinary chlorophyll-grains had in most places disappeared. Nevertheless in several cells some swollen grains were still distinct. Other cells contained fine granular or pulpy green matter collected into masses at one end. In a few other cells the chlorophyll-grains had run together, forming a continuous green rim with a sinuous outline attached to the walls. In fresh leaves the guard-cells of the stomata include grains of chlorophyll; but these, after the leaf has been immersed in the carbonate, almost always become fused into a few nearly colourless spheres.

Sections made from leaves which had been left for 22 hours in a solution of 4 to 1000 exhibited, in the upper and lower epidermal cells of the disk, and in the cells of the parenchyma near the bases of the exterior tentacles, greenish spheres; and in such cells there were no chlorophyll-grains, but they were still present in some few of the epidermal cells which did not contain aggregated masses, and they abounded in the parenchyma in the middle of the disk, where there were only a few green spheres. These sections were irrigated with the solution of iodine, and the green spheres became yellow; and many minute elliptical particles of starch, coloured blue, could now be seen. Such particles were not visible in the sections of fresh leaves, and I believe that they had been imbedded within the chlorophyll-grains, from which the enveloping protoplasm had been withdrawn to form the green spheres.

One of the above leaves was left in the ammonia solution for three days, by which time it had become flaccid, being evidently killed. The numerous green spheres were blackened, but perfectly retained their outlines. No chlorophyll-grains could be seen, but many particles of starch. When leaves were left for some time in a solution of 7 to 1000, much pulpy green matter and innumerable spheres were sometimes formed, but no large aggregated masses; so that in these cases the solution appeared to have been too strong. The degree to which the grains of chlorophyll are acted on varies much from unknown causes; for in some tentacles, which exhibited strongly-marked aggregation after being left for 36 hours in the stronger solution, the grains could still be seen, but only after they had been cleared by immersion in acetic acid.

A leaf was laid on a glass plate kept in a damp chamber, and two or three tentacles at one end were covered with thin glass, so as to prevent their bending, and were irrigated with the ammonia solution of 7 to 1000. After 24 hours and 48 hours these tentacles included many dark-purple aggregated masses; nevertheless plenty of chlorophyll-grains were still visible. In the disk of this leaf, however, near the bases of these tentacles, there were some spheres of a fine green tint, and others purple in the centre surrounded by a distinctly defined green zone; and in most of the cells containing these spheres not a grain of chlorophyll could be distinguished. That the green surrounding zones had been derived from the chlorophyll-grains is, I think, certain; for the purple colour of the central spheres showed that the cell-contents had not been originally green. Other cells in these same sections included irregularly-shaped masses of a purplish-green colour; and these were observed slowly to change their forms in the usual manner. When acetic acid was added to them, the green transparent spheres and the zones of similar green matter round the purple spheres instantly disappeared, either from being dissolved or, as seems more probable, from being killed and suddenly disintegrating. On another occasion boiling water and alcohol produced the same effect on the spheres. Tentacles still retaining their chlorophyll-grains, but with many very pale-coloured homogeneous aggregated masses (which were seen in movement), were irrigated with acetic acid; and it was curious to observe how instantaneously they became filled with small transparent spheres. In a short time, however, the outlines of the larger masses were alone left; then these disappeared, and finally the small enclosed spheres. On the other hand, some dark-coloured solid aggregated spherical masses did not disappear when left for 24 hours in acetic acid.

The effect of the ammonia solution (4 and 7 to 1000) on the epidermal cells of the upper surface of the disk was now more especially observed. In some cases all these cells which, as already stated, invariably contain many chlorophyll-grains, included after immersion in the solution only a single or several green transparent spheres; but more commonly the spheres were very dark purple or brown. Sometimes a central sphere, which was so solid that it could be cracked, was surrounded by a well-defined paler zone. Numerous gradations could be traced, showing that several small spheres and irregularly shaped globules often coalesce, and thus form the larger rounded masses. It was repeatedly observed that when the epidermal cells contained only one or two large spheres, not a single grain of chlorophyll could be seen. It is surprising that dark purple or brown or almost black spheres should be formed in the epidermal cells of green leaves; for before immersion the cell-contents were colourless, with the exception of the chlorophyll-grains; but the fact is less surprising when it is known that these cells turn more or less red as they grow old if they are exposed to a bright light. In some of these leaves the basal cells of the longer exterior tentacles had become beautifully transparent from the aggregation of their contents into green or greenish-purple masses; and here no chlorophyll-grains could be seen; but in other parts of the same tentacles, where the aggregated masses were of a purple tint, the chlorophyll-grains were still plainly visible.

Finally, it appears certain that in the leaves of *Drosera* the grains of chlorophyll, if left long enough in a weak solution of the carbonate, sometimes break up and form translucent greenish globules, which are much smaller than the original chlorophyll-grains; and that these, by coalescing, form larger masses, which again coalesce into a few spheres or into a single one. In other cases the chlorophyll-grains swell and coalesce without having previously broken up into globules. During these various changes the aggregated masses often become coloured by the modified cell-sap, more especially in the case of the epidermal cells; or they may form a zone round the already aggregated cell-sap, in which case a dark central sphere is surrounded by a less dark or by a light-green transparent zone of matter.

It remains to be considered whether the grains of chlorophyll, after complete fusion or aggregation, are ever reformed and reassume their normal positions on the walls of the cells. Although the purple aggregated masses within the tentacles are soon redissolved, the cells becoming refilled with transparent purple fluid, it by no means follows that the chlorophyll-grains should be reformed; and such a capacity would be an interesting point. To ascertain whether this occurred, drops of a weak solution of carbonate of ammonia (2 to 1000) were daily placed during 5 days on several leaves on a growing plant; but, to my surprise, the tentacles remained after the first day expanded, with their glands bright red and copiously secreting, and they exhibited little aggregation. Large drops of a solution of 4 to 1000 were next placed on three reddish leaves, fresh drops being added in about 18 hours. After an interval of 41½ hours from the time when the drops were first placed on the leaves, three short central tentacles on one leaf were examined, and the cells were seen to be filled with quickly moving aggregated masses, and not one grain of chlorophyll could be distinguished. In 66 hours after the drops had been given the leaves were well syringed with water; and now the central tentacles of a second leaf were examined, in which there was much aggregated matter and no chlorophyll-grains. A third leaf was examined 5 days after the drops had been given, and the aggregated masses appeared to be breaking up into small highly transparent spheres. In two, however, of the short central tentacles of this leaf the cells at their bases contained no aggregated matter and plenty of chlorophyll-grains. It is probable that if these tentacles had been examined two or three days earlier, an opposite state of things would have prevailed. In a third central tentacle from this same leaf there was still much aggregated matter in the basal cells; and here a few irregularly shaped chlorophyll-grains could be seen. In other tentacles from this same leaf, and from two other leaves which had been similarly treated, some of the aggregated masses had become granular, discoloured, and opaque; and this indicates that the solution had either been too strong, or that too large a quantity had been given.

Drops of a strong filtered solution of raw meat were now placed on 7 reddish leaves, the tentacles of which all became much inflected and their glands blackened. After 22½ hours they were syringed with water, and one leaf was cut off for examination. The contents of five short central tentacles from this leaf were aggregated down to their bases, and not a grain of chlorophyll could be seen. Some of the aggregated masses were almost white with a faint tinge of green, and were moving quickly. In the long exterior tentacles which had not at first been touched by the infusion (that is, not until they had become inflected), the aggregation had not as yet travelled down to the basal cells; and here the grains of chlorophyll were quite distinct. The infusion was too strong; for after five days one out of the six remaining leaves was dead; two others were much injured, with the outer tentacles killed, those on the disk, though immersed for a longer time, being still alive; the fourth leaf was considerably injured; the fifth and sixth looked fresh and vigorous, with their glands, now of a red colour, secreting freely. Five of the short central tentacles from one of these latter leaves were now (i.e. after the five days) examined: in three of them only a trace of aggregation was left, and plenty of chlorophyll-grains could be seen; in a fourth tentacle there were still some aggregated masses and a few chlorophyll-grains; in a fifth there were many aggregated masses and some fine granular matter, and here no chlorophyll-grains were distinguishable. There can hardly be a doubt that in four out of these five tentacles the chlorophyll-grains had been reformed. On one of the much-injured leaves, in which the glands of the central tentacles were still opaque, the cells in their footstalks contained some aggregated and some brownish granular matter; and here minute globules were arranged along the walls of the cells in the places where chlorophyll-grains ought to have stood; but whether these were remnants which had never wholly disappeared or new grains reforming could not be ascertained.

Drops of a weaker infusion of raw meat were next placed on seven reddish leaves, which were all greatly acted on; but the infusion was still rather too strong. In from 24 to 25 hours afterwards all the leaves were well syringed; and small pieces having been cut off two of them, several of the short central tentacles were examined. In one of these leaves a very few chlorophyll-grains could be seen in some few cells in one of the tentacles which had not undergone so much aggregation as the others. In the piece from the second leaf not a single chlorophyll-grain could be distinguished in any of the short central tentacles. The sections were then immersed in alcohol, and in a few minutes all the aggregated masses were broken up into very fine granular matter; but no chlorophyll-grains could be seen, except in the one tentacle above mentioned. In three days after the drops had been first given, four of the leaves (including one of those from which a small piece had been cut off) looked vigorous, and were fully or almost fully expanded. The fifth leaf, from which a piece had likewise been cut off, appeared somewhat injured. The sixth had its tentacles still inflected and seemed much injured, and was apparently almost dead.

Four of the central tentacles on the vigorous leaf, from which a piece had been cut off, after 24 hours, were now (*i.e.* on the third day after the drop had been given) examined. In most of the basal cells of three of these tentacles only a trace of aggregation was left, and many chlorophyll-grains could be seen in them; but these were not so regular in shape or so regularly placed as are the normal grains; so that I presume they were in the act of reforming. Two basal cells in one of these tentacles still contained large quickly moving aggregated masses, and not a grain of chlorophyll could be distinguished in them. When this section was irrigated with the solution of iodine, the aggregated masses in the two just-mentioned cells instantly broke up into brownish granular matter, and the irregular and, as I supposed, just reformed chlorophyll-grains in the adjoining cells ran together and became confluent, forming narrow rims along the walls.

After intervals of 4, 6, and 8 days from the time when the drops were given, 15 central tentacles on three of the leaves were examined; and in all of these tentacles, excepting one in which there was still much aggregated matter, chlorophyll-grains could be seen. After 11 days one of the leaves, from which a small piece had been cut off after an interval of 24 hours, and in which most of the central tentacles then included no chlorophyll-grains, was now reexamined. The central tentacles appeared perfectly healthy and were secreting: in 8 out of 10 of them, the cells included chlorophyll-grains having the usual appearance; in the other two tentacles there was still much aggregated matter and no ordinary chlorophyll-grains, but some few irregularly shaped chlorophyll-grains. With respect to the second leaf, from which a small piece had been cut off, and in which the central tentacles did not then (*i.e.* after 24 hours) contain a single chlorophyll-grain, only a very few of the central tentacles now (*i.e.* after 11 days) appeared healthy; but in two of them, which appeared quite uninjured, there were innumerable perfect chlorophyll-grains in all the cells from the glands down to the base.

Considering the whole of the evidence here given, there can hardly be a doubt that with the leaves of *Drosera* as soon as the aggregated masses break up, and even before they are wholly redissolved, grains of chlorophyll are reformed.

Drosophyllum lusitanicum.—The footstalks of the tentacles are bright green, from the large number of chlorophyll-grains which they contain. Two leaves were immersed in a solution of carbonate of ammonia (4 to 1000) for 23 and 24 hours, and the cells of the footstalks now contained innumerable spheres, some much smaller and some much larger than the grains of chlorophyll, and other oddly shaped masses, more or less confluent, of translucent bright-yellow matter, which, when irrigated with alcohol, instantly broke up into fine granular matter. I looked in vain in several of these tentacles for grains of chlorophyll. Another leaf was immersed for only 16½ hours in a weaker solution of 2 to 1000; but this sufficed to produce an abundance of yellow translucent bodies, which were seen to change their forms greatly, though slowly. In many, but not in all, of the cells of this leaf the grains of chlorophyll were still quite distinct. The several leaves were left both in the stronger and weaker solutions for 48 hours; and this caused the yellow spheres and masses to disintegrate into brownish granular matter. In this respect the aggregated masses in *Drosophyllum* differ from those in *Drosera* and *Dionaea.* Leaves were also left for 24 and 48 hours in an infusion of raw meat; but no yellow aggregated masses were thus produced, and the grains of chlorophyll remained perfectly distinct. This singular difference in the action of the infusion of raw meat on the tentacles, as compared with those of *Drosera*, may perhaps be accounted for by their serving in *Drosophyllum* almost exclusively for the secretion of the viscid fluid by which insects are captured—the power of digestion and of absorption being chiefly confined, as I have explained in my 'Insectivorous Plants' (pp. 332–342), to the minute sessile glands on the disks of the leaves.

As in the three foregoing genera the grains of chlorophyll tend to aggregate into moving masses under the long-continued influence of a weak solution of carbonate of ammonia, I thought that the grains would probably be similarly acted on in all insectivorous plants; but this did not prove to be the case. The immersion of leaves of the common *Pinguicula* in a solution of the ammonia and in an infusion of raw meat did not cause any aggregation of the chlorophyll-grains, though numerous transparent spheres were formed within the glandular hairs. Again, the immersion in carbonate of ammonia of pieces of young and old pitchers of a *Nepenthes* (garden hybrid variety) caused the appearance of innumerable more or less confluent spheres of various sizes in the glands on the inner surface of the pitcher and in the exterior epidermal cells. These were formed of translucent matter, either almost colourless or of a brown, orange, purple, or greenish tint; but the grains of chlorophyll were not acted on.

Sarracenia purpurea.—The pitchers of this plant are evidently adapted for catching and drowning insects; but whether they can digest them, or may have the power of absorbing matter from their decaying remains, is doubtful.[11] Many observations were made; but one case will suffice. A piece of a pitcher was left for 24 hours in a solution of 4 parts of the carbonate of ammonia to 1000 of water, and for 24 additional hours in a solution of 7 to 1000. In the cells of the parenchyma, especially in those close to the vascular bundles, there were many spheres and aggregated masses of bright orange transparent matter. Spheres of the same and of various other tints were present in the epidermal cells, more especially in those on the inner surface of the pitcher; and some of these spheres were of exactly the same pale greenish colour as the swollen chlorophyll-grains which were still present in some places, being often collected together into rounded masses. In many of the epidermal cells which contained spheres no chlorophyll-grains could be seen, though they were abundantly present in the epidermis of fresh leaves; and it is this fact which chiefly leads me to believe that the chlorophyll-grains sometimes become so completely fused together as to form spheres, being often blended with the aggregated and coloured cell-sap. When a solution of iodine was added to these sections, the pale-coloured spheres and irregularly shaped aggregated masses became bright orange, and they were sometimes sprinkled over with blue particles of starch. The iodine did not cause their immediate disintegration and disappearance, nor did alcohol or acetic acid. In this respect they differ from the recently aggregated masses in *Drosera*; though in this latter plant the older and more solid aggregated masses are not acted on by these reagents. Many of the cells contained green granular matter, formed either by the chlorophyll-grains having been mechanically smashed or by their disintegration; and acetic acid sometimes caused this granular matter to change instantly into the same orange tint as that of the aggregated masses.

The orange spheres and variously shaped masses were seen in many sections of pitchers which had been exposed for different lengths of time to solutions of the carbonate of different strengths; and in many of them swollen grains of chlorophyll had become more or less confluent. The original nature of the latter could be recognized by the sinuous outlines and greenish tint. They were not seen to change their shapes spontaneously; but this could not have been expected in sections. Portions of a pitcher left in distilled water for nearly three days did not exhibit a single orange sphere or aggregated mass; but there were some colourless oil-globules which were dissolved by alcohol; and the chlorophyll-grains, though generally much swollen, were still distinct. It may therefore be concluded that in *Sarracenia* the chlorophyll-grains often undergo aggregation under the influence of carbonate of ammonia, but that they are less easily acted on than those of *Dionaea* and *Drosera*.

Leaves with Glandular Hairs and Other Leaves.—I had formerly observed, as described in my 'Insectivorous Plants,' that the glandular hairs of some plants absorb carbonate of ammonia and animal matter, and that aggregation is thus caused in them. Consequently such leaves and others without hairs were immersed in solutions of carbonate of ammonia (4 and 7 to 1000) generally for 24 hours. No marked effect was produced on the chlorophyll-grains, excepting their occasional displacement, in the following cases (plants were selected almost by hazard, but which belong to different families):—first, of leaves not bearing many or any glandular hairs, namely those of *Brassica*, *Fumaria*, *Fuchsia*, *Robinia*, *Oxalis*, *Tropaeolum*, *Euphorbia*, *Stapelia*, *Beta*, *Allium*, *Lemna*, a fern (*Nephrodium*), a *Marchantia*, and a moss. Nor were the grains acted on in two species of *Saxifraga* (except on one occasion, when they formed masses shaped like a horseshoe, presently to be described), nor in *Primula sinensis*—although the leaves of these three species are clothed with glandular hairs, which absorb carbonate of ammonia and undergo aggregation. Young leaves of *Dipsacus sylvestris* were immersed for 24 hours in a solution of 7 to 1000, and large yellowish highly refracting spheres were formed in the upper epidermic cells which do not include any chlorophyll-grains, and the grains were not at all aggregated in other parts of the leaf. When the sections were irrigated with acetic acid or with alcohol, the spheres in the epidermal cells disappeared quickly, in nearly the same manner as occurs with recently aggregated masses in the cells of *Drosera*.

Leaves of *Cyclamen persicum*, which bear hardly any glandular hairs, were left in a solution of 7 to 1000 for 43 hours, and this caused the chlorophyll-grains to collect into heaps; in some parts the grains retained their outlines distinct; but in other parts they formed perfectly homogeneous bright-green masses of the shape of a horseshoe. These were cleared by alcohol; and it was evident that the grains had become completely fused together. It is remarkable that many of the central cells near the vascular bundles contained spherical or oddly shaped confluent globules of pale-blue transparent matter. In the preceding paper an analogous result from the action of carbonate of ammonia is described in the underground stems and rhizomes of *Mercurialis perennis*. The leaves were left for 24 additional hours in the solution, and now the horseshoe masses disappeared, being converted into pulpy matter. The immersion of the leaves of this *Cyclamen* in water for 47 hours caused the chlorophyll-grains to accumulate into heaps, as is know to follow from any injury there was hardly a trace of their confluence, and none of the pale-blue globules were present. Similar horseshoe masses were seen, but only on one occasion, in the leaves of *Nicotiana tabacum* after their immersion in the solution; and so it was with the stems of *Euphorbia Peplus*. Portions cut from a leaf of *Mirabilis Jalapa* were left for 16½ hours in solutions of 4 and of 7 to 1000, and the chlorophyll-grains in many of the cells became completely confluent, forming horseshoe masses or rings; and they were sufficiently solid to project when the cells were torn open. When these horseshoe masses and rings were irrigated with acetic acid, they became so transparent that even their outlines could hardly be distinguished. If in these plants, and more especially in *Cyclamen* and *Mirabilis*, the confluent chlorophyll-grains forming the horseshoe masses are still alive (and this is rendered probable by their bright-green colour, and in the former plant by their breaking up when left for an additional day in the solution, and in the latter plant by the action of acetic acid on them), we have in these cases a first step in the process which in some plants leads to the formation of spontaneously moving masses lying free in the cell-sap.

Pelargonium zonale. —The effects produced by the immersion of the leaves of this plant for 24 or 48 hours in solutions of 4 or 7 parts of carbonate of ammonia to 1000 of water are not a little perplexing. The leaves are clothed with glandular hairs, which absorb the ammonia and undergo aggregation. Moreover, numerous almost colourless, shining, translucent spheres generally, but not invariably, appear in most of the epidermal cells in which there are no grains of chlorophyll, and in the palisade-cells, in which they abound, and likewise in the parenchyma. The smaller spheres blend together, and thus form large ones. A solution of only 2 to 1000 sometimes sufficed to produce the spheres. Usually the spheres are not acted on by alcohol, but occasionally they were dissolved by it. If after immersion in alcohol they are subjected to the iodine solution, they soon almost disappear; but this, again, does not invariably occur. Acetic acid always caused their rapid disappearance, and without any apparent effervescence, a slight granular residue being sometimes left; and this occurred with leaves which had been kept so long in the solution that they were dead. The acid dissolved, of course with effervescence, the crystalline balls of carbonate of lime which occupy many of the palisade-cells. When sulphuric ether was added, the smaller spheres of transparent matter disappeared in the course of a few minutes, while the larger ones became brownish and granular in their centres; but this granular matter disappeared after a time, empty transparent bag-like membranes being left. Traces of similar membranous envelopes could sometimes be detected after the administration of acetic acid. Caustic potash did not act quickly on the spheres, but sometimes caused them to swell up. I do not know what ought to be inferred from the action of these several reagents with respect to the nature of the spheres and aggregated masses in which I never saw any movement.

On two or three occasions the palisade-cells of leaves which had been immersed in the solutions, instead of containing large transparent spheres, were gorged with innumerable, often irregularly-shaped, more or less confluent globules, many of them being much smaller than the chlorophyll-grains. This occurred with a leaf which had been immersed for only 18½ hours in a solution of 4 to 1000. After sections of this leaf had been cleared with alcohol, it was irrigated with the solution of iodine, and the globules rapidly ran together or became confluent, forming irregular amorphous masses.

It was difficult to ascertain whether the chlorophyll-grains ever or often became blended with other matter, and thus aided in the formation of the transparent spheres. The difficulty was partly due to the grains being easily acted on by water. Thus, in some sections made and placed in water, and then cleared in alcohol, no grains could be distinguished; while they were distinct in sections of the same leaf which had not been wetted before being placed in alcohol. Many grains were also found in a disintegrated condition in uninjured leaves which had been kept for 47 hours in water. It may be here added that not a single sphere could be seen in these leaves; nor were they present in leaves slightly injured by being kept for 24 hours in a very weak solution of osmic acid. Nor, again, in a leaf which had been immersed in an infusion of raw meat for 24 and for 50 hours; and in this leaf the chlorophyll-grains were still visible in many places, but were sometimes heaped together. Notwithstanding the difficulty of ascertaining the effects of carbonate of ammonia on the chlorophyll-grains, chiefly owing to the action of water on them, I am led to believe, from the gradations which could be followed, and from the absence of chlorophyll-grains in the cells in which one or two large spheres were present, that in the case of the palisade- and parenchyma-cells matter produced by the disintegration of the grains first aggregates, together with other matter derived from the cell-sap, into minute globules, and that these aggregate into the larger spheres. I will give a single instance:—A leaf was immersed for 22½ hours in a solution of the carbonate of 4 to 1000, and sections, after being cleared in alcohol, exhibited in many places distinct chlorophyll-grains, and in other places only very fine granular matter, and in a very few cells minute transparent globules. The leaf was left for 24 additional hours in the solution; and now sections cleared in alcohol exhibited numerous minute shining translucent globules, many of which were smaller than the few remaining chlorophyll-grains. There were also other much larger transparent spheres, more or less confluent, which, when irrigated with acetic acid, instantly disappeared.

A leaf was immersed in a solution of 4 parts of phosphate of ammonia to 1000 of water, and after 23 hours there was no trace of aggregation. It was left for 24½ additional hours in the solution; and now sections cleared in alcohol exhibited not only minute shining colourless globules, smaller than the few remaining chlorophyll-grains, but plenty of large spheres, more or less aggregated together; and in the cells containing such spheres no chlorophyll-grains could be seen. The spheres, both large and small, disappeared instantly when acetic acid was added, as in the case of those produced by the carbonate. It appears, therefore, that these two salts act in the same manner, but that the phosphate acts more slowly than the carbonate, as is likewise the case with *Drosera*. A leaf immersed for 45 hours in a solution of 2 parts of nitrate of ammonia to 1000 of water was a good deal infiltrated and darkened in colour; but no spheres were formed; some of the chlorophyll-grains had, however, become confluent while still adhering to the walls of the cells.

Spirogyra (*crassa?*).—When filaments of this alga were placed in a solution of carbonate of ammonia (4 to 1000), the cell-sap became in a few minutes cloudy from the formation of innumerable granules, and the green spiral chlorophyll-band soon began to contract. A filament was irrigated under a cover-glass at 11.10 A.M. (Oct. 4) with the solution; and by 11.25 the cell-sap had everywhere become granular: in two of the cells the pointed ends of the chlorophyll-band and the irregular lateral projections were retracted, so that these bands now appeared much smoother and blunter than before. In two neighbouring cells the bands had become converted into circular masses surrounding the nuclei.

At 12.50 two cells were selected for further observation: in one of them the original spiral band now formed a layer of nearly uniform thickness, except in three of the corners where there were rounded lumps, which adhered closely to the two transverse and to one of the longitudinal walls of the cell. By 4 P.M. the layer on the longitudinal wall had become in the middle so thin that it consisted of a mere thread, which at 4.15 broke and disappeared; the upper end (with reference to the observer) of the layer then rapidly contracted into a pear-shaped mass. The layer at the lower end of the cell had by this time assumed a dumb-bell shape, which, however, soon afterwards became cylindrical. At 7.10 P.M. the appearance of the cell was utterly different; for there were now at the upper end two ill-defined masses, and at the lower end two somewhat irregular balls of green matter connected together by a thin band. At 8 A.M. on the following morning there was a large oval mass lying obliquely across the upper end of the cell, with its two extremities connected by bands with two spheres in the lower corners.

The changes in the other cell, which was observed at the same time, were almost equally great. The spiral band was first converted into two layers lining the two transverse walls, and these were connected together by a sinuous longitudinal band. At 4 P.M. there was in one of the corners a large pear-shaped mass, which contracted while it was watched into an oval mass, and at the opposite corner a small dark-green sphere. By 7.10 P.M. there were two spherical masses and an oval one, which latter by the next morning formed a much elongated dark band; and instead of two there was now only a single separate sphere. At this same time two adjoining cells included four and five oval or spherical chlorophyll-balls; but one cell still retained a spiral band. Alcohol and acetic acid produced only the same clarifying effect on these masses as in the case of ordinary chlorophyll-grains.

Filaments of this alga were left for 26 hours in a solution of only 1 part of the carbonate to 1000 of water; but this sufficed to cause some granular deposition in the cell-sap, and many of the cells included, instead of the spiral band, spherical or oval or pear-shaped masses (and in one instance a half-moon-shaped mass) connected together by the finest threads of green matter, one of which was seen to break, and the pear-shaped mass quickly became almost spherical. The changes of form and the movements of the chlorophyll-band in the foregoing several cases, under the influence of the ammonia solution, closely resemble in most respects those which may be seen within the tentacles of *Drosera*. The above weak solution seemed to be favourable to the health of the plants; for after six days' immersion they looked greener and more vigorous than other plants of the same lot which had been kept in plain water. The cell-sap still contained brownish granular matter, and many of the cells oval or spherical masses.

The brownish granular matter is always precipitated quickly; and when three young cells, which were as transparent as glass, were irrigated with a solution of 7 to 1000, the precipitation seemed to be instantaneous. After a time the granules are either deposited on the protoplasm lining the walls of the cells, or they collect into one or two spherical masses in the middle of the cell. These spheres apparently consist of a delicate membrane lined with granules and enclosing cell-sap. They distinctly lay within the spiral band of chlorophyll. Their appearance reminded me of the bag-like masses sometimes produced within the cells of dark-red leaves of *Drosera* when acted on by ammonia. In one instance the granules became collected into a spiral band. They were not acted on by alcohol, sulphuric ether, acetic acid, or a solution of iodine. Alcohol caused the protoplasm lining the walls to contract, by which means the granular matter and chlorophyll-bodies were all carried towards the centre of the cell.

Three other kinds of Conferva were immersed in a solution of the carbonate, and were casually observed. In the first, in which the cell-walls were dotted over with chlorophyll-grains, there was at first some slight degree of aggregation, and then the grains all became disintegrated. In the second species, the filaments of which were extremely thin, the solution produced no effect. In a third the chlorophyll-bodies became aggregated into spheres. If the species in this family are difficult to distinguish, systematists might probably derive aid by observing the different actions of a solution of carbonate of ammonia on them.

Conclusion. —From the facts given in this paper we see that certain salts of ammonia, more especially the carbonate, quickly cause the cell-sap in various plants belonging to widely different groups to deposit granules apparently of the nature of protein. These sometimes become aggregated into rounded masses. The same salts and, in the case of *Drosera*, an infusion of raw meat tend to act on the chlorophyll-bodies, causing them in some few species to become completely fused together, either in union with the aggregated cell-sap or separately from it. Aggregation seems to be a vital process, as it does not occur in recently killed cells; and any thing which kills a cell causes the already aggregated masses instantly to disintegrate. These masses, moreover, display in some cases incessant movements. The process of aggregation is not rarely carried so far that the masses lose the power of movement; nor do they then readily disintegrate when subjected to any deadly influence. From these facts, from other considerations, and more especially from the action of carbonate of ammonia on the chlorophyll-bodies, I am led to believe that the aggregated masses include living protoplasm, to which their power of movement may be attributed. The most remarkable point in the whole phenomenon is, that with the Droseraceae the most diverse stimuli (even a stimulus transmitted from a distant part of the leaf) induces the process of aggregation. The redissolution in the course of a few days of the solid aggregated masses and, especially, the regeneration of the chlorophyll-grains are likewise remarkable phenomena.

1. [Read 6 March 1882.] *Journal of the Linnean Society (Botany)* 19 (1882): 262–84.†

2. Pfeffer, in his recent admirable work 'Pflanzenphysiologie' (B. ii. 1881, p. 248), speaks of the phenomenon as being in many respects interesting; and Cohn writes ("Die Pflanze," Vorträge aus dem Gebiete der Botanik, 1882, p. 361) in still stronger terms.

3. Quart. Journ. Micr. Sci. vol. xvi. 1876, p. 309.

4. Van Tieghem, 'Traité de Botanique,' 1882, p. 596. See also p. 528, on masses of protoplasm floating freely within the cavities of cells. Sachs ('Physiologie Végétale,' p. 74) and Kühne ('Das Protoplasma,' p. 103) have likewise seen small freely-floating masses of protoplasm in the hairs of *Tradescantia* and *Cucurbita* which undergo amoeboid changes of form.

5. 'Insectivorous Plants,' p. 58.

6. 'Pflanzenphysiologie,' Bd. ii. p. 248.

7. 'Studien über das Vorkommen . . . von Gallenbestandtheil' (Giessen, 1862).

8. See his interesting papers in the 'Botanische Zeitung,' 1880, pp. 298–413, and more especially p. 361.

9. Van Tieghem, 'Traité de Botanique,' 1882, p. 493.

10. These sections and many others were made for me by my son Francis, to whom I owe much information and other assistance.

11. See an interesting account of the inner epidermal cells by A. Batalin, "Ueber die Function der Epidermis in den Schläuchen von *Sarracenia* &c." 1880. Reprinted from 'Acta Horti Petropolitani,' t. vii. (1880).

∕⚭ On the Dispersal of Freshwater Bivalves[1]

The wide distribution of the same species, and of closely-allied species of freshwater shells must have surprised every one who has attended to this subject. A naturalist, when he collects for the first time freshwater animals in a distant region, is astonished at their general similarity to those of his native European home, in comparison with the surrounding terrestrial animals and plants. Hence I was led to publish in Nature (vol. xviii. p. 120) a letter to me from Mr. A. H. Gray, of Danversport, Massachusetts, in which he gives a drawing of a living shell of *Unio complanatus*, attached to the tip of the middle toe of a duck (*Querque-dula discors*) shot on the wing.[2] The toe had been pinched so hard by the shell that it was indented and abraded. If the bird had not been killed, it would have alighted on some pool, and the Unio would no doubt sooner or later have relaxed its hold and dropped off. It is not likely that such cases could often be observed, for a bird when shot would generally fall on the ground so heavily that an attached shell would be shaken off and overlooked.

I am now able to add, through the kindness of Mr. W. D. Crick, of

Northampton, another and different case. On February 18 of the present year, he caught a female *Dytiscus marginalis*, with a shell of *Cyclas cornea* clinging to the tarsus of its middle leg. The shell was .45 of an inch from end to end, .3 in depth, and weighed (as Mr. Crick informs me) .39 grams, or 6 grains. The valves clipped only the extremity of the tarsus for a length of .1 of an inch. Nevertheless, the shell did not drop off, on the beetle when caught shaking its leg violently. The specimen was brought home in a handkerchief, and placed after about three hours in water; and the shell remained attached from February 18 to 23, when it dropped off, being still alive, and so remained for about a fortnight while in my possession. Shortly after the shell had detached itself, the beetle dived to the bottom of the vessel in which it had been placed, and having inserted its antennae between the valves, was again caught for a few minutes. The species of Dytiscus often fly at night, and no doubt they generally alight on any pool of water which they may see; and I have several times heard of their having dashed down on glass cucumber frames, no doubt mistaking the glittering surface for water. I do not suppose that the above weight of 6 grains would prevent so powerful an insect as a Dytiscus from taking flight. Anyhow this beetle could transport smaller individuals; and a single one would stock any isolated pond, as the species is an hermaphrodite form. Mr. Crick tells me that a shell of the same kind, and of about the same size, which he kept in water "extruded two young ones, which seemed very active and able to take care of themselves." How far a Dytiscus could fly is not known; but during the voyage of the *Beagle* a closely-allied form, namely, a Colymbetes, flew on board when the nearest point of land was forty-five miles distant; and it is an improbable chance that it had flown from the nearest point.

Mr. Crick visited the same pond a fortnight afterwards, and found on the bank a frog which appeared to have been lately killed; and to the outer toe of one of its hind legs a living shell of the same species was attached. The shell was rather smaller than in the previous case. The leg was cut off and kept in water for two days, during which time the shell remained attached. The leg was then left in the air, but soon became shrivelled; and now the shell being still alive detached itself.

Mr. F. Norgate, of Sparham, near Norwich, in a letter dated March 8, 1881, informs me that the larger water-beetles and newts in his aquarium "frequently have one foot caught by a small freshwater bivalve (*Cyclas cornea?*), and this makes them swim about in a very restless state, day and night, for several days, until the foot or toe is completely severed." He adds that newts migrate at night from pond to pond, and can cross over obstacles which would be thought to be considerable. Lastly, my son Francis, while fishing in the sea off the shores of North Wales, noticed that mussels were several times brought up by the point of the hook; and though he did not particularly attend to the subject, he and his companion thought that the shells had not been mechanically torn from the bottom, but that they had seized the point of the hook. A friend also of Mr. Crick's tells him that while fishing in rapid streams he has often thus caught small Unios. From the several cases now given, there can, I think, be no doubt that living bivalve shells must often be carried from pond to pond, and by the aid of birds occasionally even to great distances. I have also suggested in the "Origin of Species" means by which freshwater univalve shells might be far transported. We may therefore demur to the belief doubtfully expressed by Mr. Gwyn Jeffreys in his "British Conchology,"[3] namely, that the diffusion of freshwater shells "had a different and very remote origin, and that it took place before the present distribution of land and water."

1. *Nature. A Weekly Illustrated Journal of Science*, vol. 25, 6 April 1882, pp. 529–30.†
2. See p. 214, "Transplantation of Shells."†
3. Gwyn Jeffreys, *British Conchology, or an Account of the Mollusca which Now Inhabit the British Isles and the Surrounding Seas*, 5 vols. (London: Van Voorst, 1862–69).†

⚓ A Preliminary Notice: "On the Modification of a Race of Syrian Street-Dogs by Means of Sexual Selection"[1]

Most of the naturalists who admit that natural selection has been effective in the formation of species, likewise admit that the weapons of male animals are the result of sexual selection—that is, of the best-armed males obtaining most females and transmitting their masculine superiority to their male offspring. But many naturalists doubt, or deny, that female animals ever exert any choice, so as to select certain males in preference to others. It would, however, be more correct to speak of the females as being excited or attracted in an especial degree by the appearance, voice, &c. of certain males, rather than of deliberately selecting them. I may perhaps be here permitted to say that, after having carefully weighed to the best of my ability the various arguments which have been advanced against the principle of sexual selection, I remain firmly convinced of its truth. It is, however, probable that I may have extended it too far, as, for instance, in the case of the strangely formed horns and mandibles of male Lamellicorn beetles, which have recently been discussed with much knowledge by W. von Reichenau,[2] and about which I have always felt some doubts. On the other hand, the explanation of the development of the horns offered by this entomologist does not seem to me at all satisfactory.

In order to ascertain whether female animals ever or often exhibit a decided preference for certain males, I formerly inquired from some of the greatest breeders in England, who had no theoretical views to support and who had ample experience; and I have given their answers, as well as som published statements, in my 'Descent of Man'.[3] The facts there given clearly show that with dogs and other animals the females sometimes prefer in the most decided manner particular males—but that it is very rare that a male will not accept any female, though such cases do occur. The following statement, taken from the 'Voyage of the Vega,'[4] indirectly supports in a striking manner the above conclusion. Nordenskiöld says:—"We had two Scotch collies with us on the 'Vega.' They at first frightened the natives very much with their bark. To the dogs of the Chukches[5] they soon took the same superior standing as the European claims for himself in relation to the savage. The dog was distinctly preferred by the female Chukch canine population, and that too without the fights to which such favour on the part of the fair commonly gives rise. A numerous canine progeny of mixed Scotch-Chukch breed has arisen at Pitlekay.[6] The young dogs had a complete resemblance to their father; and the natives were quite charmed with them."

What the attractions may be which give an advantage to certain males in wooing in the above several cases, whether general appearance, such as colour and form, or vigour and strength, or gestures, voice, or odour, can rarely be even conjectured; but whatever they may be, they would be preserved and augmented in the course of many generations, if the females of the same species or race, inhabiting the same district, retained during successive generations approximately the same general disposition and taste; and this does not seem improbable. Nor is it indispensable that all the females should have exactly the same tastes: one female might be more attracted by some one characteristic in the male, and another female by a different one; and both, if not incompatible, would be gradually acquired by the males. Little as we can judge what are the characteristics which attract the female, yet, in some of the cases recorded by me, it seemed clearly to be colour; in other cases previous familiarity with a particular male; in others exactly the reverse, or novelty. With respect to the first appearance of the peculiarities which are afterwards augmented through sexual selection, this of course depends on the strong tendency in all parts of all organisms to present slight individual differences, and in some organisms to vary in a plain manner. Evidence has also been given in my book on Variation under Domestication showing that male animals are more liable to vary than females; and this would be highly favourable to sexual selection. Manifestly every slight individual difference and each more conspicuous variation depends on definite though unknown causes; and these modifications of structure &c. differ in different species under apparently the same conditions. Statements of this nature have sometimes been misinterpreted, as if it were supposed that variations were indefinite or fluctuating, and that the same variations occurred in all species.

In reference to sexual selection, I will here only add that the complete manner in which the introduced dogs and other domestic animals in South America and other countries have been mongrelized, so that all traces of their original race have been lost, often appeared to me a surprising fact. This holds good according to Rengger[7] with the dogs even in so isolated a country as Paraguay. I formerly attributed this mongrelization merely to the breeds not having been kept separate and to the greater vigour of cross-bred offspring; but if the females often prefer strangers to their old companions, as seems to be the case, according to Nordenskiöld, in Siberia, and in Syria as shown in the following essay, then we can readily understand how rapid and complete would be the progress of mongrelization. I will now give without further comment the essay[8] which Dr. W. Van Dyck, Lecturer on Zoology to the Protestant College at Beyrout, who has had excellent opportunities for observations during a residence of twenty years, has been so kind as to send me.

1. Pp. 367–69 in W. Van Dyck, "On the Modification of a Race of Syrian Street-Dogs by Means of Sexual Selection: With a Preliminary Notice by Charles Darwin," *Proceedings of the Zoological Society of London*, no. 25, 1882, pp. 367–70.†

2. "Ueber den Ursprung der secundären männlichen Geschlechtscharakteren &c.," Kosmos, Jahrgang v. 1881, p. 172.

3. The Descent of Man, second edit. (1874), part ii. Chap. xvii. pp. 522–525. See also Chap. xiv., on choice in pairing shown by female birds, and on their appreciation of beauty.

4. 'The Voyage of the Vega,' Eng. translat. (1881), vol. ii. p. 97.

5. Siberian Americanoid people of Chukchi peninsula.†

6. Pitlekay: village on northeastern shore of Chukchi peninsula, Bering Strait.†

7. 'Naturgeschichte der Sängethiere von Paraguay,' 1830, p. 154.

8. In his essay, Van Dyck describes examples of Syrian bitches which mated with foreign dogs in preference to their own breed.†

⟨ Prefatory Notice: Studies in the Theory of Descent [1]

The present work by Professor Weismann, well known for his profound embryological investigations on the Diptera, will appear, I believe, to every naturalist extremely interesting and well deserving of careful study. Any one looking at the longitudinal and oblique stripes, often of various and bright colours, on the caterpillars of Sphinx-moths, would naturally be inclined to doubt whether these could be of the least use to the insect; in the olden time they would have been called freaks of Nature. But the present book shows that in most cases the colouring can hardly fail to be of high importance as a protection. This indeed was proved experimentally in one of the most curious instances described, in which the thickened anterior end of the caterpillar bears two large ocelli or eye-like spots, which give to the creature so formidable an appearance that birds were frightened away. But the mere explanation of the colouring of these caterpillars is but a very small part of the merit of the work. This mainly consists in the light thrown on the laws of variation and of inheritance by the facts given and discussed. There is also a valuable discussion on classification, as founded on characters displayed at different ages by animals belonging to the same group. Several distinguished naturalists maintain with much confidence that organic beings tend to vary and to rise in the scale, independently of the conditions to which they and their progenitors have been exposed; whilst others maintain that all variation is due to such exposure, though the manner in which the environment acts is as yet quite unknown. At the present time there is hardly any question in biology of more importance than this of the nature and causes of variability, and the reader will find in the present work an able discussion on the whole subject, which will probably lead him to pause before he admits the existence of an innate tendency to perfectibility. Finally, whoever compares the discussions in this volume with those published twenty years ago on any branch of Natural History, will see how wide and rich a field for study has been opened up through the principle of Evolution; and such fields, without the light shed on them by this principle, would for long or for ever have remained barren.

1. Pp. v–vi in August Weismann, *Studies in the Theory of Descent: With Notes and Additions by the Author*, Raphael Meldola, trans., ed. (with notes) (London: Sampson Low, Marston, Searle, & Rivington, 1882).†

Appendix

On the Ova of Flustra, or, Early
Notebook, Containing Observations Made by C.D. When He Was
at Edinburgh, March 1827[1]

March 16th 1827

(1) Procured from the black rocks at Leith a large Cyclopterus Lumpus
(common lump fish). Length from snout to tail 23½ inches, girth 19½. It
had evidently come to the rocks to spawn & was there left stranded by
the tide; its ovaria contained a great mass of spawn of a rose colour.
Dissected it with Dr. Grant. It appeared very free from disease & had no
intestinal worms; its back however was covered with small crustaceous
animals.—Eyes small. Hence probably does not inhabit deep seas?
Stomach large. Liver without gall-bladder. Kidneys situated some way
from the Vertebrae: an unusual fact in cartilaginous Fishes. Air bladder
was not seen. Brain very small; the optic nerves being nearly as large as
the spinal cord, neither the brain or spinal matter nearly filling its cavity.
The valves in the heart were very distinct; the peduncle strong. The body
was not covered with <skin>[?][2] scales, but slimy & remarkably thick. The
sucker on its breast was of a white colour. I believe it is generally a
reddish yellow? The plebs differ whether it is edible.

(2) Procured a small green Aeolis[3] & a Tritonia.[4]

(3) Examined the ova of the Purpura Lapillus[5] & found them out of
their capsules & of this shape [*Fig. 1*].

18th

(4) Found these [*Fig. 2*] growing out of an Alcyonium.[6]—?

(5) Some ova from the Newhaven rocks said to be that of the Doris,[7]
was in every respect similar to that of the Univalves & in rapid motion, &
continued so for 7 days.

19th

(6) Observed ova in the Flustra[8] Foliacea & Truncata, the former of
which were in motion.

28th

(7) Adhering to the Fuci[9] one frequently finds whitish circular masses

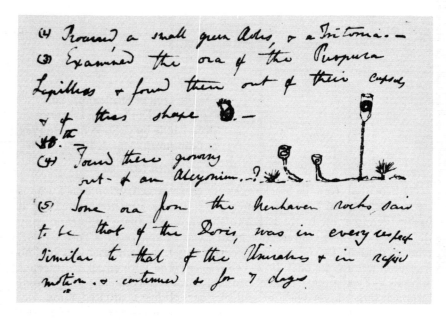

Fig. 1. Ova of *Pupura Lapillus*.   **Fig. 2.** Growths on Alcyonium.

of Ova, of an extremely viscid consistence,—& have the appearance represented at A [*Fig. 3*], when magnified however, it appears to be a mass [*of*] capsules P[10] containing animals d united together by a transparent gelatinous matter. In this species I believe I was the first to observe both the animal d, & its ciliae, x, in most rapid movement. By

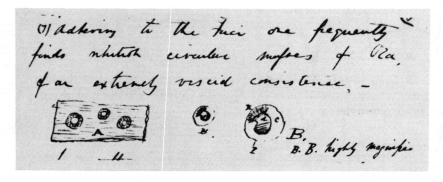

Fig. 3. Ova adhering to Fuci.

the aid of these ciliae it could revolve in its capsule & when freed from it moved so quickly, as to be discernible to the naked eye at some distance. To what animal these ova belong. I am ignorant?

(8) I found also another mass of ova, larger & of a browner colour, the capsules also being considerably larger. I could perceive no motion in these [*Fig. 4*].

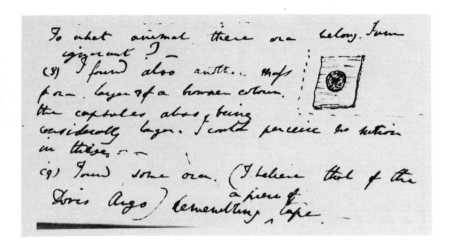

Fig. 4. Mass of brown ova.

(9) Found some ova (I believe that of the Doris Argo) resembling a piece of tape.—the capsules were rather irregular, containing from 1 to 3 angular shaped bodies.—in which I could perceive no motion.—the capsules had the *appearance* of being united, & of an oblong shape [*Fig. 5*]. These capsules were arranged in regular rows—in this manner [*Fig. 6*].

April 15th

(10) One frequently finds on the Fuci a gelatinous mass of this appearance [*Fig. 7*] containing a number [*of*] ova, which when magnified consist of A [*Fig. 8*], an outer capsule B a gelatinous mass, & c the young animal on which at its anterior end are situated numerous ciliae. These by their constant motion cause the young animal to turn rapidly round within the capsule,—& when freed from its capsule to move to & fro in the water with the greatest ease. I kept some of these ova in a bottle of the same water & at the end of 30 days were yet in motion.—

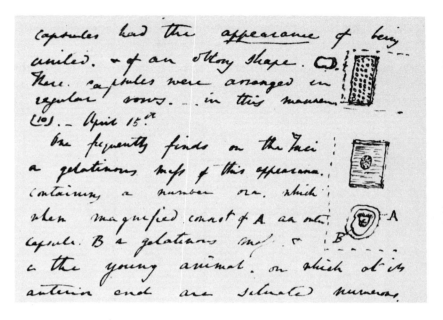

Fig. 5. Oblong capsules.
Fig. 6. Rows of capsules.

Fig. 7. Gelatinous ova on Fuci.
Fig. 8. Magnified ova.

20th

(11) Having procured some specimens of the Flustra Carbocea (Lam.) from the dredge boats at Newhaven, I soon perceived without the aid of a microscope small yellow bodies studded in different directions on it. They were of an oval shape & of the colour of the yolk of an egg, each occupying one cell. Whilst in their cells I could perceive no motion: but when left at rest in a watch glass, or shaken they glided to & fro with so rapid a motion, as at some distance to be distinctly visible to the naked eye. When highly magnified, the ciliae, which were chiefly distributed on the broader end, were seen in rapid motion; the central ones being the longest. I may mention that I have also observed ova of the Flustra Foliacea & Truncata in motion. That such ova had organs of motion does not appear to have been hitherto observed either by Lamarck Cuvier Lamouroux or any other author. This fact although at first it may appear of little importance, yet by adducing one more to the already numerous examples will tend to generalise the law that the ova of all Zoophites enjoy spontaneous motion.

This & the following communication was read both before the Werner-ian & Plinian Societies.

(12) One frequently finds sticking to oyster & other old shells small black globular bodies, which the fishermen call great Pepper-corns. These have hitherto been always mistaken for the young Fucus Lorius to which it bears a great resemblance. Having opened some of these they at first appeared only to contain an extremely viscid fluid without any traces [of] organisation; but on examining some others I found that this fluid by degrees acquiring a vermicular shape. when matured was the young Pontobdella[11] Muricata (Lam.) which were in every respect perfect & in motion. Each ovum consisted of two parts, the outer capsule being cori[a]ceous & of considerable thickness, whilst the inner consisted merely of a thin black membrane. This bag never contained more than one animal, in which it differs remarkably from that of other Molluscous animals such as the Doris Buccinum Purpura &c. &c., for in these one capsule generally contains numerous ova. At each end there is a prominent orifice, which appears to be the outlet of the young animal, but hitherto mistaken for the branches of the Fucus. The adult animal bears a considerable analogy to the Leeches & was even placed by Linnaeus in his genus Hirudo with the specific name of Muricata. Most of the leeches are viviparous & therefore the fact of the Muricata being oviparous, besides on its own account, is of value as it shows to what a great extent the mode of generation differs in the lower animals.

(13) Procured on 15th of April from deep water in Frith of Forth a good many specimens of the Pennatula[12] Mirabilis. The Polype were situated on one side of the bony axis in alternate lunate fillets in number from 70–80. Each fillet consisted of about 12 polype. Towards one end of many of the longest specimens a yellowish appearance, which upon examination turned out to be numerous ova. They were situated between the fillets towards the bare side of the stem. They were easily separated in great number from the gelatinous axis upon its being torn. But I could perceive no motion.

23rd

(14) Procured from the Frith of Forth numerous specimens of the Pennatula Phosphorea. differs from the Mirabilis in there being only 20 rows or Fillets of polype, & in these rows about 12 Polype. These fillets are opposite & decrease in size towards both end of the axis. The bony axis does not appear at either end of the Zoophite as it does in the Mirabilis, but gradually tapers into two filiform soft & flexible points embedded in the fleshy matter. Inclosed in & at the base of the fillets were

several ova of a large size & of a yellow colour could perceive no motion. I may remark that each fillet is broardest in the middle & tapers toward both ends. The whole Zoophite has a soft <glu> slimy feel, & of a red colour. The long axis in both of the above-mentioned species effervesced rapidly with nitric acid.

(15) Observed, with Mr. Coldstream at the black rocks at Leith, an Asterias[13] rubens doubled up as it were, so that the disk part formed pouch, in which were numerous loose ova, which the animal was in act of discharging from its mouth. The double Ovaria in each of the animals limbs contained a mass of ova of a small size & of an orange colour.

(16) Having taken a grain of pollen out of the Anther in an unopened Geranium flower: I placed it in spirits of wine: it was of a spherical shape & of a yellow colour: after remaining a minute in the Spirits three transparent cones were protruded from its side: these in the course of a few minutes burst, & sent, with great violence, from one of the cones numberless granules: By the next morning (the Geranium being kept in water) the Anthers had deshisced & the pollen was scattered about. A grain now being placed in < water> Spirits, emitted its contents with such force that the grain itself moved very rapidly in the liquid so rapidly indeed, that I could not follow with the microscope: When placed in water it exploded almost instantly but not with quite such force.

The Epidermis of the Petals in the Geranium is very curious; it consists of 6 (or occasionally 7) sided cells) on the sides of these cells; these [had] 12 small projections which alternate with those of the neighbouring cells: it has the same appearance, both on upper & under side: no stomata: In the Stamina, the cuticle [cells] of the Filament were Rhomboidal: in the covering of the Antherii the cells had knobbed sides: The pistil full of Tracheae. Cuticle with Rhomboidal cells. Sepals full of Tracheae. Cuticle with oblong cells. The cells in the cuticle of the Bracteae very irregular oblong: in the Pedicel rather more regular:—A Transverse section of this latter part gives a star-like appearance, this is owing to about 10 groups of ducts set within a ring of them: by dissecting a portion of the pedicel vertically these ducts were very easily seen: without this darkish ring came a circle of rather irregularly celled parenchymatous matter: then ring of green matter: then cuticle.—Examined the grain of pollen in Orchis morio. they are of a green colour & of a wedge shape with the sharp end truncated. They are fastened at their narrow ends one to the other by a highly elastic thread.—

1. Cambridge University Library Handlist (1960) no. 118. Acknowledgment is due the Cambridge University Library for microfilm copies and for permission to publish this transcription. Parts of this paper were transcribed and published by J. H. Ashworth in "Charles Darwin as a Student in Edinburgh, 1825–1827," Proceedings of the Royal Society of Edinburgh, 55 (1934–35): 97–113.

Accounts differ on the exact time, place, and subject of the paper's presentation. In the paper Darwin says (page 289), "This & the following communication was read both before the Wernerian & Plinian Societies." In his autobiography (written in his sixty-seventh year) he says, "I made one interesting little discovery, and read, about the beginning of the year 1826, a short paper on the subject before the Plinian Society. This was that the so-called ova of Flustra had the power of independent movement by means of cilia, and were in fact larvae. In another short paper I showed that the little globular bodies which had been supposed to be the young state of *Fucus loreus* were the egg-cases of the wormlike *Pontobdella muricata*." The "minute-book" records of the Plinian Natural History Society (now in the Edinburgh University Library) show that on 27 March 1827 "Mr. Darwin communicated to the Society two discoveries which he had made:

1. That the ova of the Flustra possess organs of motion.
2. That the small black globular body hitherto mistaken for the young Fucus lorius is in reality the ovum of the Pontobdella muricata." (Ashworth, *ibid.*, p. 103).

Some of the notes in the paper are dated 15 April or later, suggesting this manuscript was not the copy used by Darwin for his presentation. Possibly it was used at a later meeting not recorded in the "minute-book." Ashworth provides a more complete discussion of historical circumstances surrounding this paper.†

2. The word *skin* seems to have been written in, then lightly crossed through. Note: angular brackets enclose words crossed through in the original manuscript.†

3. *Aeolis:* a nudibranchiate mollusk.†
4. *Tritonia:* Gastropoda.†
5. *Purpura lapillus:* Grostropoda.†
6. *Alcyonium:* an Actinozoa of the Coelenterata.†
7. *Doris:* a nudibranchiate mollusk.†
8. *Flustra:* a Bryozoan.†
9. *Fucus:* brown algae; Fucaceae.†
10. Probably should be "B." Darwin in haste perhaps added "P" to the drawing, after inadvertently saying "P" in the text.†
11. *Pontobdella:* Hirudinea.†
12. *Pennatula:* sea pen; Pennatulidae of the Actinozoa.†
13. *Asterias:* a starfish.†

◀ *Coniferae*[1]

Pinus Hartwegii becomes a large tree. All such plants like a sandy peat to grow in; but they will succeed in any soil which is neither clay nor chalk. As to P. palustris, we should not anticipate any success from planting it. It might grow for a few years, but we fear it would die suddenly at last. Such, at least, is often its fate in situations much more favourable than one of clay on chalk, 560 ft. above the sea.

1. *Gardeners' Chronicle and Agricultural Gazette*, no. 16, 1844, p. 248. This is an answer published in the section, "Notices To Correspondents," obviously in response to a letter from Darwin to the editor.†

◆ Coleoptera at Down[1]

We three very young collectors have lately taken, in the parish of Down, six miles from Bromley, Kent, the following beetles, which we believe to be rare, namely, *Licinus sitphoides*, *Panagus 4-pustulatus* and *Clytus mysticus*. As this parish is only fifteen miles from London, we have thought that you might think it worth while to insert this little notice in the 'Intelligencer.'

1. Francis Darwin, Leonard Darwin, and Horace Darwin. *Entomologist's Weekly Intelligencer*, no. 143, 25 June 1859, p. 99.†

◆ Variations of Organs[1]

My father finds that in his letter, published in your number for September 25, he did not give with sufficient clearness his hypothetical explanation of how useless organs might diminish, and ultimately disappear.[2] I therefore now send you, with his approval, the following further explanation of his meaning.

If one were to draw a vertical line on a wall, and were to measure the heights of several thousand men of the same race against this line, recording the height of each by driving in a pin, the pins would be densely clustered about a certain height, and the density of their distribution would diminish above and below. Quetelet experimentally verified that the density of the pins at any distance above the centre of the cluster was equal to that at a like distance below; he also found that the law of diminution of density on receding from the cluster was given by a certain mathematical expression, to which, however, I need here make no further reference. A similar law obtains, with reference to the circumference of the chest; and one may assume, with some confidence, that under normal conditions, the variation of any organ in the same species may be symmetrically grouped about a centre of greatest density, as above explained.

In what follows I shall, for the sake of brevity, speak of the horns of cattle, but it will be understood that my father considers a like argument as applicable to the variations of any organs of any species in size, weight, colour, capacity for performing a function, &c.

Supposing then that a race of cattle becomes exposed to unfavourable conditions, my father's hypothesis is that, whilst the larger proportion of the cattle have their horns developed in the same degree as though they had enjoyed favourable conditions, the remainder have their horns somewhat stunted. Now, if we had made a record of the length of horn in the same species under favourable conditions, we should, as in the case of the heights of men, have a central cluster, with a symmetrical distribution of the pins above and below the cluster. According to the hypothesis, the effect of the poor conditions may be represented by the removal of a certain proportion of the pins, taken at hazard, to places lower down, whilst the rest remain *in statû quo*. By this process the central cluster will be slightly displaced downwards, since its upper edge will be made slightly less dense, whilst its lower edge will become denser; and further, the density of distribution will diminish more rapidly above than below the new central cluster.

Now, if horns are useful organs, the cattle with shorter horns will be partially weeded out by natural selection, and will leave fewer offspring; and after many generations of the new conditions, the symmetry of distribution of the pins will be restored by the weeding out of some of those below the cluster, the central cluster itself remaining undisturbed.

If, on the other hand, horns are useless organs, the cattle with stunted horns have as good a chance of leaving offspring (who will inherit their peculiarity) as their long-horned brothers. Thus, after many generations under the poor conditions, with continual intercrossing of all the members, the symmetry of distribution will be again restored, but it will have come about through the general removal of *all* the pins downwards, and this will of course have shifted the central cluster.

If, then, the poor conditions produce a *continuous* tendency to a stunting of the nature above described, there will be two operations going on side by side—the one ever destroying the symmetry of distribution, and the other ever restoring it through the shifting of the cluster downwards.

Thus, supposing the hypothesis to be supported by facts (and my father intends to put this to the test of experiment next summer), there is a tendency for useless organs to diminish and finally disappear, besides those arising from disuse and the economy of nutrition.

1. *Nature. A Weekly Illustrated Journal of Science* 8 (1873): 505 (written by George H. Darwin).†

2. See p. 177, "On the Males and Complemental Males of Certain Cirripedes, and on Rudimentary Structures."†

Bibliography I
Species Collected
by Darwin

[Insects Collected by C. Darwin at Cambridge, North Wales, and Shrewsbury.] In James Francis Stephens, *Illustrations of British Entomology; or, a Synopsis of Indigenous Insects* . . . , 11 vols. (London: Baldwin, Cradock, 1828–35.)

"Communication on Viviparous Lizards, and on Red Snow." [Read 14 December 1835.] *Cambridge Philosophical Society Minutes.*

G. R. Waterhouse, "Descriptions of Some of the Insects Brought to this Country by C. Darwin, Esq." [Read 2 January 1837.] *Transactions of the Entomological Society of London* 2(1837–40):131–35.

W. Martin, "Observations on Three Specimens of the Genus *Felis* Presented to the Society by Charles Darwin, Esq., Corr. Memb. Z.S." [Presented 10 January 1837.] *Proceedings of the Zoological Society of London*, pt. 5(1837), pp. 3–4. *L'Institut, Journal général des Sociétés et Travaux scientifiques de la France et de l'Étranger* 6(1838):210–11.

J. Reid, "Notes on Several Quadrupeds in Mr. Darwin's Collection." [Presented 10 January 1837.] *Proceedings of the Zoological Society of London*, pt. 5(1837), p. 4. *L'Institut, Journal général des Sociétés et Travaux scientifiques de la France et de l'Étranger* 6(1838):210–11.

J. Gould, "Remarks on a Group of Ground Finches from Mr. Darwin's Collection, with Characters of the New Species." [Presented 10 January 1837.] *Proceedings of the Zoological Society of London*, pt. 5(1837), pp. 4–7. *L'Institut, Journal général des Sociétés et Travaux scientifiques de la France et de l'Étranger* 6(1838):210–11.

J. Gould, "Observations on the Raptorial Birds in Mr. Darwin's Collection, with Characters of the New Species." [Presented 24 January 1837.] *Proceedings of the Zoological Society of London*, pt. 5(1837), pp. 9–11.

W. Martin, "Observations upon a New Fox from Mr. Darwin's Collection (*Vulpes fulvipes*)." [Presented 24 January 1837.] *Proceedings of the Zoological Society of London*, pt. 5(1837), pp. 11–12.

W. Martin, "Observations on a Specimen of *Dasypus hybridus*, Desm., from Mr. Darwin's Collection." [Presented 24 January 1837.] *Proceedings of the Zoological Society of London*, pt. 5(1837), pp. 13–14.

G. R. Waterhouse, "Characters of New Species of the Genus *Mus*, from the Collection of Mr. Darwin." [Presented 14 February and 28 February 1837.] *Proceedings of the Zoological Society of London*, pt. 5(1837), pp. 15–21, 27–29. *Isis, oder Encyclopädische Zeitung*, 1839. Pp. 140–42. *Archiv für Naturgeschichte* 6(1840):174–80, 281–85.

J. Gould, "Exhibition of the Fissirostral Birds from Mr. Darwin's Collection, and Characters of the New Species." [Presented 14 February 1837.] *Proceedings of the Zoological Society of London*, pt. 5(1837), p. 22.

Charles Darwin, "An Account of Fused Sand Tubes Found Near the Rio Plata, along with Several Other Specimens of Rocks." [Presented 27 February 1837.] *Cambridge Philosophical Society Minutes*, 1837.

G. R. Waterhouse, "Characters of Two New Genera of Rodentia (*Reithrodon* and *Abrocoma*), from Mr. Darwin's Collection." [Presented 28 February 1837.] *Proceedings of the Zoological Society of London*, pt. 5(1837), pp. 29–32.

Richard Owen, "A Description of the Cranium of the *Toxodon Platensis*, a Gigantic Extinct Mammiferous Species, Referrible by its Dentition to the *Rodentia*, But with Affinities to the *Pachydermata* and the *Herbivorous Cetacea*." [Presented 19 April 1837.] *Proceedings of the Geological Society of London* 2(1838):541–42. *Annales des Sciences Naturelles*, 2d ser., 9(1838):25–45. *Notizen aus dem Gebiete der Natur- und Heilkunde*, vol. 2, 1837, col. 118–19; vol. 8, 1838, col. 1–9, 22–25.

F. W. Hope, "Descriptions of Some Species of Carabidae, Collected by Charles Darwin, Esq., in His Late Voyage." [Read 1 May 1837.] *Transactions of the Entomological Society of London* 2(1837–40):128–31.

J. Gould, "Exhibition of Mr. Darwin's Birds, and Description of a New Species of Wagtail (*Motacilla leucopsis*) from India. [Presented 25 July 1837.] *Proceedings of the Zoological Society of London*, pt. 5(1837), pp. 77–78.

William Buckland, "Note sur quelques ossemens fossiles de l'Amérique méridionale." [Translated from p. 603 (supplementary notes), vol. 1, of *Geology and Mineralogy, Considered with Reference to Natural Theology: With Supplementary Notes. The Bridgewater Treatises*, 2 vols., 2d ed. (London: Pickering, 1837).] *Annales des Sciences Naturelles*, 2d ser., 7(1837):319–20.

G. R. Waterhouse, "On a New Species of the Genus *Delphinus*." [Read 28 February 1838.] *Proceedings of the Zoological Society of London*, pt. 6(1838), pp. 23–24.

John Stevens Henslow, "Florula Keelingensis. An Account of the Native Plants of the Keeling Islands," *Annals of Natural History, or Magazine of Zoology, Botany, and Geology* 1(1838):337–47. *Neue Notizen aus dem Gebiete der Natur- und Heilkunde*, vol. 10, 1839, col. 257–59.

Francis Walker, "Descriptions of Some Chalcidites Discovered by C. Darwin, Esq.," *Entomological Magazine* 5(1838):469–77.

J. S. Henslow, "Description of Two New Species of Opuntia; with Remarks on the Structure of the Fruit of Rhipsalis," *Magazine of Zoology and Botany* 1(1837):466–69.

Richard Owen, "Description d'une mâchoire inférieure et de dents de Toxodon trouvées à Bahia-Blancha, a 39° de latitude sur la côte Est de L'Amèrique méridionale," *Annales des Sciences Naturelles . . . (Zool.)* 9(1838):45–54. *Notizen aus dem Gebiete der Natur- und Heilkunde*, vol. 8, 1838, col. 308–12.

Richard Owen, *Fossil Mammalia. The Zoology of the Voyage of H.M.S. Beagle, under the Command of Captain FitzRoy, R.N., during the years 1832 to 1836. Edited and Superintended by Charles Darwin* (London: Smith, Elder, 1839–43); [hereafter cited as *ZVB*; see C. Davies Sherborn, *Annals and Magazine of Natural History*, 6th ser., 20(November 1897):483; 1(February 1838):1–40; 7(March 1839):41–68; 8(May 1839):69–80.]

George R. Waterhouse, *Mammalia. ZVB* 2(May 1838):1–16; 4(September 1838):17–32; 5(November 1838):33–48; 10(September 1839):49–100.

John Gould, *Birds. ZVB* 3(July 1838):1–16; 6(January 1839):17–32; 9(July 1839):33–56; 11(November 1839):57–96.

Francis Walker, *Monographia Chalciditum, Species Collected by C. Darwin, Esq.*, 2 vols. (London: Baillière, 1839.)

Charles Darwin, "Ueber die Luftschifferei der Spinnen." [Translated from pp. 187–88, Charles Darwin, *Journal of Researches into the Geology and Natural History of the Various Countries Visited by H.M.S. Beagle* (London: Colburn, 1839.)] *Neue Notizen aus dem Gebiete der Natur- und Heilkunde*, vol. 11, 1839, col. 23–24.

M. J. Berkeley, "Notice of Some Fungi Collected by C. Darwin, Esq., during the Expedition of H. M. Ship Beagle," *Annals of Natural History, or Magazine of Zoology, Botany, and Geology* 4(1839):291–93.

G. R. Waterhouse, "Descriptions of Some New Species of Carabideous Insects, from the Collection Made by C. Darwin, Esq., in the Southern Parts of S. America," *Magazine of Natural History, and Journal of Zoology, Botany, Mineralogy, Geology, and Meteorology* 4(1840):354–62.

G. R. Waterhouse, "Description of a New Species of the Genus *Lophotus*, from the Collection of Charles Darwin, Esq.," *Annals of Natural History; or, Magazine of Zoology, Botany, and Geology* 5(1840):329–32.

G. R. Waterhouse, "Description of a New Species of Lamellicorn Beetle,

Brought from Valdivia by C. Darwin, Esq.," *Entomologist* 18(1842): 281–83.

Leonard Jenyns, *Fish. ZVB* 12(January 1840):1–32; 14(June 1840):33–64; 16(April 1841):65–96; 17(April 1842):97–172.

Richard Owen, *Fossil Mammalia. ZVB* 13(April 1840):81–112.

John Gould, *Birds. ZVB* 15(March 1841):97–164.

M. J. Berkeley, "On an Edible Fungus from Tierra del Fuego, and an Allied Chilean Species." [Read 16 March 1841.] *Transactions of the Linnean Society of London* 19(1845):37–43. *Proceedings of the Linnean Society* 1(1849):97–98. [Summary.]

G. R. Waterhouse, "Descriptions of Some New Coleopterous Insects from the Southern Parts of S. America, Collected by C. Darwin, Esq. and T. Bridges, Esq.," *Proceedings of the Zoological Society of London* 9(1841):105–28.

Adam White, "Descriptions of New or Little Known Arachnida," *Annals and Magazine of Natural History, including Zoology, Botany, and Geology* 7(1841):471–77.

G. R. Waterhouse, "Carabideous Insects Collected by Mr. Darwin during the Voyage of Her Majesty's Ship Beagle," *Annals and Magazine of Natural History, including Zoology, Botany, and Geology* 6(1841):254–57, 351–55; 7(1841):120–29; 9(1842):134–39. [Title of article varies slightly in continued parts.]

M. J. Berkeley, "Notice of some Fungi Collected by C. Darwin, Esq., in South America and the Islands of the Pacific," *Annals and Magazine of Natural History, including Zoology, Botany, and Geology* 9(1842): 443–48.

Francis Walker, "Descriptions of Chalcidites Discovered by C. Darwin, Esq., near Valparaiso," *Annals and Magazine of Natural History, including Zoology, Botany, and Geology* 10(1842):113–17.

Francis Walker, "Descriptions of Chalcidites Discovered in Valdivia by C. Darwin, Esq.," *Annals and Magazine of Natural History, including Zoology, Botany, and Geology* 10(1842):271–74.

Thomas Bell, *Reptiles. ZVB* 18(August 1842):1–16; 19(October 1843): 17–52.

Francis Walker, "Descriptions of Chalcidites Discovered near Conception, in South America, by C. Darwin, Esq.," *Annals and Magazine of Natural History, including Zoology, Botany, and Geology* 11(1843):30–32.

Francis Walker, "Descriptions of Chalcidites found near Lima by C. Darwin, Esq.," *Annals and Magazine of Natural History, including Zoology, Botany, and Geology* 11(1843):115–17.

Francis Walker, "Descriptions of Chalcidites Discovered in the Isle of

Chonos by C. Darwin, Esq.," *Annals and Magazine of Natural History, including Zoology, Botany, and Geology* 11(1843):184–85.

Francis Walker, "Descriptions of Chalcidites Discovered in Coquimbo by C. Darwin, Esq.," *Annals and Magazine of Natural History, including Zoology, Botany, and Geology* 11(1843):185–88.

G. R. Waterhouse, "Description of a New Genus of Carabideous Insects Brought from the Falkland Islands by Charles Darwin, Esq.," *Annals and Magazine of Natural History, including Zoology, Botany, and Geology* 11(1843):281–83.

Francis Walker, "Descriptions of Chalcidites Discovered by C. Darwin, Esq.," *Annals and Magazine of Natural History, including Zoology, Botany, and Geology* 12(1843):45–46.

G. B. Sowerby, "Description of Fossil Shells." Appendix, pp. 153–60, in Charles Darwin, *Geological Observations on the Volcanic Islands, Visited during the Voyage of H.M.S.* Beagle. *Being the Second Part of the Geology of the Voyage of the* Beagle (London: Smith, Elder, 1844).

W. Lonsdale, "Description of Six Species of Corals from the Palaeozoic Formation of Van Diemen's Land." Appendix, pp. 161–69, in Charles Darwin, *Geological Observations on the Volcanic Islands, Visited during the Voyage of H.M.S.* Beagle, *Being the Second Part of the Geology of the Voyage of the* Beagle (London: Smith, Elder, 1844).

Christian Gottfried Ehrenberg, "Über einen die ganze Luft längere Zeit trübenden Staubregen im hohen atlantischen Ocean, in 70° 43' N.B. 26 W.L., und dessen Mischung aus zahlreichen Kieselthieren," *Bericht über die zur Bekanntmachung geeigneten Verhandlungen der Königl. Preufs. Akademie der Wissenschaften zu Berlin,* 1844. Pp. 194–207.

G. R. Waterhouse, "Descriptions of Coleopterous Insects Collected by Charles Darwin, Esq., in the Galapagos Islands," *Annals and Magazine of Natural History, including Zoology, Botany, and Geology* 16(1845):19–41.

Christian Gottfried Ehrenberg, "Über eine aus feinstem Kieselmehl von Infusorien bestehende Schminke der Feuerländer," *Bericht über die zur Bekanntmachung geeingneten Verhandlungen der Königl. Preufs. Akademie der Wissenschaften zu Berlin,* 1845. Pp. 63–64.

Christian Gottfried Ehrenberg, "Weitere Untersuchungen des atmosphärischen Staubes aus dem atlantischen Ocean an den Capverdischen Inseln," *Bericht über die zur Bekanntmachung geeingneten Verhandlungen der Königl. Preufs. Akademie der Wissenschaften zu Berlin,* 1845. Pp. 64–66, 85–87.

Christian Gottfried Ehrenberg, "Über einen bedeutenden Infusorien haltenden vulkanischen Aschen-Tuff (Pyrobiolith) auf der Insel Ascension," *Bericht über die zur Bekanntmachung geeingneten Verhand-*

lungen der Königl. Preufs. Akademie der Wissenschaften zu Berlin,
1845. Pp. 140–42.

Christian Gottfried Ehrenberg, "Über einen See-Infusorien haltenden
weissen vulkanischen Aschen-Tuff (Pyrobioloth) als sehr grosse Ge-
birgsmasse in Patagonien," *Bericht über die zur Bekanntmachung
geeingneten Verhandlungen der Königl. Preufs. Akademie der Wissenschaften zu Berlin,* 1845. Pp. 143–57.

G. B. Sowerby, "Descriptions of Tertiary Fossil Shells from South
America." Appendix, pp. 249–64, pl. II–IV, in Charles Darwin,
*Geological Observations on South America. Being the Third Part of
the Geology of the Voyage of the* Beagle (London: Smith, Elder, 1846).

E. Forbes, "Descriptions of Secondary Fossil Shells from South America." Appendix, pp. 265–68, pl. V, in Charles Darwin, *Geological
Observations on South America. Being the Third Part of the Geology
of the Voyage of the* Beagle (London: Smith, Elder, 1846).

Joseph Dalton Hooker, "Description of *Pleuropetalum,* A New Genus of
Portulaceae from the Galapagos Islands," *London Journal of Botany*
5(1846):108–9.

Joseph Dalton Hooker, "An Enumeration of the Plants of the Galapagos
Archipelago; With Descriptions of Those which Are New." [Read
4 March, 6 May, and 16 December 1845.] *Transactions of the
Linnean Society of London* 20(1851):163–233. *Proceedings of the
Linnean Society of London* 1(1849):276–79. [Summary.]

Sidney J. Hickson, "On Some Alcyonaria in the Cambridge Museum,"
Proceedings of the Cambridge Philosophical Society 20(1921):366–73.

Sydney J. Hickson, "Darwin's Cavernularia," *Nature. A Weekly Illustrated Journal of Science* 137(1936):909.

Bibliography II
Books Written by
Darwin

Journal and Remarks. 1832–1836. Vol. 3 of *Narrative of the Surveying Voyages of His Majesty's Ships* Adventurer *and* Beagle, *between the Years 1826 and 1836, Describing Their Examination of the Southern Shores of South America, and the* Beagle's *Circumnavigation of the Globe.* 3 vols. London: Colburn, 1839. Reissued as *Journal of Researches into the Geology and Natural History of the Various Countries Visited by H.M.S.* Beagle, *under the Command of Captain FitzRoy R.N., from 1832–36.* London: Colburn, 1839.

The Zoology of the Voyage of H.M.S. Beagle, *under the Command of Captain FitzRoy, R.N., during the Years 1832 to 1836. Edited and Superintended by Charles Darwin.* London: Smith, Elder. Pt. I: *Fossil Mammalia.* Richard Owen. [With a Geological Introduction by Charles Darwin.] 1840. Pt. II: *Mammalia.* George R. Waterhouse. [With a Notice of Their Habits and Ranges by Charles Darwin.] 1839. Pt. III: *Birds.* John Gould. [With a Notice of Their Habits and Ranges by Charles Darwin, and an Anatomical Index by T. C. Eyton. Many Descriptions by G.R. Gray.] 1841. Pt. IV: *Fish.* Leonard Jenyns. [With Notes by Charles Darwin.] 1842. Pt. V: *Reptiles.* Thomas Bell. [With Notes by Charles Darwin.] 1843.

The Structure and Distribution of Coral Reefs. Being the First Part of the Geology of the Voyage of the Beagle. London: Smith, Elder, 1842.

Geological Observations on the Volcanic Islands, Visited during the Voyage of H.M.S. Beagle. *Being the Second Part of the Geology of the Voyage of the* Beagle. London: Smith, Elder, 1844.

Geological Observations on South America. Being the Third Part of the Geology of the Voyage of the Beagle. London: Smith, Elder, 1846.

A Monograph of the Fossil Lepadidae; or, Pedunculated Cirripedes of Great Britain. London: Palaeontographical Society, 1851.

A Monograph of the Sub-class Cirripedia, with Figures of All the Species. The Lepadidae: Or, Pedunculated Cirripedes. London: Ray Society, 1851.

A Monograph of the Fossil Balanidae and Verrucidae of Great Britain. London: Palaeontographical Society, 1854.

A Monograph of the Sub-class Cirripedia, with Figures of All the Species. The Balanidae (or Sessil Cirripedes); the Verrucidae, &c. London: Ray Society, 1854.

On the Origin of Species by Means of Natural Selection, or Preservation of Favoured Races in the Struggle for Life. London: Murray, 1859.

On the Various Contrivances by which British and Foreign Orchids are Fertilised by Insects, and on the Good Effects of Intercrossing. London: Murray, 1862.

"The Movements and Habits of Climbing Plants." *Journal of the Linnean Society (Bot.)* 9(1865):1–118; 2d ed., rev. London: Murray, 1875.

The Variation of Animals and Plants under Domestication. 2 vols. London: Murray, 1868.

The Descent of Man, and Selection in Relation to Sex. 2 vols. London: Murray, 1871.

The Expression of the Emotions in Man and Animals. London: Murray, 1872.

Insectivorous Plants. London: Murray, 1875.

The Effects of Cross and Self Fertilisation in the Vegetable Kingdom. London: Murray, 1876.

The Different Forms of Flowers on Plants of the Same Species. London: Murray, 1877.

Erasmus Darwin. Preliminary Notice. With Ernst Krause. London: Murray, 1879.

The Power of Movement in Plants. Assisted by Francis Darwin. London: Murray, 1880.

The Formation of Vegetable Mould, through the Action of Worms, with Observations on their Habits. London: Murray, 1881.

Index

Abrothos (Abrolhos), *Beagle* at, 1, 3, 4
Acasta (cirripede), in sponges, 2, 179
Accelerated inheritance, 2, 230
Aceras longibracteata (orchid), fertilization, 2, 140
Achenia, of *Pumilio argyrolepis*, 2, 36–38
Acineta (orchid), unknown fertilization, 2, 150
Aconcagua, volcano, 1, 63, 65, 66
Acropera (orchid): atrophied ovules, 2, 65; hermaphrodites, 2, 150; separation of sex, 2, 69
Actineae, on Pernambuco sandstone, 1, 140
Action of sea-water on germination of seeds, 1, 264–73
Adapted, best, 2, 13, 17–18
Adie and Son, hand-level, 1, 230
Adlumia, flowers sucked by bees, 2, 183
AEgiphyla, dimorphic, 2, 62
Aërial dust, 1, 199–202, 244
Affection, in infant, 2, 195
Affinities, serial: barnacles, 1, 252
Agaricus muscarius, contractile filaments, 2, 207
Agassiz, Prof.: broken glacier boulder, 1, 164; creation of species, 2, 90; granite blocks on the Jura, 1, 156; moraines of ancient glaciers, 1, 159; work on glaciers, 1, 229, 241
Agency of bees in fertilization of papilionaceous flowers, 2, 19–25
Aggregation, in cells, 2, 256–76 passim
Agouti, bones, 1, 7, 18
Alcippe: borrowing barnacle, 1, 250–

51; rudimentary males, 2, 178
Alison, Mr.: shells of Chili, 1, 41, 42
Allan: *Phillips's Mineralogy*, 1, 229
Alternation of generations, animals and plants, 2, 127–28
Ammonia, on *Pelargonium*, 1, 198
Ammonia carbonate: on chlorophyll-bodies, 2, 256–76; on roots, 2, 236–56
Amsinckia spectabilis, dimorphic flowers, 2, 62
Anacamptis pyramidalis (orchid), fertilization, 2, 139–40, 144
Anaitis plagiata (Lepidoptera), with orchid pollinia, 2, 144
Analogy: hermaphrodites in cirripedes and plants, 2, 178; in classification, 1, 215; of volcanic rocks to glaciers, 1, 193–94; resemblance, examples, 2, 88–89
Ancient gardening, 2, 93
Ancient glaciers of Caernarvonshire, 1, 163–70
Anderson, Mr.: *Dendrobium cretaceum* (orchid), flowers, 2, 149
Andes, origin of, 1, 17
Andrena parvula (bee), on *Cypripedium*, 2, 152–53
Anelasma (cirripede): in skin of sharks, 2, 179; ova, 2, 85
Anemone apennina, crosses freely, 2, 42
Anger, of infant, 2, 194
Anglesea, geology by Henslow, 2, 74
Anser cygnoides (Chinese goose), fertility, 2, 219
Antarctic seas, icebergs, 1, 137–38